LIKE GOOD STEEL

Like Good Steel

The China Letters

of

Margaret Bailey Speer

NORTH CHINA, 1925-1943

SELECTED AND EDITED
BY
Caroline Smith Rittenhouse

The Round Table Press
Berwyn, Pennsylvania
1994

The Round Table Press

PO Box 475
Southeastern, PA 19399

261 Dayleview Road
Berwyn, PA 19312

Like Good Steel:
The China Letters of Margaret Bailey Speer
North China, 1925-1943

PRINTED IN THE UNITED STATES OF AMERICA

FRONT COVER: *Margaret Bailey Speer (inset) at Yenching University with background of the Western Hills and roofs of the University in the foreground, taken from Yenching's landmark water tower pagoda.*

MAP OF CHINA reprinted from endpapers of John Service, *Golden Inches: The China Memoir of Grace Service* (Berkeley: University of California Press, 1989) with permission from the Regents of the University of California.

LIBRARY OF CONGRESS CATALOGING -IN -PUBLICATION DATA

Speer, Margaret Bailey, 1900-
      [Correspondence. Selections]
      Like good steel : the China letters of Margaret Bailey Speer,
North China, 1925-1943 / selected and edited by Caroline
Smith Rittenhouse.
           p.   cm.
      Includes bibliographical references and index.
      ISBN 1-882275-05-5
      1. Speer, Margaret Bailey, 1900- --Correspondence. 2.
College teachers--China--Correspondence.   4. Students--China--Politi-
cal activity.   5. China---History--Republic, 1912-1949.   I. Rittenhouse,
Caroline Smith. 1931-   II Title.
LA2317.S68A6   1994
951.04--dc20   94-26488
                                                          CIP

Dedicated to China's students

D r. T'ing was arrested and held for fifteen days in a room with ten women prisoners. She was questioned for hours on end. Apparently the only charge against her was that the censors didn't like the messages she had written on Christmas cards to friends in America...such reprehensible statements as: "The Chinese are like good steel; you can bend them but you cannot break them."

MBS Letter, March 14,1939

Contents

Editor's Preface

Margaret Bailey Speer's letters from China are available to researchers in the Special Collections in the Mariam Coffin Canaday Library at Bryn Mawr College. In 1982 MBS privately published "Letters from Yenching," excerpts intended only for family and close friends, a project inspired by her brother, Bill Speer. Reading the letters after they came to Bryn Mawr, I became convinced that they deserved a wider audience, especially since her advocacy for women at Yenching University is virtually ignored in published histories.

MBS with Charlotte Tinker as her "eyes" has reviewed my selections and editing of the letters. I have omitted much that was meaningful mainly to the family and added paragraphing. Cramming as much as she could into letters from China, MBS did not waste space. We agreed that Wade-Giles romanization of Chinese was appropriate.

For chronological clarity I have divided the letters into chapters with date ranges in headings, and I have tried to add continuity and historical context in italic notes, anchored to authoritative sources. The bibliography is in no way comprehensive but offers guideposts for readers. I have written a biographical introduction, "Going to China," and an afterword, "The End Is Where We Start From," to introduce MBS, set the scene, and then to bring her story up to 1993.

Many thanks to MBS for her patience and good cheer; to Charlotte Tinker for many good suggestions along the way; to Trina Vaux for her good work in the *Recollections of Miss Speer*.

I am particularly grateful that MBS sent me to Ithaca in 1987 to meet her Yenching colleagues and friends, Harold Shadick, Y.P. and V.K. Nyi Mei, and Knight Biggerstaff. They shared their memories and friendship generously. Thanks also to Margaret Sailer for material on Randolph Sailer.

Researchers depend on the kindness of curators of collections: thanks above all to Manuscripts Librarian Leo M. Dolenski at Bryn Mawr College for help of many kinds, to Archivist Martha L. Smalley at the Yale Divinity School Library, to Wilma Slaight at the Wellesley College Archives, and to Fred Burwell, College Archivist at Beloit College in 1990 when I visited.

Attentive research friends are also indispensable: thanks to Helen Lefkowitz Horowitz for steering me toward a far better format than I began with, to Barbara Sicherman and other researchers in the Bryn Mawr College Archives for listening and advising. My archival cohorts, Eleanor Beatty and Claire Liachowitz, helped with final details unavailable at the end when I was in Maine.

Special thanks to Florence Newman Trefethen, retired editor at the Council on East Asian Studies at Harvard, for her close reading of the manuscript. Her firm, "This must be published" heartened me. Thanks to Dolores Brien for editorial guidance and imaginative design. I am indebted to Charles Putnam Dethier for eagle-eyed proofreading.

Thanks to my daughters Sarah and Kate for listening to my progress reports and to my husband Jim for daily cheer and for doing endless chores and errands that freed my time.

Caroline Rittenhouse

LIKE GOOD STEEL

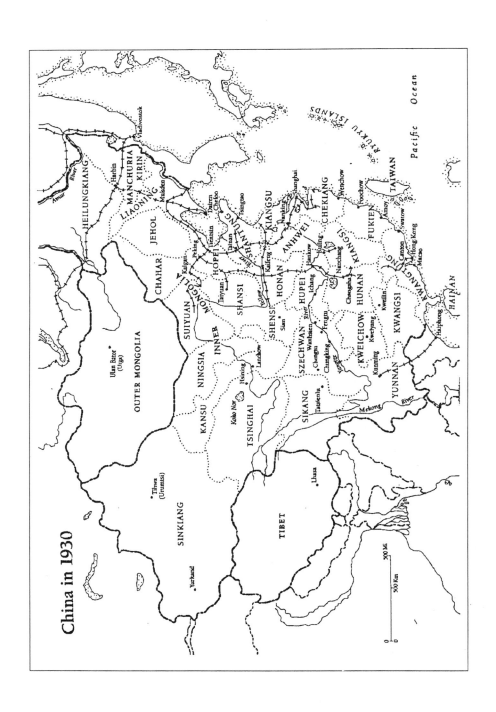

China in 1930

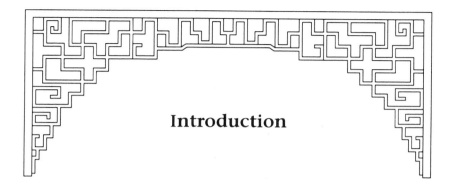

Introduction

Going to China

A feminist bred in the bone, Margaret Bailey Speer went to China in 1925 not, as earlier mission women went, to preach the gospel of gentility nor to make the world her household,[1] but to teach English at Yenching University. As a member of the faculty of the Women's College, she soon found that she was vigorously fighting to preserve the autonomy of the Women's College as the Western and Chinese men in the University sought to merge the funds of the Women's College into the University's budget, thus placing money and power in the hands of the male administrators.

"How much of an advocate for women did I feel? Completely, wholly for the women students and for the women faculty. The funding was all. If there had not been special funds for young women, I doubt if there would have been any women on the faculty, Chinese or otherwise. There were these funds, and it was the feeling of the Women's College Faculty that we needed to have women!

"My feminism over the years has never been so much militant as just bred-in-the-bone. I had a mother who was a match for my father. She was very different from him but she was certainly a match for him. Mother's whole life was: 'Women are important, and women are going to be important, and they're going to be worth being important.' It really never occurred to me that I would have to be a feminist or a suffragist or anything. This was just the way it was: women had rights, and women were going to get their rights, and women were going to be worthy of their rights."[2]

MBS's feminist mother, Emma Doll Bailey Speer, came from a family with Quaker sympathies (her father was a Friend until he married), and her mother believed that young women should be able to earn their living. This made Bryn Mawr, still viewed as a Quaker college, a natural choice for daughter Emma.[3] Just because she was the only girl in a family of five did not mean she would not go to college. Her four older brothers all went to Yale. According to MBS, one of them said to Emma, "We've all gone to college. You should go to college too!"[4] From their home in Harrisburg she was sent to Miss Stevens School in Germantown where she was prepared for Bryn Mawr College—not Yale, since in the 1890s Yale did not accept women.

At Bryn Mawr Emma Doll Bailey found English and Greek absorbing.[5] She also made many friends, among them Margaret Hilles. When a summer conference for the Student Volunteer Movement for Foreign Missions was restricted to male college students, Emma and Margaret persuaded Mrs. Hilles to chaperone them on a visit to Northfield. There they met some of the young men at the conference, among them handsome young Robert Elliott Speer, one of the speakers. A graduate of Andover and Princeton, he was campaigning to enlist college students as missionaries to bring about "the evangelization of the world in this generation."[6]

When Emma Bailey returned to Bryn Mawr for her sophomore year, she suggested to Dean M. Carey Thomas—and perhaps also to President of the College James E. Rhoads—that Robert Speer was a personable young man who was speaking at many colleges and might be invited to speak at Bryn Mawr. And so he was. Miss Bailey also managed to hear him speak in Germantown and in Philadelphia.

She put on record her interest in Home and Foreign Missions as a member of the College Missionary Society, which met occasionally "for the purpose of learning more about the methods and results of missionary work." There was, she wrote in June 1892, "a deepening interest in the work."[7] She also had a deepening interest in Robert Speer, who had been named Secretary of the Board of Foreign Missions of the Presbyterian Church. They became engaged and on April 20, 1893 they were married.

Robert Speer's work involved a great deal of traveling. Young Mrs. Speer went with him on one great trip round the world in 1896 and 1897, a rugged trip going across Russia, riding horseback through Persia, then through India and China, visiting mission stations. Many of those they met in China in a few short years would be brutally wiped out by the Boxers, the fiercely anti-Christian secret society (they practiced a prescribed ritual of Chinese boxing that they believed made them indestructible) which in 1900 burned missionary stations and killed missionaries and Chinese Christians, mostly in North China, culminating in a siege of the Peking foreign community and the Boxer War with Western powers.

After the Speers returned to the United States, they settled in Englewood, New Jersey. Five children were born: Elliott, Margaret (Marnie to her family and friends), Eleanor, Constance, and William. They grew up in a house where missionaries came as visitors, missionaries from Japan, India—and China. Some stayed for long periods of time. "We profited by the people who came and went. It was a rich life, more interesting than just ordinary families in Englewood."[8]

Robert Speer continued to travel, leaving Emma Speer to raise her children alone for long months. Undaunted, she found time and energy also to become a charter member and then president of the YWCA for sixteen years. This did not spoil family life, MBS said, because "we profited by all the contacts and the things Mother was doing."

Although Robert Speer was away a great deal, MBS remembers him as a father who "gave himself to his children when he was there in a way that many fathers don't." Summers they went for a month to Diamond Pond, near Colebrook, New Hampshire. There both boys and girls learned to camp rough. Robert Speer, his daughter recalls, "liked nothing better than to go down the stream camping, everybody carrying equipment, Father carrying the heaviest load. Mostly there were hard trips for the boys, but he always had one slightly easier trip in the summer when he would take some ladies young and old along with him. He loved to fish, he loved to tramp, he loved the hills and streams."[9]

Formal education in Englewood was also important for the Speers. MBS went first to public elementary school and then to the Dwight School, a private school for girls in Englewood. She graduated when she was sixteen, which her mother felt was too young for college, so she packed her off to Abbot Academy in Andover, Massachusetts. Many Abbot girls went to nearby Wellesley, some to Smith and Vassar.

But Bryn Mawr alumnae mothers quite often sent their daughters to Bryn Mawr. Mrs. Speer, however, was not sure. M. Carey Thomas, since 1894 the president of the College, had in 1915 and 1916 been the object of a faculty rebellion at Bryn Mawr, condemned for her highhanded ways with appointments. The contretemps was thoroughly reported in *The Philadelphia Ledger*, which distressed Mrs. Speer. Maybe Margaret should go, with other Abbot girls, to Wellesley. "My father just scoffed at that," she remembers. "'Wellesley? Certainly not Wellesley.' He had a firm idea that Bryn Mawr was a good place: it had produced my mother. I had Bailey cousins there. Certainly I was going to Bryn Mawr, as I did, and as my sister Constance did."[10]

All four of the Speer children (the fifth child, Eleanor, died when she was very young) went to their parents' colleges: Margaret and Constance to Bryn Mawr, Bill and Elliott to Princeton. At Bryn

Mawr MBS majored in history and economics, graduating in 1922. She viewed the College's president, colorful feminist M. Carey Thomas, with a mixture of awe and amusement. It was Constance Applebee, field hockey coach and director of physical education, who won MBS's affectionate admiration as the only member of the administration who encouraged and supported the Christian Association.[11] MBS became its president, following M. Carey Thomas's niece Millicent Carey, a true adherent of muscular Christianity. "Oh clever Milly, to leave us Marnie," sang their friends.[12]

MBS's years in college came at a time when there was, as she remembers, "a great feeling of internationalism." Among the speakers for the Christian Association were some who described the work to be done in China by missionary educators. President Edmunds of Canton Christian College spoke on "Modern China and its needs, and the needs of its women." "The Christian educated woman is the hope of China," he concluded.[13] Internationalism was part of the mission. From a Student Volunteer conference at Des Moines in December 1919 MBS brought back memories of dances, a snowball fight—and a speaker who urged that "Missionaries are to be considered in the light of practical statesmen molding an international morality."[14] By the time she was a senior, MBS was fairly sure she would go abroad.

The Presbyterian Mission Board, however, would not send people abroad until the year in which they were going to be twenty-five. In the three years she had to wait, MBS worked. She was secretary to Maud Royden, the English lay preacher and suffragist, during her lecture tour in the United States. MBS also taught a year at Sweet Briar College, and she spent a year doing graduate work at Bryn Mawr. "But I guess I was a little too much of an activist at that time to be much of a scholar."[15]

To MBS "Going to China was no big deal. I'd known many people who had gone. The kind of interest that there was in China in the 1920s was very much like the interest in Africa of more recent years: a continent that was opening up, people coming and going, more contacts, so that it was far away but never struck me as being dangerous." And how else could she go to live in China if not as a missionary? "It was a very natural thing to be a missionary. It wasn't as though some sudden bolt of lightning from heaven came and said to me 'You must go out and evangelize the world.'"

MBS was recruited to teach in China by tall, handsome John Leighton Stuart, an admirer of Robert Elliott Speer.[16] Stuart was the president of Yenching University in Peking, and he visited the Speers when he was in the United States fundraising. MBS's family knew that she would not be completely among strangers at Yenching: Ran Sailer[17] and George Barbour, friends of the Speer family, were teaching there. "I guess they just said, 'Marnie, come along to Yenching.'"

Yenching University was an "amalgamation" of four small denominational colleges in Peking. The intent of amalgamation was to centralize the missionary educational effort. From 1919 until 1926 the University buildings were scattered throughout the city of Peking, a makeshift until the grand new campus west of Peking could be completed. In 1920 the Women's College (founded as Bridgman Academy) became part of Yenching University, but it retained a good measure of financial and administrative autonomy.

Yenching drew young American college women, newly emancipated, eager to educate their Chinese "sisters over the sea".[18] The dean of Yenching College for Women in 1925 was Alice Browne Frame, a Mount Holyoke graduate. Alice Boring, a Bryn Mawrtyr with a Ph.D. in biology, had also been recruited by Leighton Stuart, who persuaded her to leave her teaching position at Wellesley.[19] Grace Boynton, Class of 1912 at Wellesley, daughter of Congregationalist minister Nehemiah Boynton, had been teaching English in Peking since 1919. Augusta Wagner, also from Wellesley, went out soon after MBS as a secretary and eventually became Professor of Economics after completing her Ph.D. at Columbia University in New York. Nancy Cochran came later from Smith, and others were at Yenching for brief times.

The young American women teaching at Yenching were undaunted by the unsettled political situation in China in the 1920s.[20] China was no longer the remote, romantic land described by Marco Polo, grand traveler of the 13th century. Walled in for centuries from intrusion by barbarians beyond her borders, China had tranquilly assumed herself the center of civilization. Foreigners were unwelcome but 16th century Jesuit missionaries came by land and 18th century European traders came by sea, seeking silk and tea. They had little to interest the Chinese until the British seductively introduced opium from India. Dismayed by the destructive addiction, the Imperial Government of China tried to oust the Westerners, but, no match for western warfare, lost the Opium Wars in mid-19th century.

The opening of China by treaty began, unequal treaties giving Western powers advantages over China. Extraterritorial rights were established for foreigners, merchants, diplomats, and missionaries, placing them under laws of their countries, not Chinese laws. In 1895 the Japanese fought with China over Korea and won, beginning a new imperialism. Western powers began to seize more concessions and hint at dividing China among themselves. The United States opposed this through the Open Door policy, maintaining the principle of equal opportunity in trade for all powers in China and the preservation of China's integrity as a nation.

But the Chinese resented and eventually raged against foreigners, seeing no reason to distinguish missionaries from others, in a rebellion led by the Boxers from 1899 to 1900. In North China they murdered missionaries and their families and attacked the foreign legations in Peking. The Western powers rescued the besieged Legations from the Boxers, defeated them, and imposed penalties and prohibitions, levying a $333 million indemnity against China.

If foreigners destroyed China's serene seclusion, they also stirred awareness of the need for modern education in order to survive in a modern world. Among those urging education for all of China's people, not just the elite, was Western-educated Sun Yat-sen, leader of the republican revolution that overthrew the Ching dynasty in 1911.

Even before the revolution Protestant missionaries had established schools, including some for girls. Chinese students also studied abroad, often in Japan. In 1908 the United States remitted a major portion of the American share of the Boxer indemnity to educate students for study in the United States. The "Returned Students" brought Western educational methods to China. Students also had inherited the tradition that scholars should advise those in power in the state.

The Empress Dowager, last of the Ch'ing Dynasty, was overthrown in the 1911 revolution, but Sun Yat-sen's new republic was not strong enough to resist continuing Japanese imperialism when Japan seized German rights in Shantung in 1914, forcing Twenty-One Demands on China. After World War I, the Chinese, who had declared war on the side of the Allies, hoped to persuade the Treaty Powers at Versailles in 1919 to force Japan to give up its claim to Shantung; however, it was decided to leave the German concessions to Japan.

The anger and anguish of the Chinese students over this decision was expressed in a massive protest in Peking on May 4, 1919. The Chinese student movement marks May Fourth as its first historical demonstration. Students condemned the Japanese imperialism, the Treaty of Versailles, and Chinese political submission. Peking students gathered at the Gate of Heavenly Peace, T'ien-an-Men, endorsed a manifesto, and organized for political action.

Leighton Stuart, president of Yenching University in Peking, viewed the student protesters with hope that the leadership would be Christian, a patriotic movement dedicated to uniting China.

Introduction

"The Christian movement will save not only the individual Chinese but China....And as go the students, China will follow with all its vast population."[21] Yenching's students were potentially the future leaders of China.[22]

Yenching, shaped by John Leighton Stuart's vision, had Westerners like Alice Boring on the faculty, but MBS remembers the faculty as being about three-quarters Chinese. The dream was to have Chinese and Western faculty teaching and living together on equal terms.[23]

The student body at Yenching was almost wholly Chinese, and Chinese students, after World War I, had their own dreams as they began a search for power. Some were recruited by the Chinese Communist party, formed in 1921, some by Chiang Kai-shek, rising leader of the Kuomintang, the "National People's Party."

But there was no unified nation of China. Its government was unstable, and in North China power was in the hands of the warlords, local military leaders feuding with each other, each with his own army living off the land. Sun Yat-sen in 1924 struggled to reach agreement with the warlords but he was unsuccessful and ill, and he died in March 1925.

Rancorous warlords did not interrupt the life of the new Yenching University in Peking. Alice Boring wrote to Bryn Mawr alumnae, "Political change and war makes much less difference in China than it would in any other country...The farmers have suffered by the war more than the city people, as their carts and mules were ruthlessly requisitioned by the army, but they are used to floods and famine and this is just one more piece of hard fate.

"The war has disturbed foreign trade and used up money, so that China is getting into a worse condition financially. This prevents the development of natural resources and education, but it does not make the condition of the average Chinese very different from usual. Even here in Peking, the capital of the country, the war has scarcely touched us. Everything has gone on as usual for those of us in educational work." [24]

But in Shanghai, shortly after Alice Boring wrote this letter, there was an anti-foreign demonstration and demonstrators were killed on May 30 by police. This led to a massive movement throughout China, which came to be known as the May Thirtieth Movement. It was a time of protest and instability in China but also, at Yenching, a time when student dreams of saving China were supported. To this world of political civil war and university idealism MBS came in 1925, eager to teach and eager to learn about China.

MBS's letters home from China to her parents are full of her observations about the Chinese people—she felt, increasingly, that Westerners could never totally know and understand the Chinese—her admiration for strong women she met, Western and Chinese, her fascination with architectural design (and with Yenching's architect) her adventures on walking trips into the hills, as well as descriptions of her garden, the festive rituals and friendships which sustained her in a land where there was often fighting near the University. "If it wasn't the warlords, it was the Japanese."

Only a book could hold all that she wanted to tell her dearly loved parents, but letters would have to do.

"Dear Mother and Father," she wrote, and sometimes "Darling Mother," sending the letters off "With a world full of love." Aware of the significance of historical events, she often tried to send home a record. Emma and Robert Speer must have read the letters with intense interest, often laughing, probably less agitated than many parents at the adventures and intrepid independence of their daughter.

Her story began as she set out from Diamond Pond in New Hampshire, where her family had been spending the summer. Her brother Elliott drove her to Montreal. There Henry and Jo Sailer Welles, on their way to the North China Presbyterian Mission boys' school, joined MBS on the Canadian Pacific for Vancouver. Jo Sailer's family were the Speers' next door neighbors in Englewood, and she had spent two years in Peking teaching at the North China College for Women. Henry had visited Peking briefly when he accompanied Robert Speer around the world in 1922 to 1923, so MBS was traveling with old friends and old China hands. They sailed from Vancouver on the *Empress of Australia* to Yokohama, Japan, where the ship steamed through the Japanese fleet on maneuvers, the travelers' first sight of Japanese military power. From Japan they went by boat to Korea and by train to Mukden in Manchuria and then to Peking. In Mukden they saw the soldiers of the warlord, Chang Tso-lin. Neither the Japanese nor the warlord interfered with the travelers, and they arrived safely in Peking.

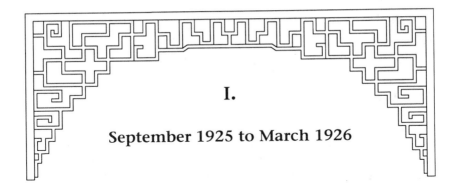

I.

September 1925 to March 1926

Taking a Whack at Chinese

*M*argaret Bailey Speer's *train was met at the dusty Peking station by a throng from the Presbyterian Mission, who escorted her sedately by ricksha to the Mission Compound, where she was to live with a family named Steinbeck. To her missionary elders she was a treasure, daughter of Robert Speer, Secretary of the Board of Foreign Missions of the Presbyterian Church.*

No doubt she was cheered to be met also by one of her own generation, George Barbour, who came barreling along bareheaded on his bicycle, shouting a greeting. There were others too, like John and Barbara Hayes, from the Mission, who were to lighten her life.

The first task for Westerners who came to teach at Yenching was to learn Chinese—or at least to tackle it! Language School was a trial, but MBS was not condemned to live in the drafty old Chinese palace, the T'ung Fu, which housed the Women's College. Not content to study only the language, MBS set out to learn about China: to hike in the Western Hills, wander about old temples, and taste strange Chinese delicacies. At Western dinner parties she listened attentively to conversations about the unsettled military and political issues that caused friction between Chinese and Westerners. She found time also to describe her adventures to her family.

September 25, 1925

Everyone had warned us, dismally, that from Mukden to Peking would be the worst part of the journey, but it was all perfectly serene and our train rolled into Peking exactly on time. It's true that there were other inhabitants of the sleepers beside the passengers, but since the troops have been using the trains that was only to be expected.

There were lots of people down at the station to meet us. I was informed a thousand times that there had been a battle royal over where I was to stay, but it had finally been decided that I was to live at the Mission with the Steinbecks. We therefore stopped on the way to the compound to visit the T'ung Fu (as the Women's College is always called) so that Jo could see her old friends and I could see the whole shooting match.

As we were all riding solemnly along in rickshas and the older missionaries were apologizing for the dust storm which greeted us, our respectability was shocked by a shout from the rear, "Well, Marnie, what a funny old woman you'll be!" and George [Barbour] came flying down on his bicycle, getting in the way of the rickshas and looking very thin but as young as he used to be. He flies about bare-headed and does other things that most missionaries are careful not to.[1]

After all the tales of Chinese discomforts I feel as if I were living in a palace. The Steinbecks' house is gray stone, built very much like any American or English house of thirty years ago. There are electric lights and a real bathroom, and what greater luxury could anyone ask. The compound is full of green trees and children and is altogether a very happy place.

You've been in Peking yourselves, and there's not much point in my writing you a book to describe the taste of the dust, and how you find you have a dirty face just when you want to look most fetching, or how helpless you feel when you can't speak Chinese to the ricksha coolie, or how horribly the beggars whine, or how

13

fascinating the markets are, or what a nuisance it is always to wear a hat and never to drink unboiled water, or how pathetic a funeral procession, or all the other thousand and one first impressions.

The weather is really heavenly, cool and sunny, and breezes that are very nice in the compound, though of course they mean dust in the streets.

September 28, 1925

I'm staying for several days at the T'ung Fu to get acquainted with the Women's College faculty. It is awfully funny how everyone tries to give me an impersonal view of China and yet how each group tries to make me see that its work and its outlook is the most important thing in the whole country. I'm very glad that I'm really living at the Mission compound. Quite aside from the fact that it's the most comfortable place to live it will give me a more peaceful winter, a better chance at the language, and a more general view of the work in Peking than I would have had anywhere else.

The Presbyterian Mission in the North part of Peking was a typical mission compound with six or eight western-style houses behind a high wall with a spirit screen inside the gate. It seemed to MBS in 1925 a wonderful oasis. "Later," she wrote in 1982, "we often commented on some of the unfortunate effects of missionaries living in such foreign style in the middle of Chinese towns and cities all over the country. It was the custom, however, and perhaps no other arrangement would have been possible, in Peking at least."[2]

Like most new missionaries, MBS spent her first year in China studying the Chinese language. Her struggle to learn to speak Chinese was to be a constant in her life in China, but she never let this deter her from trying to talk with the Chinese people she met.

From the start, she faced her life in China from a position of strength. Her sense of humor kept her from taking missionary work too seriously, and her self-confidence and common sense, seasoned with an eagerness for new experiences, made her willing to experiment and explore. Above all, her well-educated mind (a history and economics major at Bryn Mawr) and her lively intellectual curiosity led her to find civil and international turmoil in China fascinating rather than frightening.

October 11, 1925

The days are frantically busy. Sunday morning we went to the Boys' School service where Allan Hunter[3] spoke on what young people everywhere could do for peace. They told us afterwards that the interpreter had left out entirely all his remarks about the wickedness of America. Mr. Steinbeck seemed to think the interpreter was justified, but I don't see any hope for future understanding if the Chinese aren't told that there are a few of us at any rate who are ashamed of the iniquities of the West.

Sunday afternoon Henry [Welles] and I wandered about the Temple of Heaven. Jo didn't go with us, as she has had a miserable cold ever since she got here, and has had to take things slowly. Henry and I had a splendid time, revelling in the color and lines of the Temple and the altar and roaming through the woods around it.

No one seems to have thought it unusual for a young female missionary to wander alone through the Temple of Heaven with a married man, so long as they both were part of the Mission. MBS's expeditions with husbands of the Presbyterian Mission were in keeping with the mission tradition: "Circumstances in China encouraged camaraderie which extended across sexual lines."[4] In any case, most of MBS's time was taken up with Language School.

Don't worry about our keeping up this terrific pace all winter. We are being thoroughly looked after, and besides, next week we will have to begin studying in the evening. So far we have had nothing to do outside of school hours.

Just going to school is tiresome enough, though, as the person who designed the seats evidently bore a great grudge against all future students. The first few days I writhed in agony trying to find a suitable angle for my long spine and the hard bench back. Then suddenly I had an inspiration. Now I blow up an air cushion and sit in sumptuous ease.

Language School lasts every day from 8:45 to 12, and 2 to 4; and twice a week we are there till 5:15. I try to walk at least twice a day, but it takes at least half an hour to sprint the two miles (more if you stop to pick up the babies you trip over) so that it's rather a rush, as well as bad for the digestion to rush right off after breakfast and lunch every day.

Actually studying Chinese is fascinating. The teachers do not speak a word of English and yet they make us understand a dozen or more new Chinese words every day. It's great sport, and though the tones seem hopeless, still it's very exciting to try a few laborious phrases and find that the ricksha coolie understands.

Harold Shadick, an Englishman, who had also arrived at Yenching in the fall of 1925 and was in MBS's language class, recalls that the Language School was fairly new and had a principal who was somewhat of a tyrant. He was feared by the Chinese tutors, who were ordered to drill on words already studied and not to introduce additional words. Shadick felt the need of more "street" words and persuaded the tutor to pass on "contraband" words surreptitiously.[5]

Street words were useful in speaking Chinese, but at Mission dinner tables the language was that of diplomacy and the problems of extraterritoriality. A few years earlier, in 1921 and 1922, China's problems had been discussed at the Washington Conference. The post-World-War-I treaty powers hoped to encourage a stable government in China, and the Nine-Power Treaty had affirmed support for the Open Door policy and the territorial integrity of China. It also proposed conferences on the Chinese customs tariff and extraterritoriality, but the tariff conference was not held until 1925-26, and neither this meeting nor that of the extra-territoriality commission in 1926 resolved the issues.[6]

October 18, 1925

The Missionary Association has appointed a committee to draw up resolutions concerning our stand on the questions of tariff autonomy, extraterritoriality, unequal treaties, etc. When these are brought up for a vote, the people who have been hedging and talking about "explaining" will have to take a definite stand. John Hayes seems to me to have more "dope" on the situation than anyone else out in this compound. Other people seem to think they can shut their eyes and maintain the status quo, but he sees all the questions that are inevitably going to be involved.[7]

This morning's paper is full of rumors of war, and apparently the situation around Shanghai is serious. General Sun Chuan-fang, who apparently cares nothing for the present government and would like nothing better than the failure of the Conference, is making the most of his chances and taking over Shanghai. He wants Nanking too, and though the other warlords are docilely withdrawing their troops, realizing the value for the present of peace at any price, they are not likely to let him go on forever. If General Feng or Marshal Chang send troops to meet him and are not able to rout him at once, there will be serious civil war, and the Tariff Conference won't be likely to accomplish much.

MBS was concerned about the international conferences and conflicts, but her own special struggle continued to be with the Chinese language. She wrote about it to her younger brother Bill.

November 7, 1925

I have a Chinese name, spelled in English Sang Mei-te. If you pronounce it one way it means "Beautiful virtuous abundance" and if you pronounce it another way it means "Half-baked mulberry tree." So you see how careful you have to be. There is a girl next door whose name is "Lovely pearls" but if you pronounce it just a little bit differently it means "True pig." If you say *Shu pu yao* in one tone of voice it means "I don't want the book" and if you say it in another it means "Bats don't bite." So if you think Latin is a terrible language, just come and take a whack at Chinese.[8]

The next week MBS went to the Western Hills for the first of many weekend retreats. The Hills were often to be a sanctuary from urban and University pressures. MBS had been brought up by her father to hike and camp joyfully.

November 15th 1925

Yesterday was the most heavenly day we've had since we got to Peking. For a long time we've been planning a weekend in the Western Hills, and we thought we had arranged for quite a large party to go out yesterday for the night. But for various reasons— Christmas shopping and rumors of war—everyone dropped out but Jo and Henry Welles. I have had a bad cold, so I decided I would just go for the day and come back early with John Hayes.

We got up at the crack of dawn yesterday morning and started out in rickshas for the Hsi Chih Men station, where the trains leave for the Hills. The stars were out and a little new moon was just rising. It was bitter cold. I had on two sweaters and my leather jacket and my old coat, as well as my handsome silk and wool underclothes (it was the first time I had worn them and I was very glad to have them on as we spent the day alternately getting hot and cooling off). John went ahead on his wheel and persuaded the conductor to hold the train for us, as our ricksha men simply would not hurry. The train left at seven, and we traveled with a few shivering coolies in an open horse car so that we could see the sunrise.

The Western Hills were unspeakably lovely, all violet and blue in the early morning light, with deep velvety shadows in all the hollows. In the middle of the day the bright sunlight seems to bleach the color out of everything, but the air is so clear that the morning and evening lights are particularly beautiful.

By eight o'clock we were at Shih Chin Shan where Jo and Henry were going to spend the night and where we left their cots and blankets.

We started out on foot and wandered around for a while on a sandy stretch of ground between two river beds, so flat and sandy that the foreigners all call it Mespot. While we were waiting for a boat to carry us and a few donkeys across one of these streams we watched a man in a hut administering morphine to several men through a hypodermic needle of questionable cleanliness. John says they use it out in the country for all sorts of diseases, but of course most of the people who take it are not sick at all.

We had a gorgeous morning wandering across the fields and stopping to eat persimmons. As these were very soft and we had no spoons, we had a most hilarious time trying to eat the insides without covering our whole anatomies with sticky persimmon juice. We were absolutely unsuccessful and amused the whole village with our antics. Everyone gathered around to watch and wondered why we were such idiots as to try to suck out the insides instead of eating skins and all like sensible people.

Finally we struck up into the hills to Chien T'ai Ssu, a Buddhist Temple high up in the hills in a lovely grove of oak trees. All the trees were red and russet, the first great patch of autumn coloring I've seen in China. We had our luncheon there and talked to the priests who were all very friendly and not nearly so eager for coppers as the priests in the temples nearer Peking. The temple buildings are very well kept up and are all really beautiful, climbing up the hillside in terraces, with the courts full of tremendous old gnarled trees. Some of the buildings are supposed to be seventeen hundred years old.

While we were eating our lunch, we heard the priests chanting their noonday prayers. Then we climbed still higher up the hillside and while the men went on up a very steep slope to "The Peak of Perfect Happiness" Jo and I lay in the sunshine looking across the hills and plains to the range of eastern mountains almost ninety miles the other side of Peking. Everything was tawny in the bright sunlight, and the nearer hills with their steep bare sides looked very like the Highlands. I kept thinking of that verse in Isaiah "Thine eyes shall see the King in His beauty, they shall behold the land of far distances."

At last we had to think of going home and here lay the great problem. Jo and Henry were going back the five miles to Shih Chin Shan, but the only train we could get from there would bring us into Peking after the city gates were closed. (Since the latest war scare Feng's soldiers have been guarding several of the gates, and they are shut at five o'clock.) So John suggested that we strike south to Ch'ang Shin Tien, a station on the Hankow Line, where we could catch a train that comes straight through the wall to a station inside the city.

We said good-bye to Jo and Henry and started leisurely down the mountain, thinking we had about seven miles to go and more than three hours before train time. We stopped several times to look at the view and to eat persimmons, and in one little village we went into a shop and sat down and drank tea while everyone came up and chatted with John. He explained thousands of Chinese customs, and I felt that I was learning more about China in a few hours than I could learn in weeks of Language School.

But just outside the village we got a bad shock. We stopped to ask the way, and a friendly traveler who had just come up from the town toward which we were headed, told us that we still had fifteen *li* (that is five miles) to go and that the last train for Peking left at half past four. Since it was then half past three, we looked at each other in despair and John asked if I was good at a dog trot. I said I could walk as fast as ever he wanted, but running was absolutely beyond me. So he set the pace and off we started.

Conversation stopped, and I didn't see any more of the view but kept my eyes glued on his heels in the path in front. The fastest "speed queen" on the Colebook Road never equaled our long strides. Five miles an hour doesn't seem such terrific speed when you are fresh and have a smooth road before you, but just try it when you've already done ten or twelve miles and when you're not sure of your way on rocky Chinese footpaths.

We decided that if we missed the train, I could impersonate Barbara Hayes for a while and we would try to get donkeys and strike up along the river the ten miles to Shih Chin Shan where we could spend the night with Jo and Henry who had already begged us to share their blankets with them; but we made up our minds that we were not going to miss the train.

When we were still nearly a mile from the station, a small boy told us that the train was already there. I wish you could have seen us go! As we were striding up the last hill we met a whole flock of Chinese school boys with their books under their arms, and they all fell in behind us with shrieks of laughter, imitating our ridiculous foreign stride.

Just as we got within sight of the station we saw a train go by, and our hearts sank, but we made one final spurt and found our own train sitting peacefully at the platform not expecting to go for twenty minutes. But it was just half past four, so that if it had gone on time we would have made it! We were so hot that we didn't like to risk the open car, and the regular second and third class carriages were so unspeakably stuffy that we climbed into a freight car and sat on some lumber where we could look out the door at the sunset over the hills we had just left and watch the camel trains moving by in the dusk.

Today I'm a little stiff, and John decided that he would get to church before the congregation this morning so that he wouldn't have an audience while he hobbled into the pulpit. He and Barbara are certainly two of the finest people in Peking. They are always full of fun and they know more about Chinese psychology than anyone else I've met.

The next week Augusta Wagner, a Wellelsey graduate, arrived to be secretary to the dean of the Women's College. When she arrived, MBS wrote to her mother, "We fell on each other's necks with great feeling." MBS had met Augusta Wagner when she was working for the National Board of the YWCA with Mrs. Speer before going to Wellesley. In 1925 Augusta's sister had recently died,(her mother had died earlier) and her father and brother, MBS recalled, thought it quite mad for her to go off to China. MBS remembered her as "naturally adventurous, meeting serenely the inconvenience of traveling alone on delayed ships and trains from Yokohama to Kobe to Tientsin to Peking, but quite unprepared for the strains of life at the T'ung Fu, the Women's College."

The T'ung Fu, where the Women's College was housed, was "a sprawling picturesque series of courtyards that had been the palace or residence of a family named T'ung. It was cold and drafty, built like most Chinese houses without enclosed corridors so that to go from one room to another (bedroom to bathroom, for instance) one had to run across the courtyard braving the icy North China wind. Such discomforts were minor, however, compared to the discomfort of being thrown into the midst of older women who were set in their ways and whose attitudes too often were narrow and censorious. Individually they meant to be helpful to the newest recruit, but collectively they were forbidding."[9]

Life outside the T'ung Fu included constant speculation about the complicated relationships of the Chinese and Westerners in Peking.

December 12, 1925

Last evening I had a very interesting time at dinner at the T.T. Lews'. Dean Lew is certainly one of the finest men in Peking.[10] His frail little body seems ready to collapse at any minute, but there is nothing frail or weak about his spirit. In speaking of the Customs

Conference, he said that neither he nor any other Chinese in any sort of public position could make any public statement about the present situation that did not demand full and immediate customs autonomy and abolition of extraterritoriality, even though many of them know that any such immediate step is impossible. The reason for this, he said, was that they had learned from long experience that in dealing with Anglo-Saxons they were dealing with legalists who stick to the letter rather than to the principle.

If the Chinese delegates admit that they think only partial autonomy is wise just now, the Western diplomats will go home and say, "Why, the Chinese themselves don't want autonomy. We went to the Conference ready to give those fellows anything they asked for, but they themselves agreed that they wanted us to stay on and help manage things a little longer."

And as a result it will be impossible to secure any other change or modification for the next twenty years. It is in the same spirit that foreigners are saying now that the present tariff rates weren't imposed upon China, but that the Chinese themselves wanted and asked for them. A fact which is true, of course, but doesn't make the present conditions any more tolerable to the Chinese. Dean Lew said that French influence is growing rapidly in China, largely because the French psychology is similar to the Chinese. The French are willing to discuss and agree to principles, realizing that adjustments and compromises must be made later and that the details must be left flexible, instead of insisting, as the Anglo-Saxons do, on working out a detailed and concrete plan which they forevermore cling to tenaciously.

His opinions about General Feng Yü-hsiang were very interesting. He thinks he is the only one of the present warlords who is disinterested, and that if he can avoid the advice of too many politicians, he will really be able to gain control and restore order. He says that if the combination of Feng and C.T. Wang can't succeed, nobody can.

Food for the mind was important, but MBS was also interested in what was on the table, and she unhesitatingly tried new delicacies. She wrote to her brother Bill about some of her experiments with Chinese food.

December 13, 1925

I've had a lot of Chinese food lately. I've had most of the queer things to eat that you read about in books except birds' nest soup, and that costs about twenty dollars a dish, so you see why we don't have it for lunch every day.

Sea slugs are supposed to be a great delicacy, but I don't like them much. They look like snails with a lot of horns, and they just taste like any old kind of fat. Thirty-year-old eggs are simply delicious. The white is a clear transparent red color, the yolk looks like gray-green clay, and the taste is most surprising! Ducks' windpipes are another delicacy, at least when I've been out to dinner in Chinese houses the host has fished them out of the dish and presented them to me with great ceremony, but they really haven't any taste at all.

The best thing of all, that we always order when we go out to dinner in a Chinese restaurant, is what we call "ducks in doilies." You put a round thin pancake made out of bread dough on your plate, and then you pick up a piece of raw onion in your fingers. Using this as a spreader, you smear your pancake with a spicy sort of sauce just the color of apple butter. Then you make a little pile of onion and duck and delicious vegetables in the middle of your pancake, which you then roll up neatly and eat with your fingers. There are two difficulties about eating it: if you don't fill your pancake full enough, you have to eat an awful lot of dough for a very little bit of duck; and if you fill it too full, it's likely to spring a leak and the juice runs down your arm or gets sprayed all over the table.

But table manners in China are a great comfort. You don't have to bother about polite conversation. It's perfectly polite not to say a word but to devote yourself entirely to stuffing yourself as full as possible. All the dishes are put in the middle of the table, so you grab for yourself and reach in front of your neighbors and spill as much as you like. After a feast is over, the table is so covered with scraps that it looks as if there had been a fight or as if the cat had been walking over it and upset all the dishes.

I have pretty nearly mastered the art of eating with chopsticks except when it comes to noodles. They are very popular here and are served in a way that makes them seem particularly long and slippery. Most people don't even try to eat them neatly. You grasp a few of them firmly with your chopsticks, stuff them into your mouth, bite them off, and let the remaining six inches of them fall back onto your plate with a splash.[11]

Warlords

Although Peking was reasonably safe for Westerners investigating Chinese restaurants, the city's residents were always aware of the fighting not far away in the countryside between the Chinese warlords, who pillaged the countryside, disrupted transportation, and thus eroded the economy. Warlords repeatedly fought with each other, changing partners and betraying each other. Three were well known: Chang Tso-lin was known as the "Warlord of Manchuria"; Wu P'ei-fu had been trained by the Japanese; Feng Yü-hsiang was the "Christian General."[12]

December 20, 1925

After two and a half months of Language School our Christmas vacation has begun, and I feel just about ready for a little excitement. Moreover, it looks as if we might get it. The horizon seems to contain two events ready to relieve the monotony of life—the war and the Anti-Christian movement. I wish I knew what the papers at home were saying about us here—nothing at all, if they are wise, for there is really little real news; but Peking is a perfect hotbed of rumors, and all sorts of wild reports are circulated every day.

First I'll explain why the war is getting exciting. Not because there is any chance of the fighting coming any nearer to Peking, though people in the South City say they can hear the guns, but simply because Feng's wounded are being brought back here, the worst cases to the PUMC[13] and the others to the base hospital at Nan Yuan just a few miles south of us. There have been calls for volunteer nurses, doctors, and chauffeurs, and for people to make surgical dressings.

It is simply sickening that so many of Feng's men are being hurt—most of the reports are unreliable but apparently nearly five thousand have been killed and wounded. And here again, foreigners are at the back of it, as of so many of China's troubles. As you probably know, the present fighting is between Feng and Li Chinglin and started after Li and Kuo had deserted Chang Tso-lin. When it started everyone thought it would be over in a few days, as it was just the usual Chinese bluff on both sides. Li only started it for personal reasons, and Feng sent his troops toward Tientsin because Li had been breathing out fire against him and it seemed time to maintain peace and order. But the trouble came because Li has as advisor an English soldier of fortune named Sutton who takes war more seriously than Chinese soldiers do, with their safety pins and umbrellas. So it turned out that on Sutton's advice Li's men had dug themselves real trenches, and that Li had a good supply of six-inch guns. Now with all this preparedness for real war, Li, just to save his face, has to keep on fighting.

Most Chinese soldiers are a pretty rum lot and the fewer there are in China the better off the country would be, but it's rather sad to have Feng's men getting the worst of it, for they are decent and well-trained. Wherever they go they pay for what they take, business picks up, and the districts through which they have passed are better off for their having been there, while all the other troops leave desolation in their wake. The care that is being given to Feng's wounded is something perfectly unheard of in Chinese warfare. They are actually being looked after at the front instead of being left to die where they fall.

The most serious outcome of all this fighting—not just the Feng-Li campaign but the whole business—is probably going to be in Manchuria. The Japanese have already taken advantage of Chang Tso-lin's fall and have calmly taken possession of Mukden, and they'll soon find a good excuse to take over even more of Manchuria than they already have. China will probably object in vain. Russia may object more forcibly. Of course you mustn't take anything that I say too seriously—it's all just repetition of other people's opinions, but politics is the most absorbing subject of conversation at every Peking dinner party.

The second excitement is the Anti-Christian movement. For months we have known that they have planned special propaganda for Christmas time, but lately all the wild rumors have been growing a little more definite. Most of the rumors are hysterical and perfectly absurd, and each person believes what he pleases—that nothing is going to happen or that by the end of this week not a Christian will be left alive or a church standing in Peking. A lot of silly people go around saying this will be just like 1900, but they forget that there is this difference: in 1900 it was the missionaries who said ahead of time that there was danger and the Legations who poohpoohed the idea, but now half the people in the Legation Quarter are scared out of their wits while most of the missionaries agree in saying that half the rumors are tommyrot and the other half bunk. However, most of the Christian institutions are taking precautions, not against any attack so much as against any panic among the Christian students or church members.

It's hard to imagine anything more absurd than most of the rumors: that Tsing Hua is going to be burned because it was built with American indemnity money,[14] that Yenching is also to be burned to the ground, that the agitators have quantities of sulphur bombs ready, that every Christian Christmas celebration will be broken up, and that all Christian schools and churches will be burned. It's all perfectly ludicrous and the majority of missionaries and Chinese Christians treat it as simply ridiculous exaggeration.

On Friday there was a meeting of the Anti-Christian leaders to plan the demonstration, and in spite of wide advertising only thirty people came, which was scarcely a dangerous showing. Moreover, General Lu Chung-lin, the Defense Commissioner for Peking, has ordered that there shall be no demonstration of any kind, no parades, no mass meetings, no public Anti-Christian gatherings, and he has even gone so far as to forbid the use of fire-crackers in any celebration for fear the noise might be mistaken for gunfire and start a panic! So you can see that actually there is very little danger.

But the combination of the war and the Anti-Christian agitation makes one stop to consider the real significance of Christmas. This morning, Dr. Y.Y. Tsu preached at the PUMC service. He is the director of religious work there, and his wife, who was one of the Hui girls, is one of the nicest girls in Peking. He preached a splendid sermon, but the most significant thing he said was that in the present situation we should be very careful to attribute only the highest motives to our enemies and to realize that the Anti-Christian agitators are absolutely sincere in thinking they must attack Christianity both as a tool of imperialism that has been used to help in the break-up of Chinese culture and as a religion of superstition. He is quite right.

Of course a few of the agitators are only radical Communists who are looking for any sort of a row, but a great many of them are absolutely sincere in thinking Christianity a menace to Chinese civilization, and if we will only realize that, it ought to challenge us to make sure that our work is not in any way an agent of imperialism or an attempt to substitute Western religious superstition for Chinese superstitions. It makes one stop to consider how much of our ordinary Christmas celebration is just a mass of tradition, valuable only because it has associations that we love, and how much of it is the real beauty and truth of the Christmas message that God's love has entered the life of men.

Those who feared the Anti-Christian Movement most intensely were doubtless the members of the mission community who remembered clearly the Boxer Rebellion in 1900, when the fiercely anti-Christian secret society killed North China missionaries and attacked the foreign community in Peking.

The impact of the Anti-Christian Movement in the 1920s on Yenching was to force Westerners to ponder the intercultural nature of the University.[15] Trustees of Yenching in New York urged the Western faculty to leave China, but Leighton Stuart insisted that the Chinese and Westerners were working together in time of crisis, seizing the challenge "to practice international fellowship and Christian principles."[16]

MBS approached this challenge by looking for opportunities to see at first hand China's civil war casualties, since she knew that her students were undecided in seeking to build a strong China through military strength or through pacifism.

Sunday Morning [after Christmas, December 27, 1925]

It is a nice sunny morning and I am making the most of a day of peace before I start out tomorrow for adventures. I'm not sure yet where I'm going. We have another week of vacation at Language School, and I had been planning to go out to visit some of the country villages.

Yesterday, however, word came from the emergency hospital at Nan Yuan that they are in desperate need of workers—anybody with a strong back and presence of mind. The nurses and doctors who have been down there for the last two weeks are all being laid low with flu, and the wounded soldiers are still coming in. There isn't any equipment, the men are lying on straw, or on the stone floor, or just out in the yards. I've been eager to go from the beginning, but at first they only needed nurses. So I told Margaret Barnes I couldn't go with her, and got all set to go down to Nan Yuan this morning. But Dr. Bash heard about it and said I'd be sure to get the flu and that she would send down two Chinese nurses from Dow hospital who would be more useful than I. I was terribly disappointed, but there was nothing to do but submit gracefully. There is no course for a new missionary except to heed politely the advice of all the old hands and be thankful when all the advice isn't contradictory.

There is still hope, though, for John Hayes has gone down today to look the ground over and see what the station can do as a unit. He is going to bring back a report tonight, so I can decide then whether I can go to Nan Yuan; otherwise, I'll go off with Margaret to Ma Fang.

My reason for wanting to go to Nan Yuan is not just wanting to rush off to excitement or simply because there is need for emergency relief but it will really be valuable experience, especially since I'm going to be working with students who are young and enthusiastic and wavering between pacifism and the feeling that strong military preparedness is China's only hope.

For instance, there is a tremendous difference of opinion among the missionaries. Allan Hunter has come back from work at Nan Yuan convinced that Feng's Christian propaganda is on a par with Sutton's contributions to Gen. Li of Swiss guns and foreign military tactics—merely a more effective method of warfare. It's a real question whether Feng's Christianity is going to bring peace or more war to China. However, we're all exceedingly thankful Feng's troops came out ahead this time.

Barred from helping with wounded soldiers, MBS went instead out into the countryside to visit members of the Mission who were living and working in a rural Chinese village.

January 3, 1926

School begins again tomorrow, so I'm spending today trying to get caught up with letters, for I found my desk piled high with American mail when I came home last night from the country. We had a most wonderful time in spite of the bitter cold, and I wish there were time to write a book about all our adventures.

We started out last Monday with the thermometer at 8 degrees, the coldest day so far this winter and colder than any day in Peking all last year. There were three of us: Margaret Barnes, a nice girl in our mission who has been out here a year and a half and whose family are now living in Harrisburg, Janet (Jennie) Mackay, a Scotch doctor, who is full of devilment and is in particularly high spirits just now as she is to be married in a few weeks, and I.

Grace Boynton was with us the first lap of the trip. She is Nehemiah Boynton's daughter and is assistant professor of English at Yenching, but is spending this winter all by herself out in a country village studying Chinese. We took the train from Peking out to Tunghsien, less than ten miles from the city wall, but as far as the train would take us toward our destination. The third class car was of course not heated and that was really the coldest part of our whole trip.

You would have had to see us to appreciate our clothes, but I'll send you some pictures as soon as they are developed, which will show you how outlandish we looked. Margaret had on, over the part of her anatomy between her waist and her knees, not counting coats and outer coverings, nine layers! Since I was wearing knickerbockers, I wasn't quite so heavily swaddled, but I wore all the sweaters I owned, topped by a most ridiculous old Chinese coat, fur inside and silk outside. It seems odd, but heavy Chinese silk is much the best for the outside covering because it sheds the dust.

At Tunghsien we hired a cart for our bedding rolls and started out across the river valley in a dust storm that was simply blinding. Though the first river to be crossed was not more than fifty feet wide, it took us more than half an hour to get across, since it is a slow business to load carts, mules, donkeys and horses, onto the little flat-bottomed ferry. Once across the ferry, we trudged along beside the cart, thankful that the wind was blowing from the west so that the dust was not right in our faces, and got to Yenchio, seven miles away about three o'clock.

Grace's cook was expecting us and had water piping hot for us to wash our dusty faces with, and a lunch of delectable hot *chupopos.* Grace has two tiny Chinese rooms with regular paper windows and stone floors, but with foreign stoves she manages to keep very warm and cosy. At six o'clock we all went to the service in the little street chapel next door. Pastor Li, an enormous man with a most engaging smile, who is the country evangelist for that district, played the hymns on an accordion, and a young student preached. Naturally I couldn't understand more than a few words here and there, but the audience, made up mostly of small boys and donkey drivers and carters, listened very attentively.

That night the only place where there was room for the three of us to sleep was on the *k'ang* in Grace's room. The *k'ang* is the most important part of every Chinese house; it is a raised brick platform that can be heated underneath, and is used for sleeping, eating, and sitting, Chu P'u, Grace's servant, was so anxious to make us comfortable that he built a roaring fire underneath, and we had to spend the night turning over and over to keep from scorching in any one spot.

On Tuesday we started on to Ma Fang, seventeen miles away, where the Gordons are living. Mr. Gordon had sent his cart in to Yenchio for us, and Jennie and Margaret rode in it most of the way, but I walked along with the carter making feeble efforts in Chinese.

It was still bitter cold, but there was no wind, and the sun was very bright. The air was so clear that we could see the whole semicircle of mountains that surround Peking on the west, north, and east. It was a glorious day. Every mile or so we went through a little village where the women and the donkeys were grinding corn, while the men were sunning themselves against the mud walls, and the children were busy gathering fertilizer and scraping the fields for any bits of grass that might do for fuel.

Every little while a little cavalcade of men on donkeys would pass us, looking for all the world like the Canterbury pilgrims in their gray coats and black hoods. Mr. Gordon came part way to meet us on his bicycle bringing sandwiches and a thermos full of cocoa, but we had to eat quickly before our toes and fingers froze.

We got to Ma Fang in the middle of the afternoon and were thankful for the sight of a foreign house. Our mission has had an outstation at Ma Fang for a long time, but the results have not been very encouraging. In 1900 there were about three hundred Christians in the whole district called the East Field, but most of them were killed by the Boxers.

The next year the church there had an even worse blow because the Italian troops which were sent out there to punish the Boxers were led about by a Christian elder who behaved in a most heathenish manner and made the most of his opportunities for blackmail. For the last four years there has been no missionary out there, though we own a good deal of property there, and a foreign house built about ten years ago was standing empty. This fall the Gordons moved out there, though it is a day's journey from a doctor or any other foreigner. Mr. Gordon is doing agricultural work, trying to improve native methods of farming and experimenting with native grains and stock.

But they need a doctor there desperately. They already have a dispensary that is fitted up with all the necessary equipment, but it had to be closed some time ago for lack of funds. The two days that we were there, Jennie looked over all the girls in the little school and treated some of the women in the outlying villages, but that was such a tiny drop in the bucket that it only made one realize more than ever how much a doctor is needed. Everywhere we saw children with trachoma and all sorts of horrid skin diseases.

We spent two days in Ma Fang, visiting some of the houses, and playing with the Gordon children in our spare minutes. It was a very good glimpse of what life is like in a missionary outstation. The Gordons can get kerosene and some varieties of food right there in Ma Fang, but coal has to be hauled from Tunghsien and everything else from Peking. Mail comes by messenger three times a week, but there is no parcel post. The only method of locomotion is bicycles for Mr. Gordon and cart for Mrs. Gordon and the children. They all seemed very busy and happy, but life must often be very cold and lonely.

On Friday, New Year's Day, we started home, this time taking donkeys instead of a cart. The wee beasts were so completely covered by our *rutaos* (bedding rolls) that it seemed wicked for us to climb up on top. The whole village assembled to watch us mount, and I was glad for our reputation that Margaret was an accomplished rider. She sat so securely on top of her trotting steed that we christened her "Queen of the Donks," but Jennie and I felt very precarious indeed.

We hadn't gone more than a mile when we came to a pond covered with ice. Our donkey boys took a short cut across the middle and left us to our fate as our animals tried to pick their way around the slippery path by the edge. Suddenly Jennie's mount refused to go any further on such a questionable expedition and lowered his head, leaving Jennie standing neatly on her feet in front of him.

While we were laughing at her, my donkey decided to turn at right angles and ascend an absolutely perpendicular bank. Since I was helpless to stop him, there was nothing to do but turn a back somersault. I had on so many clothes that I merely bounced across the ice with my feet in the air. After that we found it was speedier for me to walk, though I did ride a little bit later in the day.

We spent that night at Yenchio again with Grace [Boynton]

and started for Tunghsien yesterday morning in a somewhat milder dust storm than the one we had had on Monday. They had told us in Yenchio that the train for Peking left at twelve thirty, but at twelve o'clock just as we were helping our donkeys to disembark from the ferry we heard the engine whistle as it departed up the line. There was not another train until five, so we were a little disconsolate, but we decided to go on two miles into the town of Tunghsien East where the American Board Mission is. We felt like such awful looking sights in our old clothes covered with dust that we didn't like to present ourselves in civilized society, but Margaret said she knew some people who wouldn't mind appearances. But all the houses in the compound look alike, and we landed by mistake at the Burgesses. They are always cordial and welcomed us in with open arms.[17]

It turned out that they were in the midst of a New Year house party and some of the guests who had been expected on the morning train hadn't turned up, so they had plenty of luncheon for us. Dick Ritter and several other Peking people were there, and our awful looking clothes only added to the general merriment. Mrs. Burgess is the only woman in China who is as tall as I am, and she was so pleased at the prospect of seeing someone else wearing her clothes that she begged us to stay over Sunday. But we really were too disreputable for that, and besides we knew there would be piles of home mail waiting for us in Peking, so after seeing all the sights of Tunghsien we came in on the evening train.

Tunghsien itself is full of Feng's soldiers, but we didn't see any out in the country except on the roads leading south from Tunghsien and Peking. They march along singing "Hark the herald angels sing" in a sort of quick step time.

Altogether we had a splendid time. Best of all we got a real idea of what China is like outside the cities. The people in the villages even fifteen miles from Peking are absolutely unaffected by the ups and downs of the political situation, except when taxes are raised or troops are quartered on them.

Everyone was extremely friendly. Most people thought I was a man because I was walking and because of my extraordinary height. Most of the men by the side of the road would hail me and pass the time of day, which consists in China of asking where you are going, where you have come from, and whether or not you have eaten.

After nearly a week out of doors and in sight of the mountains, and after so much exercise—I walked considerably more than sixty-five miles—it seems terribly shut in here among Peking's gray walls, but it is pleasant to be back where one does not have to break the ice on the water pitcher in order to wash in the mornings, and where one does not have to wear so many clothes that one's arms stick out at right angles.

Mr. Chi

In this first year in China, when she was not yet entangled in teaching schedules, committee work, and administrative responsibilities, MBS not only explored life in China outside Peking, but also intrepidly seized a chance to observe the customs of a Chinese family at home.

February 28, 1926

I'm enclosing a letter to amuse you. Also it may explain my disappearance in case you never hear from me again. I "picked up" this Mr. Chi on the street car last Monday, on Tuesday I received the enclosed note, on Wednesday I wrote to him declining his invitation to tea, on Friday he came to call, and today I am going to his house to dinner. He really is a most respectable youth, a Christian, married, and very proud of his small son. His chief aim in life is to practice speaking English, and he apparently has a mania for making friends with foreigners.

36

I feel a little trepidation about going to dinner today because it is the first time I have gone to a meal at a Chinese home except to places like the Lews' where they are used to foreign customs. I'm afraid my Chinese is pretty inadequate for conversing with all the members of the Chi family who do not speak English.

February 28, 1926

I mailed a letter to you just a few hours ago, but I simply must write you about my adventures this afternoon while they are still fresh in my mind. I've just come in from my visit to Mr. Chi, and I'm bubbling over with excitement. It was the first time I had been in a Chinese house for a meal, except in the houses of some of the University staff who were educated in America.

Mr. Chi had asked me to come at half past one to have dinner and to stay as late as I could. When I started out I was afraid that my Chinese wouldn't be adequate for conversation with the rest of his family, but I need not have worried about that. They were all so friendly that it would not have mattered if I had not been able to speak a word.

The only thing that worried me after I got there was that I would make some perfectly inexcusable break. It is so easy to sit down by mistake in the seat of honor, or to go through the door first before one has been sufficiently urged, or to do something else that is fearfully bad manners, and I have not yet had much training in Chinese etiquette.

To begin at the beginning, Mr. Chi met me at the gate and ushered me into the house, which consisted of five small rooms, pretty poor and dirty. Three girls bowed and smiled most politely, but since it is very bad form for a Chinese man to refer to his wife, it took me a long time to discover which one was his wife and which were his sisters. His four-month-old son was exhibited proudly, a pale little thing, dressed in the red and blue clothes that all Chinese children wear.

Mr. Chi and I then sat down on the *k'ang* and drank tea and ate nuts and sweetmeats while his sisters and his wife, who was a pretty girl with rouged lips and a dirty face, disappeared into the background.

Mr. Chi's father came in to chat for a few minutes and then disappeared, probably to a wine shop. He was a villainous looking old rascal, who used to have some kind of official job but like a lot of other Manchus has drifted along pretty shiftlessly since the Revolution.

My conversation with the family was limited to questions about the weather and America and how I liked Peking, but Mr. Chi and I discussed everything under the sun. He tried to talk in English and I tried to talk in Chinese, but we both talked pretty much of a mixture.

Finally at four o'clock it was dinner time, and I expected that we would all sit down at a table together, as the modern families do, but no indeed. In spite of being Christians, they still follow all the old customs. The *lao t'ai t'ai* (that is the term for the old woman who is the wife of the head of the family) and I sat down on the *k'ang* with a little table between us, and it looked for a while as if we were going to be the only people who were going to have anything to eat. But in a few minutes Mr. Chi went out, and I gathered that he and his father were served in another room. I suppose his father would not think of sitting down at the same table with a woman.

The three girls stood up and served us, not eating anything until we had finished. It was a very simple meal of vegetable dumplings and fried bread. If it had not been for me, they would probably only have had the dumplings. My chief problem was to know how much I was supposed to eat. I didn't want to eat too little and seem unappreciative, and yet I was afraid if I ate too much there wouldn't be enough for all the girls who were watching us hungrily.

As for hygiene, I hate to think of all the germs I ate. Of course the *lao t'ai t'ai* kept serving me with her chopsticks, but even worse than that was the method of feeding the baby. Young Mrs. Chi was nursing it when we began to eat, but after a little while the grandmother began to feed it. She would chew up a little dumpling, spit it out on her finger and then stuff it into the baby's mouth. If the poor wee mite didn't swallow it all at once, the grandmother would help it with her chopsticks, and then with the same chopsticks would give me some more dumplings.

Various neighbors and relatives came in during the afternoon, and I was very much impressed by the neatness of all the older women. Their clothes were all immaculate, and the way their hair is brushed smoothly back from their foreheads gives them a very distinguished air. The older women have a look of serenity and peace that comes, I suppose, from years of patient self control. Many of the girls look restless and unhappy. It must take a long time to become thoroughly resigned to being silent and submissive, even when you have always known that you would have to be.

After dinner Mr. Chi asked if I would mind stopping on the way home at the house of a friend of his, a Mr. Ch'en, who was very anxious to learn English. I couldn't help wondering as I said good-bye to old Mrs. Chi and young Mrs. Chi and they cordially urged me to come again, what they really thought of a foreign woman who walked around the streets with men and went wherever she pleased.

The Ch'ens lived in a much more well-to-do courtyard than the Chis, and Mr. Ch'en, after chaining up a very fierce dog who tried to eat us alive, ushered us into the house. The first sight that met my eyes made me wonder whether I hadn't better leave as soon as possible. In the main room were four old men, silently and earnestly playing Ma Jongg. They were typical old school Chinese gentlemen, wearing their little silk caps and old-fashioned carved spectacles, and smoking long pipes. I was afraid they might not relish having a foreign woman breaking into their sanctum, but I need not have worried, for between interest in their gambling and the fact that it is very bad manners to look at a strange woman, they paid absolutely no attention to me at all.

We went into a side room, where I was made to sit down in the seat of honor, and Mr. Ch'en's daughter, an exceedingly pretty girl of about seventeen, brought me cigarettes, which I refused, and tea and nuts and candied fruit, which I nibbled at. One must eat something when one is offered food, and yet one feels very piggy when no one else touches anything.

Mr. Ch'en is a very nice looking man of about thirty-five, with a quiet shy manner. He is the head of a whole series of government primary schools. He has studied both German and English, but only from books and with a little help from Chinese teachers. Since he has no contacts with foreigners, he is very bashful about trying to talk in English at all. His younger brother and two friends who were there do not speak any English at all, and since they were all very friendly, we carried on a fluent conversation in Chinese, with Mr. Chi interpreting when I got stuck.

I felt as if I were in a fairy tale. I am sure I was the first foreigner who had ever been in the house, and yet all of them (except the four old codgers playing Ma Jongg) were as cordial as could be. Parts of our conversation were awfully funny. I have grown used to the curiosity of the people out in the country and some of the coolies and servants, but it still startles me to have someone who is really educated stop in the middle of a sentence to ask how old I am, or how much I paid for my stockings! I finally had to tear myself away and come home, but they all begged me to come back, and I felt as if I were leaving old friends.

In less than a month, any semblance of fairy-tale life in China would be harshly smashed for MBS.

40

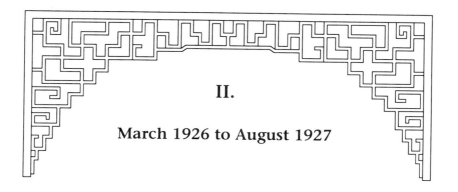

II.

March 1926 to August 1927

Three-Eighteen

The city of Peking, where MBS was living and studying Chinese in both orthodox and adventurous ways, was in 1926 seething with conflict between Chinese students, Japanese soldiers, Chinese warlords—the provisional governors of Peking—and the Western Powers. The student protests of May 4, 1919, condemning Japanese imperialism and the weak response from Chinese government, had grown into the May Fourth Movement of university students perceiving themselves as leaders whose duty was to save China from domination by Japan and Western Powers.[1]

By 1926 students viewed warlords and Western Powers as equally the enemies of a united China. Occasions for student agitation were not difficult to find, and the Chinese Communist Party seized its chances to incite students to demonstrations for the salvation of China. The May Thirtieth 1925 incident in Shanghai, when students who were protesting the killing of a Chinese worker by a Japanese foreman were fired on by British-led police, is well-remembered. Many were injured and several killed, and the atmosphere of violence linked to student protests was intensified. A similar skirmish on March 18, 1926 in Peking was to be commemorated in years to come at Yenching. MBS had been in China only a few months when, on the way to Language School, she *rode her bicycle into the midst of the brutal scene.*

March 19, 1926

No doubt there have been full details of yesterday's demonstration in the New York papers, but I'd like to go back to the beginning and tell you just what has happened, at least as far as we can get it straight from all the conflicting reports here.

Last week the Kuominchun (Feng's army) fortified the forts at Taku (the Tientsin port), laid mines in the channel, and said that they would allow no vessels to go in or out of Tientsin. This action was directed entirely against the anti-Kuominchun forces, in this case represented by Chang Tso-lin's fleet from Mukden, but nevertheless it violated the Protocol of 1901 in which China promised the Powers that free communications between Peking and the sea should always remain unobstructed. Since there was an immediate protest, the port was reopened as far as foreigners were concerned, and foreign ships were to be allowed to go in and out during the daytime.

Then came the unfortunate incident of the forts firing on two Japanese destroyers which were proceeding up the channel and which returned the fire. The Kuominchun authorities claim that there was a misunderstanding and the shots were fired merely as a warning to the destroyers to stop, there was also a report that the Japanese fired first, though I don't believe that was true. Of course the Japanese were furious and protested at once, demanding a formal apology and indemnity for the men on the destroyers who were wounded. I suppose such an apology will eventually be given, though the radical Chinese leaders think that the Japanese should pay an indemnity for the men who were wounded in the Kuominchun forts.

The next development came last Tuesday, the 16th, when the Ministers of the eight Powers sent an ultimatum to the Chinese Foreign Office demanding that within forty-four hours the port of

Tientsin should be entirely opened according to the stipulations of the 1901 Protocol. This caused a perfect furor among some of the liberal Americans in Peking, since it meant a virtual appeal to force whether gunboats were actually used or not. It certainly seemed like a most unnecessary step, since the 1901 Treaty is one of the unequal treaties that everyone has been agitated and agitating about all winter, and its sole justification, if it has any, is the protection of foreign lives, yet in this case foreigners were in no danger whatsoever, and the arming of the Taku forts was merely part of the Chinese civil war.

A delegation consisting of Roger Green, Lucius Porter, Dr. Stuart, Mr. Gleysteen and several others went at once to the Legation to protest to Mr. MacMurray against America's participation in the ultimatum, but Mr. MacMurray was perfectly adamant in holding to what Mr. Green calls the "gun boat policy".[2] So various cables were sent home protesting, and this same group of men made a statement of their position for the newspapers at home, though out of deference to Mr. MacMurray they did not publish their protest in the papers here. I can't think of anything that might more easily stir up anti-foreign feeling just now than this ultimatum, giving as it does the impression that the Powers are ready to use force merely to enforce the treaties, instead of reserving it as a last resort in case of real danger to foreign lives. And apparently Mr. MacMurray acted without consulting any of the people here who know far more about the situation than he does.

Still, whatever one may think of the unwiseness of the ultimatum, the incident seems to be settled now, for the Foreign Office has agreed that the terms of the 1901 Protocol must be kept and the commanders on both sides (both of the Taku forts and of the Mukden fleet) have agreed to the Powers' demands. I don't know whether there will be any further developments or not, but certainly every bit of influence and pressure should be brought to bear on the Department of State, so that Washington will make it quite clear that America will not countenance a gunboat policy here in the East.

Yesterday's student demonstration started as a protest to Tuan C'hi-jui, the head of the present provisional government, against the ultimatum of the Powers, but there was not the slightest sign of ill feeling against foreigners. Whatever ill feeling there was, was directed entirely against the government. This is briefly what happened. Day before yesterday a small group of students had gone to the Cabinet Office to protest about the ultimatum, and in a clash with the guards several students had been injured.

Yesterday a large mass meeting of students was called, and the Yenching and Tsing Hua students asked for a holiday in order to attend. The Yenching faculty (I don't know about Tsing Hua) granted it. About six thousand students went to the mass meeting, representing the Peking Students' Union, the General Labor Union, the Kuomintang (the People's Party), the Dare-to-Die Corps (a group of very radical students) and a good many others.

Mr. Hsü Ch'ien, who is the President of the Sino-Russian University, and the leading Communist in Peking, presided, and did his best fairly successfully to arouse the students and to persuade them to go to Tuan C'hi-jui's office to protest against the ultimatum and to urge him to take a firm stand in his dealings with the foreign demands. After Mr. Hsü had got the students well started on their parade to the Executive Office, he himself drove in his car to a nice safe place in the Legation Quarter. Although most of the students thought that they were in a perfectly peaceful parade, there were evidently a number of Communists who hoped to make as much trouble as possible for Tuan C'hi-jui.

Altogether a crowd of about a thousand went to the Cabinet Offices, and when Marshal Tuan (or Premier Chia) refused to see any representatives of the students, they tried to force their way past the guards. The soldiers, who were Tuan's own bodyguard, not the police or the Kuominchun soldiers in charge of the city, then fired into the air or else fired a round of blank cartridges.

The crowd immediately began to move, but since they were inside a compound with a high wall, they could not disperse quickly, and without giving them time, the soldiers began to fire directly at them, keeping the firing up after the crowd had definitely broken. Of course people were knocked down and trampled on in their efforts to get away from the soldiers who came on, using their bayonets and rifle butts. At least thirty students were killed, two of them girls, one a sophomore at Yenching, and a great many more were wounded, some of them fatally.

It just happened that I passed by within twenty minutes after the shooting, and I'm afraid I can't forget it. The Executive Offices are on Hat-amen Street, just half way between our Compound and Language School, and I go past them four times a day. I had lunch yesterday at the Leynses', and since we were a little late starting for school, I started ahead on my wheel, and Henry, who rides faster than I do, said he would soon overtake me.

As soon as I got out onto Hatamen Street I knew that something had happened or was about to happen. The streetcars had stopped. (Later I found out that the shooting had torn down the trolley wires.) There were very few rickshas and on every corner there were crowds of quiet people. They were the sort of crowds one could find only in the East—men, women, and children, curious to know every detail of whatever excitement was in the air, but perfectly silent.

What first made me realize that something really serious had happened was that no one was running toward any one scene of action, but that everybody was standing at the corners of the *hutungs* (alleys). I realized afterwards that this was so they could dive down the side streets to a place of safety in case the shooting started again or the soldiers came in sight.

I had heard nothing about the student demonstration so I had no clue as to what the demonstration might be. I naturally wondered whether it might be an anti-foreign demonstration, but since I was the only foreigner in sight on the whole length of the street and no one was paying the slightest attention to me, I knew it couldn't be that.

Then as I went further down the street, I saw the trolley wires down, the ground littered with papers, which turned out to be hand-bills, and then suddenly I came to the gate of the Executive Offices with fifteen or twenty boys lying dead across the entrance. I still didn't understand what had happened and my first thought was that a bomb might have exploded. I feel now that it was awfully cowardly of me not to stop to see whether I could help, but I have grown so used to being unable to understand or to make myself understood in the ordinary excitements of the street that it never occurred to me that there was anything I could do.

Moreover, it was not until I had gone on several blocks and saw a detachment of soldiers running up the street toward me that I began to comprehend what had actually happened. As soon as the reinforcements of Kuominchun troops arrived, people began to run hither and yon and the excitement broke out in great waves, but by that time I had got to school.

The ten minutes that I was on Hat-amen Street were an extraordinary period of dead calm in the midst of a storm. Five minutes later the soldiers had formed a cordon around the scene of the shooting and stopped all traffic on the street, but at the time when I came by, the shooting was just over, the students who had escaped unhurt had miraculously disappeared, and the bystanders, dumb with terror, were waiting with the patience and curiosity of the Orient to see what was going to happen next.

This afternoon I went down to the T'ung Fu to the memorial service for the Yenching student who had been killed by a bayonet gash across her breast. Timothy Lew led the service which was entirely in Chinese except for the few words that Mrs. Frame[3] and Dr. Stuart said at the close. The great Chinese coffin stood in the

46

center of the Chapel, piled with the wreaths of paper flowers that are always used here. There had been no time to arrange a carefully planned processional for the choir or anything of that sort, but one felt no need for any extra aids to solemnity in the face of such true grief. It was heartbreaking to see the boys and girls, their faces set and drawn until they could bear it no longer and began to sob quietly.

No one knows how the feeling will turn in the next few days, but as far as I can learn today, most of the students feel that they were unsuspectingly caught in a trap yesterday and were just used as the tools of the Communists. Feeling is running high, no longer against Marshal Tuan, but against this rascal Hsü Ch'ien. It is all tragic, and the attitude of many of the foreigners in the Legation Quarter who say "Oh well, it served them right; they are a lawless good for nothing lot," makes one sick at heart. Some of the students are wild and reckless and hard to manage, but who can blame them for feeling that China has suffered enough, and they must do anything to help her? Student demonstrations are not a very helpful way of solving China's problems, but neither is a massacre the proper way to check the demonstrations.

Many forces were at work in the struggle for power in China in 1926. The Chinese Communist Party had been organized in 1921 by Mao Tse-tung at about the same time that Sun Yat-sen was making efforts to strengthen the Kuomintang, the nationalist Republican party, by recruiting students. Sun died unexpectedly on March 12, 1925, but in the spring of 1926 Chiang Kai-shek, Sun's disciple, was emerging as the leader of the KMT and was already making plans for the Northern Expedition, a campaign to defeat the warlords in North China and thus to create a unified nation.[4] MBS was very much aware of the threat of fighting in Peking and throughout the province of Chihli in which the city was located.

April 4, 1926

Our latest excitement is air raids. For the last three days, every morning at ten o'clock, one of Chang Tso-lin's airplanes has circled over the city, dropping half a dozen bombs. Apparently the aviator is trying to hit one of the places where the Kuomintang troops are concentrated, but he flies so high and has such poor aim that the bombs have so far done no particular damage. It is an odd sensation to stand out in the compound in the warm spring sunshine watching the machine slowly circling and hearing the dull thud as the bombs explode. If the plane should fly directly over our heads, I suppose we might grow anxious, but as long as one can see it plainly flying over other parts of the city, one can only rage at the cowardliness and wickedness of bringing these Western methods of warfare to China.

Chinese warfare is a funny thing. Every day this week there has been a rumor that the Kuomintang were expecting to evacuate Peking that very night and that looting would begin, but every morning dawns serene and peaceful, and it seems as if this part of the war were going to peter out. At least it looks as if the Wu-Chang alliance were going to break up any day. Wu P'ei-fu sees that if the Kuomintang is beaten, Chang Tso-lin will take Chihli for himself, so before it is too late, Wu wants to have it out with Chang and send him back to Manchuria where he belongs.

Fighting and Festivities

Chinese warfare was seen and heard in Peking, but Yenching University was still a peaceful community which mourned its dead and continued to work for the living. In the spring of 1926 the new campus was under construction in Haitien, about five miles northwest of Peking and outside its city walls.

All the different parts of the University, scattered throughout Peking, were to be brought together on one extensive campus at Haitien. The new campus of Yenching University (the name, chosen with much thought, was an old name for Peking) included the grounds of an old prince's palace almost halfway between the new Summer Palace and the ruins of the old Summer Palace.

The architect for Yenching was an American, Henry Killam Murphy.[5] His plans, MBS recalled many years later, "were innovative, for he had followed traditional Chinese patterns but with modern building materials," thus combining the strengths of Western concrete and Chinese architectural design. Mr. Murphy was clearly charmed by young Miss Speer.

April 18, 1926

Yesterday morning there was snow on the Western Hills, a rare occurrence even in winter and a perfect miracle for April. It was such a gorgeous day that Jo Brown and I, who had planned to go out to the Summer Palace, couldn't bear to stay inside just because the city gates were shut and there were rumors that Chang Tso-lin's troops were likely to enter the city in more or less disorderly form at any minute. So we put on our walking clothes and set out to see for ourselves whether or not we could persuade the guards to let us out the gate. But our sweetest smiles were unavailing, so we had to content ourselves with wandering around the old Winter Palace which is in the center of the city. The lake and the sky and the wildflowers and the temple roofs were all glorious in the sunshine and we felt at peace with the whole world when we came home at four o'clock.

I played two hard sets of tennis and was just thinking how pleasant it would be to spend the evening in bed with a book when the telephone rang and a masculine voice asked persuasively if I would not like to go down to the Peking Hotel to dance after dinner. It turned out to be Mr. Murphy whom I had met at dinner at Mrs. Frame's the week before, Henry Killam Murphy of Murphy and Dana, the architect who is doing the new Yenching buildings.

His wife, who did not come out with him on this trip, was in Bryn Mawr shortly before my day. He is very charming, a thoroughgoing Yale man and New Yorker and interested in lots of interesting things. I told him that I wasn't particularly keen about dancing and he said to come down and have dinner with him at any rate.

He came to get me in a car, very swanky indeed for one who is used to bicycles and rickshas. On the way down to the hotel we passed a good many soldiers, not all of whom were under perfect discipline, but on the whole the streets seemed as quiet as usual. However, when I remarked at half past eleven that it was time for me to go home, we found that there were rumors that the streets were full of Chang's soldiers, who were likely to commandeer any vehicle and who were behaving like marauders. There was not a car to be had that was willing to go outside the Legation Quarter, much less the three miles north to our Compound.

The hotel clerks said it would be idiotic to try to go in rickshas and that no ricksha men were able to go, so there was nothing for it but for me to stay there over night. The hotel is crammed jammed full of Chinese people who think that it is safer at the moment than their own homes, but I finally got a room where I got a good sleep. I have seldom felt odder than coming home in an evening dress at nine o'clock Sunday morning. The people at the Mission were all very decent about it, for which I am duly thankful, for I was afraid some of them might think my behavior a little scandalous.

After I had put on more suitable clothes for the daytime, I went with Mr. Murphy to look at some of the old Chinese palaces and temples on which he is basing his Yenching designs. I learned more about Chinese architecture in a few hours than I had learned in all the time since I came to Peking.

May 8, 1926

Mr. Murphy left Peking this morning and, after inspecting the buildings he has designed in Canton and Manila and Kobe, will get back to New York early in July. He is a most amusing person, quite a ladies' man, and must have been born on the Blarney Stone, but he really does know most of what there is to be known about Chinese architecture and its adaptation to modern buildings. He gave a ripping lecture at Language School, that I wish he could repeat to all Mission Boards at home, so that they would see how important it is to use Chinese rather than foreign architecture when they put up new buildings in the field. I've seen quite a lot of him these last three weeks, and it's been great fun to hear his New Yorker's point of view and also to learn at first hand some of the principles of Chinese architecture.

Murphy's innovative combination of traditional Chinese patterns with modern building materials would eventually produce a beautiful campus, but in the spring of 1926 the construction was incomplete and there was more chaos than campus.

May 25, 1926

Everything in the faculty residence compound at Haitien is in an awful mess. The houses are finished, but the light and water aren't ready, and there are no good roads. In about ten years, when everything at Haitien is completed, the new campus is going to be heavenly, but this summer and fall, with a lot of the buildings only half done and the grounds covered with pipes and ditches, it is going to be an unholy mess. Augusta and I are responsible for furnishing two of the faculty suites in the dormitories, and we both feel woefully lacking in imagination and knowledge of interior decorating.

In addition to concerns about construction of the new campus, the Yenching community recognized with distress the gravity of the pressures on the University's president, Leighton Stuart, who had become the force that sustained Yenching and allowed it to flourish.[6]

51

May 29, 1926

Mrs. Leighton Stuart has been very ill for weeks, with a strepto-coccus heart infection that is absolutely hopeless. It has been aw-fully hard for Dr. Stuart who has had all the University burdens: the problem of moving, the ordinary strain of Commencement, and the question of getting the students safely over May 30th. He has aged tremendously this winter and must be fairly near the break-ing point, but he still keeps his wisdom and his vision.

Stuart's wife, Aline Rodd Stuart, had been a semi-invalid for some time, Stuart says in his autobiography, adding with masculine complacence that she was "chiefly concerned that my work was not interfered with by her weakness and fairly frequent ailments. She and my mother supple-mented each other admirably. My mother's interests were intellectual or in public affairs, my wife's in housekeeping, notably in desserts up to New Orleans standards, in the beautiful products of Chinese craftsman-ship, in simple kindly deeds for people in trouble." Stuart's mother had come to live with Leighton and Aline in 1913 after his father's death and, he says, "naturally had accompanied us to Peking." Stuart adds that his mother's "energy seemed inexhaustible, but it was never of the bustling kind. Rather it was benign. It carried her into the hearts of us all...for the whole Yenching community, faculty and students alike, she was known as 'Mother Stuart.'"[7]

Alas for Leighton Stuart, his mother died in 1924, aged eighty-three, and his wife died June 6, 1926, so that he lost his female support system just at the time of the planning and move to the new Yenching campus. But the University itself became the source that sustained him.[8]

The University's move from the city buildings took place during the summer of 1926 while MBS was on vacation in Peitaiho, a favorite ref-uge from the summer heat in Peking. MBS heard about it and remem-bered many years later that "People, households, library books, pianos—everything that the University needed" was moved, "mostly with carts and during the rainy season when no one could know from day to day whether there would be a downpour or not."

But at the time, MBS's mind was on the approaching visit from her parents and her younger brother Bill, who were planning to spend several months in China and would come by way of Japan as she and many travelers did at this time. It was left to Augusta Wagner to help with the move and to furnish the dormitory suite to which Dean Frame had assigned them. But interior decorating gave way to cleaning up the buildings, which had been opened in the spring of 1926 to women and girls who had fled from the soldiers of the feuding warlords who were ravaging the countryside around Peking.

June 20, 1926

The dormitories at Haitien were used for housing refugees in April and May, and Augusta wrote me last week that she had just been out to look at our suite and found it to be the last to be evacuated. She thinks it will take all the Lysol in the PUMC and all the incense in China to make it habitable. But the whole campus at Haitien is still in such a state of confusion that there is nothing to do but wait patiently and trust to Providence that by September we will have a place to live.

There is desperate need for someone to take charge of things and check up all the failures of the Construction Bureau. But Dr. Stuart, if he is to be saved for the future, needs a complete vacation now. He hasn't yet had a chance to get away since Mrs. Stuart's death.

From July until late November MBS wrote no letters home, first because her parents and her brother Bill were en route to Japan and China and then because she could report her adventures and concerns to them in person. She traveled in Japan with her family and then by train across Korea visiting mission stations. They got back to Peking in time for her father to be the speaker at the dedication of the new Yenching campus and buildings.

Robert Speer then went on to conferences in other parts of China while Emma Speer and Bill stayed in Peking, spending part of the time at the Presbyterian Mission and part of the time on the Yenching campus. Mrs. Speer did a good deal of shopping, helping Augusta and MBS furnish their rooms in the new dormitory. They found a Chinese amah to work for them and christened her Little Treasure.

MBS's mother and brother left just before Thanksgiving. MBS and Augusta had dinner with the Fergusons "whose lovely big Chinese house was our home away from home during all the Peking years." Mary Ferguson, like Augusta a Wellesley graduate, was registrar of PUMC. Her father, Dr. John C. Ferguson, was "the patriarch of Peking's American community," respected for his knowledge of fine arts and familiar with local politics.[9] "Life at the Fergusons' was a lovely mixture of formality and luxury on the one hand, and a simple home life on the other," and MBS and Augusta felt that they were taken in as adopted daughters.

MBS and Augusta Wagner both missed Mrs. Speer, regretting that she left just before the party at which MBS celebrated her twenty-sixth birthday with Alice Boring, Grace Boynton, Freddy Giang, Hsieh Wan-ying, and Camilla Mills. Miss Mills taught home economics at Yenching. Freddy Giang had returned from Vassar to teach at Yenching on the same ship with MBS. She and Hsieh Wan-ying, a brilliant young teacher, protégée of Grace Boynton, shared a faculty suite, as MBS and Augusta Wagner did. These four were regularly invited for "Friday Lunch" at the small house shared by Miss Boynton and Miss Boring. "We talked about almost anything," MBS recalls. "It was interesting because there were two older people, two younger foreigners, and two younger Chinese. We talked about anything under the sun!"[10]

But Miss Boring and Miss Boynton were no substitute for Mrs. Speer, and after her visit MBS and Augusta Wagner continued to miss MBS's mother. Letters from Augusta Wagner show her immense affection for Mrs Speer, and Augusta's references to herself and MBS as "your children" define her relationship to MBS as a sister. "So many things your two children in Peking do to the tune of 'Oh if Mother could only be here with us!'" she wrote.

MBS and Augusta seem to have considered theirs as a sisterly rela-tionship, an attachment that was "one of the major axes along which the narrative of their life experience unfolds." [11] This is a recognized pattern for missionary women in China: writing about the "centrality of female friendships in China," an historian notes that "The prototypes for female friendships were relationships between natural sisters."[12]

December 17, 1926

The great event of the last forty-eight hours is that Augusta and I have bobbed our hair. We have been discussing it for weeks. Augusta looked like a little tough from Broadway at first, but now that her hair has been washed and dried properly it's stunning. As for me, when the ends get used to being cut and when my unruly forelock is trained out of my eyes, I won't look quite so much like a wire-haired fox terrier. Dr. Brown says ruefully that I've lost all my dignity. The few people who think my hair looks nice say I look like a flapper and a tomboy, which does not strike me as being my line.

January 23, 1927

Exams will be over in a few days and then we have two weeks holiday to celebrate Chinese New Year. We have made several plans but have had to give them all up and will probably stay right here, perhaps going to T'ungchow or the Hills for a few days.
First we had thought we would go down to T'ai Shan, going on to the tomb of Confucius at Chufoo and stopping on the way back at Tsinan, but John told us that we must on no account pay our hom-age to Confucius because the country between T'ai An and Chufoo is infested with bandits. We also heard that there is so much snow on the Sacred Mountain that no one can climb it. I wish you could see the Hills today. A week ago we had the heaviest snowfall there has been in Peking since 1908, and the Hills are still white with it.

There were often bandits and fighting not far from Yenching, but MBS writes of festivities at this time and throughout her years in China. Her friend and colleague in Yenching's English Department, Harold Shadick, recalled that there were those who thought the revelry frivolous in a serious time,[13] but the young members of the Yenching community were rarely morose and perhaps that is what preserved their sanity. MBS's letters are sometimes about trips to the Hills and house parties at Yenching, but she was never unaware of the dangers and rumors of danger.

January 30, 1927

The only gaiety of this last week was a party at the Boring-Boynton house for Freddy Giang and J.C. Li, her fiance. An enormous red Chinese invitation was sent out, and we all went in Chinese clothes. Since they were short one man, and since I could find no feminine attire to fit me, I went as a man. I wore my own blue mandarin coat with the gold dragons and the biggest Chinese satin cap that Little Treasure could find in Haitien (with a charming red button on top.)

If I knew any more than you do about the political situation, I'd tell you, but no one here knows anything really. We live on rumors. Sometimes the British seem to have a little sense, as in their suggestion to give up the Tientsin concession, but it seems to me the maddest folly for them to be sending so many troops to Shanghai.

But Shanghai was distant from Peking, and MBS spent the Chinese New Year holiday early in February on a trip to the Western Hills with her Yenching elders: President Leighton Stuart, Dean William Hung,[14] Alice Boring, and Grace Boynton. With this group MBS thought of herself as "Little Marnie," a tongue-in-cheek description because, although a generation younger, she was considerably taller than all except Dr. Stuart. The weather in the Hills was cold and snowy, but finally there came a "heavenly day" when some from Yenching took lunch and started straight up over the Hills.

February 13, 1927

We went first to T'ien T'ai Ssu, the loveliest temple in all the Western Hills. It is the only temple I have seen in China which is perfectly kept up like the Shrines at Nikko. It is famous for a figure which the priests there claim is the mummy of the father of the Emperor K'ang Hsi, who came to the throne in 1661 when his father became a hermit in a little cave back of the temple. The figure does not look in the least like a mummy; it is sitting upright and is wrapped in a magnificent robe of yellow silk. The face is smooth and dark brown, as if it were covered with highly polished lacquer. There was a nice young priest there who brought us tea in the sunny courtyard while we ate our sandwiches and who was very much set up because we took his picture and promised to send him a copy.

We went on three miles from there to Lung Men Ssu, the Temple of the Dragon Gate, which is not really a temple at all but the tomb of an early Manchu prince. There are wonderful marble carvings and a long avenue of gorgeous white pines. Numberless fresh little boys sprang up out of nowhere offering to show us the sights and suggesting that they would be glad to have their pictures taken for a remuneration of two mao. We gave some coppers to two silent little urchins, the most unkempt of all, who the donkey driver told us were "children of bitterness."

Trips to the Western Hills were a source of restoration and perspective for Yenching Westerners, but there were other diversions.

February 20, 1927

Although of course it is reprehensible in the extreme, the chief parlor sport in Peking now is suggesting wives for President Stuart. Everybody is backing a different candidate, and there is great hilarity about the possibilities. Dr. Yamei Kin thinks Camilla would be ideal, Dean Hung is all for Augusta, and I hear that the Porters have had their hearts set on me. Other candidates range from

Mrs. Zwemer to some of the young Chinese faculty. The only safe bet is Miss Boring.

The diaries and correspondence of Grace Boynton reveal that both she and Alice Boring were eager for Leighton Stuart's attentions;[15] but Stuart did not remarry. Many years later he wrote about his wife: "Our married life was so richly satisfying a memory that she unfitted me for caring to repeat the experience. Apart from personal disinclination, this was probably no disadvantage. Yenching had become my rapidly growing family. Several faculty wives took turns in overseeing my domestic needs. I was free to travel constantly both abroad and in China."[16] Stuart remained a fascinating widower, married only to Yenching.

But a letter written in 1941 by Alice Boring, not long before Pearl Harbor, suggests that she and Leighton Stuart had a close if complex relationship: On August 29, she wrote to her family: "Last Friday was Aline Stuart's birthday (Leighton's wife), so as usual he asked me to go to the cemetery with him to take some flowers, and then we hiked across the plain for the rest of the afternoon. The calmness and faith with which he meets the daily problems in connection with this situation, one by one without worrying, is a constant marvel to me."[17]

If there was to be no wedding for Leighton Stuart, there were other celebrations. The February 20, 1927 letter in which MBS confided to her mother the gossip of Peking dinner tables continues with an account of a joyful Chinese ceremony.

Last Wednesday was the Lantern Festival which marks the first full moon of the Chinese New Year. We had a splendid celebration beginning with a parade of the whole University carrying lanterns, small ones for individuals, gorgeous big ones for every class and club and faculty group.

The students from Amoy had made a dragon more than fifty feet long, which had flashlights in its tummy to illuminate its writhings over the heads of the crowd, and which spit out mouthfuls of sparks that would have struck terror to the heart of the most intrepid Saint George.

America may pride herself on being democratic, but she will never catch up with China. The ropes and red lanterns and admission by ticket of a college celebration at home are a far cry from a Chinese festival. All the coolies in the neighborhood were here, not to watch the procession but to join it, and the policemen who had come to keep order pushed and shoved with the village children to get the best view of the great finale.

No imperialist MBS,[18] nor a romantic evangelist. She did not pretend to understand the Chinese completely, but she never lost sight of the purpose of Yenching, to be a predominantly Chinese University.

Restless Days

Planning ahead for an essentially Chinese institution was vital, but in 1927 Western women must also be considered. As chairman of a faculty committee for planning future faculty residences, MBS found herself designing houses, a responsibility she felt was nearly turning her into an architect.

March 8, 1927

The question of housing for single women is difficult, as you know, and it is further complicated by the fact that any house which we build must be suitable to Chinese as well as foreigners. The two absolute requirements for housing accommodations for the Chinese are that they shall be sufficiently pretentious to give the occupant plenty of face and yet that they shall be extremely economical to live in. It is difficult to meet both requirements.

The latest inspiration that Mrs. Frame and I have had is to put up two small Chinese houses, each to hold two people, but close enough together so that in case the occupants wanted to they could have their meals together. A house for two is the ideal arrangement, but the great drawback is expense. It is undeniable that it has cost Miss Boring and Grace Boynton a great deal more to live this winter than it has cost any of the rest of us.

Living arrangements were overshadowed shortly by the civil war: six Westerners were killed in a violent incident on March 24, 1927 in Nanking by the Nationalist Hankow government (which included Communist advisors) in order to discredit Chiang Kai-shek with foreign countries. The army attacked foreign consulates, and Dr. John F. Williams, an American who was Vice President of the University of Nanking, was killed with five others from three countries. Many were wounded. In April Chiang Kai-shek ousted the Hankow government from Nanking and a moderate Nationalist government was established,[19] but in March it was the brutality that made headlines.

March 27, 1927

I have come to the conclusion that the most pernicious factors in the modern world are military officers, politicians, and newspapermen. This horrible business at Nanking has blotted the sun out of the sky for the time being. Dr. Williams' death still seems incredible.

It's ghastly to think of the schools and houses that were looted and the places that have been burned. But worst of all is the way in which people have lost their heads, going perfectly mad with panic, returning to all the old idiocy of war time propaganda. Yesterday's *Leader* had glaring headlines: "Cantonese Troops Murder Foreigners in Nanking," giving just as false an impression as the Chinese papers' statement that British and American marines had killed two thousand Chinese soldiers and civilians in Nanking. Even today though the reports are toned down, the foreign papers play up the fact that foreigners have been killed, utterly ignoring the fact that for the five foreigners who are known to be dead, nearly five hundred Chinese were killed when the British and American boats shelled Nanking. I wish to goodness every American boat in our navy would go back east of Honolulu where they belong.

Of course, so far we have been utterly peaceful and undisturbed here in Peking, and therefore it is easy for us to talk. Nevertheless, all this bunkum about this being a second Boxer outbreak and China seething with anti-foreignism, is half newspaper propaganda, and the other half the panic of Shanghai business men. But if they don't stop talking they soon will arouse an outbreak of anti-foreign violence that all the gunboats in China won't be able to stop.

I'm enclosing a page from the inside of the *Leader*. The statements here are as close to the truth as anything that is known yet, but all the headlines and front page dispatches have been sensational to the nth degree. You can see from this that the cause of the original disturbances in Nanking is not yet known. Refugees from Nanking say that if it had not been for the Navy they would all have been killed. Possibly. But also if it were not for gunboats and navies the situation might not have been so serious. If in order to evacuate the foreigners from Nanking in safety, five hundred Chinese are killed, who can blame China for feeling a slight distaste for foreigners.

All this twaddle of the foreign governments about protecting life and property makes me sick. China is in the middle of a revolution, and it is perfectly inevitable that there will be a loss of life and property. It is deplorable, and everyone would like to avoid it, but even so, the loss of foreign lives is negligible compared to what the Chinese themselves are suffering.

This is China: if foreigners don't like it, they can go home; if they want to stay here, they will have to take the risks. Of course I think that the fewer risks they take the better. I have about come around to the view that if the consuls order foreigners to evacuate, they had better go, chiefly because a dead foreigner is likely to cause even more trouble for China than a living one!

The Yenching Board of Trustees in New York urged that the Western faculty withdraw to Japan or Korea, but President Leighton Stuart replied that there seemed to be no immediate danger. "Our Chinese advisers do not anticipate any danger except during the interval between change of governments, which is not probable in the near future."[20]

March 30, 1927 (March 27 letter continued)

Everything here is quiet and is likely to remain so for three or four weeks at any rate. Also, all the old-timers are convinced that even when the Nationalists do get here there will not be the same excitement there has been in the South. In the first place, the Northern temperament is not so excitable and in the second place, there has never been the same antagonism between foreigners and Chinese that there has been in the Yangtze valley.

Reports coming in from Shanghai and Nanking are meagre but horrifying. Miss Treudley told me yesterday that the only thing that saved the foreign faculty at Ginling was that the Chinese faculty stood between them and the troops. But worst of all is the apparent hatred and misunderstanding that is being stirred up at home. Please don't let people blame all this on the Chinese, and please help people to understand that foreign intervention is the very worst thing that could happen.

April 8, 1927

These are restless days, but you must not worry about us. You may be quite sure that when any real danger looms up, we will remove ourselves to places of safety. War psychology hasn't a patch on the present excitement in Peking. The beginning was about March 29th, when we began to get the first reactions to the Nanking Affair. The first break in Peking morale came when, with Dr. Houghton's assent, there was a general exodus of wives and children from the PUMC. Then last Sunday Mr. Pettus called a meeting of representatives of the different Missions who decided that they would suggest to the various groups which they represented that all mothers and children begin to get ready to go. There were various reasons for leaving. Some felt that Chang Tso-lin's troops might pull out any day and that we would have a repetition of Nanking, others were merely mildly apprehensive of a possible railroad strike that would cut us off from Tientsin.

Some people honestly feel that it is best for the Chinese to have foreigners get out now, so that there will be no possibility of any international complications as a result of harm coming to foreigners in case conditions grow disturbed later on. The situation is, of course, complicated by many factors which there is no time to write about, but I cannot help recalling a phrase that "many people were glad God was calling them home." It seems a little naive for us to expect the Chinese to take seriously and in good faith this sudden realization on the part of so many foreigners that this is the ideal moment for us to turn all the work over to the Chinese.

Here at Yenching we are carrying on as usual for the present. In spite of Dr. Stuart's passionate hope that we will go on normally whatever happens,[21] I cannot feel that there is real unanimity among the foreign staff. About half of the women with children are leaving, but many are staying on. We are all determined to go on with the regular work for the time being, but if there should be an official order from the Legations for us to leave, I think there are quite a number of the faculty who would feel they ought not to go.

There is also a division of feeling as to whether it would be right or not to accept the protection of the Legations in case of danger. My own feeling is that it would be disgraceful to leave now. The students do not feel that as yet there is any danger to foreigners which is not shared by the Chinese. There is the probability of looting and a few days of disorder if Peking changes hands, but that is something which the faculty and students must face together.

For us to go now would mean the complete disrupting of the University, and the students would have no possible interpretation except that we were running away at the first hint of danger. I cannot reconcile this rapid evacuation of missionaries with the tales of missionary heroism on which I was brought up!

Of course there is another side to it, and I don't in the least criticize the people who have gone—I'm very thankful that Jo Welles and the baby are out of Paotingfu—but the noisy way in which Americans have been rushing out of Peking this last week has been positively affronting to the Chinese and gives us more claim to caution than to heroism.

Dr. Stuart is closely in touch with both the military situation and the feeling of the Chinese, and if the time comes for us to go, we will. The time has passed when foreigners were an asset to a Chinese community in times of disorder, and if the time comes when we are too much of a liability, the Chinese faculty may want us to go quickly. I certainly do not want to stay if my presence means extra danger for the Chinese here, but in Peking that time has not yet come.

In spite of rumors and minor panics, MBS and her friends went on teaching and, during spring vacation, continued to hike in the hills, taking picnics and finding heights where they could lie in the sunshine and look down over the plains below, forgetting, at least temporarily, the problems of Peking. By late May the threat of war seemed reasonably remote to MBS and her hiking friends, and they set off on a longer excursion.

June 21, 1927

Our trip to Miao Feng Shan, in spite of all forebodings, was a great success. There were eight of us altogether. Everyone had warned us that the last weekend in May would be too hot for mountain climbing, but we had not been able to get away before, so it was then or nothing.

We started early Saturday morning, the cart with all our luggage having started at dawn under the guardianship of Pao Hsun, the table boy. That day we walked about fourteen miles across the plain, stopping in the middle of the morning for a good drink at the Black Dragon Pool, and having lunch at some hot springs. We got to our destination, the Temple of the Great Awakening, soon after two, and unpacked in the great roomy guest house.

Next morning we went over a mountain whose insignificant name is Turnip Patch, but where the path is so steep and winding that it is called the Three Hundred Elbows. After reaching the top of this, we dropped down about a thousand feet through orchards where the hawthorn trees were all in bloom and then up again another thousand to Miao Feng Shan.

The temple there is not very imposing in itself, but there is a terrace where one feels as if one were on the top of the world with all the kingdoms of the earth spread out at one's feet. We put our cots out there for the night in spite of the lack of privacy.

The priests told us various tales about the wonders of the place. There is a rock in the middle of the temple on which the Goddess of Mercy landed when she came down to China from heaven several hundred years ago, and under this rock there is a deep and sacred cave where a large red serpent lives. Every year sometime during the seventh or eighth Moon the serpent comes out and the air around the temple is so filled with his breath that a great red light is visible through the whole countryside.

The next day we came home, walking nearly twenty miles down a long valley to San Chia Tien, the Establishment of the Three Families, where we were met by a car.

Once down from the hills, MBS faced the reality of a volatile student body at Yenching. The student movement, she recognized, would be increasingly important historically.

The next excitement was a rumpus with the students from which the University emerged victorious in the eyes of a few of the authorities, though to many of us the victory seemed scarcely distinguishable from defeat. It's a long story and scarcely worth telling at length, except that it will be interesting later on as the first chapter in the struggle that is bound to come.

My own feeling is that it would be better to be defeated with colors flying than to start in on compromise when we all know that when the radical elements really set to work against us they will keep on finding excuses no matter how many times we try to meet their demands. However, many older and wiser people than I think that the most important course for us at present is to keep going at all costs and if possible with the goodwill of all parties.

The pretext in this particular case was examinations. Our exams were due to begin on June 11 with Commencement on June 20. After a few preliminary murmurings, on June 5 the students asked that we close the University at once and that they be allowed to go home, receiving credit for their work without any examinations. Their reason was that the Southern armies were advancing rapidly toward Peking and it looked as if communications might soon be cut.

Nankai University in Tientsin and Tsing Hua had both just closed, giving the same reason, and of course our students didn't like the idea of going on. There was a great deal of discussion among the students, the girls consistently taking a more sane and sensible stand than the boys. It was very hard to sift out all the motives: first, this was the opening wedge for demands made by the radical element, giving them a chance to stir up trouble; second, the lazy students who didn't want to take exams had a good excuse; third, a small group of students were really worried about the situation and wanted to go home.

Dr. Stuart, at a mass meeting of the whole University, explained that we could not lower our standards, but that we would allow the students three choices: the University would carry on as usual, and each student could decide for himself whether he would (1) take his examination at the scheduled time, or (2) take it at once, or (3) go home at once and take his exams before college opened in the fall.

The students voted on this after several fiery speeches from impassioned undergraduates, and if the vote had been by secret ballot, no doubt they would have agreed to the faculty plan, but the vote was by hand, and many of them were afraid of the radicals, so by a majority of thirty they rejected Dr. Stuart's proposals.

After that there were many meetings both of faculty and students, and the gist of it was that we compromised, and instead of the University as a whole sticking to its avowed policy, the question of examinations was settled separately in each individual class. In classes where there were daily grades, very few exams were given; in other classes in many cases term papers were substituted for exams. The 'victory' lies in the fact that we did not close without any exams, but it seems to me it has committed us to a policy of collective bargaining on all academic matters. In these days of nationalism, we will have to be willing to have the students take a share in many decisions, but it should be through accredited representatives, not by threats, demands, and intimidation.

Student protests and the many meetings necessary to respond to the students fairly and yet keep the University open did not eclipse the excitement of the very special Chinese wedding of Freddy Giang, the Vassar-educated young faculty member who had shared Friday lunches with MBS, Augusta Wagner, Grace Boynton, Alice Boring, and Hsieh Wan-ying.

All this excitement came just at the time that we were giving many of our spare moments to Frederica Giang's wedding. We are getting so adept at managing weddings now that if we are ever sent home we can go into the business—matrimonial undertakers, or something of the sort.

Hsieh Wan-ying was maid of honor and in charge of the bridal party's clothes. Camilla Mills was caterer and made gallons of punch. Augusta and I were the Embellishment Committee, which meant that we decorated, coached the rehearsal, and did all the odd jobs, even to seeing that Miss Boring's house had a little extra cleaning for the occasion.

Some dark red rugs which Grace Boynton had ordered for the Chapel arrived just a few hours before the ceremony when we had discovered that the Chinese carpets borrowed for the bride to walk on were too narrow and varied in color all the way from cerise to magenta. The Agricultural Department sent us pink and red geraniums instead of white roses at the last minute, but in spite of such mishaps everything went smoothly. The wedding was in Dr. Stuart's courtyard and the reception afterwards at Miss Boring's house, and the weather fortunately behaved itself for the occasion.

In July MBS and AW went off on vacation in Korea to escape the heat of Peking. They stayed at Sensen for two weeks and then went hiking in the Diamond Mountains, finding the woods and streams a glorious escape from the heat and dust of North China. Those who had stayed behind became ill with malaria, which MBS and Augusta Wagner escaped, but on the way home AW had appendicitis. She was operated on in Seoul, delaying their return to Yenching until the beginning of September.

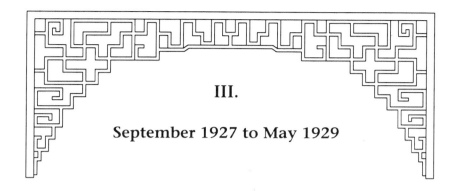

III.

September 1927 to May 1929

Independent Women

Back on the Yenching campus, MBS, at twenty-seven one of the young-est members of the Women's College Faculty, was appointed to represent that Faculty in administrative meetings. She was intrigued rather than resentful about her added responsibilities.

September 13, 1927

I seem to have broken into university administration circles. I am the Women's College representative on the Faculty Executive Committee, which means weekly committee meetings and a lot of inside dope on the doings of the University. President Stuart is going home next week to stay until Christmas, hoping to straighten up affairs in the New York Office. If you can get in touch with him, you might give him an earful of your opinions about Yenching.

Although its union with the University in 1920 was described as "a wed-ding ceremony"[1] the Women's College of Yenching University had retained a good measure of financial and administrative autonomy. Leighton Stuart, however, wished Yenching to be totally coeducational—with the men in charge! "From his point of view, the sooner we were all assimilated, the better. From our point of view, not so,"[2] recalled MBS.

Once the University had moved from Peking, where the Women's College and the Men's College had been geographically separate, there seemed to be no reason why coeducation should not be the rule in classes. The moat that had originally been planned to separate the women to-tally from the men was abandoned as ridiculous, and the idea of sepa-rate classes for women was also given up as impractical.

However, the Women's College at Yenching had substantial funds that the men in the University wished to use. The Yenching women were totally unwilling to surrender autonomy and were suspicious of plans to allow a merging of funds. Ever the shrewd negotiator, President Stuart explained in detail to MBS the complications he faced if the funds were not merged to complete the union, especially the pressure from the Chi-nese men on the faculty. She in turn wrote to her mother, who was on the Women's Committee in New York, about her dislike for strife and bitter-ness, the need for pragmatism and realism, her preference for coopera-tion over confrontation. But of course both Speer women understood that MBS would not cease to protect the women's rights.

Mrs. Speer had already corresponded with Leighton Stuart about the proposal to merge the funds. Her April 1927 letter to him is not in the Yenching files, but a letter from Dean Frame to Mrs. Speer reveals the tone: "I know at once what Dr. Stuart will say to you in answering your letter. He will say, 'But we have no idea of impairing the identity of the Women's College, dear Mrs. Speer.'" Mrs. Frame felt that Dr. Stuart, contrary to his honeyed words had a "deliberate and reasoned plan to obliterate all marks of delimitation between the colleges,"[3] thus stealing away the autonomy of the Women's College.

MBS herself confided to her mother that Mrs. Frame was part of the problem. Alice Browne Frame, the Dean of the Women's College, had been on the faculty of North China Women's College since 1912, long before it became part of Yenching University. Shortly after the amalgam-ation, in 1922, Mrs. Frame succeeded Luella Miner as Dean of the Women's College of Yenching.

As Dean she was not only accountable for the women students but also for keeping a qualified faculty (and reassuring the mothers of young faculty like MBS of the safety of their daughters), raising money—and keeping it out of the hands of the Men's College. She had had heavy responsibilities as the University moved to the new campus, where co-education in classes threatened to lead to commingling of funds. She was passionately and intensely desirous of the best possible education for Chinese women, and exhausted herself in a difficult job. She was also a single parent, raising her young daughter Rosamond alone after her husband died of typhus.[4]

November 13, 1927

Just between you and me and the gate post, we'll all be thankful when June comes and Mrs. Frame's furlough begins. Most people seem to feel a little frayed the last year before furlough, and to make matters worse she had a nasty attack of malaria during the summer. She is one of the people who gets more active as she gets more tired, and fatigue seems to stimulate her to more ceaseless attention to unnecessary detail. But in spite of all this, we will be in desperate straits when she leaves, for there is no one to take her place.

December 4, 1927

If Mrs. Frame were not leaving in June, I think Augusta and I might both come home this summer. Augusta's term is up at any rate, and I feel fairly certain that I ought to attempt a Ph.D. But it doesn't seem fair to leave the Women's College in the lurch now that we number among the oldest living inhabitants. The office would be chaos if both Mrs. Frame and Augusta left at once, and I am helping with a general reorganization of our required English courses and would hate to leave the experiment hung up in the middle. So altogether it seems more likely that Augusta will stay an extra year and that I may come home with her in 1929.

What do you think of the idea of my getting (or trying to get)

a Ph.D.? There is certainly no very vast future in a Chinese university without one.

On Christmas the frictions between the men and women were stilled, and Hsieh Wan-ying, one of MBS's young faculty friends, preached the sermon. A graduate of Yenching in 1923 with an M.A. from Wellesley, Hsieh Wan-ying was a member of the movement to write in the vernacular rather than in classical Chinese. She was invited to preach by T.C. Chao, Dean of the School of Religion at Yenching.[5]

December 29, 1927

At the Christmas Eve service in the chapel Dr. T.C. Chao was in charge, and therefore it was everything one could ask of beauty and reverence. The whole chapel was lighted with candles and was packed to the doors with students and faculty. All the hymns were Dr. Chao's own translations into Chinese, much more satisfactory than the old translations used by most missions. Dr. Chao centered the whole service around the Mother and Child, by asking women to take part. Hsieh Wan-ying's sermon, as much as I could understand, was lovely.

Christmas evening produced one of the most astonishing events we have had here. The Choral Society, made up of faculty and students, was giving a concert of Christmas carols and parts of the Messiah.

When we got to the auditorium, we found that it was jammed, not only with students but with all the old people and babies and coolies and beggars of the countryside. There had been a Sunday School entertainment earlier in the day to which all the villagers had come, partly to see their children perform, and partly to partake of the peanuts and other goodies bestowed by Santa Claus on the assembled company. Hearing that there was to be more *je nao* (excitement) in the evening, they all stayed on. Most of them had never heard a note of Western music in their lives but they sat through the evening without too much commotion. Now and then a baby wailed and several wadded urchins wandered up and down the aisles during the Pastoral Symphony!

I am keen to hear the outcome of your talk with Dr. Stuart. We hear he had the bright idea of getting the Yenching Women's College Committee in New York to lend their organization and money in a campaign to raise funds for the Men's College out here. I hope they didn't let him put it across.

Clues from MBS's letters and from other sources, including Leighton Stuart's autobiography, reveal how often he was away from the campus, usually raising money, sometimes on diplomatic ventures. MBS was soon to be one of those who assumed responsibility when the president was away.

In her first year at Yenching MBS had demonstrated unconventional independence and steady courage in a dangerous city and on expeditions into the country. Fortitude was to remain a constant in her character as she became increasingly involved in the administrative circles of the University, often with President Leighton Stuart. He was, however, frequently away from the campus on fund-raising or diplomatic trips, and MBS then worked with Howard S. Galt, the Acting President. He had been in China since 1899 and had helped amalgamate the small colleges which became Yenching University. In 1927 he had just returned from Harvard, where he was awarded a doctorate in education.[6]

As long as there are no political crises out here, it seems to me eminently satisfactory to have Dr. Stuart at home and Dr. Galt as Acting President over here. Dr. Galt is wise and sane and as straightforward as daylight, and it is a joy to work with him.

Everything is peaceful here now, but the reports of the wanton brutality after the coup in Canton two weeks ago were most distressing.[7] The quietness of the Chinese in the face of disaster is incomprehensible. One of my finest and most brilliant freshmen is from Canton. Her father is an evangelist in the villages around Canton, and her mother lives in the city itself. The student has not had one word from any of her family or friends since last July, and yet she goes about her work gaily and never lets a shadow of her own worry affect any of her friends here.

On Top of a Volcano

During the winter and spring of 1928 MBS's parents were traveling, which made catching up with them through the mails almost impossible. In May as in December 1927, politically China was a threatening place.

May 15, 1928

You can easily understand that this has not been a very happy week for China with all the old bitterness and humiliation of the Twenty-One Demands days raked up again by Japan's actions in Shantung. The only explanation of what has happened there (and reports are still not clear on some points) is that the Japanese military party has completely over-reached itself. I do not see how Japan can really expect to gain anything by stirring up the enmity that is sure to be aroused by each new detachment of troops that lands in Shantung.

Our students have been tremendously stirred, but everyone who has lived through the student agitations of the last nine years sees a remarkable gain in quietness and real purpose. There has been no shouting or wild agitating. Our own students asked for one day of no classes in order to hold a memorial meeting for those who had been killed in Shantung. The meeting was quiet and dignified, and though there were several speeches advocating a boycott of Japanese goods, there was another note sounded again and again, namely, that China's only hope lay in unification and personal and national purification.

Japanese troops, theoretically in Shantung to protect Japanese citizens, came into conflict with soldiers of the Kuomintang's Northern Expedition in Tsinan, the capital of Shantung. The Tsinan Incident of May 3, 1928 reawakened anger at the Japanese, and Chinese student protesters led the country in demonstrating against Japan and boycotting Japanese products. The Japanese consul decreed that all anti-Japanese protests should be banned, but the KMT refused, claiming the students' activities to be within the law. On May 9, thirteen years after Japan's post-World War I Twenty-One Demands, a National Humiliation Day was declared in Peking.[8]

June 8, 1928

It is hard to settle down to writing letters when one does not know whether or not one is perching on top of a volcano, and if one is, just when the eruption is going to erupt. But in spite of rumors and alarms, exams go on, and I am at present proctoring the Freshman English exam.

Ever since May 3 when the first word came of the trouble in Tsinan, we have been more or less uncertain about what would happen next up here. But after the first excitement over the Japanese ultimatum, things quieted down and we had two weeks of peace. A week ago, stirring below the surface began again.

One of my freshmen, whose father is Chang Tso-lin's chief secretary, had asked some of us to have dinner with her at the Pei Hai on Friday evening. For several weeks we had been calling her "the barometer" for her father had summoned her to Tientsin at the first sign of trouble, but had let her come back when things grew quiet again.

On Thursday her father telephoned and said she must leave at once, but finally consented to let her stay for classes Friday morning. She insisted on having the party Friday night just as she had planned. There was a full moon, and the Pei Hai was lovely in the twilight. Only a girl with generations of culture behind her could

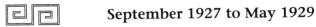

have been a perfect hostess and suppressed all excitement, all rumors, any mention of the future.

She left the next morning for Tientsin, and of course with the collapse of Chang Tso-Lin all her father's political power comes to an end, though the family position, I suppose, is not seriously endangered.

Chang Tso-lin, the Manchurian warlord, had come to Peking in December 1926 and proclaimed himself Dictator in June 1927. He left on June 3, before the Kuomintang troops occupied the city, and he was killed when his train was blown up as it approached Mukden.[9] Chiang Kai-shek's ally, General Yen Hsi-shan, marched into Peking on June 8, the date of MBS's letter.

When we left the Pei Hai, Augusta and I went to the Fergusons' for the night. As we went through the empty *hutungs*, lovely in the quiet moonlight, we laughed over a letter we had just read in the *Alumnae Bulletin* from an alumna visiting in Shanghai, who had "felt adventurous going into the native city in a ricksha."

Though we knew we might well be saying, "Dynasties pass," everything was quiet, everything seemed safe, and it was far more pleasant than going home from a party in a New York taxi. The next night Chang Tso-lin left Peking. A few days later the city gates were closed. Then the Nationalists arrived, and now we have a new flag.

When Chiang Kai-shek's Nationalist government took over Peking, the name of the city was changed from Peking, meaning Northern Capital, to Peiping, meaning Northern Peace. Nanking became China's capital, and the country was closer to being unified than it had been for many years; however, Peiping continued to be seen as the intellectual and spiritual center of the country. From 1928 to 1931 there was comparatively little disruption from military conflict.[10]

Not so for the Women's College: although Yenching's historian

Dwight Edwards calls this a time of" peace and sunshine" for Yenching, for those determined to preserve the independence of the Women's College there was need to be constantly on guard against Leighton Stuart's maneuvers directed toward taking over all authority in Women's College matters.

Although University politics was much on MBS's mind, she was also involved in creating satisfactory living arrangements for the faculty women: Myfanwy Wood, the Welsh missionary sent by the London Missionary Society to teach religion at Yenching, moved into Nancy Cochran's dormitory room in the Speer-Wagner suite; Miss Cochran moved to Mrs. Frame's, taking Dr. Brown's room; Dr. Brown moved to the infirmary. Such shifting about seemed a way to preserve amicable relations among the women.

Much more exciting was MBS's hope to move into the old Chinese house in which Lucius and Lillian Porter lived. Lucius Porter was one of the elder missionaries at Yenching, where he taught philosophy and coached athletic programs.[11]

The Porters wanted someone to housesit while they were away at Harvard in 1928-1929. The obstacle was that the Porters belonged to the Men's College and MBS and Augusta Wagner to the Women's College. Housing was limited, gender turf was tightly protected, but MBS negotiated successfully for the house by pointing out that the dormitory suite would be freed up and thus a housing problem would be settled for the Women's College. The Porters were pleased not to have unknown tenants, and MBS wrote to her mother that she and Augusta were "simply walking on air at the prospect of a house of our own and of getting away from the hectic communal existence of the Dean's Residence."

June 24, 1928

Last Tuesday we discovered that in order to let the next year's occupants of our dormitory suite move in, we would have to get our things out before going to Tsingtao. Since the Porters had gone, and our house was ready, we thought we might as well do the work at once, and on Wednesday we moved in. As yet we are still having meals at the Dean's House, but this morning we had breakfast here with Dr. Stuart as a guest, since it was the only time on his schedule that we could talk over some Women's College problems.

We are struggling with our own knotty problems in the Women's College just now. Dr. Stuart practically convinced the Yenching College Committee while he was at home that the finances of the Women's College and the University should be joined, but the explanation of all our worries on that score would fill a book.

July 3, 1928

We have laughed a good deal lately over the amount of responsibility we feel and really have for the Women's College. There are not many other colleges where junior members of the staff with only a couple of years' experience feel responsible for the whole institution. But Mrs. Frame has gone, and the young Chinese members of the faculty get married so fast that we seem to be the only ones left.

We are all very much pleased that Ruth Stahl is to be the Acting Dean; no one could be better for the job in every way. She was not willing, however, to take the complete responsibility, so we compromised by having a Dean's Committee to give her advice whenever she wants it. That committee consists of V.K. Nyi, a nice girl from Ginling who is teaching sociology, and me.

Ruth Stahl was a musician, trained at Mt. Union College in Alliance, Ohio. She too had come to North China Union College and stayed on as it became part of Yenching. She was a quiet Midwesterner, always reliable, " one of those people who would never be in the forefront" recalls MBS.[12]

I don't know how much you have heard from the members of the Yenching College Committee at home of the totally unexpected situation we found ourselves in just before Mrs. Frame left, when letters came from Mrs. Lee telling of Mr. Boyd's gift of $90,000 for the Women's College Gymnasium, with one of the conditions being that Mrs. Boyd be relieved of all future financial responsibility for Yenching.

Apparently everyone at home had already taken it for granted that the only way in which Mrs. Boyd could be so relieved, was for the Yenching University Trustees to take over the financial responsibility for the Women's College. Mrs. Lee's letter gave the impression that no one at home saw any objections to such a plan and that they would like our agreement as soon as possible.[13]

We had a meeting of the Women's College Faculty at which we all saw red and sent a letter home setting forth all the disastrous results which we felt would eventually overtake the Women's College if any such merger were effected. I'll try to find a copy of that letter to enclose even though I have changed my own point of view somewhat since then.

At that time we felt that there were two sides of the situation. First, the financial situation at home, of which we were completely ignorant. I felt that if the Committee there felt they could no longer raise the money needed for our budget, then our only course was to submit gracefully, for who are we out here to insist on somebody else's raising the money. But the other side of the situation was the practical changes that would inevitably result out here, and on that score I felt that we were much better judges than any of the women on the committee at home. Out of bitter experience in defending the rights and position of women, we put down what we felt would be the steps in the eventual loss of all the values which have been so painfully acquired in the Women's College.

This was the situation until Leighton Stuart got back. It was most unfortunate that the political changes of the moment stopped the trains so that he was delayed in Mukden and did not get here until two days before Mrs. Frame left. After several long talks with him I have come to realize that there is a third element in the situation which we will have to take into consideration, that is, the psychological attitude of the Men's College.

No one can deny that there has been a good deal of friction between us in the past. There is no use going into all the causes, though the chief ones have been (1) irritation on the part of the men due to our apparently greater wealth and to the extra red tape of a separate administration and (2) suspicion on our part due to a fear that any change might be an encroachment on our freedom and independence. Furthermore, no one can deny that there are strong forces in the Men's College all in favor of more or less complete amalgamation of the Women's College with the rest of the University.

Dr. Stuart asserts that pressure is brought to bear by the Chinese members of the faculty and that it is a matter outside his control. Whether or not that is true is beside the point, for his own sympathies are obviously with a policy of amalgamation.

Now it seems to me all this must be taken into consideration. I do not doubt that if the Yenching Committee at home could provide the funds, we could put up a good fight out here and keep our independence against all odds. It would be a constant battle but we could fight to the death and at least go down with the banners flying. I do not enjoy fighting, but I would be glad to do it in this case if I were convinced that it were worthwhile. But that is just the point. I do not think that the game is worth the candle. Such a continued campaign for our independence might be successful, but there would be a terrific cost in friction, bitterness and antagonisms. Besides, I do not think that is the way to work.

If the situation were ideal, I am convinced that it would be best for the Women's College to be a completely independent administrative unit of the University. But the situation is not ideal, and we must face the facts as they are.

Our position hitherto has been based on three points:

(1) We want to maintain certain values for the women students. (2) This can be done only by preserving the entity of the Women's College. (3) This entity can be preserved only by having a separate treasury.

I am beginning to question our logic. Since it has been the third point that has caused the friction, and we have found ourselves at loggerheads with the men over that, we have therefore jumped too quickly to the conclusion that we would never find the men sympathetic with us about anything. I think the time has come to be more optimistic and to realize that the men are no more anxious to destroy our values than we are. If we are willing to give up our outward independence, I am sure the friction will be removed and we can begin to cooperate. Surely as a general principle cooperation is much better than antagonism, and in this particular instance it is doubly so. I wish we did not have to make the choice. I wish the men were content to let us go on managing our own affairs. We weren't doing them any harm! But they are not willing, and we must make the best of it.

I am not cherishing any false hopes. It will not be easy. In giving up our independence we would be taking a risk. We must realize that we have to create an entirely new psychological atmosphere. We have been partly to blame for the friction in the past. But I feel it must be done. The old method of fighting for our rights has not been successful. The new method of cooperation will at least have the advantage of being friendly.

The old method meant that we had to protect the position of the women students against the bitterness and annoyance of the men. We shall still have to protect the position of the women, this time against economic pressure and the indifference of the men. All this means a long period of readjustment out here. We must persuade the die-hards in the Women's College Faculty; we must educate the men in the needs of the women students; and the details can probably be worked out only by painful experimentation.

Our chief danger, I think, is that the Committee at home will take some action that will prejudge the whole case. At first it seemed as if they had to act at once. Dr. Stuart now assures us that he thinks the conditions of the Boyd gift can be considered in a leisurely way and that we do not need to hurry.

The picture he gave us of the financial outlook of the Yenching Committee was very black. Because of all this, Grace Boynton and some of the others are very anxious to send a representative of the Women's College home to the Committee, in order to find out what the situation there really is and also to let them know exactly how things stand out here. I feel very strongly that it would be a waste of time for anyone to go home now. If the Committee can carry on as they are for one more year, giving us time to begin our new venture of cooperation out here, we will know very much better how we stand next June than we do now.

It is only fair to add that if anyone is to be sent home, I am to be the victim. While nothing would be nicer than a trip home and a chance to see you all, I do not relish this particular prospect, for it would be useless to go home for the November Committee meeting and then turn right around and come back. They would surely entangle me in money-raising campaigns and keep me there for the whole year. In the meantime I have a year's work mapped out here which I cannot bear to give up.

On the other hand, I should be more than pleased to go home next year (June 1929) for by that time I shall have laid the groundwork out here for whatever graduate work I am going to do in English. However, it doesn't seem to be a matter for me to decide and apparently we must wait for a decision in the fall.

In the meantime, do talk all this over with any of the Yenching College Committee people whom you see. The immediate question of the terms of acceptance of the Boyds' gift must be settled, also the future of the Yenching College Committee. And most important of all, we all need light on the best lines for cooperating with the Men's College out here so that we can preserve the values of the Women's College and be assured of a sufficient staff of women teachers and some protection for their minority opinion.

The Yenching College Committee in America (Yenching College referred originally to the Women's College when the University was still called Peking University) took very seriously its responsibility for the finances of the Women's College and for the appointment of its Western faculty. (Missionaries were appointed and paid by four Mission Boards, but some foreigners were appointed directly by the Yenching College Committee or the University Board of Managers and were paid from the funds of those two bodies.)[14]

The Women's College Faculty felt that as long as they had a separate budget and separate funds transmitted from the United States they could keep some measure of autonomy. Without a separate budget they felt that soon there would be very few women on the Faculty. "In a Yenching department with a Chinese man as the head of the department," wrote MBS years later, "any vacancy would probably be filled by one of his own protégés rather than by a young woman."[15]

In 1928 with the Men's College and the Women's College on the same campus sharing the same buildings, their independence was under review. More pressing, however, was the new government's requirements for recognition. The Chancellor, Wu Lei-ch'uan,[16] who was responsible for negotiating with the Ministry of Education, favored a unified administration for Yenching.[17] A letter from Myfanwy Wood to the Women's College Committee urged that the University not be subjected to the Chinese governmental pattern of higher education in which equality of women meant "the conforming of women to methods and standards already settled by men....

"The essence of the Yenching experiment is that it is attempting to build up in miniature the Christian ideal relationship between men and women, not as a theory but as a fundamental assumption of everyday life. It is teaching men as well as women, faculty as well as students,

the practices of cooperation as the alternative to segregation or absorption; the practice of difference in harmony as opposed to individualism or uniformity; the practice of careful nourishment of a weak minority to enable it to make its fullest contribution not at some future date but here and now in daily practice to life as a whole, showing to the majority the enrichment of life that comes from the care of a minority, as opposed to that which comes as a result of the elimination of the minority."[18]

Years later MBS reflected that "Our arguments seemed perhaps a little shrill, but there had been enough experience of the difficulties women had in making their way for us all to feel that there was danger ahead for women teachers and women students."[19]

Honest Experimentation

To escape the heat and "high tension of the Peking climate" MBS and Augusta Wagner went on vacation to Tsingtao, down the coast from Peking's port, Tientsin, and in the summer of 1928 "practically the only summer resort in China functioning as usual." The Nationalist Party had occupied Peking peacefully in June 1928, and Chiang Kai-shek arrived there early in July, but MBS was not reassured.

August 12, 1928

The political outlook seems as hopeless as ever. The Nationalists have so many factions at Nanking, all unwilling to give up their own interests, and no one strong enough to make the others fall in line. In spite of technical unity, the country is now as far from permanent peace as ever.

On the Yenching campus, however, life looked promising. Mrs. Frame had gone on furlough, and MBS and Augusta Wagner were to live for a year in the Lucius Porter house with Camilla Mills as the third housemate, an arrangement these younger Yenching women regarded as giving them delicious freedom.

September 9, 1928

Camilla arrived a week ago. It is great to have her back again and the three of us are having a wonderful time in the house. We have guests morning, noon, and night, but we'll have to slow down our pace a little when classes begin next week.

We have had the Faculty Pre-sessional Conference this week, and everything looks propitious for the opening term. Leonard Hsu, the new Dean of the University, is doing very well. We have a record enrollment of new students, and relations between the Women's College and the University are happier than they have ever been. I think the foreigners on the men's staff understand our position and the Chinese men are beginning to. There are practical questions of administration that can only be worked out in time and by honest experimentation.

We shall miss Mrs. Frame in many ways, but in our relations with the University we shall get along better without her. Her struggles to improve the Women's College and to have it recognized had filled her with more bitterness than she realized and the men all felt it.

October 28, 1928

We like our house. We have been doing quite a little entertaining for the faculty. It's so easy to have nice informal parties here— waffles and coffee after an evening meeting or something like that. The obvious advantages of this house over our dormitory-nunnery is that men can drop in. Not that we have a yearning for any particular man, but it's so much more normal and human. For instance, John Hayes just dropped in a little while ago. He had driven out with Grover Clark to see Dr. Stuart. If we had been in the dormitory, he would have had to send a message, and then we'd have had to go down to the doorstep and walk across to the Dean's Residence, which is more like a hotel than any house I've been in in my life.

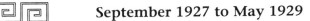

November 4, 1928

Our beloved Vice President, Wu Lei-Ch'uan, left us this week to go to Nanking as Vice Minister of Education. We shall miss him sorely, but his wisdom and his Christian point of view are desperately needed in Nanking. There is no one who can take his place here. Dr. Stuart would have liked to have Timothy Lew step in, but the students would not be very happy with that arrangement. Judge Kuo of our Political Science Department has been asked to be Acting Vice President, but has not yet accepted.

One of our chief problems continues to be the relation between the Women's College and the rest of the University. There has to be some cooperation, and we are trying to work out some plan which will protect the interests of the women students and involve the minimum amount of friction for the men of the University administration.

I wish we could settle the whole business on its own merits without having other issues intruded. The Boyds' offer of $90,000 for a women's gymnasium on condition that there be an amalgamation between the Women's College and the University has added tremendously to our troubles. I suppose people with money to give away feel they have a right to make conditions, but a thing like this seems to me like selling one's soul. In the first place, it rushes the whole business. In a case like this, where there have to be adjustments both in America and here, it takes months to reach a satisfactory working basis. Besides, we have to feel our way as we go along. It may easily be that in a year or two we'll find that a fairly complete merger with the University works all right, but I'll be hanged if I'll change my principles for ten gymnasiums!

November 11, 1928

Every day we like our house better and the things we can do because we have it. Today we have had a houseful of people and all such fun. Nancy [Cochran] came over to spend the night.

Camilla had to dash off right after breakfast to the Chinese service to sing in the choir but came back at half past ten bringing Bi (Mr. Bevan, one of our British widowers) and Dr. Faucett in for coffee.

The rest of us went to the eleven o'clock service, and then Mary Ferguson came out to lunch with Raymond Hill, a young Bostonian musician who has come to be Director of the Institute of Fine Arts. A nice lad named Biggerstaff[20] was here too. He is a Californian who has just taken his M.A. at Harvard and is out here under the Harvard-Yenching Institute to study Chinese government.

The two boys had a good time together, for they are both from Harvard, both about twenty-two, and both recently arrived in Peking and rather overwhelmed by the middle-aged community. We went out for a walk and came back to tea. The musician played for us, and we could hardly chase the other lad away when it was time for him to go back to Dr. Stuart where he was staying. You don't wonder we like our house!

December 2, 1928

We were more than ever glad to have our own house for Thanksgiving Day. Since it's not a Chinese holiday we had classes all morning and got back to the house only just in time to get ready for dinner. We had an international party—our next door neighbors the Shadicks (Harold, English and Nellie, Russian), Tom Barker (Irish), Bi (Australian) and Freddie and J.C. Li (Chinese).

We couldn't get a turkey, but we had a large bustard, and Pao Hsun outdid himself on the dinner. The Hayeses, who had been out to dinner with the Meads, stopped in in the afternoon, all four little girls very charming but Barbara and John both rather weary. In the evening all the Americans had supper together at the "Dean's Residence" after charades and an *Alice in Wonderland* skit in which Nancy, Augusta, and Camilla were Alice, the Queen, and the Duchess.

Wit and good humor were sustaining qualities in the Yenching commu-

nity, especially when MBS was required to undertake projects for which she felt somewhat unprepared.

The Christian Association at Tsing Hua has asked me to come over there once a week to lead a discussion group on College Problems. My first thought was that such a group of boys should have a man for a leader, but Ran[Sailer] says that most of them have never come into contact with educated women, and he thinks they need the feminine point of view!

We have been having a good deal of discussion about asking Mrs. Frame to come back. Of course the sooner we get a Chinese dean the better, but we have been over the possibilities with a fine-tooth comb, and there is no suitable Chinese woman available. I think the Faculty will ask Mrs. Frame to come back and that is probably wise. The only drawback is that she may not be able to fit in harmoniously to the new spirit of cooperation that we are slowly building up between the Men's and Women's Colleges.

December 9, 1928[21]

On Sunday I went over to the first meeting of my discussion group at Tsing Hua. When I asked what they wanted to discuss, one boy said Vocational Guidance. Another said, "I think the most important thing is what attitude should we take toward love affairs," whereupon all the rest chimed in and agreed that that was the pressing question.

The relationships between men and women are the most absorbing topic for all Chinese students today. They are twice as frank about it as students at home and very conscious that they are at sea. It's too bad there isn't some married woman around here to do this sort of thing, but most of them are taken up with their own families.

The general feeling seems to be that six months of peace is all that is good for us, and that we are likely to have some excitement within the next few weeks. General Yen Hsi-shan left Peking last week under rather mysterious circumstances, and the soldiers in the barracks near us here have been drilling from dawn to dark with most unusual energy. Many people think that the capital will be back in Peking before long.

Yen Hsi-shan was one of the dissident warlords who were trying to wrest popular support away from the KMT.[22] Whatever political upheavals threatened the Yenching community, Christmas was always celebrated with joy and festivity.

December 30, 1928

I began Christmas gaiety the Thursday beforehand by going into town with Nancy to dinner at the Customs Mess with one of Nancy's beaux and then to a play given by some of the young people in the American Legation. On Friday evening the Yenta Christian Fellowship had an enormous Christmas celebration lasting in true Chinese style hours longer than one would believe possible. On Saturday the Faculty Dramatic Club gave some plays in which Camilla had a leading part, and Augusta was responsible for the Christmas decorations in the chapel, so we had a busy day.

We celebrated Christmas morning breakfast by having real sausages, which were much enjoyed by the six girls who were here. We just had time to open our own things before church. After church we came back to get ready for dinner. We had six guests for dinner—Ruth Stahl and Dr. Brown, V.K. Nyi of our Sociology Department and her fiance Y.P. Mei, who is the Registrar, "Tiny" Armstrong, an enormous Welsh lad who teaches history, and Bi (that is Mr. Bevan, our middle-aged stand-by). Later in the afternoon we went over to the Hsu Shu-hsi's for the baptism of their two little boys. This is a very cut and dried account of our activities and festivities, but we did have a good time, the nicest Christmas since I've been in China. Having one's own house makes a world of difference.

Bi, who became one of MBS's and AW's closest friends, was L.R.O.
Bevan, an Englishman, educated at Cambridge and trained in law, who
considered himself an Australian after moving there and marrying an
Australian. He went to China to teach politics at Peking National Uni-
versity. After his wife's death, his children were brought up by relatives
in Sydney, but he stayed on in Peking, teaching also at Yenching. After
the move to the new campus, Bi lived there and was known to everyone
as Pi Lao Yeh (old man Bi). He was older by twenty-five years than
MBS's group of friends, but they enjoyed his company. He was, wrote
MBS later, "witty, warm-hearted, well-read, and truly humane."[23]

February 3, 1929

We hear rumors now and then that the capital may be moved
back, but that doesn't seem to faze the plans that are going on for
all the new buildings in Nanking. My old friend H.K. Murphy has
just been here on his way south. He has a three-year contract with
the National Government to lay out the city and build all the new
government buildings. He's fearfully enthusiastic of course, but
one wonders just how much of it all will actually come true.

March 10, 1929

At the moment the University is having an orgy of committee
meetings, and reorganizing all its internal administration along the
lines suggested by the Ministry of Education. On the whole the
new arrangement is a good one, but we have rushed into it in a
fearful hurry.

The "new arrangement" was in response to the opportunity offered to
Yenching and other Christian institutions in China to become part of the
national system of education. One condition was that the president should
be Chinese, or there must be a Chinese vice president to represent the
institution in applying for recognition. If the institution had a board of
managers, more than half must be Chinese. Further, the institution must

90

not have as its purpose the "propagation of religion."[24]

Yenching's diplomatic president, Leighton Stuart, persuaded the Yenching Trustees in New York to agree to greater power for a Chinese Board of Managers in Peking and revisions in the English and Chinese constitutions. At the same time Acting President Galt and Vice President Wu Lei-ch'uan met with faculty committees on campus to work out changes so that Yenching could be registered with the government.[25]

In the end, Yenching was troubled very little by the changes. Small groups of radical students, however, continued to disturb the community.

March 17, 1929

Life has been interesting enough this week, anyway, for a group of students has been trying to start a little trouble by demanding that the Dean of the College of Social Sciences be ousted. The charges against him are ridiculous, and the trouble is really political, like nine-tenths of the student troubles of the last few years. It is only a small group of students who are making a last desperate effort after a good many unsuccessful attempts to throw monkey wrenches into the machinery. I hope this will be the last appearance of these trouble-makers, for they have found this time that they have not only the faculty against them, but most of the men students and all of the women.

I am rapidly turning into an architect. The contractor begins work in a week or two on the new gymnasium, so we shall have our hands full during the spring. In the meantime, we are working hard on plans for a new faculty house for the Women's College. The problem of the best way to house a lot of single women is almost insoluble. The most important requirement is flexibility. One cannot always find a group of three or four or five or any given number of people who want to live together or could do so happily. Camilla and Augusta and I have been a perfect combination, but there isn't another such combination in the Women's College Faculty.

We already have several housing arrangements—a foreign house that holds five people, the Dean's Residence, and the dormitory suites. Our new house is to be in place of our East Compound house which the Meads are now living in. After fuming and discussing and drawing up innumerable plans, we have decided on a Chinese house, very much adapted, which will really be two complete units, each for three people, but which could if necessary be run as one unit for five or six. We have an excellent lot in the South Compound, which is close and convenient for the Women's College

March 30, 1929

I think I'll go in for architecture. We've just finished the plans for a new house for the Women's College Faculty, and it's going to be the best house on campus. We have struggled for years to find a scheme that will be satisfactory for a lot of old maids; that is, that will give each person sufficient privacy and independence and yet will not be too expensive to run. The only drawback is that I have only one chance in ten of living in it.

The Chinese women on the faculty were less likely than the Westerners to become old maids, and everybody enjoyed the parties and preparation for their weddings.

May 5, 1929

You would have enjoyed the spectacle over in the Gardens the other day. Grace [Boynton] had a shower for [Hsieh] Wan-ying, who is to be married next month. After tea, when people were beginning to wonder when the "shower" would start, there was a great commotion outside and around the lake came a miniature wedding procession. All the children, both Chinese and foreign, were marching, some with banners and horns and drums, others with trays of presents, and in the middle was a small red wedding chair (made of paper, but looking very natural) occupied by a small red-clad bride. It was a great hit, especially with the children, who had ice cream and cake as a reward for their labors.

Festive diversions did not, however, distract the Women's College entirely from its difficulties. Dean Alice Browne Frame was on furlough during 1928 to 1929, and nothing was certain about her plans for returning.

Given this uncertainty, MBS in the fall of 1928 had changed her mind about going home for three years to get a Ph.D. She had, as she said, broken into administrative circles at Yenching, and she felt that she was needed at this time of change and reorganization in the Women's College, a transition period when preserving their separate identity depended on having some continuity of leadership. If Mrs. Frame did not return, "then apparently the responsibility falls on Ruth Stahl and me, for there is as yet no Chinese dean in sight," she wrote on February 17, 1929.

Much wiser, she felt, and Acting Dean Ruth Stahl as well as the English Department agreed, for MBS to take her furlough in 1929-1930 in order to be back when Ruth Stahl and Monona Cheney, older women long in the field, were due for furlough. Going a year early would also allow her the personal pleasure of being on furlough with Augusta Wagner, who was planning to work on her Ph.D. in economics.

Fine for her and fine for Yenching, but the Presbyterian Board of Foreign Missions, of which her father was Secretary, had very strict rules: the first term abroad was to be a full five years.

Through the winter and early spring MBS agonized. Why couldn't the Board do what was sensible for Yenching? Mrs. Frame had given no assurance that she would return; there was no Chinese dean yet in sight. It seemed so simple and so much better for Yenching if MBS could go home a year early. She rehearsed her arguments repeatedly, hoping her father understood the situation, adding in her February 3 letter, "I gather that Mrs. Frame, who did not understand the conditions, went off half-cocked (as she usually does) when she heard about the plan for me to come home early."

The University did not know whether Mrs. Frame would return. MBS wrote on February 17, "We have very little light on her plans yet." By March 10, nothing had been resolved: "We don't know what Mrs. Frame's plans are. She wrote to Ruth that she probably won't come back to us and to the American Board that she probably will."

Ruth Stahl as Acting Dean had sent letters to the Board and to the China Council on March 5 (The Mission had an administrative board in the United States and another in China with Chinese members), a vexing process because of the time required for letters to go back and forth between China and the United States. It was absolutely necessary, Ruth Stahl had argued, for MBS to be at Yenching in 1930 and 1931, and "she felt the case would be very little altered even if Mrs. Frame did come back."

This brought action: "On March 12 we got the first word of Mrs. Frame's decision to come back to Yenching." But Ruth Stahl and MBS still hoped to strengthen administrative continuity by having Ruth on hand to help Mrs. Frame in 1929 (while MBS went home) and MBS "on the spot" to help in 1930 when Ruth went on furlough and in 1931 when they hoped to have a Chinese dean.

To her family, MBS poured out her aggravation: "I don't know whether you realize the position Mrs. Frame has put us in this last year. When she went home last June she completely washed her hands of Yenching and said that her resignation was final and that she was never, never coming back to us. This was in spite of all requests to reconsider and to think the matter over....By the end of two years we hope to have found a Chinese dean, but if we have not, we have not the slightest idea whether Mrs. Frame will consent to stay on or not. People seem to think that if we don't find a Chinese dean, or if Mrs. Frame doesn't stay on, I will have to be the goat."

For the present, however, the China Council found the women's arguments unconvincing, and MBS was not granted an early furlough. MBS was both personally and professionally disappointed and anxious for the

Women's College, but went resolutely on with her work.

May 12, 1929

We hear devastating rumors from home of how tired Mrs. Frame is, and of how little vacation she is going to get this summer. Naturally she wants to be here for Formal Opening, but I wish someone could persuade her to take a few months extra vacation and not try to get back here till late in the fall.

The workmen have started on the new Women's College house, so the battle has begun. Building a house in China is supposed to be the surest known way of losing your disposition. You have your choice of losing it during the building, but getting a fairly decent house as a result, trying to keep it at first or losing it when you live in the house and find out that the windows don't work and the doors have cracks and the floors lie in waves.

I may come through unscathed if I follow the latter course, for it is by no means sure that I shall live in the house when it is done. I should like to live there with Camilla or the Wards, but housing the Women's College is a ticklish business, and there are still some unknown quantities in our next year's staff.

May 26, 1929

I got back from Paotingfu Wednesday evening. On the whole, Mission Meeting was fairly satisfactory: the chance to get acquainted with other members of the Mission is far more valuable than the actual transaction of business, which is largely of an unimportant routine nature. I cannot feel that it is right or wise for the foreigners to do all the business alone without any Chinese present. We voted on at least half a dozen questions which affected the workers in our churches, schools, or hospitals. It would be so much more friendly if nothing else, to get their advice before rather than after the decision.

I was very much struck by the great difference in attitude in

Paotingfu and Shuntehfu, as compared with Yenching, toward the question of Chinese cooperation. Here in the University it is not a "question" at all; it is the natural order of things, and no one thinks anything about it. It is a much happier atmosphere to live in here where foreigners and Chinese are all on the same social, intellectual, and economic level.

The situation is very different in the other stations and inevitably so. I wonder if it is ever possible for a foreigner to work almost entirely among uneducated people without feeling patronizing and somewhat set apart, no matter how much he may "love" them.

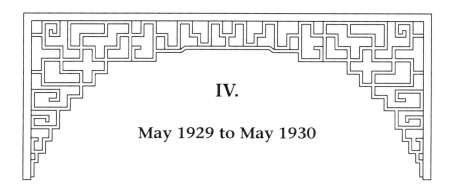

IV.

May 1929 to May 1930

Death, Love, and War

*An historic occasion—and the promise of a spectacular procession—
brought MBS and some of her friends dashing to the campus gate
to watch the coffin of Sun Yat-sen carried from the Western Hills to his
splendid tomb in Nanking. After Sun Yat-sen, leader of the Chinese Republic, died on March 12, 1925, his coffin had been kept at Pi Yun Ssu
in the Western Hills until his tomb was ready in Nanking, to which it
was to be moved with great ceremony. "His figure became the object of
a revolutionary cult reminiscent of the ancestor reverence accorded a
dynastic founder."[1]*

May 26, 1929

The great event this week is of course Sun Yat-sen's funeral.
The coffin was taken today from Pi Yun Ssu in the Western Hills to
Peking. The entombment in Nanking is to be next Saturday. After
the ceremonies are over civil war can begin! At least Chiang and
Feng are politely saying that hostilities will not start until next
week.

Minute plans have been published in the papers every day about
the pomp and ceremony of today's procession, but judging by our
glimpses of it this morning a good deal of the money provided for

it must have gone straight into a few pockets. The catafalque and the bearers' special uniforms were in the Nationalist blue and white, but aside from that there wasn't much of a spectacle. There were supposed to be more trimmings after the procession reached the city gates.

The coffin left Pi Yun Ssu in the middle of the night and was scheduled to pass the campus at four o'clock. The telephone operator called me at quarter past four saying the procession was coming, so we tore down to the gate to be greeted by the news that the gate was not allowed to be opened and that the troops guarding the road would shoot anyone who looked over the wall!

That gloomy prophecy turned out to be unfounded, for at five o'clock the gate was opened and the policemen outside said we might watch if no one stepped outside the gate. Finally at half past six the procession came by. It was not very impressive. Several of the troopers in the advance guard were eating their breakfast as they rode, and any of the officers who had cigarettes were smoking. The PUMC ambulance which came in the rear was the snappiest looking part of the procession!

MBS was disappointed by the lack of dignity in the procession bearing Sun-Yat-sen's coffin. She and her friends, Western and Chinese, were old hands at planning formal ceremonies and knew how to bring them off with a flourish.

June 2, 1929

The first of our annual crop of weddings came this week— V.K. Nyi, a very modern and feministic young member of the Sociology Department married Y.P. Mei, our Registrar, one of the finest of all the Returned Students.[2]

V.K. Nyi, after her freshman year at Ginling College, won one of the ten scholarships for women awarded by Tsing Hua to help young Chinese

college students go to the United States. She completed her undergradu-
ate work at Smith College and then went to the University of Chicago for
graduate work in sociology. There she met Y.P. Mei, a graduate of Oberlin
College, who was doing postgraduate study. She returned to China to
teach sociology first at Ginling and then in 1927 at Yenching. In one of
her courses she took her students on field trips to see coal mines, orphan-
ages, and "prostitution places." She wanted to open the students' eyes,
to have them "get into contact with real Chinese society." Alas, after she
had taught two years, she and Y.P. Mei, who was by then also at
Yenching, married and, under University rules forbidding husband and
wife to teach in the same university, she was no longer allowed to teach.
But their wedding itself was a lesson in preserving Chinese culture in
combination with Western missionary ideas.[3]

It was an interesting mixture of old and new. They are both
Christians and the actual ceremony was performed by V.K.'s father,
who is an Episcopal minister from Hangchow. But instead of copy-
ing foreign customs as most of the foreign educated brides do, V.K.
was dressed in old ceremonial garments and headdress and rode in
a red chair from the house to the chapel. We have the science of
wedding decorations all worked out now. We have done so many
we can do it with the turn of a hand.

After the festivities were over, MBS and Camilla Mills went for their
summer vacation to Peitaiho (Augusta Wagner had gone back to New
York to study for her Ph.D.) where they stayed in Henry and Jo Welles's
house and helped care for Betty and Holly, aged three and two, while
their parents, in Peking, awaited the arrival of their third child. There
were two experienced amahs, so the chief responsibility was to take the
children to the beach, and they had a diverting vacation.

July 14, 1929
    The last few weeks have been enlivened by the fact that Bi has

fallen in love with me. It was somewhat astonishing, for Camilla and Augusta and I have seen a good deal of him this last winter, but he has always behaved with the greatest neutrality. However, this sudden ardency on his part is not reciprocated on mine, so you needn't worry about my marrying a widower just yet.

Harold Shadick recalls that Bi "became really enamored of Marnie, but she did not return this"; however, MBS and Bi had an "exceptionally intimate" friendship.[4] Very likely, MBS and Bi had that rare and fortunate relationship of friendship between man and woman that enriched their lives without restrictions. In any case, in the summer of 1929 distractions of romance and visitors did not blot out the continuing political instability in China.

July 21, 1929

This tangle in Manchuria is not very cheerful. I can't understand the attitude of the National Government. They must have known just when the CER [Chinese Eastern Railway] was to be taken over, but it was done at a time when Chang Hsüeh-liang was not in Mukden, C.T. Wang was in Tsinan, and neither of them are hurrying back to where they belong. C.T. Wang hasn't yet got back to Nanking and "The Young Marshall" is still playing about here at Peitaiho. We passed him on the road the other day, driving his wife (?) in a very smart trap and followed by a mounted bodyguard. They don't seem to consider the situation as serious, and yet there seems every likelihood of a nasty outbreak.

Wang Ch'eng-t'ing was the Nationalist Government's Foreign Minister. "The Young Marshall" was Chang Hsüeh-liang, a Manchurian warlord, son of Chang Tso-lin.[5]

July 28, 1929

Affairs in Manchuria seem to be calming down a bit, and if

there are enough compromises to save everyone's face, the business ought to be settled quite peaceably. The tie-up in the railroad has caused a lot of trouble for all the people who were planning to cross Siberia. The wife of one of the Anglican missionaries here was on the train that was stopped just west of Manchouli and has had to spend about ten days trying to get around by Vladivostok. One feels that the Chinese have behaved childishly and that the Soviet has been as imperialistic (in the Chinese sense of the word) as any of the capitalistic powers. The Kellogg Pact has been a wholesome influence, however.

Part of the difficulty with the Chinese Eastern Railway involved the Russians, who had moved swiftly into Manchuria, ignoring the Open Door policy of Western powers which was intended to preserve the integrity of China. The Kellogg-Briand Pact was an agreement condemning war and urging peaceful settlement of international disputes.[6]

On the Yenching campus, MBS concentrated on housing for the Women's College in the coming year. Although the new house about which she had written earlier was not complete, she was planning to live in the finished part with Camilla Mills, Ruth Stahl, and Caroline Chen, a graduate of Mills College in California. She suspected that Mrs. Frame would object because she wanted one of them at least to live with her in the Dean's Residence—"but the plan will be happy for us." MBS hoped her mother would be an advocate for common sense with the Yenching Committee, especially concerning the swimming pool.

August 12, 1929

I see your name on the Yenching College Committee letterheads now. Do ask Augusta to explain our point of view about the Women's College swimming pool. From all Mrs. Lee's letters it appears that the Committee at home has absolutely refused to consider our opinions on the subject, yet they take Mr. Garside as an absolute authority on the questions though it is several years since he has been in China, and when he was here he was at Cheeloo and not at Yenching.[7]

It's a kind of absentee landlordism that is very trying when people at home create problems that those of us out here have to deal with. I realize that of course it is partly Mrs. Frame's fault. Naturally the Committee respected her judgment about it but apparently one year at Mount Holyoke has been enough to obliterate all her memories of Yenching conditions.

The funniest thing about the Committee's position is that they interpret our suggestion that the men students would naturally want to use the girls' swimming pool as meaning that the boys are nothing short of Goths and Vandals. They do not at all consider the sheer waste of putting up an expensive pool that can be used by less than a quarter of the college community.

The Yenching Committee, the Chinese political and military situation, and heavy rains were challenges to good humor, but fortunately MBS and her associates forgot all these problems from time to time.

August 18, 1929

Last night we had a real party. Camilla and I went into town to dinner at Shelly Gleed's. He's a nice youth in the BAT [British American Tobacco Company] whom we had lots of fun with last spring. Jimmy Faulkner of the Chartered Bank was there and Bi and a girl from the PUMC. As usual out here, all the men were British and the girls American.

After dinner we danced on the Peking Hotel roof, the coolest place about here in this weather. There was an almost full moon, and the view of the city gates and the scattered hutung lights in the moonlight was heavenly.

August 25, 1929

The Porters got to Kobe yesterday, so they will be here in a few days more. The progress on the new house is very discouraging. I go over it every morning on a tour of inspection and find something new that is wrong every day. It's a time-consuming process, but someone has to keep an eye on things.

The situation in Manchuria is very puzzling. The rumors of war come and go and are contradicted every day. Certainly the Chinese do not want war, but they appear to think the mix-up will cure itself, which is hardly likely.

September 16, 1929

Today I have been at Dr. Stuart's house again for tea, this time to meet Mrs. Woodrow Wilson and Dr. and Mrs. Tensher of Tokyo who are cousins of hers. After that Dr. Stuart and Lucius Porter and I escorted them about the campus. Mrs. Wilson was "sweet" in the accepted sense of the word, but the Tenshers were really interesting.

Camilla and I have been much amused by a serious suggestion that we go to live in Dr. Stuart's house when he goes to America after Formal Opening and take charge of entertaining all the University guests. We certainly shall not do it—for many reasons. We much prefer the kind of entertaining we can do in our own small house. We have already established a very happy custom of having a few girls in for breakfast. Almost all Chinese like foreign breakfast. The girl we are trying to fatten up comes every day, and others come very often, especially on Wednesday and Sunday, which are waffle mornings.

September 21, 1929

The new house is nearly finished. Painting and a few other odd jobs have to be finished, but of course it's the finishing touches that have to be watched most carefully. Lots of houses around here wouldn't be half bad if somebody with a little taste (or sense) had kept an eye on the painting. A Chinese painter will put on a sticky shiny varnish every time, if you don't watch like a hawk.

But I really think it's going to be a nice house when it's done.

October 13, 1929

I took a Chinese exam this week and have about eleven more to take before the end of the year. I have resigned from every committee and am not doing anything except regular teaching work and Chinese.

Of course the Mission is right to insist on the language requirements even here at Yenching where one doesn't need the language in the course of every day work. But it seems to me it's a mistaken emphasis in my case. They made no objection when I got involved in administrative work my first three years out here at Yenching, but now they have come down like a ton of bricks with the result that the last year before furlough when my knowledge of Chinese is going to be of least use and I've had enough experience to be of value on committees, I have to spend all my time with character cards and a dictionary.

October 25, 1929

On Tuesday Camilla and I went in to dinner at the Faucetts' and found ourselves in the middle of the ricksha coolies' riots. Just as we were leaving here at seven o'clock Camilla and I, Bi, Knight, and George Barbour, we met Dr. Adolph who told us there was trouble in town and we might have difficulty getting through the gates. As a matter of fact we saw only one crowd showing signs of violence, but we saw several tram cars reduced to splinters, and heard a dozen conflicting rumors flying about as rumors do here in Peking.

When we came home at midnight, the city was technically under martial law. The streets were empty and we were stopped at most corners and forbidden to go along certain streets, but we got home safely and were glad we hadn't missed the excitement. The poor coolies "broke their own rice bowls" in the Chinese phrase, for hundreds of them were arrested and held for a couple of days though they had no conception of what the riots were about.

October 27, 1929[8]

The success of Formal Opening exceeded even Dr. Stuart's fondest hopes. It was well worth waiting these three years, from the point of view of the campus alone. The first of October is always a lovely time of year, and the weather this year was flawless for the three great days. The months of hard work that the Landscape Committee had put in had all borne fruit, and the whole campus was truly beautiful. When one looks at the lake, the trees, the lawns (yes, in spots there are actually lawns) the flowers, the neat winding paths, it is almost impossible to recall the raw and barren campus, the yawning heating trenches, the piles of pipes and cement bags that surrounded us three years ago.

The best part of the Formal Opening ceremonies was the Service of Dedication held in the auditorium on Sunday morning. The actual opening on Tuesday afternoon was most impressive. There were dozens of speeches of course, a few of them holding the students spell-bound. General Shang Chen and President Chang Po-ling of Nankai made corking speeches, and the Chancellor, Wu Lei-ch'uan, in his usual quiet winning way spoke of the Christian foundations of the University and the Christian ideals for which we stand. I believe the distinguished guests were not disappointed in Yenching and the students began to feel stirrings of pride in the University and their share in it.

Mrs. Frame got back in time for the excitement of Formal Opening, and Ruth Stahl is thankful to be relieved of the responsibilities of the Dean's Office and able to spend her days in her studio again.

Housing has been a problem as usual but everyone is reasonably happy now. The new house in South Compound was supposed to be finished in September, but the contractor excuses himself for being two months behind schedule by saying the work was

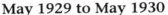

delayed by the rains—as if we had had two months solid rain during the summer.

The greatest excitement of the last week has been the trouble between the ricksha coolies and the tram men. It reached a crisis on Tuesday over the election of officers for the Peking Federation of Labor Unions.

Trouble started late in the afternoon when a tram tried to force its way through a crowd of coolies and then spread like wildfire over the city. All trams were stopped, and in the course of the evening most of them were smashed. When we went in through the Hsi Chih Men at half past seven there was a large crowd venting its feelings by throwing stones at a tram that had been turned over and was lying on its side. On Hatamen Street we passed about ten empty cars, then unmolested, but later in the evening we saw the same cars with all the windows broken and the sides smashed in. One car near the Hsi Ssu Pai Lou was reduced to kindling wood.

By ten o'clock the ricksha coolies' ardor began to cool, and troops were called out to help the police restore order. All rickshas disappeared by magic, and the police were able to feel important and stop all motor cars. About six hundred ricksha coolies were arrested and held for a couple of days. The poor devils are worse off than ever because popular sympathy is all with the tram car men, their union has been disbanded by the authorities, the police now have a good excuse to beat up any coolie who irritates them, and of course the people who engineered the rumpus have skipped safely away.

November 17, 1929

I wish I could come to some definite conclusion about my own future. I go ahead on the assumption that I'll spend my furlough getting an M.A. at Columbia and then come back here to Yenching, but I wonder sometimes whether it is right to take that for granted.

Looking ahead, I cannot see any great future for the foreigner in mission education out here. Certainly in administration the foreigner must be increasingly willing to step out. For example, when I came out (this is just between ourselves) people talked quite frankly of my being the next Dean of the Women's College. It's obvious now that after Mrs. Frame leaves we must find a Chinese dean. In fact we should have done so already. That leaves then, for me, just the field of teaching. For ten years at least, perhaps more, the Department of English here will need and want foreigners. After that, who can say?

T'ai Shan

In the midst of uncertainties, personal and political, MBS celebrated Christmas and with Camilla Mills held a housewarming party on New Year's Eve at which guests had such a good time that they didn't go home until morning. Moving into the new house was as exciting to them as the excitement in Peking over the discovery of the skull of Sinanthropus Pekinensis. MBS took time off during the Chinese New Year vacation for a long-postponed trip to China's most sacred mountain, T'ai Shan.

February 2, 1930

It's a gray, snowy Sunday morning in the middle of our Winter Vacation (it used to be called China New Year Vacation, but we politely give the rose another name now that the Government is trying to abolish the lunar calendar) and there is therefore time to take Corona in hand and tell you of my adventures.

I had planned to spend the whole two weeks' holiday studying Chinese and trying to get off a few of the exams, which I must get out of the way before I start home and with that excuse I refused Mrs. Frame's request that I be one of the Women's College delegates to the meeting in Shanghai of the Council on Christian Higher Education.

However, I didn't stay at home. During exam week Mildred Owen and Jo Brown, two YWCA secretaries with whom I had been at Language School, came out to have lunch with us. They were leaving in a few days to go back to Shanghai and were planning to stop off on the way at Tsinan, T'ai Shan and Chufu, the place where Confucius was born and buried. They said one of their party had dropped out and they had an extra reservation, and why didn't I come along? When I realized that I could make the whole trip in six days, I decided it was too good a chance to miss. For three years Augusta and I had tried to get to T'ai Shan during Spring vacation but always at the last minute we had been stopped by wars, evacuation, or broken train service. But this time nothing went wrong.

On January 24 we started off, five from the YWCA and I. I decided that I would cut out Chufu in order to have more time in Tsinan with Octavia Howard, my Bryn Mawr classmate, whom I hadn't seen since coming to China. I expected to stay with the others for the first four days, but as things turned out I lost them within twenty-four hours and pursued the rest of my way independently.

This is how it happened. We spent the first night on the Blue Express—the second class car was the best I've ever traveled on in China—and got into Tsinan the next morning. We had an hour and a half between trains and all went out to Cheeloo University (Shantung Christian University) where I had a glimpse of Octavia and her family.

At eleven o'clock we scrambled aboard what was supposed to be a third class car on the southbound train for T'aian. It really was a much battered baggage car, but we sat on our suitcases and bedding rolls and wrapped ourselves up in our steamer rugs. When we began to get hungry and cold, we bought large steaming sweet potatoes for four coppers apiece.

About three we got to T'aian and were met by kind Mr. Hansen of the Methodist Mission. Then followed fifteen minutes of frantic discussion and mind changing among the rest of the party for they discovered that the trip to Chufu would take longer than they had expected, that they could only get it in by cutting down their time at T'aian, which would mean rushing up the mountain that same afternoon and spending the night in the icy atmosphere on top. Each person had a different idea, and everybody talked at once. Patient Mr. Hansen kept urging them to hurry, and finally just as our train, which had been changing engines, started to pull out of the station, they all piled back on board to go on down the line to Chufu, leaving me in peace with the Methodists!

The next day I went up T'ai Shan by myself!

Reminiscing about climbing T'ai Shan, MBS noted that several years later she went up the mountain again and once spent a summer holiday half-way up the mountain, "but this trip was alone, and I had no one to talk to about it as the exciting day went on. It was bitter cold but I was well wrapped up and had four cheerful chair bearers. It would hardly have been possible for me to make the whole climb on my own two feet. Very light people sometimes had two chair bearers, somewhat heavier people had three, but Mr. Hansen and the head bearer looked at me and decided I needed four. I did a great deal of walking, which was not rug-ged rock climbing but up a long pilgrim trail with well-worn steps and short level stretches. Whenever I got winded I got into my chair."[9] Writing home in 1930 about the climb, MBS urged her parents to read Eunice Tietjens' poem "The Most Sacred Mountain," "for nothing else describes so well the feelings that one has."[10]

T'ai Shan is a sacred mountain, and after the day there alone, except for my four cheerful chair bearers, I felt as if I'd been converted or the way one is supposed to feel after being psychoanalyzed.

I got to the top about noon and ate my lunch sitting in the sunshine just outside the South Gate of Heaven. I wandered about the temples on the top and found the stone where Confucius stood and "found the world small." One shared his feelings and at the same time, as one stood there, one "found China great." And there in the midst of "Space, and the twelve clean winds of heaven," one thought too of "The King in his beauty and the land of far distances." Thousands of years, thousands of steps, thousands of pilgrims! And new China is there too. Just beyond the ridge where the emperors used to send their horses back there is a monument to Sun Yat-sen bearing the characters one then saw everywhere: *Tsung li ching shen pu szu:* "The spirit of the founder will not die." And on one of the old stones at the top among the inscriptions that famous poets and emperors have left through the ages are four new blue characters: *T'ien hsia wei kung,* the Nationalist slogan meaning "Everything belongs to the People" or more literally, "Under Heaven all is common."

It was a wonderful day, and I was glad I had gone alone. Coming down was a thrilling experience. The bearers prefer to have you ride, for they are very proud of their speed in running down the six thousand, seven hundred steps! My heart stood still for the first moment, and the head bearer told me I looked green and yellow, but after the first few minutes it was fun, and I got used to the extra slide and swing as at each level spot the bearers changed their diagonal and shifted the chair straps to the other shoulder.

February 9, 1930

I'm sorry Father feels so discouraged about China. There are plenty of discouraging elements, and there is not likely to be an improvement that the rest of the world can see in less than twenty years. But as individuals they are struggling desperately for better things, and their faults as a nation are the faults of an adolescent with an inferiority complex.

We had a gorgeous exhibition of fireworks in our courtyard last evening. It's the usual custom at Chinese New Year and is especially necessary in a new house. Caroline Chen got the "flower pots" in Peking and some of the girls came to see the show. The cook and the boy especially enjoyed themselves since they had the honor of setting them off.

The "flower pots" were the proper fireworks for this occasion to chase away evil spirits.[11]

March 2, 1930

Mother's report that Dr. Stuart had said I would have to take Mrs. Frame's place caused me some consternation. It is hard to know how firm Mrs. Frame is in her determination to leave Yenching in 1931. If she does go, we ought to move heaven and earth to find a Chinese woman to take her place. And though that may be impossible in 1931 it ought not to be impossible forever, and everyone hopes that Mrs. Frame will stay until a Chinese successor is found. So don't have any illusions about my settling down as Dean of the Women's College.

I have been having a little excitement this week over one of my girls who has been accused of being a Communist. The rumor spread that the police were on her trail and that she would be arrested if she left the campus. She is not a Communist or a member of any political party, but that would not make being arrested any less unpleasant. And though the Nationalist Government is not chopping off heads with quite the same nonchalance that Chang Tso-lin used to have, yet people who are suspected of dangerous tendencies disappear most mysteriously sometimes.

March 16, 1930

For the last few weeks it has looked as though we might get by without our spring war, but rumors are beginning to spread again that Yen and Feng are coming to Peking and troops are moving up and down the railroad. I hope Chiang Kai-shek can weather the storm. A corrupt government is a good deal better than none at all.

March 23, 1930

The political situation is, as usual, an enigma. Yen Hsi-Shan is at present in complete control in Peking. His men have taken over practically all the civil offices this week. On Thursday we heard that the *Leader* was the only pro-Nanking newspaper left in North China, and Thursday night five of the Kuomintang men in the *Leader* office were supplanted by Yen's men. Some rumors say that Yen is already here; others that he is on his way. It isn't yet clear whether there's to be real fighting, but people seem to think that if it comes it will be in North China this time.

In 1930 the Nanking government was challenged by warlords in both North and South China. Yen Hsi-shan joined Feng Yü-hsiang and Wang Ch'ing-shan in seizing political and military power in North China.[12]

March 30, 1930

The great sensation in journalistic circles this week is the closing of the *North China Standard* and the *Shun T'ien Shih Pao*, the big English and Chinese papers subsidized by the Japanese Government. The papers were closed on order from Tokyo, apparently, as part of Baron Shidehara's new policy—certainly a good sign for future Sino-Japanese relations.

Baron Shidehara, the Japanese Foreign Minister, had developed a policy of cooperation with Western Powers on China policy and was not in favor of Japanese military intervention in China.[13] As always in times of political uncertainty, MBS and her friends maintained their equilibrium by praying, walking in the Western Hills, and occasionally having some "un-missionaryish fun."

March 30, 1930

I'm a little sleepy today for we were up late last night. The Faculty Dramatic Club gave an informal performance of "The

Gondoliers" here at our house. The whole house was appropriated for dressing rooms and properties, and we had a grand, noisy, hilarious time, with the cast staying on long after the audience had gone.

April 25, 1930

Our Easter service was out on the island that has grown to be a Yenching tradition. Myfanwy Wood preached, and lots of faculty children and several students were baptized. After the service we went to the Shadicks' for an Easter breakfast celebrated in true Russian style.

Tomorrow at the crack of dawn we start off for two days in the Hills. It's the first weekend this year that we've gone out to a temple. The Hills look so near that we're constantly resolving to go, but we never seem to have time to pack up our beds and bedding and get off.

May 4, 1930

Our trip to the Hills last weekend was a great success. There were nine of us—Helen and Len Sweet, Jo, Dell Bryon, Ruth Rooker, Knight, Bi, Camilla and I. We walked about twenty-five miles and slept out of doors in the temple courtyard, so we came back as burned as if we'd been at the seashore. Ch'ieh T'ai Ssu where we spent the night is one of the loveliest and oldest of the temples in the Western Hills. It has a huge open terrace where all the priests in this part of China are "ordained". That night there was the most elaborate service I've ever seen in a Chinese temple, apparently part of a hundred dollars worth of services that a Peking actor had paid for!

The second day we went on to T'ai Che Ssu, a lovely temple in a green hollow of the hills, where there is a wonderful old abbot who has been there forty years. He came to talk to us after lunch. Since he talks to everyone who comes and has a splendid memory, he's a very well informed old man.

In the afternoon we came back along a ridge to Mentoukou where we took the train for Peking. Mentoukou has large coal deposits fairly near the surface, and there are several mines there both British and Chinese. For a couple of hours, walking along the ridge we could look down into the black valley. All the other valleys were green and beautiful, but this one was a hive of activity. Great black piles of coal, countless little black men toiling about, and every now and then on the path we'd meet a little black ten-year old, trudging home with his primitive miner's lamp strapped to his forehead. It's sickening to think of the cost in human weariness of the coal that keeps us warm.

Yesterday we had a most un-missionaryish day. Camilla and Knight and Bi and I went out to Paomachang to tiffin at Oscar Fiedler's. Supposedly we were going to the Spring Races in the afternoon, but we stayed at Oscar's so long playing Gilbert and Sullivan and the Gotterdammerung on his orthophonic ? that we only had about an hour at the race course. We saw "all Peking" there, and Camilla and I decided that we were as well dressed as anyone else. Then we went back to Peking to the "talkies" (they've just been installed in Peking this week). I don't know whether the one we heard was typical, but it struck me as worse than the average movie. It's bad enough to have to look at movie actresses' faces without having to listen to their voices. After that we had dinner and then went to the hotel to dance. I must be getting old—I found the day wearing.

On May 16, 1930 MBS announced with triumph that she had finished her Chinese exams. "The final ordeal was to make a public speech in Chinese. I did that on Tuesday, so now I feel like a free woman." She was also relieved of her administrative and teaching responsibility, finally going home on furlough.

MBS made the long trip home by sea: a Japanese boat from Tientsin to Kobe and then the "President Lincoln" from Kobe to Seattle. From

Washington she traveled by train to New York. There she spent most of her furlough year living with her parents at 24 Gramercy Park while she studied for her Master's degree in English Literature at Columbia, with time off for holidays in New England with her family.

At the end of July 1931 MBS began the return trip, meeting Augusta Wagner in Chicago, where she had been staying with a friend. In San Francisco they had a reunion with Camilla Mills who, during MBS's furlough year, had married Knight Biggerstaff. MBS and Augusta Wagner sailed August 6 on the new Nippon Yusen Kaisha liner, "Tatsuta Maru". When they reached Japan they took time for sightseeing. Then they boarded a little ship, the "Choan Maru" and, managing to avoid typhoons, dust storms, and missed connections, got safely back to Yenching.

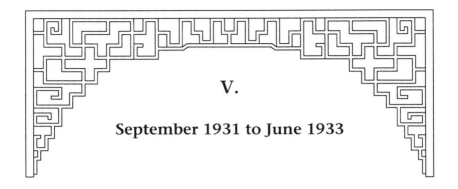

V.

September 1931 to June 1933

Seeds of Hatred

When MBS and Augusta Wagner were sightseeing in Japan, they had no inkling of the Manchurian Incident that was to change the world's perception of Japan. On September 18, 1931, shortly after Yenching opened for the academic year, Chinese troops clashed with Japanese railway guards north of the South Manchuria Railway center of Mukden. Japanese troops attacked the barracks of the Chinese soldiers and occupied the city of Mukden.[1] Students throughout China protested the Japanese assault, and Yenching students announced to the Chinese government that they were ready to fight.[2] By October radical protests took the form of a nationwide boycott of Japanese goods.[3]

September 29, 1931

Last week without any warning came the Japanese invasion of Manchuria. Political observers may discover a thousand intricacies of treaty rights and the differences between moving troops and technical "warlike acts," but to the common person the technicalities don't matter and the one thing that seems obvious is that Japan has waited till the rest of the world was concerned with its own troubles and has seized the chance to take Manchuria. It may be true that the Japanese will govern it better than the Chinese warlords of the last twenty years or that "eventually, why not now" is as good a motto in Mukden as in Minneapolis, but that only proves that might is right and that "there is no justice."

I have never seen such despondency among the students. Of course some of the hotheads want to fight and are asking for military training, but most of them feel perfectly hopeless. They have no faith in the Nanking Government, no faith in the League of Nations, no faith in themselves, no faith in the world. As Caroline Chen said the other day, "It's no fun being a Chinese." There must be a liberal element in Japan, if only there were some way to appeal to them.

October 14, 1931

Today is another unexpected holiday to allow the students to hold meetings both here and in the countryside on the "Japanese invasion." We have been thinking of nothing but this Japanese business and today are waiting impatiently for news of the League of Nation's Council meeting yesterday.

Experts seem to disagree as to whether or not Japan has broken the Kellogg Pact, but that is a mere technicality. One tries to keep in mind that it is not the Japanese people who are responsible for this aggression, but at any rate the Japanese military party has some black crimes to answer for. Their pretext that the Chinese blew up a bit of the S.M.R. line is absurd on the face of it. Even if that is true, which no one believes (lots of people we know were in Mukden at the time) the Japanese were all ready for a coup. They had been moving troops up from Korea for days. And since then they have done everything in their power to provoke the Chinese to violence while at the same time they piously protest against anti-Japanese feeling here as "unfriendly" and say that their troops must stay here to protect their nationals.

Yesterday afternoon when I was in town, I saw three Japanese soldiers marching up and down the Glacis practicing bugle blowing.

Of course a harmless enough pastime, but who would blame a Chinese student if he threw a stone at them? And of course Japanese planes bombing Chinchow is a little more provoking than bugle blowing. We all know the sins of China, her weaknesses, jealousies, and interest in face-saving, but I cannot see that there is one shred of excuse for Japan's actions.

All our Chinese faculty are perfectly sick. If the rest of the world does not step in, there seems to be no alternative between letting Japan take Manchuria and going to war, which would mean that Japan would get Manchuria and a good deal more besides at least for the immediate future. So far Peking has been very quiet, and our students have been quite controlled. They want military training at once. It won't do them any good, but they have to have some active outlet.

October 25, 1931

We are doing very little entertaining these days. The Chinese faculty and students feel that with the flood on one side and Manchuria on the other this is no time for gaiety. Consequently we have cut out all "parties". We have the students in for Sunday morning breakfast or one or two people at a time for supper.

The League of Nations is taking a long time to come to any decision. Today's papers say that England, at least, is insisting on some definite action. But nothing can undo the harm that has been done and the seeds of hatred that have been sown will grow up into a harvest of bitterness and fear. We buy no Japanese goods any more.

November 1, 1931 [4]

We have been waiting for weeks to see if war was really going to burst out in Manchuria. It seems clear enough now that there won't be war, but there's a mess that will not be cleared up in a hurry. Hatred of Japan is bitterer here than it has ever been, and anti-Japanese activities provide a good cloak for Communist propaganda of all sorts.

November 15, 1931

We went into town on Friday to the Heifetz concert. It wasn't up to what Heifetz ought to be, though of course even so it was a great treat for Peking. The city is under martial law, which means that people are supposed to stay off the streets at night, so coming home in the car we had to stop at every corner to show the guards that we were not suspicious characters.

Since the trouble of last week in Tientsin, Peking has been full of rumors. It is hard to know whether the Japanese were back of the riots in Tientsin, but of course they profit by every additional bit of disturbance, so naturally they get blamed. I think it's most unlikely that we'll have any sort of trouble here, but some of the students have been a little worried and have needed pacifying. The group of students as a whole have taken a most sane point of view. At a mass meeting on Wednesday some of the hotheads argued for a strike and other radical measures to show their patriotism, but all such proposals were voted down by a vote of 700 to 30.

December 6, 1931

This has been a thrilling week. It is probably too soon to tell what the permanent results are, but so far it has been tremendously rewarding. Ten days ago it looked as if the "national crisis" were going to split Yenching into two irreconcilable factions. Today there is a stronger feeling of unity and cooperation than I have ever known. All fall we had been marveling at the restraint and good sense that the majority of our students had been showing, but ten days ago the fever that has been spreading through the other universities infected us too. Students from Shanghai have been pouring into Nanking by the thousands to urge Chiang Kai-shek to come north to take charge of the Manchurian situation, and when the

119

Tsing Hua students decided to cut classes for two weeks and go to Nanking too, it was too much for some of our students and they decided to go along. After two mass meetings where the moderates did their best, but in vain, they voted 205 to 201 (the rest not voting) to go to Nanking.

The question before the faculty was whether to say "Classes as usual and all who do not show up will be counted absent" or to give in. We had several long sessions and joint discussions with the students and finally decided that for a week (to be made up during the mid-winter vacation) classes would be suspended, and instead we would all engage in patriotic activities. Committees of faculty and students together got busy at once, and on Monday morning Patriotic Week started with a flourish. About 100 students went to Nanking, but all the rest stayed here and used their patriotic enthusiasm constructively.

In the mornings we have had lectures and discussion groups where faculty and students have discussed together whether China should declare war on Japan, what the causes of the Manchurian problem are, what China's foreign policy should be, and what are the first steps for reconstruction in China. In the afternoon the students have divided into small groups, a few for military drill, a lot for first aid, others for surveying, radio, and chemistry; and many of the girls to knit and sew, making things to be sold for flood relief.

The activities may not be of great value in themselves, but the point is that we have shown that both faculty and students do really care about China, and both radicals and moderates among the students see that the faculty are willing to work hard with them for things that are worth while. Every other university in Peking has been having two weeks of no classes while a minority of students have gone to Nanking and the rest have lolled about with nothing to do.[5]

By this time MBS was fully involved in the administrative decisions at Yenching. Dean Frame had resigned permanently, and Ruth Stahl, the Acting Dean, was away during the fall 1931 semester. A committee of three was carrying on until a permanent dean could be found. Myfanwy Wood was chairman, and the other two members were MBS and Caroline Chen. MBS wrote that Yenching wanted her to be the chairman but she refused because she was chairman of the English Department, where she and Harold Shadick were teaching advanced courses in literature—all at a time when much of the students' attention was focused on protesting the Japanese invasion of Manchuria.

The faculty and administration of Yenching had been supportive of student protests until the students began considering a mass march to Nanking. Chancellor Wu Lei-ch'uan played a leading role in negotiating a compromise between the faculty and students at this time, and Wu and President John Leighton Stuart led a parade of about 700 students, faculty, and University officials around the neighborhood in December 1931.[6]

Stuart felt that the Manchurian Incident was "another of the turning points of history," describing it as a "faked railway accident and the barefaced rape of Manchuria." Stuart deplored the refusal of the United States and Britain to get involved when the situation could have been resolved, he believed, without loss of face for the Japanese.

"When the League of Nations finally took up the matter and sent the Lytton Commission to investigate, it was too late. The Japanese had tested out the reluctance of the Powers to get involved and their lack of cohesion. Mussolini saw the point and followed with Abyssinia. The Spanish Civil War was the next consequence. Hitler soon followed the lead. All this could probably have been averted by prompt, stern and united action in Manchuria. In China the Mukden Incident, September 18, 1931, became an anniversary observed annually, especially by students, with bitter shame and high resolve. It made a profound impression and colored the thinking of patriotic Chinese from then on. I had the feeling of a murky miasma coming in from the sea and settling down

especially upon north China with the inevitability of fate."[7]

This was written in retrospect. At the time, in spite of troubled aware-
ness of the escalating anti-Japanese feelings, life went on. Christmas
was celebrated, and MBS began planning her garden as respite from ex-
asperation and impatience with the League of Nations.

New Year's Day 1932

Out skating this afternoon in the comparative warmth of the
afternoon sun, I felt that winter is not such a bad time of year after
all,but now sitting by the fire I have been chortling over Karel
Capek's "The Gardener's Year" and I can hardly wait for spring to
come and the buds to open. After supper we'll have to get out the
University of Nanking seed catalogue and start making out our order.

This is the most welcome holiday of all the year. The government academic calendar allows us only one day at Christmas but
insists on three days of legal holiday at New Year. Academically it's
an impossible time for a vacation, almost at the end of the semester before exams, but actually it's blissful, for the weeks before and
after Christmas are like a three-ring circus. The faculty did Lawrence
Housman's "Bethlehem" in which I was Mary, fortunately with little
to do but sit still. That was the Friday before Christmas. On Saturday we had a party here for some of the boys and girls, and then
went over to Nancy Cochran's for the first of several Christmas
dinners.

We hung our stockings by the fire, and each was presented with
cheap but pointed presents by everyone else. The most ridiculous
was a yellow duck with its mouth wide open, given me by Catherine
Boyden with an insulting inscription about my voice—my singing
voice.

On Sunday a Wellesley classmate of Augusta's, who is a doctor
at the Margaret Williamson Hospital, came out; we had a candlelight vesper service, and after supper about twenty boys and girls
came to sing carols, pop corn, and eat mince pie and ice cream. We

had hoped to have the Fergusons for Christmas Dinner, but Mrs. Ferguson was not well. When we found they couldn't come, we asked Freddy and Wan-ying with their husbands and children. Bi appeared as Santa Claus to the delight of the small boys and Pao Hsun roasted the two turkeys to perfection. In the evening Caroline, Kit King, and Chen Yüeh-mei, our nice new Physical Education Director, came to supper, and we ate more than was good for us but managed nevertheless to get to eight o'clock classes the next morning.

On Wednesday we had the annual party of our household, our next door neighbors, and all the servants and children. Pao Hsun made mountains of *paotze*, steamed dumplings full of chopped meat, which were fed without fatal results to three babies as well as big children and grownups. Each youngster big enough to stand alone "spoke a piece" to the immense pride of all relatives, and we had a better time than all the rest of them put together.

January 13, 1932

The new government seems to spend its time chasing around the country looking for itself and either giving posts to people who know nothing or trying in vain to persuade people who do know something to take posts out of which they'd be turned in a few weeks anyway. It's discouraging but not quite so tragically funny as the League of Nation's way of doing nothing.

February 7, 1932

While convulsions of all sorts are going on in Shanghai and the government is moving to Loyang and schools in both Nanking and Tientsin have had to close, we have been going about our business, starting the work of the new semester and listening to nothing more alarming than the fire crackers which ushered the Chinese New Year in yesterday.

No mail is coming through from America or via Siberia and

since the suppression of the *Leader* we have no English paper. We get news from Shanghai in snippets but are totally ignorant of anything that is going on in Europe or America. If the Japanese attack on Shanghai was a "mistake" as some of them say, or if it is chiefly an attempt to cut off the source of all financial support for the government, then we can hope to be left undisturbed here. If it's part of a policy to try to get control of all the chief cities, we'll probably have some sort of a coup here before long. But it will probably be over quickly, for Chang Hsüeh-liang is so cowed by the Japanese now, he isn't likely to put up any resistance.

Chang Hsüeh-liang was the son of Manchurian warlord Chang Tso-lin. After his father's death he had committed his northern provinces to the Nationalist government at Nanking. When the Japanese invaded Manchuria, Chang was ordered by Chiang Kai-shek to withdraw troops from Manchuria because Chiang, already involved in other confrontations, could not cope with a major encounter with the Japanese.[8]

In Shanghai an exchange of shots between the Japanese troops and the KMT was viewed by the Japanese as aggression, and they retaliated by bombing Shanghai.[9]

March 1, 1932

The Japanese get worse and worse. Today they've issued an ultimatum saying they will destroy the railroads from Nanking and Hangchow to Shanghai if any more Chinese troops are moved over them. Why can't Chinese troops move where they want in China? We've taken in a lot of "guest" students (squeezed into every cranny in the dormitories) because the universities in Shanghai have had to close. Peking is full of refugees from Nanking. The consuls advised all the foreign women and children to get out—but of course Chinese women and children can't move so easily!

Leighton Stuart started for home today, so you may be seeing him before long in New York.

March 6, 1932

The Shanghai situation is eased for the moment only because the Japanese troops drove the Chinese army back beyond the twelve mile zone. We had dinner Thursday evening with six of the Chinese faculty. Our host's sixty-five-year-old aunt, who lives in a village outside Shanghai, had arrived in Peking the day before to take refuge with him. She said that the streets outside her house were covered with dead. She had seen a woman with a baby passing her door, and while she was looking a bit of shell killed the baby.

The Japanese Prime Minister says Japan's chief desire is peace in China. Japan has created enough bitterness and hatred in the last four months to make peace impossible for generations. She says she want a united and orderly China. One fails to see how deliberate destruction of universities and of the commercial press will help the forces of order and education!

Bishop Norris of the Anglican Mission here spoke the other day of the actions of the Japanese guards here in Peking as "provocative insolence." Japan is terrified of communism, yet she is doing everything in her power to make conditions here favorable for communist propaganda. She is sowing the wind, and the whole world will reap the whirlwind.

In Search of Serenity

The whirlwind would come as the Sino-Japanese War intensified, but in spring 1932 life at Yenching had not yet been disrupted. MBS and her friends rejoiced at Easter and went off on a spring vacation expedition to the mountains.

Easter, April 1932

Though a howling dust storm has blown up since noon, this morning was as lovely an Easter morning as there could be in either

East or West. We had a splendid Easter service conducted in both Chinese and English but with the sermons in Chinese by T.C. Chao. The chapel was packed with faculty and students and workmen and almost all the faculty children, both Chinese and foreign.

After the service we went to "breakfast" at the Shadicks' in proper Russian style. The host greets his guests at the threshold with three kisses and the words "Christ is risen" in Russian. Then everyone sits down to a heaping table covered with Easter eggs, spiral Russian bread, and a delicious concoction of butter and cheese.

April 11, 1932

This spring vacation I decided to let work go to the winds and went off for five days to Shantung. Five of us went off together: Augusta Wagner; Adeline Veghte of the Music Department; V.K. Mei, wife of our director of studies; Eva Wu, a student; and I. Our chief objectives were T'ai Shan, the Holy Mountain, and Chufu, where Confucius is buried and where the famous Confucian Temple is. None of us had been to Chufu before, and I was the only one who had been to T'ai Shan. It was exactly the right time of year to go, warm enough in the daytime and not too bitter cold at night. As we left the brown plains of Hopei and came into the fertile Shantung valleys we found green fields and cherry and peach orchards in full bloom.

We left on Tuesday on the Blue Express, traveling very comfortably second class. Wednesday at noon we got to T'aian where the Methodist Mission people had chairs waiting for us. It took some time in the midst of a staring crowd to undo our bedding rolls and spread the blankets over the chairs, which are really only string seats slung on a framework of poles, and to get our food baskets and other belongings properly balanced for the carriers. But soon we were off, riding the first part of the way over the rather rocky path from the station to the foot of the mountain.

After passing the First Gate to Heaven, which marks the beginning of the stone pilgrim road, we stopped now and then to look at the temples and shrines along the way and had our lunch on the balcony of a nunnery overlooking the valley and the city of T'aian. Then we went on, walking when we felt like it, being carried when we got out of breath, up past The Ridge Where the Horses Turn Back, through the Middle Gate to Heaven, along The Pleasant Mile where the path dips a bit through a pine grove, over the Snowflake Bridge, and finally to the Slow Eighteen Flights and the Steep Eighteen Flights up to the South Gate to Heaven itself. The last bit is a steep pull, so steep that one can't bear to be carried. Once through the South Gate to Heaven, one is on the top of the world.

The road goes on along the summit through a little village, past several temples, and up the last rise of the Jade Emperor Summit to the little tiptop temple where we spent the night. We got there about six, put on all our extra clothes, froze our fingers while cooking our supper, poked our noses out onto the terrace just long enough to look at the lights twinkling on the plain far below, and then rolled up like cocoons in our blankets and tried to sleep on the wooden boards that served as beds.

At five a priest called us to watch the sunrise. After breakfast out in the open we roamed about the mountain top, looking off at the mountains and plains of Shantung from the spot on which Confucius is reputed to have stood and "felt the smallness of the world below" and from the spot on which emperors sacrificed to Heaven twenty-five hundred years ago. Eva rather shamefacedly told us that her grandmother had told her she must burn some incense in the little temple, so she went off to do that, feeling she must do what she had promised but at the same time feeling that this was a rather backward thing for a girl with her education to do. We tried to encourage her.

Coming down the mountain is a good deal easier on the legs than going up but a great deal harder on the pit of the tummy. The carriers run blithely down the steepest flights while the poor pilgrim in the chair pretends to enjoy the view and tries to ignore the occasional sickening sound of a rolling stone. But it's a good deal safer than motoring. Most of the carriers make two hundred trips up the mountain a year, and accidents are practically unknown.

Early in the afternoon we got down to the Methodist Mission, and after we had seen what there was to be seen in the town they gave us an early supper, and we rushed over to the railroad station to catch the six o'clock train. Then the pleasures of travel began.

The six o'clock local was five hours late. Since the semi-express was due at twelve, we decided to abandon the local and settle ourselves for a six hour wait. The station was decorated with banners welcoming the League of Nations Commission whose special train was due the next day, but the banners added nothing to the dirty floor of the waiting room with one side open to the evening breezes.

We had just resigned ourselves to settling down on our bedding rolls when V.K. disappeared and returned with the fat station master, who benevolently unlocked for us a special room, newly swept and garnished just in case the Commission should want to get out and stretch its legs at T'aian. There was not enough light to read by, but there were a few chairs that could be slept on though the springs were a great deal more in evidence than the stuffing.

We were a pretty owlish looking lot when the train came in at twelve, but we managed to clamber on, find places for ourselves and our baggage and stay awake sufficiently to tumble off again at three o'clock at Chufu. It was inky black, and even the station was swallowed up in the darkness, but the innkeeper and some carters were there with lanterns and helped us stumble across the street to the little inn magnificently entitled "Chinese and Foreign Hotel." It was lucky that the light was dim and that we were exhausted! Our mud-floored room had two "beds" in it: one of the usual Chinese variety, wooden boards placed across a couple of saw-horses, and on this Adeline and Eva spread the oiled covering of the bedding and prepared for a nap.

The other bed must have been the reason for calling it a "foreign hotel." It was a large brass bedstead with wooden boards instead of springs, but to make up for that deficiency there was a four-poster sort of frame covered by an originally white but now grimy ruffled canopy. Comforting ourselves with the thought that the weather was still too cold for crawling creatures, V.K., Augusta, and I took off our shoes, rolled up in blankets and turned in. For an hour and a half we were dead to the world.

At five V.K. woke the rest of us. We breakfasted on eggs and noodles from the inn kitchen, supplemented by G. Washington coffee (fore-runner of Nescafé) and by six we started off in rickshas across the plain. Travelers usually take a cart for the seven miles from the railroad to the old walled city, but we had to hurry in order to get back for the noon train.

Soon after seven we got to the great Temple of Confucius. I have seen nothing to compare with it in China. Bits of it are in poor repair, but the whole place breathes peace and dignity and reverence for the wisdom of the ages. One wanders through court after court where only the birds and the wind in the old trees break the quiet, but where the great grey stone tablets with beautifully carved inscriptions show that through the centuries disciples have come to do honor to the Sage. Finally one comes to the central building where the sweep of the yellow tiled roof is upheld by the ten famous dragon-carved stone pillars. It is a place where one would like to stay all day drinking in the quiet, but we had to drag ourselves off to the Grave of Confucius. Here, except for the long avenue of ancient trees, there is little of the usual formality of Chinese architecture. The grave itself is very unpretentious, a large grass mound marked by a tall stone tablet. It gives one the feeling that wisdom has been truly honored by dignity and simplicity.

After Spring vacation the university year went quickly, very quickly considering that the problem of finding a new dean for the Women's College had not been solved. Leighton Stuart, who had been in the United States since March, was theoretically discussing a new candidate, Miss Nettie Soo-Hoo, with the New York committee of the Women's College, but he seemed not to have made it a priority.

June 5, 1932

I haven't made much progress yet with summer plans. The Fergusons have asked us to come to stay with them at Peitaiho whenever we can get away. But a great deal depends on what is finally decided about the Women's College Dean. I am in the worst dilemma I have ever faced, and I don't yet feel I have any light on it. This year there has been a committee instead of a dean, a purely temporary measure until we could find the right Chinese for the job. Until March we were hoping to get Miss Tseng, who was at the Jerusalem Conference. When we finally heard that the doctors would not consider letting her take such a position next year, we turned to a Miss Nettie Soo-Hoo, who is now in America.

Thinking that the best way to approach her would be through Dr. Stuart who was at home and could discuss her qualifications with the Yenching Committee, we cabled to him asking him to see her and present the invitation. Imagine our despair when Dr. Stuart got back last Sunday and asked casually, "What are you doing about a dean for next year?" He had heard that Miss Soo-Hoo had accepted another position but had entirely forgotten to cable that sad news to us.

We have cabled this week directly to Miss Soo-Hoo in the last desperate hope that she may still come to Yenching, but it is rather a forlorn chance, and what are we to do if she doesn't? The Women's College faculty met on Thursday to decide on an alternative arrangement in case Miss Soo-Hoo refuses. To my horror and in spite of my protests, instead of voting to continue with a committee, they invited me to be dean.

I simply don't know what to do. I've started on a job in the

English Department that is not half finished, that I really enjoy, and that I feel in some measure I can do. The Women's College job is temporary, nebulous, extremely difficult because no two people agree on its functions or its limits, and it requires a much greater fluency in Chinese than I shall ever have.

The fact that I have to make the decision is proof of something wrong in our Yenching organization. There ought to be somebody whose interest in the good of the whole university would insure a fair decision in a case like this where two separate groups are claiming the same person. My first inclination would be to let the Women's College worry along somehow until we can find the right Chinese, but as Caroline Chen says quite rightly, how can we expect to get a good Chinese for the job if no foreigner will take it. But the arguments on both sides are so even that the right course is not clear at all.

June 19, 1932

I wrote to you two weeks ago of the dilemma I was in about the Women's College deanship. We are still waiting for a cable from Miss Soo-Hoo, but our hope that she will really come is fading away. In the meantime, Myfanwy Wood leaves for England on Wednesday and somebody has got to take charge of the Women's College. After thinking it over from every possible angle, I decided that if Miss Soo-Hoo doesn't come, I'll have to take the job.

I feel very diffident about it because of my stumbling Chinese, and I hate more than I can say to give up the English Department, but it seemed as if the choice were not between the Women's College and the English Department but rather between the Women's College job alone and both of them together. For if I refused to be dean, I'd have to be chairman of a committee to take the place of a dean. Moreover, the position of dean is only a stopgap for me, for we just must get a Chinese at the earliest possible moment. And it's a nebulous sort of position with all sorts of obstacles hemming it about. In the English Department my bricks were building a firm, strong wall; in the Women's College they will probably disappear into a morass.

Another bitter thing to contemplate is that I shall have to leave this house, which I love and which seems like my own, and the garden that we've worked over all spring and go instead to that hateful Dean's Residence. I hope I won't have to live there more than a year, but there is no assurance of ever getting this house back again. But in spite of all the drawbacks, it will probably be fun part of the time anyway.

At about the time MBS was resigning herself to becoming dean, the Yenching College Committee received a letter dated June 16 from Mrs. Lucius O. Lee, Secretary of the Committee. She wrote: "Some two weeks ago I received a cablegram from Peiping signed by Miss Myfanwy Wood saying that the Women's College and the Board of Managers were extending an invitation to Miss Nettie Soo-Hoo, a graduate student in the University of Michigan to become Dean of Yenching Women's College and asking me to support the invitation by a letter to Miss Soo-Hoo. I wrote her at once and today have a letter from her saying that she is considering the invitation favorably. She had expected to return to work in Nankai University in Tientsin but changes that have taken place there recently have led to her being free to consider other work. I will let you know the outcome when it becomes clear."[10]

July 9, 1932

The last two weeks have been cheered by the pleasantest of the reversals of plans. After we had given up all hope of word from Miss Soo-Hoo, and after I had resigned myself to being Dean next year and had got ready to move out of this house and was negotiating with a substitute for my work in the English Department, lo! one fine morning a cable came saying, "Soo-Hoo accepts." So we're going to get our Chinese dean after all, and ain't it a grand and glorious feeling!

Freed from the burden of deaning, MBS left with Augusta Wagner for a vacation at Peitaiho, but almost immediately MBS was laid low by a bout with dysentery, "which is probably the most boring disease in the world." She was brought back to the PUMC hospital in Peking.

MBS's recollections of the trip from Peitaiho includes details she omitted from her letter home: at Peitaiho "Dr. Ferguson gave me a few spoonfuls of whiskey before he put me into a ricksha at the top of the hill—the first whiskey I had ever tasted in my life. When we got to the railroad station, we found Dr. and Mrs. Maxwell of the PUMC, a wonderful Scottish couple, on their way back to Peking. I had a sleeping berth and was very comfortable on the train. A car met the Maxwells at the Chien Men station, and Dr. Maxwell said he would rush me straight to the PUMC.

"At the door he put me in a wheelchair, telling the coolie to take me to E Building. The coolie thought he knew better, since Dr. Maxwell was the head gynecologist and rushed me off to the maternity ward; however, I was soon back in a more suitable bed. Most of July went by while I was lazy, living on the awful pap that is fed to patients with bacillary dysentery."[11]

July 24, 1932

I have been vegetating so long now that I feel as if my moral nature had completely disintegrated. Four weeks in bed and absolutely nothing to show for it except the slimmest figure that a Speer ever had.

Finally in August MBS had recovered sufficiently to go off again for a vacation, this time to Tsingtao, where all seemed peaceful in spite of earlier fighting.

August 17, 1932

The papers continue to suggest that there is likely to be trouble in Peiping[12] or Tientsin this fall, but so far everything is very peaceful. Everyone writes that the latest political complications haven't caused a ripple. The Japanese are hardly likely to stir up trouble as long as the League Commission is there.

September 4, 1932

We came back from Tsingtao a week ago to find the garden flourishing and our own house looking more satisfactory than ever.

My next problem is to find enough English teachers for the biggest Freshman class we've ever admitted. Perhaps they won't all actually come. There are so many rumors flying about that many people think the Japanese will march into Peking any minute, so some of the students from the South have been urged by their families not to come back.

Miss Soo-Hoo (or Ssu-tu as it should be spelled here) is taking hold valiantly. She is pleasant and capable with a good combination of American straightforwardness and Chinese manners.

September 25, 1932

Some nice freshmen were here to tea this afternoon—all from Shanghai, two from St. Mary's and two from Mary Farnham School. There is a poise and character about most of the girls who come from good mission schools that goes much deeper than their acquaintance with foreign ways. They are excellently prepared, have high standards, and have learned to think for themselves. It is odd that though in the West girls' schools are usually inferior to the great boys' preparatory schools, here in China there are half a dozen girls' schools which no boys' school can touch—St. Mary's, Keen, True Light, Mary Farnham, McTyne, St. Hilda's.

Caroline Chen is back with us in our house again and temporarily a Cantonese girl, Kit King Lei, is staying in our guestroom-study. She is an instructor in the Sociology Department. Her family have had few connections with foreigners. She went to Berkeley to college with her brother, never having talked

134

to a foreigner and knowing no one in America.

October 30, 1932

It's interesting having Kit King Lei with us. She came at the beginning of the semester expecting to stay in our guest room until another house was ready for her but there has been some trouble about the other house and she is likely to be here the whole semester. She comes from a wealthy non-Christian family, is very proud and very quick, launches into fiery arguments at the slightest provocation and is altogether a most interesting housemate. Her home was burned in the 1927 Communist reign of terror in Canton, and one of her brothers, a boy of seventeen, escaped being shot only because he pretended to be dead and lay motionless in a pile of corpses half the night.

Several weeks ago we had a most interesting weekend. The four of us (Augusta, Caroline, Kit King, and I) went out to the Western Hills to stay with Grace Chu and her uncle Hsiung Hsi-ling. They have a house and garden in the old Imperial Hunting Park, where Mr. Hsiung has started an orphanage. Mr. Hsiung was Prime Minister under Yüan Shih-k'ai before Yuan tried to restore the empire. He is a friendly elderly man, a devout Buddhist, and speaks no English. He loves his garden with its pool, its two-hundred-year-old gingko tree, and its rocks inscribed with beautiful characters written by Ch'ien Lung. He knows every tree on the hillside and just when and where the red leaves will be most glorious. We had a gorgeous time tramping in the hills, eating delectable Chinese food and in the evening playing games with Mr. Hsiung and watching the moon over the hills.

November 27, 1932

This has been a full week. We always try to celebrate home festivals, but naturally they are not holidays on the Chinese calendar so there is a rush to get work done too. We celebrated

Thanksgiving with three dinners—one here Wednesday evening for some of the Honolulu students, one in town at the Fergusons' at noon with an assorted Peking gathering, and one at night at the Dean's Residence for all the Women's College Faculty.

Miss Ssu-tu is going quietly about the job of creating an esprit de corps in the Women's College based on something more positive than the old protecting our "rights" against encroachment from the men's side of the University.

Tomorrow we have a grand celebration for the seventieth birthday of Madame Bauer in the French Department. She is the grandest character we have on the campus, a dauntless old lady, bent with rheumatism, who teaches a heavy schedule, entertains more students in her house than anyone else on the campus, never keeps a servant more than two weeks, speaks her mind to President and coolie alike, and is loved and feared by everyone. Her only son was killed in the war; she has been married twice, though no one rightly knows what happened to either husband.

She tells the students what she thinks of them in vivid language, and they take it like lambs. Last winter one romantic youth went to Nanking on a much publicized hunger strike to try to persuade Chiang Kai-shek to fight the Japanese. He came back the idol of the campus and went to call on Madame, expecting praise. She stormed at him. "You sink you are a 'ero: you are zero, stupide boy. You say you 'ave not eat; you have grown fat. Mon dieu, you should be shamed." And he was ashamed too.

Turmoil

The seasons of serenity extended through the year 1932 while the League of Nations Commission prepared its report on Manchuria. In January 1933 it became clear that the report would defend Chinese sovereignty in Manchuria.[13] Condemnation of Japan did not imply armed intervention, and the mood among the Chinese at Yenching was one of despondency.

Christmas 1932

The League of Nations may have kept us out of actual war so far, but the Manchurian question is far from being settled. The papers are full of editorials saying that China trusted in the League, but naturally imperialist powers would not turn against one of themselves, so henceforth China will have to study western militarism in earnest and will realize that Russia is the only friend to whom she can turn.

We had dinner Tuesday evening at our almost-next-door neighbors, the Meis. Y.P. is our "Director of Studies," a combination of Dean and Registrar. The other guests were his brother Y.C. Mei, the new President of Tsing Hua; the Huangs of our Economics Department; and the William Hungs; and a Mr. Wu of the Tsing Hua English Department. The conversation was about China all evening, and the feeling of the men, who are all both earnest and brilliant, was one of practical despair. The government has failed, education has failed, every hope of the last twenty years has come to nothing. Mr. Wu, the only one there who wasn't a Christian, said emphatically that the besetting sins of the Chinese are cowardice and vanity, and that the present generation of students are the worst sinners.

Politically things are quiet at the moment, but we are all waiting to see the results of the reorganization at Nanking. It's too soon to know just what is going to happen.

January 9, 1933

We are suddenly in the midst of such a turmoil that there is no knowing when I'll feel calm enough to sit down and write coherently. The semester classes ended on Saturday, and I thought there would be a breathing space during exams before I went to Shanghai for the winter vacation. This has been the quietest term since

I've been in China, no mass meetings, no devastating "movements," excellent spirit among the students, and a beginning of a much more widespread spirit of cooperation between faculty and students. On Saturday this peace was rudely shattered.

During the week news had come of the Japanese bombardment of Shanhaikuan, the port where the Great Wall comes down to the sea. Rumors spread immediately, and the students were divided into various factions. Some wanted to show their patriotism by postponing exams and getting busy in patriotic ways (making speeches, joining the volunteers, doing first aid), some were frightened and wanted to go home before the Japanese should invade Peiping, some were only too glad to seize on any pretext for postponing exams, some saw a good chance to make trouble, some wanted to go ahead with their work but were dismayed when they were called unpatriotic.

At a student mass meeting a vote was taken to ask the faculty to postpone exams one week. The faculty replied that exams would be given as usual but individual students who had "patriotic" plans could apply for excuses and make them up later. The student committee replied that the students were asking for excuses en masse. This morning exams were supposed to begin. Pickets "patriotically" tried to prevent any of the "sensible" ones from taking exams and in almost all cases succeeded. The faculty repeated that exams must go on unless individual students applied for excuses. At the moment we are at an impasse with all the signs of a regular riproaring Chinese example of "student trouble."

Dr. Stuart had gone to Shanghai and will not be able to get back before Wednesday. The whole thing is sickening. As always happens in such cases the clear issue is obscured by a dozen crosscurrents—patriotism, selfishness, fear, mob psychology, group loyalty, the old, old student-faculty cleavage that exists in every country. One can hardly bear to see sensible, promising students that last week were one's best friends, all affected by a mob spirit. A few of them have been splendid.

The Chinese members of the faculty are more distressed than we are. What hope is there for China if the pick of the students let themselves be excited and overborne and turn their energies to such wrong ends. When China needs courage and a united front against Japan, what a waste to have everyone's strength lost in a perfectly unnecessary faculty-student row. But things are so muddled, that one can't analyze the situation honestly.

And moreover what are the Japanese going to do? All the well-to-do Chinese who can move out of Peiping have started. There are rumors that China is going to declare war at last. If the Japanese think they can take Jehol and Shanhaikuan, they'll probably make a move for Tientsin and Peiping too.

The morning when the University exams were supposed to begin the patriotic pickets succeeded in preventing students from taking exams. Fifty years later MBS remembered it clearly: "I went with a number of the faculty to Sage Hall where our English classes were held to see whether there were any students there who would take examinations. Pickets barred the door—students whom we knew well and were fond of. As Harold Shadick tried gently to squeeze between two students, one of the boys shouted at him, 'Push me again, Mr. Shadick.' This became a frivolous watchword with us often in times of student upsets—'Push me again, Mr. Shadick.'"[14]

January 17, 1933

There has been a long enough lull between committee meetings and minor crises so that we are all a little more rested than we were last week and not quite so disheartened. The students are in a more reasonable frame of mind and unless the political situation takes a sudden unpleasant twist we shall probably be able to begin the second semester on time. One must expect a certain amount of hysteria in war time, I suppose. Certainly we were all mad enough at home during the War. It is doubtless much easier to go on with your regular work and not get excited when you know that the government is doing all it can. But our students felt that so little was being done through official government channels that they must pitch in and do something.

In Peiping and Tientsin schools the students packed up and went home instead of taking exams. It is something to be thankful for that the issue here at Yenching was between exams and patriotic work, not between exams and running away. But the regrettable fact was that the students' insistence on mass action made it impossible for the saner ones to act on their conviction that it was more patriotic to go ahead with their regular work than to go to mass meetings or to try to learn all about first aid in three days. It was quite impossible to go on with even a pretense of exams so we closed college four days early. I think most of them realize that their premature excitement did a lot of harm. If we can open next semester with a clearer understanding of the limits within which student activities have to be confined, the lesson will not have been too dearly bought.

February 5, 1933

Our little flare-up over University authority seems to be happily settled. I am sending you a statement of Dr. Stuart's which gives one angle of the situation. The first part of vacation was an anxious time when we had faculty executive committee meetings day and night. A good many students who went home have hesitated about coming back, for the papers in Shanghai and Hankow are full of stories of Japanese invasion. But this week we have had registration and all but a few have returned.

No student has been allowed to register who did not have an interview first with a member of the faculty and agree to the principle that final authority for all academic and university matters rests with the faculty, not the students. One has to realize that in many other universities the students run things to suit themselves and regard, often quite rightly, the faculty as people who are only interested in their salaries and not in the welfare of the students. Also that many of our students come from homes where their parents have long ago given up any idea of understanding this strange, new generation and consequently let them go their own way however mad it is. Work begins again tomorrow, and if the Japanese leave North China alone, it ought to be a good term.

February 26, 1933

Everything is running smoothly. Our enrollment is just about what it always is the second semester; patriotic activity is subordinated to studying; the students are showing an excellent spirit; the sun is so warm at noon that the gardener comes pottering hopefully about the compound; and if only the Japanese would go back where they belong we'd.all be perfectly happy. They are apparently bent on taking Jehol and the Chinese are bent on resisting, and one hears the whistling of troop trains all night long. The American Legation people think all the fighting will be confined to Jehol; the British are not quite so optimistic. We read all the Geneva dispatches eagerly and wish America could do something, though an embargo on arms to Japan seems the only thing she can do.

You'll probably see Leighton Stuart when he's in New York next month. He thought he had to go, though I think he's much more needed here.

[April 16] Easter Afternoon, 1933

It has been a lovely day, beginning with a service at six o'clock on top of the hill in the Korean Garden. The Honolulu students planned and conducted the service. The view was gorgeous of the Western Hills and the flat plains covered with the new feathery green of the willows. It was so clear that one could see the hills of Jehol to the northeast, though not the men fighting on them.

We came back to breakfast at our next door neighbors' and then went to the regular morning service on the island. Several people, big and little, were baptized and three of the foreign children were confirmed. Then, as always on Easter, we went to Harold and Nellie Shadick's for Russian "breakfast."

"Our Easter service," MBS wrote later, "was held as was our tradition on the island in the middle of the campus lake. I should explain that instead of the church or chapel or Christian Association that an American college might have had, we had an organization called the Yenta Christian Fellowship. (Yenta is an abbreviated form of Yenching Ta Hsüeh, the full name of Yenching University.) This Fellowship included faculty, students, and the Christian staff and workmen on the campus. It was a very vigorous and democratic organization."[15]

April 30, 1933

Last week when the Japanese moved south from Chingwangtao to the Luan River, there was a fresh exodus from Peking, but everything continues peaceful here and the students are as calm as if the Japanese were a thousand miles away. Actually life here is quieter and more comfortable and less troubled than it seems to be at home. It doesn't seem right to be so well taken care of when nearly everyone else in the world is in trouble.

May 7, 1933

It is a peaceful Sunday morning, much like a day in the middle of June at home. The hot dusty wind that blew for four days without stopping died down on Friday and today though it is hot in the sun here on the terrace it is shady and cool. A light breeze filling the air with the "snow" from the willow trees.

Friday was a holiday so seven of us went off to T'ien T'ai Ssu, the lovely peaceful little temple on the side of a long valley. It is the cleanest and most well-kept of all the temples in the hills. To get there we took rickshas to Pi Yüan Ssu, the Azure Cloud Temple, climbed up the worn stone road to the top of the pass, had lunch surrounded by friendly villagers, then up over the ridge, and dropped down through the Temple orchards to the Temple itself. We slept out on the terrace with the moon in our eyes and woke in the morning when the birds began to twitter in the trees around us.

Tranquility soon turned again to turmoil for MBS at Yenching as rumors became reality and signs of war were clearer.

May 21, 1933—Sunday

If I begin on a recital of all the rumors and signs of war that we've had in the last ten days it will make you think we've been leading a very exciting life, which is not the case. Work and play take their unruffled course and the tenor of our ways is as even as usual. But the latest doings of the Japanese provide us with plenty of rumors which generally turn out to be one-sixteenth part true. I'll eliminate the rumors and tell you only what has happened, but you must remember that we're as peaceful as can be, going to town, having a joint tennis tea with Tsing Hua, celebrating Augusta's birthday, providing an enthusiastic audience for the faculty dramatic club's performance of *Iolanthe.*

[May 25, 1933] Thursday

At this point on Sunday I was interrupted by the arrival of Dr. Ferguson and Mary who carried us off in their car for tea. My letter designed to tell you that the excursions and alarms about us had no effect on us, was destined never to be written, for since Sunday they have had a good deal of effect, and we are carrying on now with about half of our student body. But to go back to the beginning.

It was two weeks ago this morning that Peking sleepers were wakened at five o'clock by the hum of an airplane. While Chang Hseüh-liang was here we were used to noisy planes but never at that time of day. Since then they have come every day or two, sometimes one alone, sometimes eleven of them flying in formation. They have dropped nothing more formidable than pamphlets telling the inhabitants how foolish it is to resist Japan's altruistic efforts to bring peace to China and how sad it would be if Japan were forced to annihilate the rest of the citizens of Hopei as she was forced to wipe out the troops who resisted her at the Great Wall.

Some machine guns on the city walls popped away at the visitors the first few days but lately they have given that up. Nearly every day there were rumors that the Japanese had taken Tungchow, fifteen miles east of the city, and a few people began to think it was time to go to visit their sisters and their cousins and their aunts in the South.

Martial law was tightened up, but the streets were not completely closed. We went in one evening to hear *The Barber of Seville* sung by an Italian opera company and though our car was stopped some ten times between the hotel and the city gate, the police and the soldiers were most polite and after looking us over well, they let us go.

Last weekend troops being withdrawn from the front began to swarm in. Some were let into the city; one division was billeted on the Fergusons' *hutung*, but most of them filled up the villages outside the walls. Haitien has been full of them. Our cook has had eight men in his little court, so he brought his wife and children into our compound out of harm's way. The fear of retreating soldiers is more deeply ingrained than the fear of the Japanese, but these men have behaved very decently and have paid for all they have taken.

The tension grew a little tighter on Saturday when a sentry at the Japanese Legation was stabbed by a Chinese whose indignation had got the better of his discretion. The wonder is that it's the first incident of the kind there has been in the twenty months

144

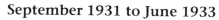

since the Japanese took Mukden.

It was on Monday morning [May 22] that panic hit Yenching. At five o'clock in the morning one of the students received a message from town saying that the Japanese were going to take Peking that afternoon at three. The rumors are always very specific about the time of day! By noon more than a hundred students had left, and since then two or three hundred more. Some of them were scared out of their wits, most of them were Southerners whose families have been reading appalling things in the newspapers and consequently have been telegraphing frantically to their children to come home.

The Foochow papers said the PUMC had been bombed, and one Canton paper said that Yenching had been burned to the ground! Scuttling students have been only a small part of the general exodus from Peking. Since Monday the trains going south have looked as the Times Square subways would look if every one of the rush hour passengers had a bedding roll and a baby.

Yesterday the tension relaxed, but it is difficult to know how much basis there was on Monday for fear or how much there is today for serenity. The Japanese delivered some sort of ultimatum and now some sort of truce has been arranged, but whether the truce is permanent or what will happen if it breaks down no one can prophesy. In the meantime classes go on cheerfully with about half the usual enrollment and the faculty finds life more fun than usual. One day last week we went out to the golf course at Pao Ma Chan with the Fergusons to see a tournament and found Chinese and Japanese playing together as happily as larks. Can you beat it!

I haven't much sympathy for the discomforts of the people packed into the southbound trains, but I have for the refugees who have come in from the villages by the Great Wall. One sees them by the dozen in Peking—dusty carts full of women, children, and bedding, everything else left behind. They say there are over 10,000 in the American Board Compound at Tungchow.

The Japanese attacks on Chinese armies in Hopei Province, Japanese planes flying low over Peking, were Japanese strategy to bring about defection and confusion among the Northern Chinese armies; the Japanese succeeded and the Chinese, defeated, surrendered in May 1933, signing the Tangku Truce, which students felt shamed China in the eyes of the world.[16]

June 18, 1933

The last time I wrote was when we were in the midst of excitement, wondering whether the Japanese were coming the last fifteen miles to Peking or not. When the truce was signed, everything calmed down quickly, most of the students who had left came back, the city has been peaceful, and the only reminder of that breathless week is that Japanese airplanes still fly over us every day or two. We had Baccalaureate service today. Commencement is on Tuesday. We are the only college in the area that has finished work according to schedule and not missed a class. In some neighboring colleges half the faculty skipped off!

Summer plans are still indefinite for the trains have not been able to start running to Peitaiho. The Fergusons are hoping to be able to get up there next week and if they get off I shall go with them for ten days. I have to be back here for most of July to get some work done and to look after the English entrance exams. Then perhaps Augusta and I will go to Peitaiho again in August to stay with the Sweets. Just now Augusta is in Shanghai, where she'll be for a hot month investigating factories.

Augusta was working on a Ph.D. dissertation on labor relations in China. In Shanghai she visited factories and the silk filatures where children of eight or nine years old stood all day long beside boiling vats, snatching the silk cocoons out of the hot water that burned their fingers to the bone.[17]

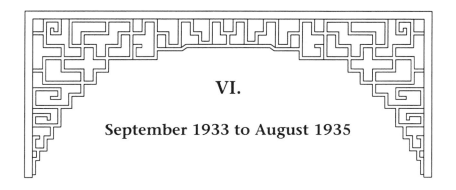

VI.

September 1933 to August 1935

Strong Women

By September 1933 MBS recognized, reluctantly, that Miss Ssu-tu, the Chinese dean the College had welcomed enthusiastically, was not forceful enough to manage a Faculty that included assertive Westerners. Looking back at this period, MBS recalled that "It was beginning to be clear to us that Miss Ssu-tu would never be the sort of Chinese dean we had hoped for. Part of the trouble may have been on our part. We were quite a group of strong-minded women and when Miss Ssu-tu found it hard to make up her mind, I'm afraid we kept pushing her, thus eroding some of her self-confidence."[1]

September 3, 1933

This has been a week of goings and comings. Mrs. Frame left for home, looking fat and buxom, but with orders from the doctor to rest for several months more. Her lungs are better than they were, but not healed. Myfanwy Wood got in last night, and we're all going to the station to meet Grace Boynton tonight. It is going to be fun to see how the old guard takes to Miss Ssu-tu. Someday I shall tell you all about Miss Ssu-tu, but not till the bust-up comes.

Meanwhile, the Yenching community kept a watchful eye on the Japanese and went on with daily life.

September 10, 1933

Yesterday we had Tom and Betty Barker to tea. Tom used to be at Yenching but is in Mukden now. He is a level-headed unsentimental Irishman, who made an urgent plea in church for cooperation between Japan and China and for the necessity for friendliness toward individual Japanese, but his accounts of conditions in Manchukuo are not pleasant.

The two curses of the country are drugs (opium) and banditry. The banditry is, of course, partly the result of the activities of the Volunteers, which gives the Japanese an excuse for atrocities and so it goes in an endless circle. The drug trade, he says, is carried on openly under the new regime, chiefly through Korean peddlers. It was there before but it has enormously increased in volume. He said he knew absolutely that in one town of 25,000 inhabitants the trade in heroin and morphine was $2,000 worth a day.

September 24, 1933

It looks as if we may be in for some new disturbances here after a peaceful summer and after opening with a whopping big Freshman class of exceedingly nice students. The bandit situation in the area from which Japanese troops have theoretically withdrawn and which government troops are not allowed to enter, has grown steadily worse. There are "renegade" generals there ready for any excuse for loot and Japanese generals with one foot already over the line waiting for any pretext to come back again.

October 1, 1933

On Thursday we went to a grand celebration in a village halfway between here and Tsing Hua. Our next-door neighbor's cook's brother's first son was a month old, and we were all invited to the feast. As each guest brings a present, the more guests you invite the grander you can make the party. A special mat shed is put up in the courtyard, actors and musicians keep up a din for two days, all the relatives and neighbors come to stay, and the baby, bundled up in red quilts, sleeps peacefully on the *k'ang*.

I enclose a few clippings about the latest activities of insurgents and Japanese. It was only a momentary flare-up. Feng's troops have been successfully routed in the last few days, but it is an indication of the conditions which our friendly neighbors know how both to stir up and to make use of. It's a vicious circle. If China were unified, she would not need to fear outside aggression, but if there were less mischievous interference, she would be more unified.

October 8, 1933

On Tuesday, for the first time in the eight years I've been here, I went to the Great Wall. Dr. Margery Fry of the famous Fry family, Principal of Somerville College, a J.P. and ever so many other things beside, is in Peking, and Myfanwy Wood wanted to take her to the Wall. There has been fighting not far away, but, though we saw a trench and a Japanese plane keeping an eye on things and lots of soldiers, we didn't see any excitements or actual combat. We were well guarded, for there was a special car of American Marines going to see the sights too. We had a very successful day, nice weather, trains not more than an hour late, persimmon trees loaded with fruit along the way, the hills clear, and the Wall looking as solid and enduring as it has for centuries.

An underlying theme of admiration for strong women runs through MBS's letters in 1933 and 1934, even as she deplores the unsettled military situation. She marvels at the capable Chinese women who are called on to cope with family emergencies and laughs at Hsieh Wan-ying's caricature of a faculty meeting.

November 5, 1933

Our household has been somewhat disrupted because Pao Hsun, our big husky cook, who looks like a fullback or heavyweight boxer, has pneumonia. The Men's Infirmary has very kindly taken him in, and Dr. Li says he is getting better.

A Chinese family is wonderful! Pao Hsun has a nice sunny three-*chien* house where he looks after his wife, two children, a sister-in-law, and a grandmother, but his wife is a frail little thing whose hands are full with the children. His sister-in-law is only a girl, and the grandmother is blind, so when he went to bed and needed a nurse, his aunt was immediately summoned. She is the sort who is always called in an emergency, the type who makes China fundamentally a great and strong nation—capable, cheerful, decent, self-reliant, her black hair slick, her round pink cheeks smiling, her blue gown spotlessly clean.

Last evening Freddy Li and Hsieh Wan-ying had a party for all the old-timers on the Women's College Faculty. (There are only five who have been teaching here continuously longer than I!) Reminiscences flowed thick and fast and we ended with a take-off of a faculty meeting in the old Peking days. Wan-ying took the prize as an early student government chairman tearfully resigning because of the embarrassment of having to have committee meetings with men students!

November 26, 1933

Friday night the *Je Nao* (the Faculty Dramatic Club) surpassed itself with a family evening of songs and recitations of the 1880's. The whole family was there—Grandpapa and Grandmama, Oscar and Adrian, Fanny and little Alice, dear daughter Emmeline and her husband just home from laboring in the Lord's vineyard in China, and all the rest. The Shadicks' house was transformed with antimacassars, aspidistras and lace curtains, and knickknacks, all complete to a copy of "The Wide, Wide World" on the table.

We are well launched on our campaign for a million dollars toward endowment to be raised in China. Most of the faculty are giving from four to nine percent of their salaries over a period of four years, and at present campaigning is going on with the students and their families. It's a new idea to most of them.

One of MBS's freshman students described the Yenching faculty as "men and women professors who teach at their ease and with what they can earn are able to lead their lives in a rollicking fashion." "Je Nao" means literally "hot noise" or "excitement" and, MBS recalls, was "a good example of our leading our lives in a rollicking fashion."[2] The Faculty Dramatic Club met at least once a month, quite often in MBS's and Augusta Wagner's house, since they had the biggest living room and there was always a large audience to applaud the cast. They did melodramas or some Gilbert and Sullivan, usually with original words referring to life at Yenching.[3]

The faculty needed humorous diversion at a time when they were being urged to give substantially from their salaries to the Million Dollar Campaign. Leighton Stuart, even as early as the 1920s, had tried to raise funds to constitute a Chinese financial base for Yenching.[4]

December 3, 1933

Wan-ying has undertaken to teach me Chinese. When she heard me telephoning the other day, she upbraided me for using inelegant expressions. I replied that since no one ever spoke elegant Chinese to me, I was reduced to the vulgar expressions that I learned from Pao Ch'ing and Pao Hsun. She is therefore coming to tea once a week, supposedly to improve my Chinese, but we usually drop into English after the first five minutes.

December 10, 1933

Miss van Asch van Wyck's visit has made this the red letter week of all the year.[5] In the first place, it's fun just to have a guest, for we don't often have anyone staying here. And then what a guest! She says the two months in bed have left her stiff in the joints, but they haven't slowed up her mental processes.

She asked so many intelligent questions about Yenching during the first half hour she was in the house that we gave her all the back numbers of the Faculty Weekly Bulletin to read. She not only read them but absorbed every detail, so that she will suddenly ask, "How is it that you have four times as many girls majoring in Sociology as in Political Science?" I don't think I have ever met any one before with a really international outlook. Even Miss Royden had a thinly veiled dislike for the French.

Most broadminded Americans are internationally minded only to the extent of having a benevolent tolerance toward Europeans and Orientals and looking forward to the happy day when all the world will have come around to America's way of doing things. But Miss van Asch van Wyck never discounts any one nation's difficulties or idiosyncrasies and assumes from the beginning that both sides (not just the other fellow) will have to make adjustments and that these adjustments will not be easy.

And how will America ever be able to understand European problems while we are all limited to one language? She remarked mildly the other day when she saw a list of books that a Faculty Discussion Group was using that they were all English books, and said that in any Dutch group there would be French and German books as well.

December 17, 1933

I feel ready for even the congestion of the next fortnight, for during the ten days that Miss van Asch van Wyck was here I felt as if I was having a holiday. I put off as much of my regular work as I could in order to stay at home, to have guests for tea and supper to meet her, and during the last few days when she was stronger to take her to the Summer Palace, the Temple of Heaven, and the

Western Hills. She has taken a place in my calendar of great women with Miss [Maude] Royden and Miss [Marion] Park and Dr. Alice Hamilton,[6] and in some ways higher than them all. Her never failing interest in everything from Mussolini's latest threat to the League of Nations down (or up!) to every student she met, her sense of humor, the quickness with which she pieced together every casual mention of our simplest problems here, the complete fairness of all her attitudes, the combination of uncompromising standards and discipline for herself with tolerance toward other people's differences—well, altogether everything about her forms a standard for judging oneself that leaves one feeling like a worm.

Underlying MBS's meditations was the uneasy awareness that the Chinese dean was not the kind of strong woman needed at the Women's College. Nothing could be done in mid-year, so MBS watched the manipulations of the Japanese in Manchuria and began planning her garden.

January 21, 1934

The long awaited announcement came from Changchun yesterday that Pu Yi (was he named especially for Gilbert and Sullivan's benefit?) has yielded to the Will of Heaven and the wishes of the independent "Manchu" people and will again ascend a Dragon Throne.[7] Before long he will be told that the only proper place for his throne is in Peiping, and then won't we all have a good time!

February 4, 1934

Today, according to the Chinese calendar, is the "Beginning of Spring." A balmy breeze this morning attested to the infallibility of the sages who base their reckoning on the moon rather than the sun. There is still skating and patches of snow in the garden melt slowly, but the "Great Cold" is over, and we've just sent a big order to Nanking for seeds.

February 18, 1934

There are constantly new proofs of the interdependence of all parts of the world. Ch'en Fang-chih is by all odds the brightest girl in the Junior class, not only the cleverest but the most thoughtful and independent. She is the eldest of eight children. Her mother comes from an old family of scholars, her father started with almost nothing and developed a prosperous silk export business. Yesterday she had word that he had failed because of the failure of an Australian firm with which he had large contracts. Her mother thought Fang-chih had better leave college, as they have lost everything, but I told her we would see her through college, as she can easily get a scholarship.

Ch'en Fang-chih not only got through college at Yenching but continued her studies at Bryn Mawr, using the name Agnes Chen. She received her Ph.D. in 1939 and returned to teach at Yenching. In 1934, when MBS was writing to her parents about Ch'en Fang-chih, MBS and her mother were also discussing the multiple responsibilities of working women; that working women were almost always single was implicit.

February 25, 1934

Mother's comment on the double job most "working" women have is something we all agree with heartily. When Miss Fry, a former principal of Somerville College, was here last fall, she said the same thing about women on the staffs of universities in England. She said there were fewer women professors than men because in the first place a woman had to be about 20 percent better than a man to be given the same rank, and in the second place, very few women had an opportunity to work uninterruptedly in their particular field as men did. During the vacations a woman usually had to look after older relatives or she had housekeeping to do even during the term times or she had sick people to look after or something else.

Here at Yenching I think there is more absolute equality of men and women with less friction than almost anywhere else in the world. Yet I think almost all the married men honestly feel that they have two jobs—they have to look after their families as well as teach. That is, they have to escort their families to Peitaiho in the summer and sometimes help their wives to fire a cook or look after odd jobs in the house and buy the coal, and so forth. But except for taking the family to Peitaiho, the unmarried women all have to do exactly the same things, besides in addition planning the meals, taking the whole responsibility for entertaining, student parties, or looking after guests, providing food for joint compound teas or suppers, house cleaning, looking after the servants and their families and a host of other things.

In addition most of them have to live with other people who are not always congenial. Keeping house as Nancy Cochran does for three other women ranging in age from twenty-three to fifty-five, not one of whom knows more than a few phrases of Chinese, who have different tastes and different friends, is a pretty demanding job in itself. Nellie Shadick helps Harold to correct his papers and if he chooses to invite a class of thirty students to supper, Nellie sees about borrowing dishes, planning with the cook, setting the table, and all Harold has to do is to stop reading in time to get dressed before seven o'clock.

But it's not a simple sum in arithmetic. A lot of professional women say that one job of teaching plus one job of being housekeeper and manager and hostess make two jobs, and sigh about how nice it would be if they could just have an office and follow a man's routine. But I don't know one woman in a hundred who wouldn't be miserable if she couldn't wash her best stockings or fuss over new furniture covers and who doesn't have the time of her life over a day of spring cleaning, all the more because she feels she's being virtuous while she's doing it!

The Blow Falls

Double jobs, deficits—the work went on, and now there were also the difficult decisions about admitting the increasing number of foreign students who wanted to come to Yenching for a year or two, children of good missionary parents who could not understand why Chinese students were admitted and Westerners not. Different exams were worked out for the foreigners—stiffer in English and easier in Chinese—and they were carefully interviewed because they caused problems unless they were really interested in China and ready to meet the Chinese students as equals.

But the most pressing problem for MBS was once again the lack of a dean for the Women's College. On May 9, 1934, Miss Ssu-tu suddenly cabled the Women's Committee that she was withdrawing as dean, that she would leave in June and return to teaching, which she believed would be "more satisfying for the development of my personal plans."[8]

May 13, 1934

We are again just about where we were two years ago with regard to a dean for the Women's College. Miss Ssu-tu has this week sent in her resignation, and there is no doubt that it will be accepted. She is a nice person, but the job has been beyond her from the beginning for she has no head for administrative details. Last year we all hoped that with help and in time she would be able to grasp the job, but this year it has become increasingly evident to everyone that she couldn't do it. She lives in a dream world and thinks that wanting to do a thing is equivalent to doing it. But she has shown a fine spirit and we are grateful for what she has tried to do.

The Administrative Committee and the Women's College Faculty will meet this week to decide what to do. We ought to have a Chinese, but I'm afraid this experience has shown that it is almost impossible to ask someone to come in from outside and there are none of the Chinese members of our staff yet ready for it. The most important problem before the Women's College is to build up the Chinese staff. We have two or three corkers but the turn-over is terrific.

The constant change among the Chinese staff was a real problem for the Women's College. "Splendid young women came for a year or two but then got married, often to men whose careers lay in other cities."[9]

May 20, 1934

Well, the blow has fallen. I have to be Acting Dean of the Women's College for the next year at least. I don't mind quite so much as I should have two years ago, for I've had a chance to have my swat at the English Department, but neither do I greet the job with shouts of joy.

Miss Ssu-tu has done her best, but the Women's College has not made much progress in the three years since Mrs. Frame left, and there are several messes that need to be cleaned up. We still need to have a Chinese dean, but there is no one on our present staff who can do it and we cannot again try to get somebody from outside until we can get a clearer idea of what the position is and should be.

There is far less friction than there used to be (that is one good thing) between the "Women's College" and the "University," but there is still no clear-cut accepted conception of what the ideal relationship between the Women's College and the University should be. We cannot be separate; we ought not to be completely lost in the larger group; somewhere between there is a state of co-operation and mutual responsibility that we must achieve. But whether that can best be achieved by keeping our "independence" or by doing everything possible to become more like all the other parts of the University we don't quite know.

Many people think we should have only a Dean of Women

rather than a Dean of the Women's College. Logically I think they are right, but actually a Dean of Women would be only a glorified matron, and it would be almost impossible to get the right sort of Chinese woman for the job.

Well at any rate, I have to take the job as it is and we'll hope that in a year or two the position will be clearer and we can find the right person for it. Harold Shadick will probably take over the chairmanship of the English Department in July. Until then I shall be pretty busy, for though Miss Ssu-tu will still be nominally in office, a lot of matters that affect next year are already being referred to me, and I have to handle them without appearing to do so. To add to the fun, Grace Boynton has suddenly had to have a serious operation and won't be able to do any work the rest of the semester, so we're having to look after her classes.

I hope that I won't have to move into the Dean's Residence. It has always seemed to me wrong to keep up such an expensive and elaborate house, when we need both the space and the money for other things. The only sort of person who can be happy in it is someone who wants to entertain continually on a grand scale. I should like to use it either as a dormitory or a music building.

In addition to tending to the administrative problems at Yenching, MBS felt responsible, reluctantly, for being an active member of the North China Presbyterian Mission.

Paotingfu, May 28, 1934

Mission Meeting is in full swing, a little later than usual this year, but with beautiful cool weather for a help. I've had to shave off a little of both ends of the meeting for it is planned on a leisurely scale not very suitable to a Yenching schedule, but by coming down Friday afternoon and going back tomorrow, I'll miss only two days of classes. The more I see of some of the members of the Mission the more I like them and admire their spirit, but the more

I feel that our minds move in totally different worlds. On Saturday I listened to Miss Logan and Miss Gould and Miss Judson tell of their preaching trips in the country. Their whole emphasis is on "preaching the gospel" to as many people as possible and "calling for decisions." Of course not everyone who "hears" "believes," but many do, and one must go on preaching so that more and more may hear and believe. Of course the gospel must be preached, but surely Christianity is not so much a story to be told as a life to be lived.

The evangelists will tell you of someone who listened to street preaching, who began coming to church, and now after a few weeks "he has torn down the idols and he believes," as if that were the end of the battle. "Thou shalt love the Lord thy God with all thy mind" surely means that part of the Christian life is to put our wits to work to make everything in life show forth the Christian way of love, and it seems to me the missionary who conceives of his work only in terms of preaching is missing the chance of his lifetime.

Mr. Shepherd of the American Board,[10] at the request of the Chiang Kai-sheks, is taking over a county in Keanglin that has been reclaimed from the Communists and is heading up the work of a Christian group who are going to try to organize the whole political and economic life of the district on a Christian basis. He has a terrific job, but one that will help show millions of people that Communism is not the only solution for Chinese problems.

July 8, 1934

The greatest event of the last few weeks has been the arrival of Camilla and Knight [Biggerstaff]. Knight, having got his Ph.D. from Harvard, has been awarded a very liberal fellowship for future research and has come back for two years in Peking. They hope to get a house in town in the fall, but for the time being they're keeping me company here. Both Knight and Camilla are the happiest sort of people to have around.

Augusta went off yesterday on what ought to be a perfectly grand trip into the Northwest. Some of the Public Affairs faculty planned a trip to study possibilities of economic development in Suiyuan and Mongolia. When the railroad heard that Wan-ying might go along with her husband, Wu Wen-tsao, they offered a private car for the trip. They'll be gone nearly three weeks, stopping all along the way, being entertained by generals and magistrates, and, if they don't get dysentery or malaria or typhus, having a chance to see everything. Ku Chieh-kang, the man whose autobiography I sent Father, is one of the group and they'll have an interesting time with each other, as well as in what they do and see.[11]

Augusta Wagner found the private car less than luxurious. It was hot and crowded and difficult to keep clean. They had a cook to prepare food for them, but they also had plenty of flies to swat. Fortunately none of them got sick. Along the way they were entertained by generals and magistrates. "They learned a great deal about the politics and economics of growing opium poppies in the Northwest. One of the generals who entertained them explained that he allowed the poppy growing to go on because otherwise he would have had no revenue with which to make the social reforms that were obviously necessary."[12]

Meanwhile, the Women's Committee was perturbed about Miss Ssu-tu's resignation, which had come as a total surprise to them.

August 7, 1934 Peitaiho

A letter from Mrs. Finley[13] in the last mail asked what the real reason was for Miss Ssu-tu's resigning. In my official capacity I can scarcely write the details to the Yenching College Committee, but since there is no one else who is likely to feel called upon to explain at all, I may as well tell you a bit, and Mother can pass it on to Mrs. Finley, so that no one will suspect anything worse than the truth!

The trouble was simply that Miss Ssu-tu, while a very nice person

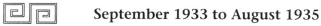

and a thorough lady, lacked every quality that an administrator needs. She had no mind for details, no ability to sum up a situation, no faculty for interpreting what people said in the light of their backgrounds or positions, no judgment as to when a situation called for immediate and decisive judgment and when it needed delay and thorough discussion. Coupled with these lacks were the more positive disadvantages of a mind that moved unusually slowly, a fear of disagreeable scenes that led her to avoid issues instead of facing them and the handicap (which is hardly her fault) of being neither Chinese nor foreign.[14] It was simply unfortunate that she was in an administrative position and especially in one that is as complex and where there are as many factors to be harmonized as at Yenching.

Probably one of her difficulties was in having a few strong-minded people (who shall be nameless!) about, who knew more about the difficulties than she did. However, we all honestly tried to help her; we all, Chinese and foreign, tried to keep our hands off and to stand by ready to help when she wanted it, but it was no good. It was tremendously hard on her, for she certainly had not asked for the job in the first place, and it's a bitter experience for anyone not to make a success of a new job. She showed a splendid attitude, and after she had resigned did everything in her power to make things easy for anyone who might come after her.

People have asked how we made the mistake of getting her in the first place. It's hard to see, but all her recommendations were excellent, with never a hint of her lack of administrative ability. She was simply a very nice person in completely the wrong place.

It is almost impossible to find a good Chinese woman for such a job. Dr. Wu at Ginling is practically perfect but there are not many like her. Most of the older women have achieved their independence and position with a struggle which has left them warped or scarred. The younger ones get married before they have enough experience.

Dr. Wu Yi-fang, President of Ginling College for Women, a Ph.D. from the University of Michigan, was known as a champion of equal opportunity for women. Later she became a government advisor and represented China in international forums. Unable to find a future Dr. Wu for Yenching, MBS carried on, taking time off when possible.

August 20, 1934 Peitaiho

Saturday night we went to a most elegant picnic of the Wheelers'—everything served on proper china plates by boys in white gowns, with as many different dishes as if we'd been eating in a dining room. I had a chance to get acquainted for the first time with Bill Fenn's wife, an extraordinarily nice girl. I gather from both Fenns and Wheelers that they have a harder time at Nanking getting on close terms with either faculty or students than we do at Yenching, and that they feel less Christian interest among their Chinese colleagues. Yenching has lots of faults, but I doubt if there is a place in all China where Chinese and foreigners live together more happily or know each other more intimately than we do on the Yenching campus.

September 9, 1934

I am writing with the latest addition to the household curled up in my lap, an eight-weeks-old wire-haired fox terrier pup. She has no name yet, for none of the twenty odd that we've thought up seems to click. Knight and Camilla gave her to us to take their place now that they're leaving us for their new house in town. It seemed a little mad to take a young and completely untrained puppy at the beginning of term when the house is full of guests and there's lots to do, but she was so adorable, I couldn't bear not to bring her home at once, and our inner courtyard is a perfect place for her to play in safety.

Most of our new students have come, and we are holding our breath in the annual week of suspense when we never know whether we're going to be able to squeeze everyone in. I've had plenty to keep me busy but all the really trying work of assigning rooms has been done by Tan Ch'ao-ying, my exceedingly nice and capable secretary.

October 7, 1934

I feel just about ready to rush off to the Hills or Peking or anywhere away from this messy house. It has been overrun with painters, plumbers, masons, and carpenters, and since there are so many men tracking in and out the boy has decided not to bother to clean any more. But in another week or two the house will be dazzling. The outside woodwork is all being repainted. The original paint put on when the house was built five years ago had faded from scarlet to a dirty pink. The job is being done now by a special guild of painters from Honan who use the oil of the tung tree, a native Chinese oil that is the base of most foreign varnishes. They are skilled workmen and guarantee their work to last for ten years. It's a lovely lacquer red now that looks gay but not garish with the gray brick.

October 21, 1934

Though there are persistent rumors that the Japanese are already practically in control of all North China, everything goes on peacefully here. Our student body is quiet and happy. I have been having conferences with the new women students this week, and they have all been very friendly and appreciative of Yenching. The students who come from the big schools in Shanghai and Tientsin are more modern and foreignized than students from government schools than ever before. It's a great relief to have a peaceful time with no temptations to excitement and hysteria.

Madame Chiang Kai-shek

Although MBS rarely remarks on it, one source of strength for women at Yenching was their common college background. Many of the Western women and also the Chinese women on the faculty (Those who were Returned Students) had connections with the Seven Sisters in the United States. An annual alumnae gathering had become a fall ritual.

October 28, 1934

This has been a week when, aside from speaking in chapel and teaching my classes I seem to have done little but entertain guests, all of them very nice. The climax came yesterday when all the Yenching alumnae of the seven women's colleges (Bryn Mawr, Wellesley, Mount Holyoke, Vassar, Smith, Radcliffe, and Barnard) entertained their fellow alumnae from Peiping. This has come to be an annual event in the fall. We have lunch in college groups, then tour the campus, and all meet together for tea.

It wasn't simply the lovely weather and having thirty odd people out from town for the day that made it a high spot, but the fact that as our most distinguished guest we had Madame Chiang Kaishek! She and General Chiang arrived in Peking by plane on Wednesday after a strenuous trip through the Northwest. Since she is a loyal Wellesley alumna, Augusta wrote to ask her if she'd come out to join the Wellesley group, and though she and her husband are both having medical treatment at the PUMC and refusing all other invitations, she came. The Wellesley group were lunching here at our house, and the servants found it hard to understand why when the greatest lady in the land was here, I should go out to lunch!

I stayed here until she arrived (very unostentatiously in a car with a chauffeur and only one guard) and then went over to Miss Boring's where Bryn Mawr and Radcliffe were meeting together. After lunch we came back here, and she talked very informally about the New Life Movement and the reclamation of the Communist areas in Kiangsi, which is her special project.

Of course I had heard a good deal about her, but I was quite unprepared to lose my heart to her so completely. She is a woman of great power and charm, with the air of a truly great lady, conscious of her position, but simple and natural and friendly, lovely to look at, alert, well-read, and very keen. She speaks perfect English with an unusually pleasing intonation. And whatever faults she may have, she is working tirelessly for the good of the country as she conceives it.

Father wrote of her article on "What Religion Means to Me," pointing out that she didn't mention the name of Christ, but after lunch talking to the large groups (among them Sophia Chen Zen, who has little use for Christianity) and then to four of our journalism students who came to "interview" her, she said again and again that China needed Christianity beyond anything else and that the young leaders who are going down to the Communist front must be filled with the spirit of Christ.

November 12, 1934

We were reading after tea when the bell rang at the gate, but before Pao Ch'ing got there, the caller had walked right in, and who should it be but Madame Chiang Kai-shek. It was surprising enough to have her come to call informally and unannounced, but more so, since yesterday's paper had said she was in Suiyuan. She had flown back to Peking yesterday and was motoring past Yenching and just dropped in. She may be ambitious and Chiang may be ruthless, but there seems to be a nearer approach to unity for China than there has been for years, and Madame Chiang has got brains and charm and an undaunted spirit, and her ambitions are as much for China as for herself.

MBS's 1982 recollections of Mme Chiang's impromptu visit add a more everyday dimension to the portrait of Mme Chiang, who announced that "she had been on quite a long trip in the Western Hills and asked if she could use our bathroom. Naturally we said yes, but when she did not reappear from the bathroom we began to worry. I went back to ask if she needed anything, and she laughingly said that she could not unlock the door. So anyone in the garden might have seen, though happily there was no one there, the strange spectacle of the Generalissimo's wife climbing out our back window by a stepladder which we had brought into the garden for her."[15]

Amid the diversions provided by guests, MBS continued her efforts to learn Chinese, celebrated holidays, and traveled further in China, this time to Shanghai and Nanking.

November 25, 1934

This fall I've been trying to study Chinese, not so much to learn any more (I've almost given up hope of that) as to keep from forgetting what little I know. I had lost all faith in the professional language teachers, but Mrs. Ch'en Ts'ai-hsin, whose husband is head of the Mathematics Department, very kindly agreed to help me three hours a week.

She's a friendly, homely body who doesn't speak any English and whose Peking dialect is perfect. My first idea was just to chat with her, but we started reading Mark and have spent two months on the first five chapters—not because I can't understand it but because she isn't satisfied until I pronounce each phrase perfectly and I almost never do! She's the only Chinese teacher I've ever had who didn't seem to think that foreign tongues can't manage Chinese anyway, so let them say it any old way. But Mrs. Ch'en is a martinet and a hundred times is not too often to try a single phrase. I may learn the tones after all. It's good fun and I'm having intensive Bible study and ear training at the same time.

December 2, 1934

Dinny the pup is growing to be a great help entertaining guests. Today my invaluable secretary Tan Chao-ying and her mother came to lunch. Old Mrs. Tan doesn't speak anything but Cantonese, so conversation was limited, but Dinny filled all the gaps and completely won the old lady's heart.

December 9, 1934

I feel as if I'd had a holiday for I got back last evening from a two-day trip to Paotingfu for a meeting of the Mission Executive Committee. The weather fortunately has been mild for December so that the trip down in an unheated train was quite bearable. I had more layers of clothes on than usual and a steamer rug to wrap around my nether extremities after the sun went down.

Since my compartment had only a flickering oil lamp, it was impossible to read for the last two hours, and I conversed with my companions—a French Sister of Mercy with a starched white head-dress two feet wide, a rosy-cheeked girl of about fifteen with her, very proud of a new rosary someone had given her, and a well-dressed Chinese gentleman. In my best Chinese, I offered the gentleman some coffee from my thermos, and then discovered he had been in America for twelve years getting a Ph.D. and learning transportation from every angle, including that of a ticket collector on the Pennsylvania Railroad. Kentucky is the only state he hasn't been in. He's now an official of the Peiping-Suiyuan Railway. He asked hopefully if I didn't think the railroad service had improved in the last two years. I said it had, but the dirty wooden car we were in was evidence enough of the room for further improvement.

Christmas Afternoon, 1934

It has been a busy Christmas time as usual. Knight and Camilla are staying out here with us. We're having dinner for eight to-night, breakfast for twelve this morning, and dinner for twelve last night. On Thursday the servants and their families all come for a meal of *pao-tze* (a kind of stuffed steamed bread) and fruit. With our household and next door's combined there will be nearly forty counting the babies.

Christmas is becoming more and more an accepted festival in Peking among the Chinese. I'm afraid that wreathes and tinsel and Santa Clauses are perhaps more in evidence than the Wise Men and the Shepherds and the Star and the Manger, but at least the spirit of generosity, of thinking of other people, of including your neighbors in your own fun, is spreading—though it is entirely foreign to any Chinese holiday celebration or festival.

January 20, 1935

On Thursday I hope to get off to Nanking and Shanghai. I shall have to go at American tourist speed to see and do everything there in a week—Council meeting, shopping, visits with alumnae, inquiries about possible Chinese deans, and glimpses of a few friends. And I'll see what China looks like outside of Hopei.

February 10, 1935

I got back from my Shanghai trip a week ago and have been busy all week with the routine of the beginning of term and catching up. It was a good trip, fun to see old friends and interesting to see Nanking and Shanghai for the first time. The weather was perfect, like late March here but without the wind. This was unusually lucky, for they had just had a month of miserable cold rain.

Some old students came across the river to meet me at Pukow with a private launch and took me to see all the interesting spots of Nanking. It's odd that in a new capital where everything looks toward a new China, the first places shown to visitors should be tombs. Outside the East Gate of the City on the side of Purple Mountain is an old Ming Tomb with its faded red walls, its approach guarded by stone animals, its gnarled old trees all seeming to belong to the mountainside. Further on is the new Sun Yat-sen Memorial, brilliant and harsh in its staring new white granite, its blue tiles, its geometrical angles, its formal planting, very clean and fresh, very well guarded by smart young police officers. Beyond this, in the new cemetery for revolutionary soldiers, marked by the Martyrs' Memorial Pagoda, a new pagoda, surprisingly successful, built by Mr. Murphy. The colors are soft, the irregular wall of the cemetery fits the hillside; though it is new, the whole plan is essentially Chinese in that it cannot all be seen from one spot. There is always something beyond that one must go farther to see and it is in harmony with its surroundings.

There are other astonishing things to see in Nanking—all proof of industry and courage and faith in the future, though some perhaps have been overhasty—the wide new streets, filled with enormous motor busses, the handsome and expensive new Government buildings, some of them jerry-built and rococo, others very happy adaptations of Chinese architecture, hundreds of new houses, most of them looking as if they might have been planned for the outskirts of Passaic twenty years ago, and the whole place full of young people busy in their offices until five o'clock even on Saturdays and keen on their jobs.

In Shanghai I had five days, four of them full of meetings of the Council of Higher Education. There are lots of nice people in Shanghai but I felt it a disturbing sort of place—a dozen different communities all living near each other but each oblivious to the very existence of the others, probably greater contrasts between luxury and poverty than anywhere else in the world with the rich taking less responsibility for the poor.

The meetings of the Council of Higher Education served the purpose of educating me, but I doubt if they will have any stupendous effect on the politics of the Christian Colleges. The first half of the session dealt with business which convinced me that the "Correlated Program" exists only in words. There was a great deal of talk about our common purposes and interests, all the speeches were buttered with politeness, but no college seemed to be considering seriously anything except its own independent welfare.

The Correlated Program was an effort to strengthen institutions of Protestant education in China and to avoid duplication.[16] MBS returned with relief to Yenching where her garden was coming up even as students were threatened in the dormitories.

March 10, 1935

I wonder if the North China climate has changed permanently. Spring is a full month early and we have had heavenly balmy days with none of the usual dry dusty wind. The lilac buds are getting green, the spirea tips are red, the roses in our protected courtyard are covered with leaves. Lao Chang has sowed the peas and in the border columbine, pinks, lilies, and larkspur are all showing their heads.

March 17, 1935

Last Monday we had quite a fluttering in the dovecotes. While I was dressing, the telephone rang and it was one of the Seniors to say that several policemen had been in the Third Dormitory looking for one of our Sophomores. Fortunately, five minutes before they came she had a telephone message from Tsing Hua and had gone out on her bicycle. But we had a few bad hours until we knew that the police had not got her at one of the gates, as we feared they might. We did not know how soon they might come back to search for her again; so I suggested that she spend the rest of that day and the night in the Infirmary. That same morning the police arrested ten Tsing Hua students, including two girls. Eight of them have since been released, but only after being held several days. Our students belonged to a discussion group with the Tsing Hua students. They obviously have radical leanings and have been seriously studying Communist literature, but I don't think that our student was a member of the Communist Party or contemplated any bomb-throwing plots.

March 24, 1935

My bones and muscles are feeling very creaky as a result of unwonted exercise with the girls in their Health Week program. There has been dormitory competition in almost every phase of life this week. Inspectors have gone about to see which dormitory is cleanest and which rooms are neatest. There has been roll call at the recreation hour every day and at various lectures on health. Everyone has kept a daily record of her "health habits." There have been posters and exhibits and games—and as a result we may be healthy, but we're also exhausted. Ch'en Yüeh-mei, our cracker-jack Physical Education Director, has been the moving spirit.

Easter Day, 1935

I was interested in what you wrote of the Independent Board Bulletin's attack on Dr. Stuart and "Chancellor Wu Lei-ch'uan." Anything more fantastic than labeling the dear old man as a Communist is hard to imagine. He is the very pattern of the old Confucian scholar with Christian virtues added. He lives very simply, refuses the salary he is entitled to, and gives nearly everything away, and is a devout Anglican.[17]

May 12, 1935

We had an interesting contrast this week. On Thursday evening a very good string quartet, which has recently been organized in Peking, came out to Yenching to give a concert. The Auditorium was simply packed with students who obviously enjoyed and appreciated the music. On Friday the men's Athletic Council put on "A Night of Fun," with a jazz orchestra, a skit by the Faculty, and some other hilarious numbers, and the hall was less full than it had been the night before. It's gratifying that the students prefer Beethoven to jazz, but at the same time it's a pity that more of them haven't learned to enjoy laughing at themselves. The skit was written by Bi and Nancy [Cochran] about a contretemps we had last summer over the bus companies that run from here to town. There was a superb scene as the rival bus drivers, complete with large paper busses, argued on the stage.

Summer brought tranquility and only occasional gunfire. MBS continued to meditate on her future in light of the uncertainties of potential political change in China.

July 14, 1935 Peitaiho

The peaceful scene around us is in contrast to the noise of big guns being fired this minute at Chinwangtao, probably target practice of the British cruisers there. Every morning we wake to the rattle of machine guns as the Japanese practice on the sand dunes to the north of us. It's all routine, not anything special this summer, but all the worse that we are accustomed to this idiocy.

July 21, 1935

I have thought a lot about the possibility of coming home next summer. It would depend partly on whether we get a Chinese dean. Unless there is somebody responsible in charge, I can't get away for the whole summer vacation plus the two very busy weeks at either end.

While there is a job here that I can do, I want to stay and do it, but I wonder seriously whether middle-aged women have a place at Yenching. There will certainly be need for foreigners for some time to come, but I wonder a little whether the slowness with which we have developed the Chinese women on the Faculty may not be because we have too many middle-aged dominant Western personalities. If that is so, I want to get out before I am a stumbling block. Of course also there are all sorts of uncertainties about the University's future if the Japanese take over North China, but it's too early to consider those possibilities yet.

China's political future has been so completely hidden during these last few years that I've thought the only thing to do was to go along from month to month and not think about what might or might not happen, but now I wonder whether I don't have to make a definite decision either to stay in China the rest of my life, no matter what happens, or to consider staying at home for good after 1938.

August 12, 1935

The two weeks since we came back from Peitaiho have gone incredibly fast. The first was taken up largely with preparations for and cleaning up after the wedding of my secretary Tan Chao-ying to Kenneth Chen, one of our young instructors. I've known them both well ever since they first came to Yenching. The wedding was here at our house. Nellie Shadick helped decorate the living room, which looked very attractive with pink lotus buds against green. And Augusta managed all the refreshments for one hundred and fifty people like a professional caterer.

It has been hot at times but August mornings and evenings have a freshness in the air that make August much more comfortable than July and the sunsets over the Western Hills have been as beautiful as any at Peitaiho across the Shanhaikuan Mountains.

We have had about the same number of applicants for entrance as in former years, though it remains to be seen how many Cantonese students will really come north. On the train coming down from Peitaiho our car had far more Japanese than Chinese in it. They were getting off and on at every station along the line and acting just as if they were at home.

MBS's letters from September and October are missing, according to a note she made at the top of the November 3, 1935 letter. The fall of 1935 was still a peaceful time, and MBS was able to continue her exploration of China. MBS recalled in 1982 a trip to see caves with famous Buddhist sculptures and frescoes. : "In October Augusta, Bi and I made a trip to Tatung. There was an Anglican Mission there, the only group of English-speaking people, and the missionaries were good enough to take in visitors to the caves. After a night on a very rackety train we arrived at the Mission early in the morning. The caves were fascinating. Many of the Buddhist sculptures had been ruined over the years by souvenir hunters who chopped off bits of the sculpture, but they were well worth going to see, and the visit gave us a taste of the cold and dirt and general dreariness of such an inland city as Tatung." [18]

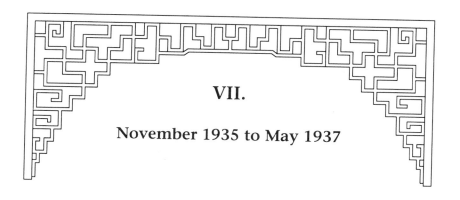

VII.

November 1935 to May 1937

Rumors and Wild Surmises

The Japanese were steadily tightening their hold on North China in the autumn of 1935, so that when the Honolulu students, whose traditions were American, noisily proclaimed Halloween on October 31, the Chinese students assumed the Japanese were attacking. The political future of Peking—and of Yenching—was uncertain. By December Chinese students organized a massive protest against Japanese power that grew into a national movement, the December Ninth Movement.[1]

November 3, 1935

If one needs to be convinced that there are certain yawning gaps between Western civilization and the Orient, all that is necessary is to be roused from one's bed at midnight to try to explain over the telephone in Chinese to an agitated dormitory matron that the pandemonium outside the dormitory gate is not the Japanese come to loot the campus but merely American students following the time-honored Western custom of celebrating Halloween. (And for good measure just try to make clear the exact nature of Halloween and its significance in the scientific and unsuperstitious West!)

Having completely forgotten the existence of Halloween I went to bed rather late Thursday night and was just dozing off when I heard distant shoutings which I first took to be the singing of marching soldiers in the village. As I woke up I recognized the strains of "Hail, hail, the gang's all here." Augusta had just called out from her room to remind me it was Halloween when the telephone rang.

First the matron of one dormitory and then of another called up to ask the meaning of the horrid and terrifying noises that were rising under the girls' windows. I tried to calm them by saying it was just a quaint American custom; called up the head watchman to ask him to go out to tell the boys to go back to their own part of the campus; and put on my clothes and went out to see if I could find the culprits.

When I got there, peace reigned in the women's quadrangle, but not within the building. Most of the girls, never having heard of Halloween, and being waked out of sound sleep by a drum, a cornet, and shouting voices, not unnaturally supposed that the Japanese were at the gates. Some of them dressed, packed their valuables, and prepared for flight.

Now in the cold light of day, large numbers of both boys and girls are angrily demanding punishment for the offenders. The celebrators were a carefree group of foreign and Honolulu students with a few rather foreignized Chinese freshmen. It shows up again the almost unbridgeable gulf between East and West. The majority of the Chinese conclude that anyone making such a disturbance is obviously bad, a real hooligan. No gentleman could do it. Most of us cannot conceive of taking a harmless joke so seriously.

Tuesday evening [November 5, 1935]

The lights blinked before I finished this Sunday night.

Japanese control of North China is getting tighter all the time. Bishop Norris has just come down from Mukden and reports miserable happenings there. And the Government seems to have started on inflation. Exchange is 3.22 today. If it stays there our

University budget will profit, but who knows when the bottom may drop out of it altogether.

November 10, 1935

Things are rather jumpy here. Rumors galore. Our friends and neighbors, or to speak more accurately, our lords and masters, seem to be having things pretty much their own way.

November 12

Today has been a holiday. Sun Yat-sen's birthday and a welcome breathing spell giving a chance to wrap up Christmas packages. Last night we had a party of twenty-four students taking advantage of the evening before a holiday—twelve foreign students (mostly American, missionaries' children) and twelve of the more foreignized Chinese, including Fong Sec's three children and three of Liang Ch'i-ch'ao's grandchildren. They were all very gay and friendly, joshing each other and us, and playing with Dinny and consuming huge bowls of *ch'ao mien* and numbers of persimmons. War and peace and the fate of nations seemed beyond their horizon entirely.

Then this morning two girls came to breakfast, one a Christian, the other not, both very ardent leaders in the Student Government Association. They can't bear not to be doing something in a time of crisis and yet what can they do? They had come for advice and yet there is so little one can suggest. How to be sane and poised, to stir up a public-spirited interest among the rest of the students without being excitable or inflammatory—it's all easier said than done. Apathy, communism, defeatism are all the wrong way, but what is the right way? Not just writing hot-headed articles, but they don't know what else to do.

November 19, 1935

Tomorrow is the date set according to the most persistent rumors for a proclamation of the "independence" of North China under the Japanese. Whether it will come off or not, you'll know as soon as we do, and also what the results will be. Predictions vary from perfect peace and indifference of all concerned to outright war between Nanking and Japan with the battle line almost anywhere between here and the Yangtze.

November 20, 1935

Well, we're not "autonomous" yet. There's a hitch somewhere and the proclamation is postponed for a while. There is a lot one could write on the subject, but no one is quite sure that letters go through uncensored. The "autonomy" if it comes, will not be "voluntary," you can be sure of that.

December 1, 1935

The political situation occupies most of our thoughts. I don't know whether you're getting any better news about North China than we are. For the most part, we get rumors and wild surmises. No one knows what is going to happen next—maybe nothing. Maybe autonomy, maybe a little local disorder, maybe war somewhere between here and the Yangtze. So far the students have been remarkably calm. Only one or two have left, and that only because of pressure from their families. Their quietness has been almost too good to be true, and is perhaps about to be shattered. Some of the student government leaders have been growing restive and have called a mass meeting for tomorrow. I hope the good sense of the majority will prevail and they won't take any unwise measures. Though really one couldn't blame them, even if they went completely wild. The things the Japanese say and do grow more galling every day.

December 13, 1935

I couldn't settle down to write letters last Sunday, nor have I been able to since. We have all been too worried and troubled about the political situation and what our students were going to do next.

All fall the students have gone on with their work with the most phenomenal calm, but at last they could bear it no longer, and though one may doubt the wisdom of some of their recent actions, no one can help sympathizing. When a week ago today seventeen Japanese planes, three of them bombers, flew back and forth over Peking, I felt as fierce and warlike as any Abyssinian.

That evening at a mass meeting our students decided to join those from other schools and colleges in a demonstration—a monster parade to protest against the autonomy proposals and to ask for an audience with General Ho Ying-ch'in, the Minister of War and the ranking official in Peiping. The time for the parade was to be kept secret, but we guessed rightly that it would be on Monday. About 140 girls and 300 boys (just about half of our student body) took part. They were very well disciplined and started off at seven in the morning to walk to the Northwest City Gate. They went across the fields, since there were scores of police on the main road to stop them. It was a bitter cold day with a northwest wind blowing. The thermometer stood at 10 degrees when they started and did not get above 32 degrees even at noon. They had a few brushes with the police but no casualties, but when they reached the gate they found it shut. There the Tsing Hua students joined them, and then they all stayed till four o'clock in the afternoon, with little to eat and with no protection from the wind.

The Chancellor did not wish to appear to give his approval, but wanted to keep in touch with developments and thought that some foreign non-administrative members of the faculty might go to keep an eye on proceedings, so Augusta and Bi went after the demonstrators and from the outskirts helped somewhat to calm the excitable and to encourage the footsore. After Ho Ying-ch'in had sent two representatives to negotiate through a crack in the gate and when the students learned that the demonstration in the city was over, they came back to the campus. Augusta said that the police on the whole behaved with admirable tact. Meanwhile, inside the city about a thousand students gathered, paraded to Ho Ying-ch'in's headquarters, distributed handbills, and were dispersed by a fire hose only when they were within a block of the Legation Quarter where Japanese troops were waiting for them with machine guns. A few students, no one knows just how many, were arrested inside the city.

The next day everyone went back to classes as usual until noon, when there was another mass meeting and they voted to go on strike until the arrested students should be released and a few other demands met. From an outsider's point of view one can ask how refusing to go to classes helps China against Japan, but one must remember that it has become the traditional method of dramatizing student opinion and showing the country at large what the students think. Of course student opinion is not always the opinion of the general public, but in a country where few groups are articulate, it is something to have even one group that can make itself heard.

Sunday, December 15

We have had no classes since Tuesday noon and it doesn't seem likely that we'll begin classes tomorrow or very soon. The University authorities have taken no formal action and all attempts to persuade the students to go back to work have been through informal discussion, with no commands or decrees laid down from above. The main intention of the student leaders now is to start a nation-wide student movement to protest against Japanese aggression and any further submission on the part of the National Government.

The most troubling aspects, to me, of the situation are, first that the strike, once started, is hard to stop. There is a Chinese proverb about riding a tiger—it's hard to get down—and the student leaders are more or less in that position. At what point now can they say they have achieved a goal and can go back to classes? And second, that we are plunged into a war psychology, with mass hysteria, fear and suspicion and hate all aroused and ready to focus at any moment on an unsuspecting victim. Since they cannot reach the Japanese, their indignation and resentment is ready to break out against anyone who opposes them or does not agree with them—the police or any fellow students who do not see eye to eye with them There is much talk of "spies" and "traitors." And if the University authorities should be forced to oppose the students in any matters large or small, we might be handy substitutes for the Japanese. And third, that there is the possibility of another demonstration and this time there will probably be bloodshed. Without any doubt the large majority of the students have only patriotic motives, but naturally there are a few whose intentions are not so pure, who would be glad to embarrass the Government or who are just out for excitement and avoiding the humdrum routine. We hold our breath from day to day and hope that the outcome will not be ruinous to Yenching or too unhappy for either the Government or the students.

That was written at noon. Now it is ten in the evening. Two students were here most of the afternoon, one from three to six, the other from four to nine. Curiously enough in both cases we started talking about the Japanese and ended up with immortality. Now the news has just come that another demonstration is planned for tomorrow morning—the students to start from here at seven. Only a miracle can prevent a tragedy. And one is utterly helpless.

December 22, 1935

When I wrote you last Sunday evening, we were holding our breath for fear the student demonstrations the next day would end in bloodshed. Fortunately no lives were lost. I'm sending you copies of letters Augusta wrote to Dr. Stuart telling of the two demonstrations on the 9th and the 16th. She and Bi went along after the students both times to keep us in touch with all that went on. The Chancellor wanted someone to go who was not Chinese and not an administrative officer so that there could be no twisting it into an evidence of University support or instigations of the parades. I think last Monday was about the most anxious day I've ever lived through.

[December 29, 1935]

This has been a very queer three weeks. The first two days were sufficiently exciting with the two student demonstrations, and the students were keyed up to a high state of tension where they were likely to pounce on any chance remark as an indication that someone they didn't like was a traitor. They almost started a riot against the woman college doctor because of something she said in haste and they misunderstood.

I was very busy keeping track of the girls, giving excuses to those who wanted to leave, checking up on those who left in a hurry without bothering about formalities and in general keeping my ear to the ground. The last ten days there has been little to do. There are still no classes, for the Peiping Student Alliance has not yet called off the strike. For the most part the students have settled down into a routine. About a third of the girls have left the campus to go home or stay with relatives in Peiping or Tientsin. Those who are left occupy themselves with writing patriotic material, discussion groups, picketing the gates, a meeting every few days to discuss how long to go on with the strike, and doing a little surreptitious studying, but their feverish excitement has died down and many would like to go back to work.

I have been spared the usual endless Faculty Executive Committee meetings that are ordinarily a part of such a crisis because the whole issue is not simply a Yenching issue. The Chancellors of the six Peking universities are acting together and within Yenching our Chancellor is taking full responsibility for everything. Everything is being handled in a purely Chinese way—the right way and the only way, it seems to me, in a situation that is national, but a way that is much more passive and involves much more patient waiting than most foreigners are used to. The students' hope has been to start a nationwide student movement, and they have been partially successful, but within their own group they are not agreed on their aims and though at first they aroused pretty general sympathy they are now in danger of making themselves ridiculous. It is far easier to start this kind of strike than to stop it. If it comes to an end soon, we shall be able to make up the work and get on to the next semester. If not, there will be very serious complications within the University.

And the whole future of Yenching is even more puzzling than the present. Many of the Chinese said gloomily on Christmas Day that they supposed this was our last Christmas in Peking. There is not the glib talking that there was six months ago about a dramatic removal of the whole University to Szechuwan, but many people feel that if we are not actually closed by the Japanese, at least life will be made so intolerable for the best men on the faculty that Yenching cannot remain here and be a real university. In that case, we would either have to close or move temporarily to somewhere further south. We can only wait and see, and I think the sane viewpoint that we should go quietly on and hang on at all costs is growing.

These have been days when one is compelled to search one's own soul. When the routine is suddenly interrupted and all that one has been working for seems suddenly threatened with complete change, if not actual destruction, one stops to ask what one's own contribution has been and can be.

I don't mean to sound discouraged or defeated, but I have realized more profoundly these two weeks than at any time since my first months in China the waste that is inevitable because of the tremendous psychological barrier between the East and the West. The waste, I mean, in what any one Westerner can accomplish in China compared with what he could do in his own country. It is not simply a matter of language, though that is no mean hurdle. But it is a yawning psychological gulf, so deep that it can never be filled up, so wide in parts that one cannot get over it all, and almost always so wide that half one's energy is used up in bridging it. For example, we have pleasant and rewarding relationships and contacts with a great many students. Many of them become our close friends, but nevertheless there is always that invisible barrier. One becomes so accustomed to it that one almost forgets all about it, until along comes a foreign student (like Margaret Hayes) or a Honolulu student (who is essentially an American) and one suddenly realizes the freedom of give and take, the completely free exchange of ideas there can be when that barrier does not exist. Is it really useful to have to spend nearly half one's time and energy in trying to bridge that gulf and often not knowing whether one has been successful?

Revolutionary Students

With the students on strike, there was a lull in the ordinary routines at Yenching. MBS found time to organize her thoughts on the students involved in the protest and also to meditate on her own uncertain future in China.

January 5, 1936

Things don't look a great deal cheerier than they did a week ago. The Chancellors of all the Peking universities have again made public announcements urging the students to go back to work. There is one chance in a hundred that a few of our students will try to go to class tomorrow, but unless the student government calls off the strike within the next twenty-four hours, which they certainly won't do, we shall announce the beginning of our winter vacation which will last until February 1, when our second semester would normally begin.

This is a pure formality. We never close our buildings or dormitories during the winter vacation, so students will be free to stay and continue holding meetings. A little over half our students have already left the campus, and as soon as vacation is announced many more will go. Most of them are quite ready to come back to classes now, but they have to follow the orders of the Student Alliance.[2] They all hope that the strike will be called off by February first, but if it isn't I doubt if individuals would go to class in defiance of the orders of the Alliance. It's both tragic and amusing that all the tactics of the Central Government which students object to are the very tactics which the leaders of their own movement use.

There was talk for a while of a mass pilgrimage to Nanking. That has been given up, but yesterday a great band of students started out on a two-weeks trip into country districts to stir up the farmers. Twenty of our girls went and about thirty Yenching boys. Apparently the students who actually joined this trip are the dupes of some cleverer leaders who stayed behind and are pulling the strings. The boys and girls who went are very patriotic but not members of any radical party and for the most part are young innocents—half of them freshmen.

The place they are going to is a Communist center. It is likely that when they get there one or two leaders will suddenly change the tone of their propaganda and begin distributing violently Communistic material. Either the students will suddenly find themselves the center of a Communist uprising or if the police take severe measures against them, some will be shot and that incident will have the effect of arousing even the lukewarm stay-at-homes to a high pitch of excitement against the government.

For the most part the students can now be divided into four groups. (1) A very small and secret group are active Communists—not more than 2 or 3 percent of the whole.

(2) A larger group are becoming definitely revolutionary. They say that Nanking is hopeless, that the whole country is too smug and contented, and that people must be roused to revolution. These students do not belong to any party, and they have no mature political philosophy. They are hotheaded and rather scatterbrained. (3) The great mass of our Yenching students did not start out as anti-Nanking and probably at heart are not opposed to the Central Government even now. But they are violently anti-Japanese and feel that Nanking must be roused to resist Japanese aggression in the North. They are willing to lend themselves to any measures the Student Alliance tells them will help toward this end. (4) The last group does not want to be involved in any excitement and has already left the campus.

Tuesday, January 7 [January 5 letter continued]

We're still waiting for news of our brave heroes who started out on the propaganda trip into the country. Rumors filter back that about 600 students from the Peking universities are walking to Ku An, about 50 miles south of Peking where they will gather for a mass demonstration.

Thursday, January 9 [January 5 letter continued]

We sent a party of four faculty members after the students. They brought back three girls who felt they had had enough of the rigors of the country. The rest of the students were in high spirits, apparently enjoying sleeping on temple floors in the cold and learning a lot about the differences between farmers and students.

January 26, 1936

Chinese New Year was on Friday and the firecrackers are still popping spasmodically. The government ban forbidding the observance of the lunar calendar is completely disregarded, and the New Year has been celebrated more thoroughly than for many a year.

We were in town on Wednesday and went to watch the crowds at Lung Fu Ssu and the big bazaar. It was like Christmas Eve in New York but with more sunlight and with less rush. People not only buy presents but are all getting ready for a real holiday, for most of the shops shut up tight for five full days. Everyone pays his bills and even the poorest people make their houses clean, buy a new picture and some gay lanterns, and the children all have new blue gowns. They were wise people who first invented holidays and festivals. A little color and the sense of something special make everybody happy.

The students have not embarked on any new activities lately. Our winter vacation is due to end this week and we are hoping all the students will be ready to come back to classes on February third. If there are no more interruptions, we hope to finish our first semester work during February, begin at once on the second semester, cut out the spring vacation, go on longer than usual in June, and have Commencement by July first. But that will depend largely on whether there are renewed Japanese activities and whether the students can manage to stick at work. By far the great majority of them want to get back to work and have no more demonstrations, but there may be complications within the politics of the Student Alliance, and one of the disheartening things is the ease with which a few leaders can apparently intimidate the large body of students. It is often easier to protest against suppression of free speech by Nanking than it is to see that free speech is allowed in a student government assembly. But they are all learning a lot by experience and most of them are fine earnest boys and girls.

February 2, 1936

We don't quite know whether tomorrow will be the beginning

or the end of our troubles. Supposedly tomorrow classes are to begin again. Most of the students who had gone to Shanghai or Nanking have come back, and all those I have talked to seem eager to get started. Everything seemed to be going smoothly until today.

Now it appears that one or two of the student leaders are making another effort to continue the strike. Their present pretext is fantastic. They say that since this is a critical period, ordinary education doesn't meet the need, and therefore we should reorganize our courses so that they will give the sort of emergency training that is needed; and to allow time for faculty and students to discuss this reorganization, we should postpone the beginning of classes for another week!

It's obviously merely a maneuver to try to keep us from getting back to work this week, so that they can call some more student meetings and cook up something more with the students from Tsing Hua and Peita. I don't believe there are two dozen Yenching students who really want to follow these particular leaders, but they are very clever politicians, and it remains to be seen whether they will be able somehow to manipulate the student body or whether this time the faculty will be able to carry the students along a more sensible road. The Chancellor is going to speak to the whole student body tomorrow at eight, and then we'll see whether they flock to classes or not. I feel pretty sure they will this time.

But even if we win this round, there will be more battles ahead. The whole political situation does not grow more reassuring. Every day the Japanese make some new demand. The city gates, which ordinarily close at ten, earlier if there is any stir or disorder, are now open until midnight because the Japanese have soldiers constantly going and coming from Tungchow, and a part of them felt insulted a few weeks ago because the gate was not opened quickly enough for them.

I've been thinking a lot this winter about what my own future should be. Some of the questions involved are these:

1. Shall I stay in China the rest of my life? Is this where I can be of most service? Are things stable enough here so it will be possible? Do you, or will you, need me at home? (I don't know the answers to most of these, but I do know that I only want to stay if I can be useful at Yenching or in some similar type of work. I'm afraid I couldn't shift very profitably to country evangelism.)

2. If I should decide not to stay here all the rest of my life, should I make up my mind soon to get started in something new at home? What sort of job could I get and am I fitted for?

3. Can I get someone to take my place here, so that if I left it wouldn't be leaving Yenching in the lurch? The Chinese dean doesn't seem any more likely to turn up. Perhaps if I got out, we'd have to find one. Am I really needed here or not? I don't know.

February 9, 1936

Classes did start smoothly on Monday; and yesterday and the day before the students registered and paid fees for the second semester, but the battles are not over yet. There is a small group of students who are advocating no examinations (final exams for the first semester are scheduled for the last week in February) and who are pressing for what they call "emergency" education or "crisis" education. Everyone realizes that in a time like this certain courses and subjects seem dull and to have little bearing on the immediate issue. We have tried to offer several new courses on Sino-Japanese relations, both political and economic, and on the history of the Far East and other such timely and important subjects, but what some of the students have in mind is something far more radical than that.

They would like to abolish certain courses which they maintain merely inculcate a slave mentality, have lectures on subjects which particularly interest them, and have plenty of time for discussion and propaganda. They are trying hard to stir up the whole student body to make demands on the faculty. Of course I hope the sane and moderate students will stand fast and refuse to be maneuvered into anything foolish, but if they don't, I hope the demands will be extreme, for in that case we'll have a clear issue and the prospect of a good fight.

The trouble will come if they make some simple, little demand that on the surface does not seem too difficult for the faculty to accede to, but that we shall have to refuse because it will surely be merely a forerunner of more impossible ones. It's got to be made clear sometime that after all it is the faculty and not the students who determine University policies. The two chief difficulties in the situation are that the great majority of the students, who really want to go ahead with work, are too timid or indifferent to fight for their position, and that the small group of "radical" student leaders is composed of two kinds of people—a few who are out simply to make trouble for the National Government, trouble for the University, trouble for anyone, and a larger number who are really sincere in their belief that this is the right thing to do both for themselves and for China, but who are more enthusiastic than wise. I have spent the whole afternoon at the Chancellor's house discussing the situation. We don't talk about much else these days.

Leighton Stuart, President of Yenching, was on a fund-raising trip to the United States during the December Ninth Strike, leaving Chancellor C.W. Luh and MBS as principal officers of the administration at Yenching.

February 16, 1936

Still we go on from day to day, not seeing a stretch of clear water ahead, but thankful that we haven't struck any snags yet. We are due to have a week of examinations beginning this coming Saturday. Our students, following the lead of the students at Tsing Hua and Peita, have asked to be excused from exams this semester. We are to have a faculty meeting tomorrow to decide, and I think everyone will vote to say a resounding "No" to the student request. Then we'll see what will happen next.

As a matter of fact, I believe that two-thirds of the students want to have exams, and if it comes to a showdown are ready to punch in the head any student who tries to stop them. They have had hot discussions in all their student meetings, and I think the moderate element is large enough and strong enough so that we won't have serious trouble, but you never can tell.

The political situation doesn't look any rosier. It is openly announced that there is a Japanese advisor (paid by Japan) for every office in the Hopei-Chahar Political Council.[3] And the sale of heroin by Japanese and Koreans continues to flourish unchecked.

Planning her garden gave MBS respite from the trying political situation.

February 23, 1936

I've just been ordering some seeds from Nanking and my garden notebook says that last year the grass began to be green on February 23 and that there were violets out on March 8. If there is any green grass today it is not visible, for it is covered by four inches of soft, damp snow. It is snowing today for the fourth day this week, the heaviest snow even old inhabitants like me can remember. The Cantonese students and the children are all very gay and the farmers are delighted.

We're all pretty proud of ourselves this week, and faculty and students are patting themselves and each other on the back. A week ago Friday the extreme students, aided by the freshmen who were shy of exams after two months of interrupted work, succeeded in passing a motion asking the faculty not to have semester exams for this term's work. The seniors and the moderates were bitterly opposed, but they could not muster enough strength to defeat the motion. The Faculty Council deliberated for some time and were unanimous in their refusal to grant the request.

At the Tuesday morning University assembly the faculty were present in unusually full force, and the Chancellor made a fine speech saying in firm strong language why it was obviously impossible to consider the request. The students tried to have another mass meeting that night but could not get a quorum.

On Wednesday morning they tried again. This time they had a quorum, and the motion to go ahead and take exams was passed by a large majority. Everyone was pleased, the students as much as the faculty. And we had good reason to be, for the next day at Tsing Hua they had rather a nasty time when a group of rowdy students forced their way into a faculty meeting and broke some of the windows. The whole group of professors at once resigned, and since then they have had no classes and the student body has been split into two groups.

Our examinations started yesterday, and everything went off smoothly. We finish them this week and start the second semester's work next Monday. The students are asking for certain modifications of the curriculum in line with what is called "emergency" or "crisis" education, but their requests are most moderate and sensible, asking for changes in credit requirements and in teaching methods in certain courses that most of us have been advocating for years. No doubt there are still rocks ahead, but every curve that is rounded without accident is a great advance.

There is less talk of war at the moment than there was two weeks ago. The Hopei Council has been taking orders from Nanking on several minor but significant points, and there haven't been any new demands from Japan for almost a month.

If Yenching is quiet within and without next month, I hope to make a brief trip to Nanking and Shanghai to get better acquainted with the way they do things at Ginling and Shanghai College and to see some of the middle schools and look around for some additions to our Chinese staff. We are losing our doctor, our physical education director, and perhaps one or two of our Home Economics staff this summer, and we would rather have Chinese than foreigners to fill the vacancies if we can find the right people.

March 8, 1936

Second semester classes have been in full swing for a week and outwardly things seem pretty calm, but I fear there are some elements working beneath the surface to foment trouble. The Government has been, to say the least, tactless. After the police raid on Tsing Hua two weeks ago, there were other raids on colleges in Peking. So far, we have escaped, but the students have been sure that sooner or later the police would come here looking for the radical leaders.

Of course such repressive measures only defeat their own ends. Many of the students who have no sympathy with the radical elements, would take delight in joining with the gang to attack the police, if they should come. And some of the hotheads would be only too glad to have such a disturbance to help on their cause by creating martyrs and arousing sympathy and widening the gulf between students and the authorities.

Every night this week the students have organized their own patrols to go back and forth around the campus all night, ready to give the alarm when the first policeman arrives. It's very disturbing to the peace and morale of the dormitories to have the guard coming and going at intervals all night, but the patrollers themselves feel immensely patriotic and important and dramatic as they give their watchword and march up and down in the moonlight.

One has to watch one's step with the greatest care these days. Did you ever hear of Women's Day on March 8, an international day, observed in many countries like Labor Day? On Friday some of the girls told me they were going to celebrate it today and asked if I would make a speech. I agreed, understanding that it was just to be a meeting of Yenching students.

I became rather uneasy today when I saw the kind of posters that were up announcing the meeting and still more so when it began and at least a third of the audience were middle school girls from Peking. After the two scheduled speeches (mine and one by a Chinese doctor, a Wellesley graduate), there were several impromptu and very fiery speeches by representatives of those middle school students. It appeared that these youngsters had been forbidden to have meetings in their own schools, so they had calmly come out to our meeting, and their violent enthusiasm, not so much for the cause of women as for arousing the country, may get us into trouble yet.

Sometime in March two Bryn Mawr friends visited MBS, and while they were there they had a taste of the trouble MBS dealt with from day to day: Wang Ju-mei, one of Augusta Wagner's students, telephoned to ask if he could spend the night. "Naturally we said yes," MBS wrote in 1982. (The incident is not reported in her 1936 letters.) "It turned out that the police were searching the dormitories for radical students, and he had been warned to get out of the way. He was arrested later on but that night at any rate he escaped the police. Our house was rather crowded, and I think we must have put up a cot for him in the living room. At any rate, he and the Bryn Mawr sophomore who was visiting spent most of the night talking, and she said afterwards that it was the first time she had met a real live Communist."[4]

MBS's next letter was written on April 5 as "a diary of the most interesting of my varied occupations" in a week she perceived as both tragic and comic as she rushed to meet visitors, changed her travel plans for Shanghai and learned that Yenching students had been arrested in Peking.

April 5, 1936

Tuesday: Usual committees and efforts to clear my desk preparatory to going to Shanghai. Disquieting news in the afternoon—the seventy students who had cut classes in the morning to go to a memorial service in town had had a brush with the police. As a protest against the death in prison of a middle school student, the Peiping Student Union called a parade after the memorial service. Seven Yenching students were arrested—four girls and three boys. Except for one boy, they were none of them radical students, but they didn't run fast enough when the police interfered. Spent an hour in the dormitories trying to find out exactly what had happened and most of the evening at the telephone.

According to another account, after the memorial meeting at Peita for Kuo Ch'ing, the middle school student who had died in prison, "participants marched down the avenue four abreast bearing a white-shrouded coffin. More than fifty of them, including the Yenching radical Wang Ju-mei, were arrested after a heated argument with armed motorcycle police who had cordoned the road."[5]

Packed my bag for Shanghai but realizing that it was probably a waste of time. At half past ten some students came in to say that a mass meeting of our students had decided on a three-day strike.

Wednesday: Faculty Executive Committee meeting. Cancelled my berth on the Shanghai Express and made a reservation for the plane on Saturday. The Bakers[6] came to lunch after a morning of sightseeing in the Summer Palace in a thoroughgoing dust storm. Went to town to see John Hayes, who has some police official friends who may be able to help get the arrested students out of jail. On Wednesday evening we always have open house for students. Only two American girls came, as the others were all at a mass meeting where the moderate students were making a vain effort to call off the strike.

Thursday: Conferences all morning. At noon a rumor began to circulate that the police were to come that night to arrest radical students. All efforts to get the report either denied or substantiated useless. Talked to father of one arrested girl and sister of another.

Went to town to take the Bakers to the Fergusons' to tea. Got home to find the rumor of a police raid universally believed by students and scoffed at by faculty. Arranged to have a member of the faculty sleep in each dormitory as the matrons were getting panicky. Many of the students went to stay overnight with relatives in town. One of the girls who has been most active came here for the night. Slept in the study with one ear cocked so that I would surely hear the telephone, but heard nothing more disturbing than Dinny barking at a cat in the garden.

Friday: The girls who had stayed in the dormitories very derisive toward all those who had run away. Faculty Executive Committee. Efforts to get arrested students released still ineffective. Canceled my reservation on the plane.

And has it been only a week? It feels like six months. There are promises that five of the arrested students will be released tomorrow. The students were back at class yesterday and presumably will go on with regular work tomorrow, but there are rumors of new Japanese demands and the Communist situation in Shansi is far from settled.

Yenching, Easter Day, April 12, 1936

The spring is a full month late, but this week at last the wild peaches and forsythia have come into blossom and the sun has enough pale warmth to make it pleasant and profitable to work in the garden. Our Easter morning service is always lovely with babies being baptized and both children and students joining the Christian Fellowship. We always go to the Shadicks for lunch, celebrating Easter in the Russian style. Tonight the chorus is singing the Messiah.

Dr. Stuart got back yesterday, apparently well pleased with the results of his months in America. If there are no more upsets here, I shall go South on Wednesday for three days in Shanghai, three in Nanking and I hope a few hours in Hangchow.

Two of our girls who were arrested are now out of jail; one was released because of family pull, the other because she got a throat infection and they let us take her out and put her in the PUMC. They keep promising that the other two will be released soon but nothing happens. Apparently they are being treated fairly decently, though for the first week they had to wear fetters on their ankles. All of them will be considerably less mild in their political views than they were when they were arrested.

General Matsumura, the new Japanese military head in this region, has been making the most appalling statements to the newspaper correspondents. He uses parables: China is the patient and Japan is the doctor. The patient must trust the doctor absolutely and must on no account listen to the advice of anybody else. China is an open field and Japan is a lake. There is no use trying to keep the water back, they will rush through dikes of every kind, but if proper channels are provided then the water will serve the land, providing life-giving springs and power houses and the whole world will profit!

April 19, 1936

We live in such a small self-contained community here that it is good for one to get out occasionally and see a little more of the world, but though I enjoyed the days in Shanghai and Nanking immensely, I was thankful to get home again and glad that it's been my lot to live in Peking instead of in that teeming Yangtze Valley.

I had three days in Shanghai during which I visited schools and colleges, saw a lot of alumnae, called on various friends of Yenching and saw a number of my own friends. In Hangchow one of our graduates met me at the station and took me to see not only Hangchow Christian College, but also temples and tombs and azalea-covered hillsides and the island of the famous West Lake.

In Nanking I had three days, staying at Ginling. Dr. Wu [Yi-fang] went with me in my call on the Minister of Education. I could not possibly have managed all the politeness and formalities of that occasion by myself. It remains to be seen whether my visit had any effect whatsoever. Last summer the Ministry sent an order that our Departments of Home Economics and Music should stop offering major work and should henceforth become short courses. I saw the Minister himself and also the heads of the Bureaus of Higher Education and Secondary Education. Each of the three gave a different reason for the order, which leads one to believe that there is no real reason.

Dr. Stuart was in Nanking at the same time and took me to tea at H.H. K'ung's.[7] Dr. K'ung made me a present of two small yellow cotton Easter chickens! Yes, honestly he did—the kind that always perch on the counters of candy stores at Easter—and put them in an envelope marked "Ministry of Finance, Nanking." He has an enormous new white stucco house, completely surrounded by armed guards, one behind each bush. Everything in the house is brand new, the modernistic furniture on the sun porch, the Victorian furniture in the living room, and the Grand Rapids furniture in the dining room. The climax of tea was an enormous chocolate basket full of eggs and Easter chickens, and it was then that Dr. Kung insisted I should not only eat the chocolates but should take away with me some chickens.

May 25, 1936

I am afraid I shall have to go on with this Women's College Dean's business a bit longer. When I was in Nanking and Shanghai, I made inquiries everywhere and came away convinced that the one person we want is Mrs. [Waysung] New. I recommended to the faculty that we make every effort to get her, and the faculty made that recommendation to our Administrative Committee (a committee of Peking women that function in relation to the Board of Managers as the Yenching College Committee does with the Trustees). This committee felt, however, that it was not wise to invite Mrs. New at this time.

The arguments boiled down to two: (a) since she has an invalid husband and a small son and does not need a position, there is not the faintest chance that she would be willing to come (I had felt that there was just one little chance if we asked her, but some of the women on the committee who are her friends say not); and (b) in the present political situation it is better to have a foreigner!

This last point is an entirely new one and of course just the opposite of what we have all felt for years. I wish I saw some way out. I feel so inadequate for this job. My use of Chinese seems more inadequate every day, and I can't get time to study.

Mrs. Waysung New was Y.T. Zee before her marriage in 1924. Born into a family of Chinese Baptists, she graduated from Ginling College in 1919, a member of its first graduating class. She was a leader of May Fourth protests at Ginling and proclaimed herself an independent feminist. She began teaching at a government school. An independent-minded Chinese Christian feminist was the Women's College forever unobtainable desire.[8]

June 7, 1936

This has been a week of sorrow for Yenching. It has shown what bonds of affection and understanding there are in this small community. On Monday there was a Memorial Service in Chinese for Mrs. Learmonth,[9] with hundreds of old and young there, each one of whom she had helped. The funeral was on Tuesday in Peking. Augusta arranged the flowers with masses of foxgloves and Canterbury bells like the English cottage garden which Mrs. Learmonth had had embroidered on so many things and which everyone associated with her.

The student strike lasted until Wednesday, and for a day or two everyone was badly worried. Rumors of a break between Canton and Nanking were thick, and even Dr. Ferguson thought something serious was about to happen. But nothing has happened yet, and the tension has disappeared for a time at least. One thing seems to be pretty clear: if there is war, the fighting won't be here but further south, but let us hope it won't come to that.

June 21, 1936

These last two weeks have been fairly full, what with guests, student demonstrations, strikes, farewells to people leaving for furlough and permanently, and five days of beastly hot weather. And we've gone through the last week not quite sure whether Yenching was going to be smashed from within or from without. There have been all sorts of rumors about the political situation. We were advised by Nanking to close early. Even unexcitable people like Dr. Ferguson said something was going to break in North China soon. And the insanity of civil war in the Southwest has grown steadily more probable.

A week ago yesterday the students held another demonstration, ostensibly against civil war, actually anti-Japan and possibly to a certain extent anti-Nanking. Our students were locked out of the city, so none were arrested or hurt. On Monday we received an order from the Hopei-Chahar Political Council, presumably acting under pressure from the Japanese, saying that all student organizations, including the self government association, patriotic groups, even literary or educational discussion groups were to be dissolved. Of course the students were furious, decided they must protest, and most unwisely declared an indefinite strike.

As always, there were mixed motives: some are genuinely patriotic and feel that if their freedom is to be taken away completely, they must put up a struggle and it doesn't matter if they lose a semester's credit in the process; others were looking for any pretext to make trouble; others feel that it would be a good thing to prolong the term so as to keep the student body on the campus, for the students are the only articulate group who tell the world what Japan is doing. The faculty sympathize with the desire to protest but feel that striking is a foolish way to do it.

Exams are due to begin this Thursday and there is still hope that the students will go back to work tomorrow. If they try to avoid taking the exams, we are in for trouble. Tsing Hua has declared an early vacation and postponed all exams till fall, but we're not willing to do that.

July 13, 1936

Commencement is over and we actually finished up the year properly, although two weeks late. I don't believe I ever wrote about the birthday celebrations for the President and how the strike ended just in time. We finished the year in good style and are having as many applicants as usual for admission. The Japanese troops demonstrate more and more frequently in Peking streets.

June 24th had been Leighton Stuart's sixtieth birthday. This anniversary was, he wrote, "made much of by my friends in accord with a gracious Chinese tradition." There was a banquet, speeches, elaborate decorations including colored lights, a birthday present from the Power House staff, "one more sign of the close fellowship which exists between the workmen, students and faculty that is a distinctive mark of Yenching life."[10]

Red Flags, White Flags

Even on vacation, MBS and her Yenching friends were now unable to escape Japanese troops. In Peking Japanese soldiers were demonstrating more and more frequently, MBS reported in a July 13 letter.

Yenching, undaunted, looked to the next academic year with as many applicants as usual. The faculty's fall retreat offered MBS

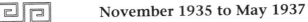

time to contemplate the future of the Women's College, her own
plans for furlough, and to wonder at the comeliness of China.

July 28, 1936, Peitaiho

I am sitting on Jo's [Welles] porch looking off at the blue sea
and the line of the hills where the Great Wall comes down at
Shanhaikuan—rather a useless Great Wall, for here in the quiet bay
half a dozen smuggling boats are lying openly and on the three
high points along the beach there are mysterious red and white
flags planted by the Japanese. No one is sure whether they mean
"Shoot here" or "Don't shoot here."

October 4, 1936

I'm sitting by myself in the back gate of the Sleeping Buddha
Temple—Wo Fo Ssu—and I wish I could put into words the beauty
of this place. The gate is a battered shabby door at the highest
point of the winding stone wall that encircles the temple. Through
the open gate behind me the bare brown hillsides rush up to the
sapphire sky. On both sides there are shoulders of the hills surrounding me like a great horseshoe, green here and there but for
the most part an olive brown. Directly below me are the roofs of
the temple, blue and yellow and gray, half hidden in the shadows
of dark green cedars and two enormous yellowing gingkos. Spread
out beyond is the Peking plain, brown where the fields have just
been plowed for the winter wheat crop, green where beans are now
ripening, grey at the far horizon, as flat and everlasting as the sea
and far more unchanging.

The Christian Fellowship is having the annual faculty retreat
out here, and most people are snoozing in the sunny courtyards
until the two o'clock meeting. It was cold this morning, but now
the sun is as hot as it could be on any August morning in New
England. Perched here in a shady corner with the sun on my feet
and the wind in my face and the rustling of the trees in my ear, I

feel that Wordsworth knew what he was talking about when he said one impulse from a vernal wood could teach you more than all the sages in their discussion groups.

Plans for the next year or two seem to be beginning to grow clearer, though they are still hazy in spots. During these last five years there have been four of us who have borne the chief responsibility for all Women's College administration—Myfanwy Wood, Ruth Stahl, Kit King Lei, and I. Myfanwy has made up her mind to retire next year. She has been in China for nearly thirty years and thinks now she is needed at home.

Ruth, Kitty, and I are all due for furloughs in 1938, me after a full term of seven years, Ruth after six years (a full term in the Methodist Board and she is not very strong and ought not to be asked to extend it) and Kitty after seven years at Yenching—but her case is rather complicated. The Women's College Executive Committee feels that Kitty and Ruth should be here while I am away and therefore sent a request to China Council so that it could be put in the Estimates for a short furlough for me in 1937 (after six years and within the Manual regulations whenever there is good reason for it).

I was electrified yesterday to get a letter from A.K. Whallon saying China Council had approved a full furlough for me in 1937, beginning next July. Even the bare possibility that I might go home next summer makes me feel breathless and rushed. And another thing, all this talk of furloughs assumes that I'm coming back to China again. How do you feel about that? I can't be certain now that it's right, but I hope I'll know when the time comes.

The political situation is very tense. Chiang's position is infinitely stronger since the Swangsi settlement but the Japanese seem determined on further demands. The behavior of Japanese troops around Peking grows more unbearable every day. They pick out holidays for their maneuvers, hold sham battles in crowded streets. A Japanese sentry pushed Myfanwy Wood into the gutter with his bayonet when she was walking quietly along the sidewalk in front of the Japanese Legation. If only the moderates can prevail over the militants.

Augusta Wagner also wrote to Mrs. Speer at this time about the situation in China: "Just now the political skies are very dark again. It looked for a time last week as if war might come, but I still believe Chiang Kai-shek will go to any lengths he can to avoid it. The Japanese are pressing him hard and are determined to come to a definite understanding with him. He is temporizing, trying to find out whether he has enough support in the country to back him in a policy of giving Japan the control of North China.

"I think Japan is insisting on the control of North China as the sine qua non for any agreement. Chiang Kai-shek, recognizing the inevitable, would be willing to accede Japan this in the hope that Japan will then not encroach on the rest of China which he will then in the meantime build up. He is afraid, however, that there might be enough opposition to this to wreck him and his government and China if he should announce this as his policy. The Japanese on the other hand want some definite understanding that this is his policy and so he is between the devil and the deep blue sea. Among the intellectuals there has been a good deal of loud talk that Chiang should fight, at any rate refuse to accede to the Japanese demands, but last week when it looked as if there might be war, with Japanese warships in the harbor and Japanese marines landed in Chapei, some of those who had been talking loudest were among the first to run.

"It is awful to see the Japanese day after day becoming ever more secure in their aggression. Of course the Chinese have brought a good deal of it on themselves, but that does not make it any better. Poor old China, whatever comes out of these discussions will not be very pleasant for her. If Chiang gives up North China to Japan (not necessarily giving public political control but giving Japan a free hand to do as she pleases) that will not be easy to bear, and if he does not, I think there is likelihood

of a break-off of 'friendly' relations and a showdown. If it comes to war, I do not think China has much show. It is all so senseless. In spite of all this, things have been quieter at the University than I have ever known them."[11]

October 18, 1936

Last Wednesday we celebrated the Double Tenth holiday (the tenth day of the tenth month, the anniversary of the beginning of the Chinese Republic) with a marvellous trip into the country to Pan Shan, a mountain about sixty miles east of Peking, beyond Ma Fang where I went my first winter here. It was a farewell trip for Bi, who goes back to Australia next month. There were nine of us: Lucius and Lillian Porter, Professor and Mrs. Ivor Richards (the great Cambridge psychologist, literary critic, author of *Basic English* and *The Meaning of Meaning*, a famous mountaineer, etc.),[12] Kit King Lei, Dora Bent, Bi, Augusta, and I, and, of course, Dinny.

We had the most perfect weather, bright sunshine, not too cold at night, and the first color glorifying the hills. We left here after breakfast in the University truck, rolled smoothly along the first twenty miles to Tungchow, but there the good road stopped. The bridges across three of the four rivers had not been rebuilt since the summer rains, and the truck had to be ferried across on a barge which was just six inches wider than the truck. At three we reached Pang Chun, the last village, where we left the truck in the chapel courtyard and started on foot, with our bedding on donkeys, across the plain to the foot of the mountain.

The hills there are far more wooded than the Western Hills. It wouldn't look like dense forest to a New England eye, but there were willow, poplars, persimmons, pears, oaks, chestnuts all along the way and on the mountain itself lots of flat topped pines. Just as dark was closing in we got to the Temple of Heavenly Completion. The abbot there is an ex-soldier and old friend of Lucius Porter and entertained us royally. From the windows of our long upper room we could look out over the valley, framed on either side by rocky hillsides that might have come out of a Sung painting, and we slept out under the stars on the terrace.

The next day we divided into three parties, each to follow its own temperament in climbing. Lucius and the Richardses started first with an Alpine rope in their rucksack and the intention of scaling every peak and running up and down every col. Lillian, Dora, and Augusta were going to set their faces steadily toward the summit and turn aside for nothing on the way. Kitty, Bi, and I were going to putter along at our own pace and stop or turn back whenever we felt like it. To our great surprise we reached the top in as good time as the others. (I have to confess it's not a very high mountain, only about 2500 feet.)

The next day on our way home the truck got stuck in the sand and the driver drove at a terrific rate for fear we wouldn't get home before dark. The dust swirled around the back of the open truck, and even though we hung on for dear life we bounded about till we were black and blue. It's a pity no one got a picture of Dr. Richards, a red bandana over his nose and his hat tied on with a piece of string. Why we weren't mistaken for bandits I can't imagine.

Another different experience was going to see the Nazi film "The Triumph of Will Power," a picture of the Party Congress and great demonstrations at Nuremberg. There was a tiny notice in the paper saying the film would be shown and anyone interested could get tickets at the German Club. Augusta thought it would be interesting to go, and we expected to find a handful of the German community there.

We were astounded to find the theater packed with Chinese, Germans, representatives of all the Embassies, swastikas flying, men in Storm Troopers' uniforms in the lobby. The picture was simply a succession of parades on a gigantic scale, torches, banners, martial music, crowds shouting "Heil," speeches to thousands, "Mein Fuhrer," "Das Volk," "Das Reich," "Deutschland," pure hypnosis but what for? Simply appalling and terrifying.

The Japanese are getting thicker than ever but the general tension is a little less at the moment. The Hopei-Chahar Political Council has issued an order forbidding all organizations of students. Fortunately we haven't yet received the order, but we can't possibly suppress all student organizations and wouldn't if we could. Everything from the Student Government Association to literary societies are supposed to be included.

November 1, 1936

We went out this afternoon with the Shadicks to the Hunting Park where the autumn coloring is magnificent. I remember stupidly writing to someone when I had been in Peking about three weeks that the Temple of Heaven was the only beautiful place here. The beauty of autumn is not very apparent in Peking *hutungs*, but out here it takes one's breath away.

The Yenching campus, which was such a waste of ditches and rock piles when you were here, is now, according to Professor Richards, the most beautiful college campus in the world. It seems as though every weekend I've written you about a different place, each more lovely than the last.

The Hunting Park (Hsiang Shan—the Fragrant Mountain) is in the Western Hills very near the Sleeping Buddha Temple. Outside its wall, which runs in a great circle from the plain up to the crest of the ridge, there are the bare brown flanks of the Western Hills. Inside the wall the hillsides are covered with pines and cedar and a low scrubby tree that is sometimes called flamebush. The Chinese simply call it "red leaves" for in October it turns a gorgeous red, every shade from orange and scarlet to a dark crimson. With the sun shining on it today it was worth going miles to see, and Chinese people do go miles to see something beautiful. Hundreds of portly Chinese gentlemen in blue silk robes were walking decorously along the main paths to enjoy the color, but we scrambled up the hillsides and soaked it in.

Preserved in the pages of this letter are three red leaves, pressed and dried.

November 15, 1936

Political conditions appear to be looking up. There is more of a spirit of unity in the whole Chinese nation than one has felt for years, and there begins to be hope that China will not have to concede everything in the Sino-Japanese negotiations.

November 22, 1936

My birthday was a lovely day. I wish you could all have been here, but I had Mother's book of T.S.Eliot which had come in good time. Grace Boynton is an authority on T.S. Eliot and says he had to go through that tortured period of expressing himself in ways that nobody could understand,but I prefer his later period of comparative intelligibility. The choruses from "The Rock" are lovely.

In the evening we had a party of the Shadicks, Wilsons, Prices, Nancy and Bi, partly to celebrate my birthday and partly as a final farewell to Bi, who left yesterday for Australia. His going has left a gap that can't be filled. He has been a good friend to old and young on the Yenching campus. The children all adored him, and probably next to Mrs. Learmonth he was more deeply and widely loved than any other member of the community. He has been a good friend to us all. (I see I have repeated myself with unconscious emphasis.)

The students have been very active this week. In Suiyuan Province to the northwest of us there is a small war going on between Government troops and "irregulars" who are apparently supported by the Japanese, who are "nibbling" surreptitiously all along China's northern frontier. To support the Government troops who are rather poorly equipped, the students have been going without heat and with very little food. It's pretty heroic to live for a week in an unheated dormitory.

Chiang Kai-shek

By 1936 MBS was saying less about women and a great deal more about Chinese politics, the overwhelming focus of life at Yenching.

December 6, 1936

The political situation changes every day. One day everyone is full of rejoicing over China's new unity and strength, the next it appears that the truce between the Government and the Communists may be shattered at any moment, and the next most everyone is filled with apprehension by something like this week's landing of Japanese marines in Tsingtao.

Is there any middle ground in the world between communism and fascism? In America and England I should think there is hope. In China it looks as though the articulate groups felt that they must go to one extreme or the other. This new alliance between Japan and Germany creates new difficulties here. Chiang Kai-shek's recent interests have been tending toward fascism, but if the big fascist boys won't let him play with them, perhaps he'll look for other playmates. Most American travellers who come this way seem to be frightened of communism. I find myself more terrified of the other extreme.

December 27, 1936

We had a lovely Christmas, but there were guests every moment. We fed over a hundred people in the course of the day, and yesterday I could hardly keep my eyes open. On Christmas Eve we went to the Shadicks where the guests represented six nationalities.

Political excitement has been very great these last few weeks. When the news of Chiang Kai-shek's detention by Chang Hsüeh-liang came, no one would at first believe it. Then there was surprise and indignation on the part of most—a general rallying to the Central Government in most quarters, but with some radical groups feeling that perhaps Chang Hsüeh-liang was striking a blow against dictatorship that the strongly organized Communists in the Northwest might be able to take advantage of. Now that Chiang is released and safely back in Nanking, there is general rejoicing, but there is an ominous note in the very enthusiasm of the celebration.

China needs unification and a leader, and Chiang is indubitably the only leader they have, and all my sympathies are really with the Central Government, but I don't like to see groups of students or other citizens demonstrating and shouting fascist slogans any better than I like to see communist demonstrations, and I don't believe a communist-fascist struggle here would be any prettier than it is in Spain.

It's too soon to know what this whole affair is all about much less what it will lead to. As usual it brings home to one that no foreigner can possibly understand the Chinese. The accounts of today's paper telling how Chang Hsüeh-liang has followed Chiang to Nanking and asked to be punished, sound as uproariously farcical as Gilbert and Sullivan. And yet it's a mistake to think it's funny. It's a deadly serious game played with great skill, but according to rules that are beyond comprehension.

Chiang Kai-shek went to North China in December 1936 to oust the Communists. Chang Hsüeh-liang had been commanding one of Chiang's armies in Sian, but he was convinced that the Japanese were a greater threat to China than the Chinese Communists. In an effort to coerce Chiang into opposing the Japanese, Chang and his soldiers took Chiang captive on December 12 and sent demands to the Nanking Government. Chiang, however, was perceived by Chou En-lai and other Communist leaders, as a more effective leader than Chang for a united China, and they negotiated Chiang's release.[13]

January 3, 1937

Our student body is like every other student group in China just now—rapidly being split into two opposing camps of Rightists and Leftists. So far there hasn't been an open break, but I don't know how much longer it can be avoided. There is a lot more behind this whole Chiang-Chang incident than any of us know, but it has had one marked effect in making the groups who support the Government more articulate than they have ever been. Some support the Kuomintang. Others support Chiang Kai-shek as a leader of the fascist type. At a parade, following fireworks on Wednesday night in celebration of Chiang's release, the students shouted slogans, not only "Long Live China" and "Down with Japanese Imperialism," but also "Down with the Communist bandits," "Down with Communist running dogs." I am afraid we are in for a period when each group will misrepresent the other and try to crush it by any tactics.

January 24, 1937

On Wednesday we sat up until two o'clock at Dr. Brown's house listening to Roosevelt's inauguration over the radio. His oath was very clear, but during his speech the static grew worse and worse until only occasional words were distinguishable. The announcer spoke of the pouring rain. Now it appears that rain has caused terrific floods. There is so much censorship we hardly know what is going on in China. Apparently much is happening that does not get into the news.

Censorship may also have dampened MBS's candor in reporting political incidents, for her letters in the next few months touch on entrance examinations, Chinese New Year, coeducational social life, and the difficulties of getting along with a large group of middle-aged female missionaries. Life at Yenching was complex and it began to look as though MBS was destined to be Dean of the Women's College.

211

January 31, 1937

Today is the last day of our vacation. I've had office hours as usual in the mornings, but the afternoons have been free for Chinese, except for the three days of the meetings of the Western Languages Association. I had to make a speech the first day about the principles underlying the construction of our entrance examinations. There were about 150 people at most of the meetings, mostly from Peiping, but with a sprinkling from Canton, Hankow, and Nanking. The mayor gave a dinner to the whole Conference in an extraordinary half-Chinese half-foreign building built by the Empress Dowager. It was fun to see the Chinese official way of doing things, but sickening to think how much municipal money is wasted that way.

February 7, 1937

We spend most of our time on this clean and peaceful campus occupied with college affairs or the students' problems, and we might almost be a thousand miles and a hundred years away from the real China of the common people, but every once in a while we realize that the China of the four hundred million is after all only just on the other side of our garden wall.

This morning when I looked out into the garden, a bit of bright color in the shrubbery caught my eye, and on going out to investigate, I found it was a bundle of cheap, worn clothes that had evidently been thrown over from the village street. When I asked Pao Ch'ing about them, he said at once that they must have been dropped by a thief, but he was very reluctant to report it to the police, saying it would be very troublesome and we would have to spend hours at the police station answering questions.

I told him that we must at least notify the University watchman, who at once came over and identified the clothes as belonging to the matron of our girls' gymnasium. She lives just across the village street from our wall, and it appears that last night a thief stole all her *pei wo*, the padded quilts that are a poor family's chief wealth in winter time, as well as most of the family's clothes. Just before Chinese New Year is always the time when thieves are most active.

At noon when the sun was warm, we went out along the main streets in Haitien to see everyone out getting ready for the New Year. The little narrow streets were packed nearly solid. Little tables were set up where writers with strips of red paper were preparing the mottoes—"Peace," "Long Life," "Observe Happiness Whenever You Come Out This Door,"—which must be put up freshly on every respectable doorway and even on wheelbarrows and coal carts. There were gay stalls selling cheap red candles and fireworks and great tubs of goldfish for the children and the old men, and piles of yellow noodles ready to be cooked, and stretched out everywhere carcasses of fat pigs, for though one may live on coarse millet and cabbage all the year round, even the poorest must have some pork on New Year's Day.

The Temple courtyard was full of peddlers and swarming with children who were spending their coppers looking at peep shows of hair-raising pictures and squatting on their heels eating fried pieces of pink mush, which is a special New Year delicacy. Everyone was in holiday mood and lots of old men and children stopped to pat Dinny, who was frantic over all the bewildering smells. I did not see any beggars and most of the shoppers looked clean and respectable. The Government declares a legal holiday on January first and abolishes the lunar calendar, but it doesn't make a scrap of difference to anyone but the politicians. The lunar New Year is the people's holiday, and it will take more than government orders to stop the celebration.

February 14, 1937

We had a heavy snow this week and the ground is still white, but my garden notebook says that the grass has begun to show green on February 23 in other years and according to the Chinese calendar we have already had the Beginning of Spring and the Awakening of the Insects.

February 21, 1937

Yesterday afternoon we decided to go on a spree, and Augusta, Louise Sailer, another friend and I went to town in a car and went to the most famous duck restaurant in Peiping for roast duck. You come in through the kitchen and eat upstairs in a little cubbyhole looking out on tiled roofs, but you choose your own duck, watch it hung in the oven, wait for ages, have it carved before your eyes, wrap the golden pieces in little pancakes with garlic and soybean sauce, have the carcass boiled with cabbage to make a delectable soup, and go away feeling full and happy.

Then we went to Liu Li Chang to the big fair that lasts for two weeks after the Chinese New Year and poked around among the stalls of jade and ivory and paintings for hours, bargaining for trinkets and each thinking our own purchases were great bargains and the other fellow's just so much junk.

We have been spending a great deal of time lately discussing better provision for social relationships between the boys and girls. It's curious how short-sighted the building plans for the University were, but nobody could have foreseen how rapidly coeducation would develop and how soon the old conventions would be pushed aside. The men's dormitories have no common rooms at all, and the girls' living rooms are so arranged that it is exceedingly inconvenient (some people think impossible) to admit men callers. The one University social room is too small and is not adapted to general sociability, playing games, music, and ordinary diversions.

It must be extremely difficult for the average Chinese girl, brought up in an old-fashioned home, but going to Western movies and suddenly faced with the freedom on the Yenching campus, to know what standards of behavior are to be considered natural and proper and what are not. Her grandmother would probably consider it improper for her even to speak to a boy, but here she can play tennis and skate with him, and go off on donkeys to the Western Hills. It is hardly to be wondered at if one girl is embarrassed to be seen walking soberly around the lake with a boy, while another sits on her beau's lap, unblushing in the public gaze. I feel that if we could make some provision for boys to come to see girls in their dormitories, at home, naturally, but with the matron and the other girls coming and going, it would be a great advance.

February 28, 1937

I got my passport this week, the first active step I've taken to get ready for leaving in July. When I got home and looked at it, I found the clerk at the Embassy had carefully put down the date of my birth as November 20, 1930. Luckily I found it out before reaching the Manchurian border, for no humorless Japanese or Russian passport officer would ever believe it was an accidental slip.[14]

March 21, 1937

I'm afraid it is several weeks since I have written. I had to make a speech in University Assembly which kept me in a lather of feverish preparation until it was out of the way. The thirtieth anniversary of the first government recognition of education for women fell on the same date as "Women's Day." Did you ever hear of Women's Day, March 8, in America? It was apparently started in Denmark about thirty years ago and is generally celebrated by Communist groups. It is a great occasion for our women students, and we have tried to save it from Communist associations.

I am becoming a little concerned by the growing old-maidishness and what might be called well-meaning spitefulness of our Women's College faculty. When I first came twelve years ago, we had two groups, an older group mostly in their forties and a younger group in their twenties. Now we have quite a number in their fifties, a sprinkling in their forties, and hardly anyone under thirty. We are beginning to eye the innocent or disturbing ways of youth over a widening gulf. But more distressing than that is the apparent fact that with a large group of our women faculty, stubbornness, distrustfulness, criticalness, and general acidity, seem to go hand in hand with and in exact proportion to religious zeal. The more "Christian" they are, the harder to get along with.

April 4, 1937

Yesterday in spite of a howling dust storm we had a very successful opening for the new playground in the village just outside the University gate. It has always seemed horrid to chase the village children off the playground here in our compound, but the mothers in the compound felt that there was too much danger of germs and insisted that we shouldn't even allow the servants' children to play there.

Augusta got the idea of raising money to establish a playground in the village, and the Y.P. Meis, whose little four-year-old son died last year, asked to have a special share in it, so it has been planned as a memorial to little Wan-tze Mei. The University gave the land, and Augusta's enthusiasm has borne fruit in swings and slides and seesaws. At the opening yesterday the village elders came to make speeches, the children from all the village schools sang songs, and then miraculously three dollars worth of cake was stretched to feed hundreds of youngsters.

Father asked about the action of the Yenching College Committee in making me Dean, and what effect that had on my work or furlough plans. It doesn't have any effect at all. I just go right on doing what I've been doing for the last two and a half years. Somebody, probably Ruth Stahl, will be Acting Dean while I'm away. We still think that there ought to be a Chinese dean and as soon as we can find one, I'll resign. The trouble is that first we must find an able Christian Chinese woman with experience in college education and the ability to get along with a mixed group of Chinese and foreigners and then she must have an opportunity to work into the life at Yenching. The experience with Miss Ssu-tu showed up the difficulties that were encountered by anyone coming in from outside.

May 9, 1937

Last week Dr. W.S. New died. You know a year ago when it seemed that he would be an invalid for life we hoped Mrs. New might come here to be Dean of the Women's College, but then he became much better, and Mrs. New felt she must help him carry on his work in Shanghai. Now I don't know what our next step should be.

Dr. Stuart is down in Shanghai now and we'll probably do nothing until he gets back. Yenching is such a democratic place that it is difficult to get anything done until one can get the whole weight of public opinion to move with one. I feel quite convinced that if we do not invite Mrs. New now, we are admitting that we will never invite a Chinese dean from outside our own faculty group. Mrs. New is the very best type of woman that we are likely ever to find. But on the other hand, the University administration see no reason for going outside the Yenching faculty and bringing in a strong-minded woman who will be unfamiliar with Yenching ways of doing things and may start a few upheavals. And within the Women's College faculty, the Chinese in particular are so polite and so loyal that they say they don't see any need to change the present Dean!

I am beginning to think that the right solution may be for me to resign flatly and loudly so as to force the issue. It has been understood all along that I would resign as soon as a good Chinese dean was in sight, but now when I suggest it people say that maybe Mrs. New wouldn't accept an invitation, that she wants to carry on her husband's work, etc. Well, we won't know until we try, and as long as I am here she may think we don't really need her, so the

best thing may be for me to clear out entirely. Dr. Stuart is in Shanghai now. As soon as he comes back I'll thrash it all out with him.

Left to right: MBS, Emma Bailey Speer, Robert Elliott Speer, and William Speer in Peking in 1926.

Left to right: L.R.O. Bevan (Bi), Augusta Wagner, Camilla Mills, Knight Biggerstaff, Yenching, 1929.

MBS, Augusta Wagner, L.R.O. Bevan, the I.A.Richardses, and friends on a walking trip, probably 1936.

MBS in hiking clothes, 1929.

President of Yenching Leighton Stuart and MBS, 1930s

The Women's College Faculty, early 1930s. MBS is third from right. To her right, Ruth Stahl, Myfanwy Wood, Grace Boynton.; to her left, V.K. Nyi (Mei) and Hsieh Wan-ying (Wu).

Madame Chiang Kai-shek at Yenching, 1934.

Augusta Wagner, 1938.

MBS in her living room at Yenching with Dinny at her feet.

Hsieh Wan-ying, her husband, Wu Wen-tsao, her son and daughters, Yenching, 1930s.

MBS outside her house at Yenching.

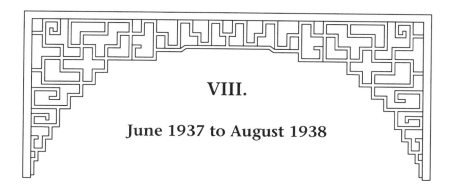

VIII.

June 1937 to August 1938

Furlough

From June 1937 until late August 1938 MBS wrote no letters from Yenching because she was on her way home for the finally allowable full year's furlough. In her 1982 reminiscences she described the trip: the land route from China to Moscow and on through Europe to England, where she spent some time with her sister at Bristol.

The plan was to go via Siberia, and there were to be four of us in one "Fourth Class Hard" compartment. Mabel Wood, a teacher from Oregon who had been at Yenching for just a year, Miss Wang, a very nice nurse from the PUMC, Augusta, and I.

In those days everyone who traveled by Siberia made the most of the experiences of other travelers who had gone before. The Congregational Mission kept a black notebook in which each group of travelers wrote down suggestions and what they had learned by experience. The chief question, of course, was food.

To get one's food in the dining car would have seemed the most natural plan. However, the Siberian trains had a custom of locking the carriages between one class and another for long periods of the day, so that to go to the dining car for a meal meant going there at a time when the train had stopped at a station and not being able to go back to one's own compartment until the next station; and stations were few and far between. We decided to take our own food. The food for the four of us cost altogether less than a dining car ticket for one person. (One could not buy meals à la carte, but had to buy a dining ticket for the whole journey.) Moreover, it was much better food than the heavy floury fare offered in the Russian diner.

In order to have hot meals we planned very carefully with a detailed menu for every day. The system for heating the food was ingenious; most people could not believe it. We had the village tinsmith make a large pail with a cover very much like a medium-sized galvanized garbage pail. Then our amah made a huge padded cover like an over-sized tea cozy. The usual schedule was for the trains to have two twenty-minute stops a day and two five-minute stops. When we knew that a twenty-minute stop was coming, our campaign was ready.

One of the four stayed in the compartment to guard our belongings. Two took the pail and one carried a teakettle and a thermos bottle. At one end of the platform there was always a huge boiler where passengers could get hot water. The only problem was that our car was the next to the last car on a long train. At some stations the boiler was near our car, but at others it was at the extreme front end of the train, so we had to rush down the platform, take our turn to get hot water, fill our great pail two-thirds full, and rush back to our own compartment.

The system then was to take about three cans, beans or sausage or whatever we were planning for the meal, tie them in a bag of cheesecloth, which then by tapes was suspended so that it was just half way down the large container of hot water. In about twenty minutes our food was nicely warm, and when the meal was over we had plenty of clean, warm water for washing the dishes.

Other passengers in our Fourth Class car began by laughing at us. They thought it was a very cumbersome process. Their plan was to heat a can of something or other on a little Sterno stove. This was strictly forbidden by the railroad authorities—quite rightly since the cars were wooden—so that they had to keep their compartment door locked while they were "cooking." Pretty soon people began knocking at our door and asking us if we would heat a can of theirs when we were heating our own. We found we could take one extra can at a time, but if we put in too many cans for our friends they cooled the water off so quickly that the whole system was useless.

The one problem of the trip was that Cook's Travel Agency had not been able to supply us with an accurate timetable. They gave us an old one, saying that it would serve the purpose if we just remembered to add twenty-three minutes, or some such number, to the time given for each station. This seemed easy enough but one had to remember that time was also changing hour by hour as we moved from one time zone to another. I was the timetable keeper and managed to keep track fairly accurately. This was important, of course, for we had to plan whether we would eat our meals early or late according to the station stops.

We had a full day in Moscow and had been invited to the Chinese Embassy there for dinner before I was to take the next train through Poland to Berlin. The Ambassador, Dr. T.F. Tsiang, and his wife were old friends because he had been at Tsing Hua and she had been a graduate student at Bryn Mawr when I was there. While we were at the Embassy, the word came through about the Marco Polo Bridge Incident. This was the beginning of a full-scale war between Japan and China. The incident itself was a minor clash between Japanese troops and Chinese soldiers a few miles from Peking. Probably the Japanese had been hoping for such an incident long before this, but I well remember the horror of people at the Embassy, feeling that all-out warfare was now unavoidable.

The Marco Polo Bridge Incident took place on July 7, 1937. The bridge was about ten miles west of Peking and in earlier times admired for its beauty. By 1937 a railway bridge beside the old structure linked the southern railways with the junction at Wanping, which controlled the rail access to the area around Peking. Japanese troops were permitted to hold maneuvers in the area by the Boxer Protocol of 1901 and on July 7 made the bridge the base of such a maneuver, firing blank cartridges into the air. The Chinese fired back; the Japanese believed one Japanese soldier had been captured and ordered an attack on Wanping, which the Chinese repelled, but by late July the Japanese were in control of the area around Peking.[1]

The increasing threat of war did not cause MBS to make any changes in her plans. She went on from Moscow to Holland and then by boat to England. With her sister and brother-in-law she traveled in Wales. From England she sailed on the "Queen Mary" to New York. She spent most of the fall of 1937 making speeches for Yenching, staying several weeks at Wellesley College, where she talked with the faculty and students about Yenching, Wellesley's sister college.

By January 1938 MBS had settled down in New York at Johnson Hall at Columbia, where Augusta Wagner was working on her Ph.D. dissertation. MBS gave speeches, worked at the Yenching office, and interviewed candidates for the Yenching faculty.

She kept in touch with Yenching. Stephen Ts'ai, the University's Controller, spent an afternoon with her in January. To her parents she wrote on January 4, 1938 that "He says outward circumstances there are fairly normal, but all the faculty are showing the strain of the last six months."

To an American visitor the Yenching campus in the summer of 1937 seemed considerably more peaceful than Peking. Eleanor Fabyan, a young Bryn Mawr alumna who was taking care of MBS's beloved Dinny, wrote that the Peking city gates were almost always closed; foreign embassies called their citizens into the Legation Quarter to protect them from bombing and bandits. From July to November 1937 the city was always aware of Japanese troops: "When off duty, Japanese soldiery could be seen swaggering down the street on foot or in great numbers of rickshas, passing by like schools of fish on their way to view the main sights of Peiping." She watched Chinese teachers, students, merchants and others, forced by the Japanese to "rejoice with each successive gain made by the Japanese army." The Chinese marched at the point of the bayonet "with tears streaming down their faces as they carried banners of rejoicing...."

Away from the city and its forced victory parades, Yenching was more tranquil. In October 1937 Eleanor Fabyan took Dinny, "that delectable wire-haired fox terrier," out to the campus for exercise. "Once in the country I realized again how confining it had been to be shut in the city and, having arrived at Yenching, it seemed like wild freedom to be able to race Dinny across the open spaces of the campus."[2]

MBS meanwhile continued to make speeches on behalf of Yenching, five a week, at schools and churches, campaigning for funds. She was also helping Augusta Wagner finish her dissertation on labor legislation in China, assisting, she wrote on April 25, with "the last horrid details of corrections and footnotes and bibliography." "Labor Legislation in China" was completed on time and defended successfully. Augusta "passed with flying colors," MBS announced on May 1, 1938. The 302-page dissertation was published at Yenching University later in 1938.[3]

MBS had put aside all thought of pursuing a Ph.D. of her own by this time. Doubts about returning to China had been resolved, and passage booked on the "Empress of Russia" sailing from Vancouver August 6 to Yokohama, which would allow MBS and Augusta Wagner to arrive at Yenching by the end of August. They would be returning to an increasingly troubled campus.

On June 16, 1938 Leighton Stuart had written a confidential letter to the Trustees of Yenching University to alert them to changes. "Within a few days of Commencement, and at the close of a session singularly free from serious complications, we have been experiencing the most disturbing threats to our tranquility since the anxious weeks of last summer and early autumn. You will have received my last report regarding the appointment of Japanese teachers and the memorandum which is being sent to the State Department. This episode led to a fresh outbreak of rumors and uneasy forebodings among our faculty and students...." Almost immediately after Commencement the Japanese began to make trouble, and the future for Yenching began to look less certain. Stuart concluded that the Japanese found Yenching, an institution with special privileges, galling: "To their minds any lack of submission to their program is anti-Japanese or communistic. It is not a happy outlook but we shall do our best to carry on, for we are having our share in a tremendously worthwhile struggle."[4]

Stuart sent with his letter one dated April 6, 1938 from Chengtu written by an alumnus who had joined West China Union University. He and other Yenching alumni felt that "It would be better for Yenching to move out of the territory under Japanese control...We think it is not very favorable to China for Yenching to create an atmosphere of peace there, as if nothing had happened in Peiping."[5]

Others argued for staying in Peking: another letter enclosed by Stuart expressed support from a former student: "We are criticized by our friends in the south and hated by our enemy here. How delicate is our present position. But I believe we are right to carry on our university as long as possible, if we are not interfered beyond our acceptance. It is very valuable to keep a group of youth to receive a liberal education here. If we close down it is just as our enemy expected, and at least part of our students will be forced to go to their side."[6]

There was no longer any discussion of MBS's resigning as dean. Asked what she remembered about "thrashing it out" with Leighton Stuart, she replied, "Nothing!" The Japanese presence in Peking had overshadowed the search for a Chinese dean, and MBS would continue to assume a major administrative responsibility at Yenching. Aware that she would be returning to Japanese-occupied territory, she wrote letters en route to China to prepare her family for a new sort of correspondence, one which must deal with censorship.

August 2, 1938, Chicago

My train got in at 6:10, Augusta's at 6:30. We are fed and tidy and reasonably cool. We have seen various people who are evidently going to be our fellow travelers across the Pacific.

The day with Ruth [Stahl] yesterday was very satisfactory, though some of her stories made me wonder whether I shall ever be able to control my temper. One of the faculty ran into a pretty sight one day outside our campus. Two Japanese were outside our wall where there were few passersby. One was dressed as a student and was writing anti-Japanese propaganda on the wall; the other was taking his picture! The next day the Japanese Embassy notified Dr. Stuart they had pictures of Yenching students' abominable anti-Japanese behavior. Imagine a Yenching student being dumb enough to write posters denouncing Japan within six feet of a Japanese camera! Heigh-ho!

August 16, 1938, at sea on the *Empress of Russia*

It's still not certain whether we'll be getting off at Kobe or Osaka or elsewhere in Japan. We'll know by the time we get to Yokohama probably.

The Nashes have a clever code in writing to people in China. They refer to two children. John and Charlie.[7] John is naturally Japan and Charlie is China. With that and with calling all the Japanese "Smiths" I think we ought to get along pretty well in spite of the censors.

Time now to go and dress for the captain's dinner. We shall be seeing the lights of Japan this evening and tomorrow we shall have to begin to accustom ourselves to self-control and to bearing up under the hissing, grinning rigidity of Japanese officialdom. Goodbye to outward freedom!

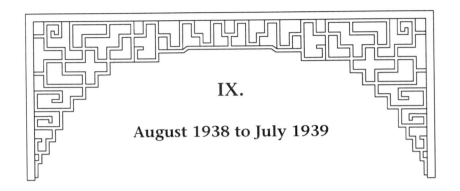

IX.

August 1938 to July 1939

Good-bye to Outward Freedom

MBS *and Augusta Wagner reached Yenching August 24, 1938. Letters home were restricted largely to reports of the weather and of socializing with other passengers. Only many years later did MBS describe her first sight in Yokohama of "crowded Japanese troop trains taking off for the front" and "a contingent of Hitler Jugend wildly applauded by Japanese onlookers." MBS and Augusta sailed from Yokohama to Kobe, visited friends there, and then they "boarded the little 'Choan Maru' for the four day trip from Kobe to Tientsin. There were seven other Western passengers, but all the rest were Japanese Army officers, quiet and well-behaved for the most part."[1]*

The Japanese were in complete control of North China, but there was a puppet Chinese government who issued the orders, and the occupation was beginning to intrude on Yenching's peacefulness. Instructions had come that the University must appoint some Japanese members of the faculty. A new agency in Peking was the Hsin Min Hui (New Peoples' Party). This was a creation of the Japanese for all forms of propagandist activity, according to Dr. Stuart, "staffed by a disreputable type of Japanese agitator and their even worse Chinese hirelings."[2] They kept issuing orders to schools and colleges in Peking as to what they must do and insisting on students taking part in the various demonstrations.

Any failure to take part was interpreted as being anti-Japanese.

MBS dared not write about this to her family, but much later described the Japanese commands: "A sheet marked 'Orders from the Ministry of Education of the Provisional Government' had instructed all students to take part in a huge demonstration in the early summer and had told what resolutions were to be adopted at the mass meeting. People were to send telegrams 'to the whole Chinese people and to all overseas Chinese' to urge them 'to extirpate Communism, to extirpate the Kuomintang, and to be unanimously loyal to the Hsin Min Hui.' Slogans were provided for the students to shout at the parade. Among them were these: 'Down with the murderous and incendiary Communists. Down with the Kuomintang which ruins the country and the people. Down with Chiang Kai-shek, the arch criminal of Eastern Asia. Let us promote Eastern culture and morality. Let us be loyal to the Hsin Min Hui of the Republic of China. Long live the peace of Eastern Asia.'"[3]

Leighton Stuart had struggled with the problem of whether to move Yenching to Free China as some urged him to do or to stay in Peking. He decided to stay. "We flew the American flag for the first time on our rather high pole," he wrote later. "Previously we had flown only the Chinese national flag or our University pennant."[4] Nothing of this was recorded in MBS's first letter from Yenching, but there are hints of the new situation between the lines and in general observations open to various readings.

September 4, 1938

We got back here on the 24th without having had any delays on the way and felt very thankful for a full measure of journeying mercies. Although most of our shipmates on the *Russia* were held up for days in Kobe waiting for passage, we got off after only one night there. While we were there, we went out to Kobe College, where we found people very well informed and understanding. There were signs of the July floods everywhere—it must have been a major calamity. Many of our fellow passengers between Kobe and Tientsin were j army officers, all very courteous and polite. From Tientsin on we were on the lookout for signs of change since we had left. At stations where once there had been crowds of well-to-do passengers getting on and off there were now greater evidences of army mules. It is not so much that people have gone away as that they stay at home and do not go out or travel more than necessary.

Here life goes on almost in a charmed circle. Gardens are green, the moon shines down on the quiet lake. We have more students than ever before and a freshman class almost twice as big as any we have ever had. The girls are more simply dressed, the boys look thinner; their entrance exams show an extraordinarily high standard. Many who in other years would have gone to government colleges are now turning to us, which means that a far smaller proportion than usual are Christians. It is going to be a big job to reach them all and give them something worthwhile this year.

Prices have gone up and the stocks of imported things in Peking are low. People are thankful for little things and are slow to talk about what they really think. An undercurrent of distress runs below all the surface commonplaces. New hymns are popular in chapel and the service this morning was thronged.

September 14, 1938

Classes began this week and all our new students are settling down to steady work. The freshman courses are swamped with the large numbers, and it is quite clear that we are all going to have a busy year. Occupied with our own routine here, it is difficult to keep clearly in mind all that is going on in the rest of the country and the world. I have only been off the campus twice, once to go to town to lunch with the Fergusons and once to go walking in the Summer Palace with Mary Ferguson. Along the road one meets little buzzing brown reminders of the opposite of peace, and sometimes during the chapel services one is distracted by the drone of some of Johnnie's playfellows. I can't think why the boy doesn't learn to be quieter in his play.

September 24, 1938

Today was the last day on which latecomers were allowed to register, so I have been taking stock of dormitory space and seeing how many of the girls on the waiting list could be squeezed in. The maximum capacity of our dormitories is 264 and we have been saving a few rooms for girls from far away who might be delayed by the difficulties of travel. The people on the waiting list have been sitting on my doorstep clamoring to be let in, and some of them have made all sorts of temporary living arrangements in the village in the hope that at the last minute there would be a vacant space. This is the first time that we have had girls who were willing to put up with uncomfortable makeshift arrangements, for coming to Yenching seems like a life and death matter to many of them now that there is no other place to which they can go. We have had one little girl staying with us for the last day or two. Her father was killed in Szechuan this summer, and T.C. Chao of our School of Religion faculty said he would take her into his house until there should be an empty place in the dormitory, but he started off to Madras yesterday. Mrs. Chao wanted to go to Tientsin with him, and the girl couldn't very well stay in the Chao house alone with their handsome sophomore son, so she is with us temporarily.

Bi found that the quiet life of Australia was too monotonous and has come back for one more year here. He got here last Saturday and is teaching a full schedule, for with our enormous freshman class it has been necessary for everyone to fall to and help with the extra sections of freshman mathematics and freshman English. The Shadicks and Augusta and I drove into town to meet Bi's train and had a somewhat astonishing encounter with Mr. Smith on the way—no harm done, just a moment of suspense and ruffled tempers.

Mr. Smith was the agreed on code for the Japanese. Later MBS explained the "encounter": at the city gate Japanese soldiers had tried to frisk Augusta.[5] The Japanese neither obstructed the funeral of MBS's beloved friend, Mrs. Ferguson, nor did they censor her letter describing it.

October 10, 1938

Mrs. Ferguson died early Thursday morning. She looked terribly frail and almost too tired to speak when we saw her just after we got back, but last week she had been better and stronger. Of course Dr. Ferguson and Mary have been prepared to lose her ever since these awful heart attacks began three years ago, and they are glad to have the long suffering over for her, but she has been the center of their life for so long that it is desperately hard for them now. I went in on Friday to see them, and yesterday Augusta and I went in early and had lunch with them before the service, which was at two o'clock. They took the coffin down to Tientsin afterwards where there is to be cremation today, and they will take the ashes home to America next month.

The funeral service was lovely and a truly great experience for us all. Dr. Ferguson is remarkable in the way he accepts and follows Chinese usages and yet never loses his own distinct American personality. He has never "gone native" and yet he adapts Chinese customs so that his Chinese friends feel perfectly at home and know just what to do. The service was in English following the Methodist ritual and with all the quiet dignity that we think right. The coffin was in the center of the main hall of their Chinese house, with Mrs. Ferguson's picture hanging over it according to Chinese custom. Ever since Friday Chinese guests had been coming to pay their respects, bowing deeply three times before the picture.

One was struck with how sensible the Chinese custom is. Everyone knows what to do; high and low do the same thing; there is no embarrassment, no difficulty about knowing what to say, no fear of intruding. Everyone who wants to show sympathy or respect can do it naturally, quietly, adequately. If the members of the family want to talk with him, the guest is asked to stay; if not he goes quietly away.

Buddhists, Taoists, Catholics, and Protestants had all been there, and many had said prayers. At the service itself the abbots of two famous Buddhist temples were there sitting quietly near the front. The courtyards were full of baskets of flowers sent by foreigners and scrolls and gay wreaths of paper flowers sent by Chinese. Everything was simple and orderly and sincere, just as Mrs. Ferguson would have liked it. If ever a life showed the power and strength of simple goodness, hers did. She was completely loving and selfless in everything that she did. I think it is her kind of meekness that inherits the earth.

October 29, 1938

Mary Ferguson is leaving tomorrow and has kindly offered to take letters, so we are all seizing the chance to write something more than the usual non-committal stuff which is all we ordinarily dare to send through the post. No one really knows how thoroughgoing the censorship is or what the results are if one is unguarded in one's statements.

With incoming mail one can tell quite clearly because so much excess paste is used when the letters are closed up again that there is never any doubt as to which letters have been opened. So far none of Father's letters have been opened—perhaps one glance at the handwriting convinces the censor that there is no use wasting his time on that. A letter from Pat and three or four letters from Mother have been opened. Whether or not the censors destroy letters that they don't like, we have no way of knowing. I think that it is likely that they pay less attention to outgoing mail, but the knowledge that any letter may be opened makes one very cautious for fear that a chance word would have repercussions on Yenching.

Today Peking has been "celebrating" the fall of Hankow and Canton. Triumphal arches have been put up on some of the main streets, every shop has to fly a flag, and a number of the tramcars were as bedecked with paper flowers as if they were floats in a Florida parade. We passed one procession—a Japanese truck with a movie camera taking pictures of the proceedings, then a military band, then a large open military car, covered with red streamers and carrying four Japanese officers who were bowing and smiling. It was on one of the most crowded streets so there were throngs of people who had stopped to gape at the brass band. I very much suspect that the whole thing was entirely for the benefit of the movie camera, for it is in marked contrast to the way high military officials usually make their way through the streets of Peking.

Ordinarily whenever a general goes from one headquarters to another, martial law is declared and the streets along which his car is to go are completely cleared of traffic. No one is allowed on the sidewalks and not even pedestrians or dogs are allowed to cross the street. If you have urgent business on the other side of the street it is just too bad; there is nothing to do but wait, sometimes for twenty minutes, sometimes for a couple of hours. One day I stood in the mouth of a *hutung* waiting for nearly an hour to go across Hatamen Street. The Chinese gendarme at the corner was very friendly, but the Japanese sentry who was policing the block would come by periodically and cram us further back into the *hutung*. When he had gone, the gendarme came up again and said confidentially, "*Tamen chen shih haipa*—They really are terribly frightened." Either that or it's a form of megalomania—all the business of the city must stop so that one general can roll up the street in his Buick to call on another general.

We have very little idea what is going on outside of this area. Of course everyone had been expecting the fall of Hankow, but hoping it might hold out a little longer. The collapse at Canton was a complete surprise, and the Chinese have been stunned by it.

232

There hasn't been such gloom since the fall of Nanking. One hopes that Canton and Hankow are not going through the same horrors that Nanking suffered last December. But if they are it will be months before we hear about it. The only paper that is available in Peking is so completely a Japanese organ that it is worthless. I subscribed to the *Peking and Tientsin Times* when I came but the same week that I sent in my subscription the Japanese banned it from the mails because of an editorial on their activities, and it looks as if the ban would never be raised. Any printed matter you can send will be welcome. Even if it doesn't all get through, some of it may arrive, and if a sufficient amount of harmless stuff is sent too, I don't believe the censor will mark me down as a suspicious character.

Peking has changed during the last year almost more than one would have believed possible. The streets are so full of dashing military trucks that whenever I venture to cross them I feel like one of the Caldecott illustrations of "John Gilpin's Ride." It is impossible to tell how many Japanese have moved in, but on the main shopping streets almost every fourth person one sees is Japanese and about every second shop has a cheap new Japanese front. Both the smells and the sounds are beginning to remind one of Tokyo.

Prices have gone sky high, partly because of the dropping (or does one call it rising) exchange rate, partly because of the worthless "Federal Reserve" currency which we are forced to use, partly because of the scarcity of goods. Coal, for instance, is already double what it cost last winter, and it is not at all sure that there will be enough to last Peking through the winter. Among many reasons for its scarcity is the fact that the Mentoukou coal mines are near one of the favorite haunts of the guerillas and in the mopping up operations the Japanese have effectively mopped up many of the mining villages.

Another shortage which is very serious for the poor people is the lack of *kaoliang*, which is usually one of the chief crops in this

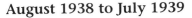

region. The grain is the chief standby in the farmers' diet, and the stalks are used for everything from fuel to making fences. There is no *kaoliang* this year for two reasons: first, the Japanese forbade growing it because when it is high it makes too good a shelter for the guerrillas; second, the Japanese ordered cotton to be grown instead. Cotton is very useful for making munitions and for keeping Japanese cotton mills going, but it is singularly un-nutritious for the local population.

The high cost of living is one of the most frequent topics of conversation, but one's Chinese friends are silent about most of the other annoyances of our new way of life. Some things can be borne but they cannot be talked about. The constant necessity for submitting to be searched is terribly galling. At the railway stations and at the city gates all baggage is turned inside out and everyone is frisked. Every time we go in or out of town, the Yenching bus has to stop at the Hsichihmen and all the Chinese must get out and be felt all over. We foreigners sit still but we usually show more outward signs of rage than the students do.

One night about six weeks ago several of us were going in to town in the evening just before the gates were shut. It was the night before the anniversary of the Mukden incident, and the army was taking special precautions. They stopped our car and made us get out. Theoretically they have no right to stop foreigners, but partly from surprise and partly from natural docility we obeyed. One burly Japanese guard made quite sure Harold had no firearms concealed on his person, but when he laid a heavy hand on Augusta's bosom, she said, "Don't you dare touch me" in such an unmistakable blaze of fury that he allowed us all to go on without further molestation.

Life goes on very quietly and in most ways normally. I think we all have many questions about the future, but for the present it is possible to be useful, so we all stick to our work, and with over 900 students on the campus it is not hard to find something that needs to be done every minute. For the last three days there has been audible gunfire, and there have been columns of troops on the roads. There is never any explanation in the newspapers. It is probably just that the mopping up has come a little nearer to the city than usual.

Within the past six months three of our men students have been arrested. One was treated very well and was released within ten days. His case was apparently merely an excuse to extort a large sum from his wealthy family. The second was kept for a month and treated very badly. His case was just a "mistake"—a former schoolmate had given his name to the police out of spite. The third boy has been in jail for about five weeks now, and no one can get any news of why he is held or how he is faring.

One thing I am growing more sure of every day is that no nation is fit to rule any other nation. The mere fact of being a ruling foreigner in someone else's land is demoralizing to the best character. And the bitterness with which we accept even the most benevolent actions of the Japanese makes me feel that the quicker Britain gets out of India the better. I trust the connection is clear!

There is no need to mark this CONFIDENTIAL for I am sure you all realize the caution which has to surround the use of such home truths as these—no extracts to be printed in the *Lakeville Journal* or elsewhere!

Jackie and Charlie

November 13, 1938

I haven't written you about Jackie and Charles for a long time. You could hardly call Charles lighthearted these days. He is beginning to realize how terribly ill he has been and that it is going to be a long, long pull before he can hope for complete recovery. He is a much soberer boy than he used to be, but he has not lost all hope and his friends and relatives hope he will be himself again before too long. Although Jackie is right here I have not seen a great deal of him. It is odd that he cannot learn even simple lessons easily. He is one of the few people in the world that could profit from association with Dale Carnegie.

At about the same time Augusta Wagner was able to send a less reticent letter to the Speers. It was carried by a young Swiss French teacher from Yenching, who agreed to mail letters in Hong Kong. "It is a sad China we have come back to. I was furious the other day when my language teacher told me that not far from us the Japanese had ordered a great wide road built right through the burial grounds belonging to him and some of our neighbors. With tears in his eyes he said, 'My father and mother and my children were buried there. They will not even let the dead alone!'

"When I was hot with anger at their callousness—for they could hardly offer a greater insult to a Chinese than to disturb the grave of his ancestors, he said to me, 'Oh there is nothing we can do, we are already a subject people!' And the road is of little use to the Chinese, though pictures of it will be taken and exhibited of what great improvements Japan is bringing to China. The road is an exceedingly wide motor road on which Chinese carts and mules and wheelbarrows may not travel. They travel on a road which already exists and serves this purpose. The new road serves the big military motor trucks. And for its labor they conscripted one person from each family in all the surrounding districts.

"It all looks so hopeless for the Chinese. They cannot possibly win a military victory. Their only hope lies in guerrilla warfare, but all that does is to keep the Japanese harassed, which of course is something, but at a most terrible cost. The guerrillas must live off the people, and they must keep things disturbed if they are to be effective; but keeping things disturbed for the Japanese means keeping things disturbed for the Chinese people too. If Japanese controlled trains are delayed and tracks torn up, Japanese military leaders and Japanese tradesmen may have diffi-

culty, but so will the Chinese merchant farmers who cannot transport their produce. Also, the line between guerrilla warfare and straight out and out banditry is a slight one in many cases.

"The organized guerrillas under the Eighth Route Army are a fine band of courageous, well-disciplined men who attempt to put down banditry and assist the country people (they have helped in the harvesting of the crops) as well as to carry on their campaign against the Japanese. They are making heroic sacrifices and living like Spartans. But there are many others who are out only to plunder."[6]

The Eighth Route Army was the Communist army, based in Yenan in northern China. The army was theoretically under Nationalist command, but the Nationalists were now based in Chungking.[7]

Augusta Wagner deplored Japanese military domination, destroying "the productive wealth" of China, and she grieved for the young Chinese intellectuals at Yenching. "We had a half dozen of the young Chinese assistant instructors in to lunch today. Such fine young men and women, and what a tragedy that they should be paying for the sins of their fathers, for China is not without guilt in all this. We were talking of the unbelievably inhuman treatment being meted out to the Jews in Germany and Austria. Who can but cringe with shame at every new manifestation of their heinous cruelty." And she feared the same for the Chinese.

"We go about the day's work holding tight to the faith that it is from places like Yenching all over the world that salvation will come, that love and truth and mercy and reason will some day rule the affairs of men."[8] In more guarded terms, MBS wrote to "Dear Friends of Yenching College for Women":

November 20, 1938

Many of our friends in America may think it incredible that an educational institution should be able to continue normally in China at the present time. To us also it is scarcely credible, yet it is true, and it is a challenge to all our powers. Yenching has been fortunate both in circumstances and in the courageous and wise leadership of President Stuart.

An interesting contrast between our seniors and freshmen throws light on changed conditions. When our present senior class entered college, it included many students from every province in China, and 30 percent of the class had been prepared by schools in the central and southern provinces. Our present freshman class is drawn almost entirely from North China, only two percent coming from schools outside the northern area. The explanation for our large numbers lies in the fact that only one other college for women is open in the northern provinces this year.

There are many problems to be faced, but we are grateful for being able to keep our doors open. In the midst of suffering and tragedy in this nation and in the world we believe that one of the great hopes for international harmony lies in the continuance of Christian institutions like this.

This was a birthday letter (although she did not say so). MBS wrote more personally to her family on that day.

November 20, 1938

Thirty-eight is not a particularly significant age, but I have had a very pleasant birthday. The Shadicks and the Sailers and Bi came to dinner last evening to celebrate. Festive meals take on a new interest these days, for butter and good meat and foreign groceries are too expensive to be used every day except with the greatest economy, but they are not yet entirely prohibitive, so we have generous portions on state occasions and therefore enjoy parties much more than we used to. Augusta is wondering what to do for Thanksgiving. We are expecting sixteen for dinner, but the cook has scoured the grocery and butcher shops of Peking and cannot find a single turkey. There is a bare chance of getting a bustard.

It has been a warm and pleasant autumn but the landscape is beginning to have a wintry look. There are still green leaves on the willows but the other trees are nearly bare. The garden is bright with dashing Shansi jays, birds a little bigger than blue jays with black heads, white breasts, grey backs, and gay blue tails. They eat the berries on the Virginia creeper that covers all our walls.

November 27, 1938

We had a grand Thanksgiving dinner party with seventeen at the table. We borrowed from the Shadicks a wonderful dining room table that has seven leaves. With candles and a great pile of fruit and vegetables in the center, it looked very handsome; the apples and persimmons were very gay and the gardener had got for us some yellow ears of corn and some large gourds. When we asked if he could get these strange things for us, he wanted to know if we must buy them or would be content to borrow them. We said borrowing would suit us perfectly. The corn we assumed came from a farmer friend, but when the gardener arrived bearing six large polished gourds, we asked where they came from. We were somewhat taken aback to hear they were the property of the priests in a nearby temple.

Both turkeys and bustards proved to be impossible to get, but we did not suffer for lack of food: tomato soup, scalloped oysters, roast chicken, baked onions, cauliflower, spinach, mashed potatoes, rolls, olives, cranberry sauce, mince pie, pumpkin pie, Sanka and fruit. We had dinner in the evening and afterwards played a game of crime and mystery that was great fun and required no special skills for such a mixed party. I am sure it is good for us to get together and have a good meal and a lot of fun, but it is dreadful to feel how much more warm and comfortable and well-fed we are than all our neighbors.

December 4, 1938

A remarkable Chinese painter [Chiang Chao-ho] had an exhibition out here several weeks ago. His pictures seem to many of us perfectly breath-taking. They are done with a Chinese brush, but not in the traditional Chinese style. Instead of being of mountains and waterfalls and pine trees, they are of beggar children and ricksha coolies and weather-beaten old men. They show the strength and suffering and quiet patience of the Chinese poor as no pictures that I have ever seen.

New Year's Day 1939

The last two weeks have been full but very happy and worthwhile. Christmas Day at breakfast we had seven boys from one of Augusta's classes to eat their fill of oranges, waffles, maple syrup, sausages, and coffee. They are boys who often come to our Wednesday evening Open House. After Church we dashed home to get the table ready for dinner for fifteen. The William Hungs and their three children were here, the Wus with their little boy, Bi, the Shadicks, George Taylor, whose wife was in the hospital with a new baby, and Michael Lindsay, a young Englishman who came out last year, son of the Master of Balliol.

Michael Lindsay was helping Yenching adapt the Oxford tutorial method in honors courses, part of Leighton Stuart's effort to make Yenching, "while becoming Chinese in a more thoroughgoing sense than heretofore—at the same time more widely and avowedly international."[9]

A few callers came in to say Merry Christmas before the dinner guests had gone, and, as the students say, "gradually" it was tea time. We had asked the Sailers and some of the Women's College faculty to come to high tea. When the tea guests left we pitched in to get ready for the onslaught of the evening.

It is now a tradition that most faculty homes are open to students on Christmas night, and practically the whole student body goes calling. They come in groups of from two to thirty; some come for a leisurely visit, some are out to make a record of visiting twenty houses. It's rather a mad scramble part of the time, but on the whole it's a pleasant custom. Altogether 165 came during the evening and had tea and cookies and cakes.

The day after Christmas we had a progressive whist party for 28 of the junior staff members who don't have homes of their own and sometimes get left out of the general jollification. The particular brand of progressive whist that we play is a great invention. It's very simple, it mixes people up and keeps them moving about, and there are certain topsy-turvy rules that keep it from being serious.

The next day we had what was probably the best party of all— the annual meal of *paotze* (steamed bread filled with meat and cabbage) for the servants. That is always a joint affair in which our household combines with the household next door. This year there were fifteen children and ten grown-ups. The Sailers showed some of George Sailer's collection of movies. The "electric shadows" were much appreciated; the children sang songs and said pieces, and then plates of steaming *paotze* disappeared in a twinkling.

One wishes one could provide hot meals for all the children in the neighborhood who are undernourished. Fortunately we have two good porridge kitchens in the village now, and the Yenching Relief Committee is able to take care of the most needy cases, but there is still a lot of desperate poverty round about.

Keeping warm is quite a problem this winter. Coal is so expensive that we all try to get along with as little as possible. We told Pao Ch'ing when we lighted the furnace in November that he needn't keep the temperature above 65 and that we would wear padded Chinese jackets when the sun stops shining in the southern windows in the afternoon. But no matter how he stoked the furnace the thermometer wavered between 52 and 59, and even with padded jackets that seems a little chilly. Finally it dawned on us that the coal for which we had paid so well was about half rock, and after berating the coal dealer on the iniquity of treating old customers so badly we have managed to get a ton that will really burn.

January 24, 1939[10]

You are certainly angelic to send so many magazines. First we read them, then they get pawed over by everyone who comes to the house, particularly by the students who come on Wednesday evenings, and finally I take them over to what the students call "Sister Hall," where they soon fall to bits under the hands of "boy friends" waiting for their "girl friends."

I am beginning to meditate on the possibility of taking a trip to the Southwest during the summer. The chief drawback is that it takes a month to get there and a month to get back, and I don't know whether I can get away for such a long stretch, since Myfanwy Wood is going home in June and Ruth Stahl is not coming back till September. But six months here make one feel as if one were in cold storage, and it seems vital to go and see what people are doing and thinking in what is left of China proper. However, the whole world may be changed by June, so we'll wait and see.

January 24, 1939

Last weekend Augusta and I went to Peking for two days to stay with Gertrude Hodgman, the Dean of the PUMC School of Nursing. It was very pleasant to get quite away from Yenching for a while, to eat different food and see different people and read different books and talk about different problems. Since it is not practical to go on any more distant journeyings, a jaunt to Peking does very well.

January 29, 1939

We have been having most heavenly weather for the last two weeks with bright sunshine and a temperature of 40 in the middle of the day, dropping to about 20 at night. One is thankful for mild weather for all the people in the villages round about.

The vacation is nearly over, and the students will be coming back this week. It is not exactly a holiday for the faculty but at

least it is a change of tempo. There have been all sorts of committees this week. We don't seem able to go through a day without
committees, but I wish the democratic process could function without wasting so much time.

I have used my Christmas presents to buy a Chinese painting
that is very satisfying to the eye and to the spirit—brown peaks
and misty valleys, a curving pine tree and a waterfall, and two scholars on donkeys crossing a bridge.

February 5, 1939

Classes for the second semester start tomorrow, and we have
just had three busy days of registration. There is usually a drop in
the enrollment the second semester, and we expected a bigger one
than usual because, after last year's upsets, there were a number of
students who finished their course in the middle of the year. I
think the men's dormitories will have some empty space, but our
four women's buildings are going to be just as full this term as they
were last, a phenomenon we have never known before.

It is quite a long time since I have told you how Johnny and
Charlie are getting along. Johnny keeps telling all his friends that
he is making good progress in his work, but it is hard to see any
signs though it is quite obvious that he has made up his mind to
stay right here no matter what happens. He doesn't seem to be
getting along with people any better than he ever did. Charlie
meets all misfortunes without ever losing his courage or his assurance that things are going to work out all right in the end. They
are both having rather a hard time financially, and their acquain-
tances spend a good deal of time arguing about which one is really
worse off. Augusta thinks Johnny's finances are a good deal sounder
than Charlie's but lots of people don't agree with her.

Although there is plenty of excitement in other parts of China,
for us here life goes on very uneventfully. Only the nearest fringes
of the Western Hills are tempting for expeditions, trips to town are

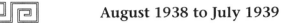

more of a nuisance than they used to be, there are very few round the world travelers to be entertained, and unless one is in a group of very familiar friends, conversation keeps to uncontroversial topics. But one feels worried and uneasy just because one is so comfortable and settled. Since I started this letter, a long account has come of air raids in Kweilin, where Central China University is, and one of our graduates has been here with a hair-raising tale of her travels with a sick baby during typhoons and cholera epidemics in 1937 and of iniquitous pressure that has been brought on her family since then.

February 12, 1939

Next Sunday is Chinese New Year, and people in the villages are getting ready for the holiday. Yesterday was the time when the old kitchen gods are taken down and burned after their lips have been well smeared with honey to ensure their taking only good reports of the household behavior. We walked through the village streets this afternoon to see the stalls where the new kitchen gods are for sale and the temple fair where there are kites and rattles and sweetmeats and other tempting things for small holiday makers.

February 19, 1939

Today is New Year's Day according to the lunar calendar and everyone is celebrating. No matter what governments say, and no matter how much modern and "enlightened" people argue for the solar calendar, this holiday is rooted in everyone's heart. All week the stalls along the village street have been gay with red candles and artificial flowers and red scrolls and strips of paper bearing legends about peace and prosperity and happiness for the new year. Today these fresh strips of paper are pasted on every respectable doorway, every wall, and even every wheelbarrow and coal-cart.

February 26, 1939

It is still cold but there is a breath of spring in the air, and the roots of grass in sheltered places are beginning to show a clear green. It makes one wander around the garden planning where to plant the peas and pondering on what else to try in that shady corner where nothing will grow.

Johnny, by the way, is getting more and more difficult to deal with. So far I haven't had any trouble with him, but a number of other people have had collisions with him that have been rather unpleasant. He just gets crankier and crankier and insists on his own way in a completely unreasonable and most exasperating manner.

March 5, 1939

On Friday night we had a party for all the foreign students. Usually we get to know them pretty well, but this year we have seen very little of them, so we thought it was time to do something for them. There are two girls and ten boys, half of them American, the rest German and Russian. We invited some of the Chinese boys and girls who speak English easily and had four others out from town. Augusta provided an ample buffet supper, and we played progressive whist, the ideal entertainment for that sort of a party.

Dr. Jenkins, our Women's College doctor, goes home this year on leave, and I am beginning to grow desperate about finding someone to take her place. We have asked almost every organization in China but haven't yet succeeded in getting any sort of substitute. Now we are looking into the possibility of finding a doctor among the Jewish refugees who are flooding into Shanghai. Mrs. Frame tells me there were nine hundred Austrian refugees on the boat she came on from India. (She got back this week after travelling around India.) They had been allowed to take some money with them but there was some sort of agreement between the Nazis and the Italian steamship line that they were to spend it all on board and were not to be allowed to take a single penny with them when they landed in Shanghai!

March 12, 1939

Mrs. Frame was here for a night this week, speaking to the Women's College faculty abut her impressions of India, particularly of the women's colleges she visited there. She was in good form, seeming very well and gay and feeling that the Madras Conference had been really successful.

Our chief subject for conversation and speculation is the new currency regulations. The authorities are trying to peg the exchange rate for the so-called Federal Reserve Bank notes which we now use in this part of the world.

Chinese national currency and F.R.B. notes and yen are all exchangeable at practically par. But F.R.B. notes are not accepted for foreign exchange at all, Chinese national currency fluctuates at about six to the US dollar, and the yen exchanges for 50 cents to the US dollar. It now appears that things equal to each other are no longer equal to the same thing. New regulations to restore the tottering theorems of geometry were inaugurated this week. So far their chief effect has been to send prices sky high. When one's salary is paid in gold one feels shamefully opulent, but in lots of businesses the uncertainty is disastrous, and for the very poor the high prices of food simply mean that they have to go hungry.

Bearing the Unbearable

When MBS or Augusta Wagner could dispatch letters that were carried by friends or diplomatic couriers to be mailed outside China, they could report more rigorously on the reality of life under Japanese occupation.

March 14, 1939

There is a chance to get a letter off tomorrow in the Embassy mail pouch, which means that I can say a few of the things that ordinarily have to be left out of my regular letters. Dr. Stacy Roberts, President of the Theological Seminary at Pyengyang, was here at Dr. Stuart's for tea and told us of some of the things they have recently been through in Korea. Things are pleasant and idyllic here compared to the constant coercion and espionage and complete lack of freedom there. But we haven't yet got used to bearing the unbearable and there is plenty here that is maddening to us and almost intolerable to the Chinese.

It sounds trivial enough to say that the passengers on our busses are searched every time they go through the city gates. Sometimes it is only a perfunctory search, sometimes every bag is opened and every pocket is turned inside out. Sometimes the girls have to get off the bus outside the gate and walk through, and this is most likely to happen on rainy days when the mud is thick. Sometimes the Chinese policewomen are replaced by Japanese soldiers who paw over the girls with a few extra pokes and nudges for good measure. One boy had an old post office savings book in his pocket; unfortunately, it bore the Kuomintang seal, and he was taken to the police station and questioned for several hours.

One of the saddest cases and one that has come close to us all is that of one of our senior boys who was arrested last fall and released a few weeks ago completely broken in mind and body. There is not the slightest evidence that he was guilty of anything. Fortunately no girls have been arrested and the few boys that have been taken into custody during the year have all been released.

The campus is conspicuous at present because it is the only area around here not flying a five-barred flag. As a matter of fact, the five-barred flag is a much nicer looking flag than the Kuomintang red, white, and blue, but we don't much care for what it stands for. Every house and shop is compelled to fly one, but the outer gaiety of the waving flags is not matched by any gaiety within.[11]

Last week the police, accompanied by Japanese soldiers searched all the houses in Haitien, just outside our gates. There was a cordon across the town, and for three hours no one was allowed to pass. There were various unofficial explanations—that they were looking for arms, for national bank notes, for ammunition stolen from nearby barracks by guerrillas, but the official explanation was that they were examining the houses for bedbugs! Pao Ch'ing told me that one of the people held up on the street near his house was a bride in her wedding chair. She could not go back, the police would not let her go on, superstition forbids the bearers to put down a bride's chair while she is in it, so there she sat for three hours cooped up inside her airless curtains. You can imagine her misery and the bearers' fatigue.

I don't know whether the papers at home had the story of Dr. Ting's arrest in Tientsin about a month ago. She is an outstanding woman physician, a former member of our Women's College Administrative Committee. She was arrested and held for fifteen days in a room with ten women prisoners. She was questioned for hours on end. Apparently the only charge against her was that the censors didn't like the messages she had written on her Christmas cards to friends in America. She had made such reprehensible statements as these: "The Chinese are like good steel; you can bend them but you cannot break them" and "We must either destroy war or war will destroy us." She refused to modify these terrible opinions but amplified them instead and finally they let her go.

The guerrillas are not very active near the city, but of course railroads are their chief objective and every now and then they tear up a bit of track. My old Chinese teacher tells me that the village where he lives is divided into groups or blocks and each group must send three able-bodied men each night to guard the railroad from dusk to daylight. They are not supplied with lanterns or even with sticks (certainly not with arms) but the Japanese hold them responsible if a foot of the line is tampered with.

One gets varying reports of the success of the guerrillas in southern Hopei and Shansi. This kind of warfare is fearfully hard on the innocent country people but continued Japanese domination is going to be worse.

Here on the campus we are well and comfortable and as happy as anyone can be in this sort of a world. The real test of whether or not it is right for us to go on here will come after a year or two when we see what our graduates are able to do. I've been having interviews with all our senior girls these past two weeks about their plans after graduation. The best ones want to go either to the Southwest or the Northwest and are prepared to do anything however hard. A few feel that for their families' sakes they must stay here. For many the cause of Christianity and Chinese nationalism are identical, a dangerous position!

MBS was concerned about the future of the women graduating from Yenching, but she was also seeking new students, interviewing them with care for their ability to cope with the challenge of Yenching. Traveling was taxing but necessary.

March 22, 1939

On Friday Augusta and Dr. Jenkins and I are going down to Tientsin for the weekend. I have to see the senior girls in one of our preparatory schools and find out from their teachers more about them than we can learn from entrance examinations. Our spring vacation comes the third week in April when the weather, which is still wavering, ought to have made up its mind that spring must eventually come. We are wondering whether to try the new railroad to Jehol. There are lovely old palaces there, but there is no use trying to go unless the present inhabitants feel welcoming toward visitors.

March 28, 1939

We spent the weekend in Tientsin, and though it is always pleasant to have a change, getting back to Yenching from Tientsin grime and sordidness was like stepping from the Times Square subway station into the light and air of Lakeville. I don't know whether or not Tientsin is a sink of iniquity but it certainly is grim and grimy, a center of rumors, fears, and suspicions, and is full of long blocks of the ugliest houses that the mind of man ever devised.

We stayed with friends at the Methodist Mission, which is in the Chinese city on flat reclaimed land (all of Tientsin is flat), and the dust from filthy streets and heaps of refuse blows back and forth across the compound all day long. The Mission compound itself is hideous, no one has made an attempt at a garden and the buildings are cheaply built and with no taste whatsoever. Yet one prefers even that barrenness to the comparative cleanliness and comforts of the Concessions, for at the Mission one is solidly in touch with reality, while the Concessions are artificial products of Western—well, all its imperialism. The Methodist girls' school, for all its shabbiness, is practically the best girls' school in China, and the dean of the magnificent new municipal school for Chinese children in the British Concession, said that if he had a daughter he would send her to the Methodist school instead of to his own.

I visited schools, and Augusta did a little shopping. We both had dinner with Dr. Ting, the wonderful little woman doctor about whom I've written before. Two weeks in jail did nothing to lessen either her courage or her good spirits.

But traveling anywhere in this country these days is hardly a pleasure. We went down third class quite comfortably, but coming back even with second-class tickets was like four hours in the New York Shuttle during the rush hour. First an hour in the Tientsin railroad station (you have to allow plenty of time wherever you go in Tientsin because you may be held up interminably by guards who may stop and search everyone at the barriers surrounding the

Concessions) and then three hours on the train where we stood wedged in the corridor until we finally managed each to sit on a suitcase. Yenching looked like heaven when we got back.

Unable to write about the increasingly threatening events outside Yenching, MBS turned to spring bloom and Easter services, and her spring vacation in Peitaiho.

Easter Day (April 8) 1939

The late afternoon is growing chilly and it looks as though we would have a dust storm before tomorrow, but it has been a lovely day and the weather since Friday has been heavenly. The North China spring is all too short, but these three days have been perfect. March was unusually cold this year and the flowering peaches were slow to blossom. Now they have suddenly burst open all at once, the flowering peaches and cherries, the forsythia and redbud. The ground is blue with violets and the lilacs will be out in a day or two.

Morning chapel and the special Holy Week services after supper have been crowded. On Thursday there was a Communion Service in Chinese and on Friday night a service in English largely of music. This morning we had the service out of doors in a green hollow in the hills beside our lake. Everyone was there—students, faculty, children, alumni, workmen and their families, and many onlookers from the village who did not join the worshippers but sauntered quietly around the edges, staring. After the service there was a picnic luncheon for everyone, but we didn't stay for that since it has become an institution for us to have Easter dinner in Russian fashion with the Shadicks.

April 19, 1939 Lotus Hill, Peitaiho

I'm sitting in the sun on a terrace near the top of a pine-covered hill. A mile to the south and three miles to the east is the sea.

Off to the northeast is the slope of the hills where the great wall comes down to meet the sea at Shanhaikuan. At the foot of our hill between us and the mountains and the sea lies the brown North China plain. In a few months it will be green, but now it is all a tawny yellow, darker here and there where it has been freshly plowed.

We had been wondering what to do during this spring holiday week. At first we thought of trying the new railroad to Jehol, but when an epidemic of scarlet fever broke out there the railroad stopped selling tickets. Our neighbors, the Wiants, suggested we come down (up!) here to their hillside cottage with them.

This is the loveliest part of Peitaiho. (Most of it is flattish barren shores with houses packed close together.) In the summer the whole beach is thickly populated, but now the whole sweep of sea and sky and hills seems to belong to us alone. We take our luncheon down to the seashore and lie in the warm sun, watching the sea gulls, and are undisturbed by the occasional quiet passing of a Japanese soldier.

Returning from a serene spring vacation, MBS found Yenching dusty and grim. Inflation and the costs of living were wildly unpredictable. Staffing was a problem as older faculty left the Women's College on furlough or forever. MBS and Augusta Wagner would soon be among the last of the old timers. The College's new doctor was an Austrian refugee, one of thousands of Jews who had fled Hitler's Germany.

April 30, 1939

Here it is April rather than March that goes out like a lion. The wind is howling this evening and the dust is seeping in through all the windows and doors. On the floor there are little heaps of dust like anthills along some of the cracks where the draft has blown up from below. The wistaria has been at its loveliest today, but I fear it will be blown to bits by tomorrow morning and the poor little

seedlings in the seedbed will be parched and bruised.

Now that spring vacation is over we feel that we are on the last lap of the year. Dr. Stuart has gone down south to a meeting of the China Foundation or something of the sort, but things have gone on uneventfully in his absence.

Our chief excitement these days is speculating about (not with) the present currency. Augusta understands its intricacies better than I do, but anyone can see that like Dickens' famous character it is "highly volatile." All the consequences of inflation are demonstrated under our noses. Those of us who are paid in gold are well off, but soaring prices and the uncertainty of what anything will be worth in terms of money next week or next month make life pretty grim for families with small fixed incomes. As for people who were living on the margin before, well, what does happen to such people when the cost of food increases more than 100 percent in six months? We are trying to do something for the university workmen, and sooner or later something will have to be done about faculty salaries.

May 7, 1939

This is the time of year that always surprises one by being much busier than one had expected. It suddenly becomes imperative to take desperate measures to fill the staff vacancies for next year that one has been vainly trying for months to fill (I think now we are going to get a Viennese refugee for our Women's College doctor. There are 10,000 German and Austrian refugees in Shanghai). The Scholarship Committee meets day after day trying to decide which candidates really need help. The Admissions Committee meets and there are visits to be paid to our accredited middle schools. Mission Meeting suddenly looms ahead, in Peking this year fortunately, so that no time need be spent on the journey. And invitations begin to come in and go out for farewell parties for the faculty leaving on furlough. This year about half of our senior members of the Women's College faculty are going away, so we are going to have to double up a lot of responsibilities for next year. I hope we are going to have some good new young Chinese. Agnes Chen is coming and two or three others about her age.

May 21, 1939

For our Women's College doctor we are making arrangements to get an Austrian refugee who is now in Shanghai. There is a young Austrian woman here now helping in the *kungch'ang* (Yenching Craftwork) who left Vienna in December and who is starting on her new life here without a word of complaint. She came to dinner with us a few nights ago, and though we didn't discuss conditions in Europe, she told us about the weeks she spent in Shanghai in the refugee camp there. There are more than 10,000 Jewish refugees there. Most of the newcomers are housed in big barrack-like buildings. She told us that for the first month she slept in a room with eight other women and that there were 350 of them who had to use one toilet and one washstand. And she is one of the lucky ones.

MBS enclosed with this letter the annual report she wrote for the Presbyterian Mission. She wrote that "Yenching's life seems almost a charmed life, but the more peaceful and free from unwelcome political interruptions it is, the more danger there is of unreality, of self-deception, and of missed opportunities. So it is with a mixture of thankfulness and misgiving that I say that the last eight months have been spent in the usual quiet routine of office work and teaching."

She described the daily activities, growing Christian life among the students, and interviews with the women who would graduate in June. Many of the original class were unable to return to college "and have finished their course elsewhere or have found opportunities for patriotic service in the interior." Some of those who remained were more mature, some still self-centered, others who gained much from Yenching but not as much as the best, "who are ready to go out to obscure places and to meet any sort of unpleasantness, not with perfect self-confidence, but with a sustaining and living sense of God's guidance and direction...They will make some mistakes and they will not become leaders overnight but they are the stuff that China needs and Yenching will be proud of them and God will use them."[12]

May 29, 1939

Our chief preoccupation this week has been the sufferings of the Austrian refugees, and our sympathies have been broadened by a sharing of their troubles. Most of us don't have the faintest conception of how rare and precious our heritage of freedom is. For several weeks we have been negotiating for a doctor to come to take the place of Dr. Jenkins, who is going on furlough. Through correspondence with our China Council office we secured Dr. Singer, a woman about fifty, who had her mother with her. We asked her to come up early to get acquainted with the situation while Dr. Jenkins is still here and also to get a start in studying Chinese. They arrived on Wednesday, and I have been able to think of little else since.

Dr. Singer is a little birdlike person with an intelligent, tragic face. Her mother is about seventy and for the last three or four years has been totally blind. Their English is halting but adequate. The first day almost all that Mrs. Singer said was, "Oh, I am so glad that I am here," and Dr. Singer's eyes filled with tears whenever anyone spoke to her. She kept saying "What a beautiful place! How quiet! How clean! I cannot believe I shall not wake up soon in Shanghai or Vienna." There is never a word of bitterness against the people who have driven them from home. "This madness must sometime pass," she says, and again and again she says that America and England must not go to war in Europe, for she lived through four years of war, watching her children starving, and she knows it creates more suffering than it can cure. We can give them security

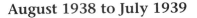

for a year and friendliness and affection, but what about the millions of others who have found no friendly Yenching garden?

And one night this week we had another visitor, a gentle girl in a dark kimono and gay obi. She was with her father, who is a distinguished scholar, and she herself is a scholar and writer. We asked about the rest of the family. She is separated from her husband—no need to ask the reason why—but is not divorced because the divorce courts of her country seldom give the mother custody of her children. Her brother, who is also a scholar, is now in Central China "on military service." After breakfast when she had left, the servants asked eagerly about her and the boy said, "Then the people of her country are not all bad people."

June 30, 1939

Now the last of the people going on furlough and all the students who do not have to stay for summer school have left, so at last we are through with farewell parties. No, not quite, for Bi goes on Sunday, but he is really the last.

Lots of interesting things have happened since I last wrote a real letter but some of them so long ago now that it hardly seems possible to write about them—people coming back from the western provinces and describing narrow escapes in the Chungking air raids, people going off on adventurous trips to the Southwest, Senior Banquet, Baccalaureate, and Commencement, luncheons, the wedding of two of our seniors combining the most astonishing features of new and old—a brass band and the Mendelssohn wedding march, a white dress and veil and red neon lights behind a temple altar! We've had struggles with painters over repairs in the dormitories and with the printer over Augusta's book, not to mention excitement over the "situation" in Tientsin and everyone's interest in the peculiar behavior of our currency.

Vacation plans are still uncertain, but I'm beginning to think we'll stay right here. Augusta gave up her idea of going to Kunming when the exchange rate went sky high and is busy here with proof-reading. We have thought of going to Japan for a hasty trip, chiefly to see the lay of the land, but now I do not see how I can get away for there are simply no old-timers here who can take over my job while I'm away.

July 17, 1939

I haven't looked at the thermometer today but I should think the mercury and the humidity must both be about 97. Until last week we were having very cool nights, but now according to the infallible Chinese calendar we are in the "Little Heat" so we can expect to steam for the next two weeks.

Augusta and I have just come back from a weekend in the lap of luxury at the American Embassy. Mrs. Johnson and the children came back to Peking about a month ago, but the Ambassador is in Chungking and she is rather lonely, I think, in that big house. She is a charming friendly person and the children are energetic little sprites. There were guests for several meals and it was a pleasant change to meet new people, but on the whole the caliber of the foreign service of our government is not very impressive, at least on casual acquaintance.

Myfanwy Wood came back this week from a visit to a London Mission Station down on the Hopei plain with interesting and heartbreaking tales of the life of the country people now. Crops have not been good, and no one can think of anything but the daily struggle to get enough to eat. We saw Myfanwy off on the six o'clock train yesterday morning, the last of the furlough travelers to depart.

Next year we are to have a Japanese professor on our faculty, an elderly scholar, who is a Catholic and who is noted for his research in Chinese archaeology. He and his family were not expected to arrive on the campus till fall, but his daughter arrived unexpect-edly last week to get the house ready for him. Unfortunately the house is still occupied by last year's inhabitants. There are a number of complications which your imaginations can supply.

Yenching had been under pressure from the Japanese to allow the occupation government to appoint three professors to the faculty, but Leighton Stuart stood fast and declared that Yenching would make its own appointments. He received funding from the Harvard-Yenching Institute to support a Japanese archaeologist, and, after a search, offered the position to Professor Ryuzo Torii, an older and experienced man who had done research in China and whose work was known to the Yenching faculty. He became a member of the faculty in the fall of 1939, a quiet, dedicated scholar, "absorbed in Chinese archaeology and not politically involved in Japanese war policies."[13]

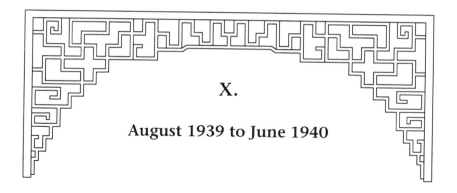

X.

August 1939 to June 1940

Oasis of Freedom

Multitudes of young Chinese men and women sought the education Yenching was still courageously offering inside occupied China, but only about one-tenth of those who applied could be accepted. Finances were uncertain, the weather cold, and hunger widespread outside the University. Yenching offered what relief they could to Chinese villages nearby, but the Japanese were making themselves increasingly present even on the campus. Americans at Yenching wondered what stand the United States might take and when.

August 21, 1939

About thirteen hundred candidates took our July entrance exams, but we are only able to accept about one hundred and fifty. As long as you deal just with the records, it is fairly simple to admit one applicant and exclude another, but when one of the rejected girls sits in your office and tells how her family have worked and schemed to make it possible for her to come to college and how there is no other place within a thousand miles to which she can possibly go and you see what an excellent student and fine girl she is, then you wish our dormitories were made of elastic instead of brick and plaster.

Johnny Smith has been manifesting a somewhat inconvenient interest in our students lately. He insists on making the acquaintance of boys and girls who are not in the least interested in him and who are totally unable to answer the questions that he puts to them by the hour. Of course he only succeeds in making himself more unpopular.

"Johnny" was always with the Yenching community, but they also had the threatening war in Europe constantly on their minds, "wondering how soon the word would come that the mobilized nations were actually at each other's throats." With imagined bombings in mind, MBS and Augusta Wagner viewed the explosion of their kitchen stove as "a minor demonstration of what a little devastation can be like." The Chinese stove, made of bricks and mud with an iron oven at one side and a watercoil around the fire box to heat hot water for baths, blew up, smashing the ceiling and windows, making MBS realize the damage a small bomb could do.

September 24, 1939

The next mail ought to bring word of what the war is meaning in Bristol and Connecticut. The radio news is very meager and it is hard to picture what changes in daily life may suddenly have come in familiar places. Here we are all guessing about Russia's next move, for that will probably affect us more than anything else.

So far, the chief things we notice are the fluctuations of exchange and the prices and shortage of many necessary things. Tin is almost impossible to find. In our kitchen explosion a few weeks ago among the things that were smashed was the large tin hood that hangs over the stove to carry off the soot and coal gas. The rest of the kitchen has been repaired, but the tinsmith cannot find us anything to make a new hood of. Fortunately we have an Arcola, but most middle-class Chinese keep warm in winter with stoves.

We have stopped using butter at eight dollars a pound, and

other foreign foodstuffs are practically unobtainable. The flood in Tientsin spoiled a lot of the stocks that were kept there, and most of the provision shops don't find it worthwhile to order any more supplies when exchange is so uncertain and the difficulties of transportation so great.

We are very fortunate to have our winter supply of coal already safely laid in, though when fourteen tons all arrived at once and unannounced at lunch time on Thursday, I felt a little taken aback. I had ordered it in July, but since our cellar is likely to be flooded in the summer and does not hold more than six tons in any case, I had asked the company to deliver half in September and half in the middle of the winter. But suddenly without warning nine mule carts arrived at the door, and the coal-covered drivers insisted on unloading at once. The sacks had to be dumped in the handiest spot, so now the clothes on the line flutter between heaps of coal, and I fear that wind and passersby will diminish the piles long before we light the furnace fire.

Now that the last date for late registration is over, we are all astounded at our final registration figures—978, about forty more than we have ever had before. Of these 289 are girls, fifteen more than we have ever had. Quite a number are living with their families outside the campus, but we have squeezed 276 into the dormitories, although we have always maintained that 270 was the maximum capacity.

MBS was housing a new faculty member in her guest room, and, to add a bit of joy in troubled times, Dinny, the wire-haired terrier, gave birth to five healthy puppies who were using MBS's closet as a canine nursery.

October 22, 1939

Dinny's puppies continue to be a great source of entertainment and delight, though we are feeling quite bereft with only two of them left. The two who are still here we call

"Dinna Ken" and "Dinna Care."

We are living in luxury today, having recklessly started our furnace yesterday. Last year with Spartan heroism we put off starting the fire until ten days after everybody else but the chief result was that the cold made us irritable and the nobility made us unbearably self-righteous, and the coal bill didn't show the slightest benefit. So when the thermometer dropped more than thirty degrees this week, we started the furnace without the slightest qualms. The University doesn't turn on the heat in the classrooms until the first of November, no matter what the weather.

October 28, 1939

This has been a week of endless committee meetings, chiefly working over budgets. The University budgets made out last spring showed huge deficits, but we were not greatly worried because the exchange rate seemed designed to give us more and more money in local currency. Now that the rate is going the other way and prices are steadily rising for almost everything, we are going to have to do something drastic soon.

Last night we had dinner with the Galts, our near neighbors. They first came to China in 1899 and went through the Boxer siege in the Legation. I had never been able to get them to talk of it, but last night among the other guests was Mrs. Stelle of the old Sheffield family at Tungchow, who had also been through the siege, and a Chinese girl, wife of one of our young instructors, whose parents were among the Chinese Christians who were in the Legation. Her grandfather, having refused to leave his farm, was killed by the Boxers. Somehow the company seemed conducive to reminiscences, and we heard story after story of those ghastly weeks.

November 14, 1939

The lovely warm autumn days are over and there is a wintry wind blowing. The house is warm and we have a comfortable supply of coal and of flour, but the people in the villages round about have no fuel and often cannot get even a day's supply of cereals. Three years ago a laborer could keep his family alive on the regular wage of forty cents a day. Now he needs a dollar a day to buy what forty cents used to buy and of course he hasn't got the dollar. Again and again you hear them say, "We poor people will just have to starve." We are able to do a lot of relief work for the people about us here, but we can hardly bear to think of the flooded villages around Tientsin.

MBS's letters were now perforce about the commonplace, since censorship made it unwise to write about current political and military events. But at about this time Doris Cummings, Leighton Stuart's secretary at Yenching, was able to send a letter to the United States in some way that bypassed the censors. Dated November 23, it describes more forthrightly the situation in China than MBS could do in her letters. "China will not make a peace that does not call for the withdrawal of troops and the return of North China to its status before the war. There may be interesting results if America will take a firm stand, in which case American-Japanese relationships may be strained, or worse, with consequent effects on Americans and American property out here. Today's paper and an 'underground' wireless message state that America is fortifying herself in the Far East with more warships and forty submarines in Manila, so it looks like business. What would happen to Yenching and to the Americans here would not be hard to figure out....

"We have a constant flow of Japanese visitors to the University, who seem to cast an appraising eye upon all they see. There have been no annoyances with them from the student or administrative view this term so far—an ominous silence?

"We have a Japanese member of the faculty now, a cultured scholar, with an attractive and well-educated wife and daughter. Dr. Stuart told a story about him and his wife. When they first arrived from Japan a few weeks ago, they were requested by the Japanese to attend an educa-

tional meeting in the city. Dr. Stuart said they were not expected to go, suggesting they might give as an excuse that they had to attend to their luggage. They did not go to the meeting but took a train and rode down to Tientsin and back, not a very comfortable trip either, in order to play the game! So you can see how we live a life of subterfuge and caution."

From Chunking by an underground route, Cummings obtained a summary of a recent speech by Chiang Kai-shek, which she enclosed. Given November 12, 1939, the speech set forth Chiang's unfaltering conviction that "In spite of offensives in military, political, and economic fields, Japan's desperate attempts to conquer China are every day becoming more and more doomed to failure."[1]

MBS's letters continued to be censor-proof reassurances to her family that life went on at Yenching. Visitors were entertained, the dogs were companionable diversions, and Americans heard enough news from the United States to know that a new date had been decreed for Thanksgiving. MBS's Yenching circle of friends celebrated by making fun of missionary life.

November 26, 1939

We celebrated Thanksgiving this week on President Roosevelt's date and had a grand party. Of course it is not a University holiday, but most Americans manage to take the afternoon off. We had dinner for fourteen here. There were no turkeys or bustards on the market, but chicken tasted just as good, and the guests provided their own merriment. We planned to have a "family reunion" and told each person the role he was to have. The rest went off by spontaneous combustion.

Augusta and I were the two maiden aunts. Our nephew had been off to "furrin" parts and brought home a foreign wife. One of our nieces was a widow with two demon children in their teens, the other niece was a missionary to China. She brought back her husband, their own child and four adopted Chinese children. A lace scarf, a shawl, or a hair ribbon were sufficient costumes to make everyone feel in character, and an hilarious time was had by all, with a real air of New England Thanksgiving in spite of the fact that only half the guests were American, the rest Chinese, English, Russian, and German.

Hilarity was a bulwark in the face of increasing Japanese oppression in North China. Augusta Wagner wrote on December 7 (the date itself an unsuspected foreshadowing) to a friend who sent a copy of the letter to the Speer family, a letter which either circumvented the censors or deceived them with subtle diction and irony: "You remember I said I would send you every evidence I could see of how the Japanese occupation was benefiting the Chinese people, of how the widely-publicized Japanese aim of cooperating with the Chinese people to improve their former wretched condition was working out. I have seen the cooperation at work!

"Many of the servants, the janitors, the coolies who work on the grounds, the men who work in the power house, the clerks, and the ricksha coolies who serve the University live in the villages of Haitien and Chengfu just outside the University walls. In recent months they have been feeling the full brunt of Japanese goodwill and love for the people in these parts. The Japanese military want the people to have good roads. The fact that the roads are five to ten miles away from the villages of the people who are impressed into building them or that their mules and wheelbarrows are not allowed on them makes no difference."

The letter describes in detail the suffering of the people conscripted to construct the roads, the destruction of family graves, the cold hungry people. "Such is the much heralded goodwill and cooperation as it works itself out in practice....However is reconciliation to come out of all of this?"[2]

However anguished Augusta Wagner and MBS felt, they kept up their courage by partaking of Yenching gaiety. MBS described their festivities in details which must have puzzled the censors.

December 10, 1939

We have just been making our plans for the various meals of the Christmas weekend. Students and faculty have all agreed to have a meal the week before Christmas such as the refugees around us eat all the time—a bowl of millet with a little pickled turnip.

On Christmas Day itself we shall have students for breakfast and our plans for dinner seem to expand every day; we are expecting now to have the Shadicks, all five Sailers, our Viennese doctor and her mother, Michael Lindsay, Chou Kuo-ping, and Mary and Dr. Ferguson.

On Friday we had a wonderful celebration of the fortieth anniversary of the arrival of Dr. and Mrs. Galt in China. He was for many years the president of the North China Union College, which twenty years ago joined with two other institutions to make Yenching. Since then he has been head of our Department of Education and on many occasions has been Acting President and Acting Bursar and Acting Controller and Acting almost everything else. He has provided the balance to Dr. Stuart's vision and is well beloved by everybody for his absolute fairness and integrity. The whole university turned out to do honor to him and to Mrs. Galt.

First we had a dinner in one of the men's refectories, with such an array of all of us in our best clothes as has never been seen before. After serious speeches there, we adjourned to the small auditorium for some fun. As Dr. and Mrs. Galt had arrived in Tungchou forty years ago with Dr. Galt riding on a donkey and Mrs. Galt in a chair, Stephen Ts'ai had the bright idea of providing the same conveyances for them Friday night. They made the short trip across the campus in great style with the corps of landscape coolies providing a guard of honor beating gongs and drums.

Nancy [Cochran] and Ran [Sailer] had concocted a wonderful skit with scenes of the high spots of the last forty years as recalled by the Galts' friends. The stage properties were managed in the conventional Chinese manner, relying on the imagination of the

266

audience to turn a chair into a tree and from the sight of a whip to supply a horse.

Augusta and Harold [Shadick] impersonated Dr. and Mrs. Galt in wonderful clothes of the turn of the century. Incredible as it now seems, one of the first student strikes in China was against Dr. Galt, so one of the scenes showed marching students with banners bearing such protesting gems as "Dr. Galt's marks are too passingless," "Dr. Galt is too love budget," and ending with a large placard which brought down the house, "Exolude Dr. Galt." "Exolude" is one of our favorite words these days since the Anti-British movement plastered "Exolude the British" all over the walls between here and the city gate.

December 31, 1939

Christmas at Yenching always manages to be very busy and very gay. It has become a tradition for most of the faculty to keep open house to students on Christmas evening. The students rush around the campus in packs seeing how many houses they can visit and getting a lot of fun both from the competition between their groups and from being free to call and eat at lots of different houses.

The next occasion was the annual party for our servants. Three households, whose servants are all related to each other, combine. We have dumplings and candy and fruit, and the fifteen children sing songs and tell stories while their parents look proudly on. Old Lao Chang the gardener acts the clown and keeps everybody in stitches.

It is peaceful and calm here, and the winter sunshine is pleasantly warm, but the windows of the house rattled two or three times this morning from the explosion of bombs in the Western Hills where some unfortunate villages are being mopped up.

Only occasionally do MBS's letters say much about the cruelties she observed among the Chinese, but she was not unaware of the effects of violence, opium addiction, and family feuds, which continued uninterrupted by shortages, cold weather, disease, and the sad prospect of a Chinese New Year without even the once-a-year treat of chopped meat.

January 27, 1940

These last ten days are supposed to have been vacation, but there has been one crisis after another. It would sound like lurid headlines if one put it baldly—quarrels, opium, suicide, attempted murder—but how little indication the words give of the suffering and the tragedy for all the people involved.

The quarrels have been in our kitchen. Our cook ordinarily seems a good-natured soul, but apparently he is noted among his friends for an unruly temper, and this week his fury has flared up twice over trifles. The first time he went for the boy with a poker, the second time he relieved his feelings by smashing some of the best china on the kitchen floor.

The opium has been taken by our dear old Chinese language teacher. A YW friend of mine once said she wished she could be as good as old Mr. Huang looked. He goes to chapel regularly and he loves to interrupt my Chinese lessons with most noble observations of life. Recently he came down with tuberculosis, and we sent him to the Presbyterian hospital for treatment, where he disgraced us by trying to bribe the coolie to go out and get him some opium.

The suicide was a nice girl in our junior class who apparently became despondent over her low grades and took poison last Sunday night at home. Her brothers and sisters had all done well in college, and her father seems to have been continually reproaching her for being the stupid one of the family. Her friends were a nice bunch of girls, but no one realized how deeply she was brooding over her work.

The other catastrophe is almost more tragic. One of our nicest sophomores went to town on Sunday to visit an aunt, expecting to come back to college that same evening, but the aunt persuaded her to spend the night. About midnight the aunt apparently went out of her head and with the murderous meat cleaver that is part of the equipment of every Chinese kitchen she attacked our student and her own little adopted daughter, a girl of twelve.

The younger girl was not badly hurt, but our girl was dreadfully cut up, the worst cuts being an ugly deep gash across her cheek, the cutting off of her right thumb and such a deep slash on the back of her right wrist that her hand may be totally useless. There is still some danger of infection, but we hope we can bring her back from the hospital to our infirmary soon. But worse than the physical suffering and danger is a complicated family situation whose dark depths of jealousy and greed and bitterness we only catch glimpses of.

February 4, 1940

Chao Shu-fen, the girl who was chopped up by her poor crazy aunt, is back from the hospital and is resting in the infirmary. We hope she will be in shape to go back to classes in a week or two. Her face is healing nicely and though the scar will be noticeable, it won't be too disfiguring. We still don't know whether she will be able to use her right hand or will have to learn to manage with her left.

The snow is coming down thickly. Augusta and our guest Suzanne Bien and the dogs and I are cosy by a blazing fire, but what about the people on the other side of our garden wall? The Chinese New Year Day is on Thursday. It is the one day when even the poorest people expect to have a little meat, but Pao Ch'ing tells me it is impossible to get even a pig's head or feet at a price they can afford and they'll feel lucky if they can get enough millet.

February 11, 1940

A week ago it seemed as though the bitter cold of winter would never break; then suddenly the Chinese calendar announced the Beginning of Spring. On Monday the cold seemed less, Tuesday it was almost warm at midday, today it is positively balmy. Of course we shall have a lot of horrid dusty cold winds in March, but we can count on the noonday sun being warm and comforting until the end of May when it will be so hot as to be distinctly uncomforting. One is thankful for the sake of the village people that the chief problem of fuel is past, for the greater problem of food becomes daily more acute.

This past week has been Chinese New Year, but we have not heard the usually universal sound of meat choppers preparing the *chupopo* that are a special New Year dish. No white flour has been obtainable at all in the village shops and meat has been so expensive that the poor people who ordinarily have it only once a year at New Year time have had to forego that treat. New Year without *chupopo* is like having nothing but shredded wheat for Christmas dinner. And now worse even than high prices there is an epidemic of diphtheria in the refugee camp at our gate.

Vanished Glory

MBS continued to lament inequalities between the University and the people outside its walls, but she was also increasingly irritated by committee meetings and Mission Meeting. She was a doer and resented time wasted in discussions. When there was a problem, she got busy and solved it, whether it was dormitory cooks on strike or missionaries set in their ways in a changing world.

February 18, 1940

This has been an unusually hectic week. The President is leaving tonight for a longish trip to the South, and there has been a great rush to get University business attended to before he goes. There have been committee meetings every day and a particularly long and nasty one on Friday about next year's budget. There are differences of opinion about how much money we have a right to ask the Trustees for and even greater differences of opinion as to whether or not we are spending wisely the money that we have.

The skyrocketing cost of living continues to be everyone's chief concern. For us it is far less serious than for most people. The University budget and those of us who are on missionary salaries profit by the rising (or falling—depends on the point of view) exchange rate, which for nearly everyone else is a calamity.

Grains and cereals of all kinds are growing harder and harder to buy at any price. We were fortunately able to get supplies early for the dormitory dining rooms, but Grace Yuan told me this week that they have only enough in her school to last for another month and no prospect of being able to get more.

I don't know whether it would be better or worse if we were all poor together. It seems dreadful that people who have a little gold can be so disproportionately better off than their neighbors, and yet if nobody had a margin at all, there would be far greater suffering all the way round. Today's paper speaks of a possible prohibition of almost all imports. If that happens we shall give up foreign food almost entirely and live on a Chinese diet, which will be hard on our cook but not at all hard on the palate.

Foreign food provided the cook with greater margin for "squeeze," the commission taken by Chinese servants on purchases for their employers.

February 25, 1940

Dr. Stuart went off this week on a trip that will take nearly two months, and we're hoping to get along with a minimum of committee meetings while he is away. The last few weeks before

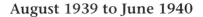

his departure were hectic, for it seemed as if all University business for the next year had to be discussed with him before he left. We had conferences from breakfast to bedtime. Now perhaps we can stop talking and get a little work done!

Leighton Stuart in the years 1937 to 1941 engaged in extensive efforts at reconciliation, "convinced that trying to bring about real friendship between the Japanese and Chiang Kai-shek was the best protection for the University." He had complicated relationships with the Japanese military and with the government in Tokyo and a long-standing friendship with Chiang Kai-shek, which gave him a unique, if ultimately futile, diplomatic advantage. The trips south to which MBS refers were made to Chiang's wartime capital of Chungking seeking response to Japanese propositions. He was, in these diplomatic missions, ultimately the champion of a free and united China, and "he made it clear to the Japanese that any negotiations with the Nationalist government were conditioned by the independence of China."[3]

Stuart noted in his autobiography that his trips were a "way of demonstrating to all concerned that Yenching, although carrying on under Japanese occupation, was none the less loyal to the Chinese cause. I wanted also to learn first-hand how that cause was faring. We had only Japanese-controlled news. The morale of our campus would be sustained by authentic information, especially if—as proved in the main to be the case—the news was reassuring."[4]

Authentic information might sustain morale, but in day-to-day living the major and minor crises absorbed MBS's time and energy as she coped with the University's food service and, with some impatience, plotted to encourage the Mission to face reality.

March 10, 1940

This has been a pretty busy and somewhat worrisome week. Tuesday might be taken as a specimen cross section, though thank goodness not a typical one. Our kitchen stove needed some minor repairs and therefore was not functioning for the day. After chapel I stood in line to get a ticket for the supply of rice and flour the Controller has fortunately been able to get for the faculty and workmen.

At about quarter to twelve one of the matrons telephoned in great excitement to ask if I had heard that the dormitory cooks were going on strike and would not serve any lunch. There were a few moments of frantic telephoning and rushing about before we collected the responsible people. Hasty consultations, the decision to ask the matrons and students to serve their own lunch, a polite but firm sally to the kitchens, the discovery that three of the cooks were quite ready to produce a meal and the fourth soon capitulated; and lunch appeared without more ado and only five minutes late!

After lunch I found our neighbor Nellie Shadick in a state of great indignation because she had been to town and Johnny had been most unnecessarily and unpleasantly rude to her. I rushed back to the office for an Administrative Committee meeting, a meeting with dietitian, manager, and cooks to explain for the tenth time that we knew the cost of living had gone up and we were going to keep our promise to raise their wages, but that we had to wait to discuss the wage scale with the management of the men's dormitories so that everything would be fair. Then a Mission Committee meeting to make plans for the program for Mission Meeting, which is to be held at Yenching this year. Then with a perfectly clear conscience spent the evening reading Lin Yutang's *Moment in Peking*, much his best book and makes Pearl Buck's books seem like the work of an ignorant and sensation-mongering foreigner, which no doubt they are.

March 17, 1940

I have been working this week on the program for our Mission Meeting which is to be here at Yenching in May. We are trying to cut out the endless, overlapping, and repetitious reports on the work of the past year and concentrate on a little more constructive thinking about the future. Times and conditions and opportunities have changed enormously in the past few years and are going to change still more, but the work of the Mission goes on in the same old channels. It is not because they are the best channels but simply because they are familiar that we are content to stay in them.

March 24, 1940, Easter Sunday

We were afraid that with Easter coming so early this year it might be too cold for our usual outdoor services, but nothing could have been more exactly right than the temperature and the sunshine this morning. The hillside hollow by the lake was sheltered from any wind, and though the first flowering shrubs have hardly begun to open, the clever landscape coolies had forced great armfuls of forsythia and peach and planted them early this morning on the edges of the hill so that only the closest examination showed they had not always been growing there. The congregation was nearly eight hundred, not counting the village children who wandered around the edges listening to the hymns and staring at the strange happenings. Lucius Porter preached a good sermon in good simple Chinese (good because it's the only kind I can follow) saying just the things that ought to be said on Easter morning.

March 31, 1940

Yesterday ten of us celebrated Saturday afternoon by going for lunch to a little Mohammedan restaurant in the village by the Summer Palace and then walking around the lake there. In the main courts there were crowds of sightseers looking at the blossoms and the famous magnolias, but on the far side of the lake we had the whole world to ourselves.

April 7, 1940

Yesterday was Ching Ming, the festival of Clear Brightness, but there is nothing clear or bright about the weather today. The air is full of flying dust, and the dry wind never stops blowing, so that one despairs of ever being clean again.

We are hoping for better weather next week when we have our spring holiday. Eight of us are hoping to be able to make a four-day trip to Jehol over the new railway that was opened across the mountains two years ago. There is an interminable amount of red tape to go through, but if passports, permits, visas, and passes can all be secured for all of us, we'll have two days there and a day on the train each way.

We went to the Toriis' for dinner Thursday night. Dr. Torii is our Japanese member of the faculty, an exceedingly nice old gentleman who spends his time in archaeological research. His wife, two daughters, and a small granddaughter are here with him. The whole family is extremely appreciative of the slightest kindness. The dinner the other night was a triumph of hospitality. Can you imagine that we would ever go to the trouble to provide Chinese or Japanese food for Chinese or Japanese guests? The two daughters had spent the day in the kitchen and produced a delectable meal— seven courses of foreign food, all cooked in French style. Mushroom soup, fish, chicken, steak, salad, dessert, everything served beautifully and tasting delicious.

The papers are full of our new government. We are rather bewildered by sudden changes in flags on the street, but otherwise it's just a question of a rose (or a leek) by any other name.

MBS and Augusta Wagner were always revived by trips, and even the Japanese occupation did not keep them from traveling to Jehol, north of Peking in what was now called Manchukuo. Here, reflecting on the ruins of the temples, MBS pondered what seemed to her the waning of Chinese civilization.

April 21, 1940

We are back again after a successful trip to Jehol. There were ten of us altogether. We left here at five in the morning and had plenty of time to get ourselves and our baggage comfortably settled in a third-class car on the 6:30 train. I don't think I've ever had such a comfortable third class train journey in China before. There were enough fellow passengers for interest, but we were not squeezed in three deep.

Jehol is on the other side of the Great Wall about a hundred and fifty miles from Peking, but the train moves along over the new roadbed at a leisurely pace, and the journey takes just over twelve hours. At Kupeikou (the Ancient North Pass) one comes to the Great Wall and the Manchukuo customs and passport inspection. Although we had been warned of unpleasantness and heard tales of other travelers for whom one experience had been more than enough, we met only the utmost courtesy.

There was a little bright-eyed interpreter who, to make doubly sure, repeated every question on the blanks we had already filled out. "Are you Miss S.? Are you a teacher? Are you going for pleasure? Are you 39? Are you single?" And then looking up from his notebook, "Why?" I shouted with laughter, and after a moment's surprise he laughed too and then said, "In Japan...." but there was no need to finish his sentence.

From Kupeikou the train goes up over the mountains in a series of spectacular switchbacks. There is not room in the steep little valleys for even hairpin bends, so the train has an engine at each end and goes up in zigzags. It is a remarkable engineering feat and was built by the Japanese in record time.

When we got to Jehol, it was beginning to get dark. A kind Belgian priest to whom we had written was at the station to meet us, but he said that his guest quarters at the Mission were full, so he had engaged rooms at a Japanese inn and had ordered the town's only taxi to meet us. Ten of us and mountains of bedding rolls and rucksacks and lunch baskets seemed too much of a load for any taxi, but since the station was several miles outside the town walking was out of the question, so we waited to see how much we could pile into one car.

We waited and we waited, and the stars came out and the station guards closed up the station. Dozens of military trucks pulled into the nearby barracks, but no taxi appeared. Finally a solitary rickety droshky appeared. We loaded the Hanwells and some baggage into it and they clattered off into the growing dusk. A half hour later two rickshas appeared from the darkness, and two more of us climbed in and disappeared after the Hanwells. And so, two by two, in half hour installments, we managed to get ourselves transported into the town to a neat little Japanese establishment called The Great Harmony Travellers' Inn, where the floor on which we slept seemed to grow softer each successive night.

We had two days there to see the great temples that are falling into decay but that still bear witness to the strength and grandeur of the early days of the Manchu Dynasty under K'ang Hsi and Ch'ien Lung. The hills, that were said to be fully covered with thick forests when K'ang Hsi first chose the Jehol river valley for a place for a summer palace, are now completely bare. Except for green cedars in the temple courtyards, everything that the eye sees is a tawny brown in the bright sunlight with darker reddish patches where the erosion has been recent. After the summer rains the hills are green, and the fields, so they say, are gorgeous with profitable poppies.

The Empress Dowager's Summer Palace in Peking is for the most part tawdry and garish, the great courts of the Forbidden City are evidence of military and dynastic power surrounded and bolstered up for centuries by armies of retainers and courtiers, but the palace and the temples and the lamasery at Jehol seem to be the work of two great men who had not only power but also culture and imagination and a love of beauty that could make magnificent architecture almost an integral part of the hillsides and the lakes. Nothing else I have seen in China has impressed me so deeply with the vanished glory and strength of this people.

One keeps turning over in one's mind all the possible reasons for the decay of such greatness. Is it the inevitable crumbling of a civilization that cannot withstand the forces of the modern world? Is it because of corruption and selfishness in high and low places? Can it be revived in a form that will benefit the humble as well as the mighty? And what about the new, uninvited rulers who have brought all their tools and belongings with them and seem to have settled down for a permanent visit?

The scant news of the war in Europe that reached Yenching was depressing. The horrors of war made MBS impatient with the Mission's aimlessness, and she took the annual meeting firmly in hand. She had less success in holding Yenching to educational standards. Maybe, she said, she was just cranky. In any case, she and Augusta needed a summer vacation, which—astonishingly—they planned to take in Japan.

May 12, 1940

The news from Europe casts a blacker and blacker shadow over everything. The fact that the invasion of Belgium and Holland has been expected doesn't make the news any more credible or bearable. Groups huddle around the radio as they did last summer, but very little news comes through except very late at night. One only hopes that the indiscriminate bombing can be postponed a little longer.

May 29, 1940

The chief business filling up the last week has been Mission Meeting. About thirty Presbyterians from Peking, Paoting, and Shunteh were here for five days. I was chairman of the Program Committee, which kept me busy, but everyone was kind enough to be enthusiastic about two great "innovations" in the program, the simplest sort of changes that should obviously have been made years ago.

In the first place, instead of going to sleep for three successive evenings while someone read aloud written station reports, we had a number of oral reports each evening on the most significant pieces of work done this past year in each station. And in the second place, instead of letting the business sessions meander aimlessly along with no committees ever ready to report when they were called on, we boldly said that the three major committees must have their reports ready at a certain day and hour. Both these schemes were regarded as the most startling new inspirations!

June 10, 1940

The European news gets no better. The radio tonight reports the capitulation of Norway. Who are we to blame the small countries for crumpling up when we are out of the thick of things? But it is horrible to think of one more victory for Hitler.

It is a little premature to be making plans now for next summer, but since it takes so long to settle things across the ocean I have started the necessary negotiations for a long enough summer vacation next summer to make a flying trip home. I'm speaking in terms of a quick trip, but if things go on the way they have lately I may be considering coming home for good.

It may just be that I'm feeling cranky at the end of term time, not having had a vacation last summer, but every committee meeting I go to I come away feeling more and more out of sympathy with the policies of spending money and the lack of sound educational policy which seem to prevail in our administrative councils. There seems to be more and more emphasis on the growth and glory of the University and less and less on the quality of character and scholarship among our students. The caliber of the students we are turning out this year is very discouraging, and yet most of the faculty don't seem to realize it. And this horrible high rate of exchange which gives everyone with a little American money nearly ten times the income he used to have seems to have deprived us of all sense of values.

We'll be off for Nojiri in two weeks. We leave here by boat on the 24th, spend a few days in Kyoto and Tokyo, most of July at Nojiri, and get back the first of August.

Japan Holiday

MBS noted in 1982 that a letter must have been missing about this time explaining why she was planning to go to Japan for the summer holiday. "It may have seemed queer to go off to Japan when we had been feeling so much animosity and rage about the Japanese occupation of North China. Japan at that time was the only possible place to have a cool holiday. Many people from North China went to Japan feeling that they wanted to size up the situation there and also to offer friends there some interpretation of our feelings in North China.

"A Japan holiday at that time was extraordinarily cheap. The exchange rates for US dollars into yen and into our Chinese FRB were different, but the Japanese had pegged the rate between yen and FRB so that if one exchanged gold into FRB and then into yen one got an extraordinarily good rate. If this seems complicated, indeed it was!

"Furthermore, we had entertained a good many people from Japan in the past few years, and they were happy to help us make our plans in Japan. Two families in particular, the Hannafords of our Mission and the Botts of the Canadian Mission, had offered to take us in or find a place for us to stay in Nojiri. Japan and the United States were not yet at war. Our feelings were still that the Japanese people were a fine people and good friends of ours. Our anger was against the military."[5]

June 28, 1940, Kyoto

We got to Kobe this morning about eleven, fortunately with skies sufficiently overcast so that Japan summer heat is not at its unbearable worst. The nice Toriis, Japanese members of our Yenching faculty, had thoughtfully sent word to the Japan Tourist Bureau to meet us, so a young man was on the dock with reservations already made for us on the noon express to Tokyo. These we did not want since we had planned to come here for a few days first, but one of them was eagerly taken by a pleasant young American army officer who had been our table-mate across from Tarpku and who had been bewailing the fact that with crowded traveling conditions he wouldn't be able to get a reservation until midnight and wouldn't get home to his family in Tokyo until tomorrow.

We had a leisurely lunch in Kobe, got a fast train to Kyoto and have had a bath and are getting settled in a big pleasant airy room. When we were here in 1926 we had rather small newish rooms with a blazing sun shining in the window, but this time we are in a wing of the hotel with a lovely green garden at our door and green tree tops outside long open windows that run the length of the room. For about the first time in my life I seem to be in that luxurious position of being able to stay for a few days in an elegant hotel without having to worry unduly about the bill! We are in the totally undeserved position of being able to profit by the two favorable rates of exchange at once, so that a vacation that would have been prohibitive a few years ago is quite possible now.

We go up to Tokyo on Monday to stay with Mrs. Hannaford for a few days before going on to Nojiri for three weeks.

It was great fun reading all the letters from Pat and Bob at once. But one's heart stops at the thought of what England must be like in these dark days. The collapse of France still seems incomprehensible, and we long to know what America is feeling and is going to do. Is she going to be paralyzed by her own preoccupation with presidential politics? For the five days on the China Sea we

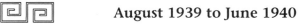

had no news at all and a few Japanese papers at Moji (all gloating over the predicament of the Allies) and here haven't sufficed for us to get caught up.

July 3, 1940, Tokyo

This morning's papers say there have been air raids on Bristol. I wonder whether Pat and the children are there or in Newquay or whether these latest developments have made them think it wise to come to America after all. One can only hold one's breath for all of Britain and pray that they can stand fast under the terrific onslaughts that are sure to come. One wishes that America would help in every way and would wake up enough to see the issues clearly.

The fundamental stupidity of our divided approach to life everywhere has been dramatized for me in the last half hour. I am sitting in the Hannafords' comfortable guestroom here on the school compound. Through the open windows in front of me have been coming the strains of "Holy, Holy, Holy" sung in boyish voices from the middle school chapel. Through another open window at my elbow I can look out at the college drill ground where a squad of college boys are practicing rifle charges with fierce yells!

We have been in this country about five days and have met nothing but courtesy and kindliness. The people one sees on trains and trams are hard working, self-respecting, dignified, kindly. The children are happy and smiling. What strange forces can bring about the metamorphosis that we have seen around us during the last two years?

China and Japan each has much to give to the other—tolerance and pride, acceptance of life and the energy for reform, the toughness of the reed that can bend, the strength of the ramrod that cannot be broken—each should complement the other.

We go to Nojiri tomorrow to the adventure of having a two-room house all to ourselves and a Japanese cook. Since we have

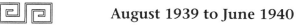

learned how to say scrambled eggs and have discovered that the word for vinegar is the same in Chinese and Japanese, we shall not starve!

July 7, 1940 Nojiri

Each day the newspaper has headlines of some new turning topsy-turvy of what had seemed established and sure, and fifteen minutes with *Life* or *Time* is enough to rouse the most sluggish imagination to the unspeakable agony that seems the only lot now for millions. One longs to be able to do something, however infinitesimal, to make that suffering less. It certainly does not seem right that with such misery on every side we should be sitting idly here in this heavenly place. Yet here we are having, if only we could share it with others, all the setting for the most perfect vacation.

For years I have heard of Nojiri as the perfect vacation place, but I was still unprepared for the actuality. After the dust and heat and flatness of our North China plain, one can hardly believe in these steep green hillsides of pine and chestnut, cherry and larch, in the blue lake that turns silver in the afternoon, in the afternoon breeze from the Japan Sea, in the blue and snow-streaked heights of this great volcano Mt. Myoka that is visible on clear days. There is a settlement of about a hundred houses, but though they are close together on the hillside they are so small and the trees are so close that each house is screened from its neighbors. We can hear the shouts of the children swimming below us but only one roof is visible from our window.

Mrs. Hannaford and Mrs. Bott from the Canadian Mission contrived to get for us for a month one of the nicest houses in Nojiri and procured for us an elderly saint, Saito San, who was the Hannafords' cook for fifteen years and the Botts' cook for five years. She knows all the ropes of Nojiri housekeeping, so though we are babes in the wood as far as language goes, we are taken care of at every turn.

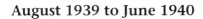

Saito San is an excellent cook (beef steak and strawberry shortcake for Sunday dinner today!) and though she talks to us in streams of Japanese, we get along beautifully by nodding and smiling and daily visits from sixteen-year-old Hugh Hannaford provide opportunities for solving any knotty problems. Fortunately by changing "L" to "R" and adding an "uh" after every consonant, almost all foods get their Japanese names. "Milk" is "miraku," "apple pie" is "appuru pai," "beets" are "bitsu," "chocolate" is "chokoratu," "lard" is "rardu," etc.

A few weeks in this peace and beauty should make one ready for anything.

Augusta Wagner also wrote to Mrs. Speer of the peace and beauty of Nojiri and the "delectable chocolate layer cake" and other delights produced by Saito San. Augusta and MBS both admired the friendly Japanese people they met and felt that they complemented the Chinese. "Together," Augusta wrote, "they could make a new order in East Asia but the heritage of hate that this war is leaving will make it impossible for them to come together as friends for many a long year, I fear."[6]

July 22, 1940

Another happy and fairly lazy week has gone by in this lovely place. The rain, which was nearly continuous for the first eight or nine days, has stopped, and we have had warm sunshiny days and some moonlit evenings. A number of times we have taken our supper out with the Hannafords and eaten it in our boats, just drifting in the middle of the lake where we could see the sunset light on the mountains.

One morning Augusta and Mrs. Hannaford and I walked around the lake, or at least nearly around it. Altogether it's about nine miles, but after walking the seven interesting miles, we cut out the last two, which are hot and flat, by coming across the lake in a motor boat. There is a fascinating variety in the path around the lake, level bits where the sun shines warm on the pine needles, places where the path is dark and shady under tall cryptomeria, spots where one looks down from a high bluff onto the waves sparkling in the breeze, clearings where the ferns and wildflowers smell spicy in the blazing sun. There is a little village surrounded by its terraced paddy fields on the steep hillsides where every thatched-roofed house rustles with the sound of thousands of silk worms eating in their shallow trays of mulberry leaves.

The newspapers are full of the new cabinet and the shift to a single party, but the men I have talked to disagree as to whether this will mean a seriously stiffer policy in China and a more irreconcilable attitude toward Britain and America. In the Japanese papers there is undisguised gloating over the fate of the Allies. The drive against extravagance in the use of rice shows that the situation in regard to food supplies is causing the government concern. The rationing of sugar and matches is not due to shortage but to the need for exporting large quantities to get foreign exchange. Practically all real cotton is exported too, and a staple fibre substitute which wears out quickly is all that can be bought here. The sheets on the boat coming over were made of a harsh fibre in a sort of porous weave.

August 11, 1940

Our trip across the China Sea was prolonged by typhoons so that instead of getting here Friday morning we did not arrive until midnight Sunday night. On Wednesday morning the purser announced that we would meet a strong typhoon that evening, or rather that it would meet us. It seemed incredible, for we were steaming along in sun and calm through the Korean islands.

At about five in the afternoon we anchored in a sheltered spot with islands all around us and no sign of storm anywhere. Another small steamer came to share our shelter and some fishing junks came by with fresh fish for sale which Augusta and another

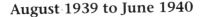

enterprising passenger bought. They tasted very good indeed at lunch the next day. There we stayed until Friday morning while the wind grew stronger and stronger.

When we started on our way again, the high waves that were still running out beyond the protection of the islands and the wreckage of some junks showed that we had missed a real gale. Saturday night we were told that we would get to Taku Bar at three in the morning and would be at the Tangku wharf in time to catch the early morning train, providing that the customs officers would be obligingly on hand at six o'clock. Breakfast was to be at four a.m. sharp.

The gong rang at 3:30, and I could see the Taku Light through the porthole, so we dressed and closed our bags, only to be met with total darkness when I stepped outside the cabin door. I heard the sepulchral voice of the cabin boy saying, "You musto sleep. No go now." So back to bed and the practice of cultivating patience. Evidently the offshore gale was so strong that it was blowing too much water off the bar, and we had to wait for the next high tide at three in the afternoon.

We did at last get in in time to catch the six o'clock evening train. Tangku is still the worst port in the world, but the station and dock are slowly being improved, and the baggage coolies were extremely good-natured though still piratical in their prices.

When we got to Peking at 10:30 we were embarrassed by our friends' thoughtfulness, for Dr. Ferguson had sent a servant to meet us and to say beds were ready for us at their house, and Dr. Stuart had sent a car and a gate pass so that we could come straight out to Yenching. We stopped at the Fergusons' to thank them and to say we had better come straight home and got out here after the campus lights were out. But our faithful Te Lin was soon wakened to unlock the door and provide candles for us, and the dogs were riotous in their welcome. Margaret Hayes and Ruth Stahl had taken good care of both house and office, and there has not been too much work piled up waiting for me. Even if there were mountains of it, I think I should not feel daunted, for the vacation seems to have renewed me completely. I feel ready for anything.

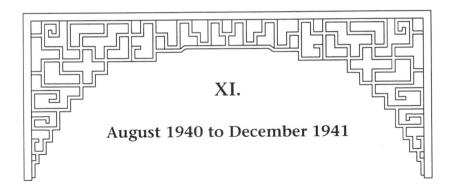

XI.

August 1940 to December 1941

Haven of Peace

U nder Japanese occupation many universities in North China closed or were under Japanese control, and applications rose sharply for Yenching, where academic freedom endured under Stuart's skillfully diplomatic hand and the persistently raised American flag. Outside the University the environment was hostile, but academic life continued largely uninterrupted, although living quarters were crowded.[1]

August 18, 1940

There have been a terrific number of arrests in Peking this past week or two. One of our students who was apparently held by mistake for a few days has just come back in a fairly distraught state, though she was treated very well. No one knows just what is back of it all, but such things do not add to the general sweetness of summer time.

September 1, 1940

We are now in the middle of registration and have already assigned 292 girls to dormitory places, although 276 is the largest number we have ever had in the dormitories before. There are still a few more to be tucked away and about thirty on the waiting list for whom I fear there is very little hope. We have put in twenty-two double-decker beds to take care of this increase, and the freshmen do not seem to mind the overcrowding since the alternative is no college education at all. But it does seem to me that four girls in a ten-by-fourteen room is fairly close quarters for college life. The maidens of Bryn Mawr and Vassar would probably agree but perhaps not those of Kunming and Chengtu.

After the first year of Japanese occupation quite a few of the Yenching faculty moved to Kunming in Southwest China, because they were unwilling to live in occupied territory.

Kunming was the capital of Yunnan, neighboring province to Szechwan where Chiang Kai-shek had made his headquarters at Chunking. Into Kunming came many refugees in 1937 and 1938, and it became "a vital intellectual center and the wartime home of the new Consolidated University for refugee scholars and students from North China."[2]

Hsieh Wan-ying, MBS's friend from earlier days at Yenching, and her husband, sociologist Wu Wen-tsao, were among those in Kunming. She wrote to Grace Boynton that her house had become a meeting place for Yenching friends. "The letters from Yenching certainly make us very, very homesick. I'm glad we stayed in Yenching for one year after Peking was occupied, and we understand perfectly now how hard you people must have struggled. We—you and we—have only one faith, that is, China will fight till the last man and the final victory will be ours. Materially we are less comfortable yet mentally we know you have harder times than we have. We just have to encourage each other and do our best for the country."[3]

In September of 1940 it was still possible to travel from Kunming back to Peking, and in her Fortnightly Letter at the beginning of the month MBS noted the response to T.C. Chao, who had been in Kunming. She also tried to make clear to the friends of Yenching the impact of the growing number of students packed into the University.

September 9, 1940

The first classes of the term began this morning, and we are just trying to finish up the last untidy threads of late registration. Again we are able to report "the largest enrollment in the history of the University." It is a very simple phrase and very satisfactory for the President to cable to the Trustees, but it is nothing to be taken lightly by those of us who have been busy with preparing for and receiving the new students.

We always used to speak of 800 as the University "quota." Last year our initial registration of 980 soon shook down to about 950. This afternoon 1040 students had completed registration, and by the end of the week, when the period of late registration is over, we expect to have close to 1100, not counting the 100 boys in the new affiliated middle school established in the Wei Hsiu Yüan across the road from our front gate.

Of the 1040, just over 300 are women. Each of our four dormitories was originally designed for fifty students, and last year we thought we had reached our maximum capacity when we tucked away 276 girls, so you can imagine that another ten percent increase has meant hurried plans for double-decker beds, additional equipment for bedrooms and dining rooms, not to mention such vital matters as reading room desks and classroom space. From a rather limited first inspection I would say that our new class is well worth the trouble it has caused us and is quite the equal of any of its predecessors in its intelligent appearance, its good manners, its good-tempered adjustment to new conditions, and its general air of quiet good sense.

Ninde Chapel was packed yesterday morning when T.C. Chao, recently returned from his year in Kunming, preached on "The Foundations of Life." Judging by the interest in chapel and the Christian Fellowship reception for new students, they are eager to take advantage of Yenching's open doors to Christian life and fellowship.

In all the arrangements for new students, both academic and social, there has been a marked improvement over other years both in efficiency and in the general good spirit, which comes from the good work of our excellent new Director of Studies, Lin Chia-t'ung, whom some of you may remember as a student in the Psychology Department ten years ago and who now has a Liverpool Ph.D. Our thoroughly admirable new Student Welfare Committee is headed by Ran Sailer and made up of young Chinese members of the faculty who are admired by the students for their sound academic standards and who are genuinely interested in the students and in raising all levels of university life. Ch'en Fang-chih is taking hold of her job as freshman doyen for the girls with a great deal of gusto. Altogether it looks as though internally this were going to be a fine year.

There are, of course, many improvements we could wish for in our external surroundings. Several students have been taken into custody by the police this summer and, although they are now reported to have been released, they have not yet turned up to register. The examination of all bus passengers at the Hsi Chih Men continues to be a nuisance but varies in severity according to the degree of military activity necessary against the guerrillas in the nearby hills. We are thankful beyond words that last year's floods in the Tientsin area have not been repeated this year, but other agencies have recently interrupted railroad traffic almost as seriously as the floods did last year.

September 12, 1940

We are in the midst of the first week of classes and already have more than 300 women students tucked away into every available corner of the dormitories. The fourteen girls on the waiting list whom we have not yet been able to take in haunt my office and send all their friends and relatives to plead their cases. It is one thing to sit in a committee and say cold-bloodedly that our maximum capacity is such and such; it is quite a different matter to see the girls themselves who feel they are losing their last chance to prepare for something useful if Yenching does not take them in.

Our visitors, Muriel Bott and her father, will be going back to Tokyo on Sunday. A number of friends whom we saw there in July—Mrs. Uemura, Miss Kawai, and Taki Fujita—told us they hope to come to Peking in August, and we of course told them to be sure to come out here to see the University, but none of them turned up. We are wondering whether the regulations against incoming visitors are meant to keep out such people, or whether they just found the whole trip too difficult to make.

October 6, 1940

A few weeks ago we had a glimpse of man's inhumanity to man which we will not soon forget. Bi has come back for another winter at Yenching, and Augusta and Harold and I had gone into town to meet two late trains on which we thought he might be arriving. He was not on the first one, and we were strolling off the platform when we noticed a bully sort of Chinese chap with a group of about ten ragged, wretched looking coolies. He was trying to herd them all from one platform to the other, and they kept straggling and straying.

Suddenly two of them, carrying their poor little bundles of bedding, bolted like rabbits across the tracks to the freight yards. There were shouts and yells, the big bully and half a dozen station armed guards raced after them, and in a few minutes they were caught and dragged back again.

Then there was a great to do with much talking and gesticulating and a large crowd gathered. Finally the whole bunch were herded into the police station, and Harold asked one of the station porters what all the row was about. It appeared the bully was a contractor who had gathered some poor coolies up in Tientsin and promised them good work on the new roads in Peking.

Now that they had arrived in Peking, one of the men found

that they were really being taken up to the Tatung mines where, according to the porter, the coolies die in a few months and no-body even bothers to bring the bodies out of the mines for burial. And worst of all in the porter's eyes was the fact that though the contractor got three dollars a day for each man, he had not given them any food the whole day long.

There was no question that everybody on the platform was on the side of the coolies, and there was general satisfaction when through the door into the police station we saw the contractor being knocked about a bit. When the coolies were told by the police that they could go, they melted off into the darkness in no time. Harold ran after them to give them some money, but I'm afraid it was not enough to get them back to Tientsin.

The possibility of war between Japan and the United States brought once again, as during the warlord years, thoughts of evacuation of Americans from China, but, as earlier, married women and children were first on the list, and MBS philosophically lived a week at a time.

October 13, 1940

Our chief topic of conversation these days is the evacuation of the Far East by many Americans. The State Department notice which came to us all was very cannily worded, and the general watchword seems to be caution but not alarm. All the wives and the children at the Embassy have to go, of course, and people like Mrs. Johnson are rushing about getting packed and feeling very provoked and ill-used.

No one pretends to be a prophet, and so we don't know whether we are wise or foolish to be remaining calm and making no plans at all for leaving in the near or distant future. There seem to be three possibilities: that nothing will happen at all; that there will be anti-American demonstrations—there have already been posters linking us with the British as people to be spontaneously opposed; or that Japan and the USA will go to war.

To expect the first is perhaps overly optimistic; the second we can bear up under; if the third catches us unaware, we'll be out of luck, but everyone feels that it's better to run the risk of internment than to run off too soon because of a false alarm. But in the meantime, no dinner table conversation goes very far before someone says, "If we evacuate," or "If we're interned." At times like this it's good to have a naturally placid disposition and to be content to live a week at a time. The most annoying part of it all is that this seems to put an end to any serious plans for my flying trip home next summer. Of course if things blow up, we'll probably all be home, but if they go on this way I can't very well come home for a brief visit for fear the State Department wouldn't let me come back again.

October 27, 1940

What a world this is! The copies of *Time* and *Life* that have come this week have pictures of London after the September air raids that make one's hair stand on end, and one is very conscious that those pictures were taken more than a month ago and the raids have been going on ever since.

Our nice boy has just been telling me that he is without winter clothes because conditions are so disturbed in his country district not far from here that the relative who was going to bring his few padded clothes up to him before cold weather does not dare to travel. He says there is simply not enough to eat in that county so each man tries to steal from his neighbor.

Here in Peking people are all a little nervous and edgy and each day brings a fine new crop of rumors about evacuation. The first contingent of Embassy wives and children leaves on Tuesday.

The Peking Association of University Women had planned to have an informal Gilbert and Sullivanish sort of entertainment later in the winter to raise money for our scholarship funds, but when it became clear that a number of the leading spirits were going to have to join the exodus in the next few weeks, we decided suddenly to get it over quickly. Everything was done in a little over a week and the occasion was a great success last night.

Four or five groups put on skits, so there was a minimum of having to get together for rehearsals. The Yenching skit in which Bi and Augusta starred brought down the house. Bi, as Professor Drydustus, made a magnificent speech in quasi-Latin, parodying academic mannerisms, and Augusta, as Mrs. Swashtout, was a perfect gushing culture-seeking clubwoman out of one of Helen Hokinson's devastating *New Yorker* cartoons. We arranged a special bus from Yenching with a special pass to come back through the gate at midnight. It was the first such gaiety many people have had for a couple of years and perhaps the last for even longer.

November 5, 1940

The first of the Peking evacuees have been going off. The *Mariposa* is coming up to Chingwangtao so that people from Peking do not have the troublesome trip to Shanghai or by way of Tangku, but in spite of all the urging of the Embassy, the boat is apparently not going to be full. A few people from Yenching are going but not enough to make much of a dent in our population.

The whole business is most mysterious. If the State Department really has reasons for wanting us to clear out, why don't they stop talking through their hats and give us at least a hint of what it's all about? The chief effect on me at the moment is that the departure of two of my staff makes necessary some readjustment in our Women's College housing plans, and it's no joke to have to make all those delicate decisions twice a year. Once is quite enough!

November 10, 1940

The boatload of Peking evacuees is leaving this week from Chingwangtao, and I'll try to send this letter by one of them. We have been busy farewelling the people who are leaving, and conversation still turns frequently to a few missionary families with children who cannot seem to make up their minds whether to go or stay. It is funny how contagious the jitters can be. It probably is a good idea for the families with small children to go, but the people with jobs to do all assume that there is nothing in the situation serious enough to warrant closing up institutions or stopping work.

General conditions are not very different from last winter. Prices are not much higher but people have used up their reserves and have less to fall back upon, so that clothes are shabbier and relatives are less able to help poorer members of their families.

Our nice boy has gone down into the country to the village about seventy miles away where his wife and children live to see if they are all right since he has not heard from them for months. We suggested that he bring them back here to live, but he said it was so much easier to make ends meet in the country that he would only bring them back if they were really desperate. I hope he gets safely back; the country districts are so full of bandits and soldiers of both sides that traveling is perilous for even the humblest pedestrian.

There are rumors that the Japanese are abandoning Canton and Swatow and burning the cities behind them as part of a new policy of getting out of south and central China and consolidating their position here in the north. Luman Shafter, who has just been here from Japan, says that the more untenable the Japanese position gets, the deeper in they will go. As American policy stiffens towards Japan, Japanese policy will stiffen in return, and we will come closer and closer to war. He says two things to remember about Japanese psychology are that they never think, they only blindly follow what they have been told, and they commit hara-kiri rather than admit that they have been wrong.

The Chinese children playing on the village streets have a song that they sing very quickly in such a high nasal tone that the ordinary passerby cannot make out the words. It can be roughly translated: "The Japanese mend the roads, but the Chinese walk on them. Before long the Japanese themselves will be eaten by our Chinese dogs." The longer they stay and the more so-called improvements they make, the more they are hated. The ordinary farmer, who only wants to be left alone, could have been won over to their side if he had really been given good government. But the people in control are no better than gangsters and foreign gangsters are always even less popular than the native variety. In this case they are worse because they are more thoroughgoing, more powerful, and there is absolutely no redress.

What do you think of Roosevelt's re-election? There is general rejoicing among the Chinese. The Japanese papers seem to consider it a direct threat, a warlike action of the American people aimed directly at them.

Franklin Delano Roosevelt's re-election in November 1940 was seen as confirmation of American opposition to the Japanese aggression in Asia and equally to the European war, but the United States continued to hold to a foreign policy commitment not to go to war. Throughout this period the Japanese were in communication with the U.S., principally through Foreign Minister Matsuoka and Admiral Nomura, Ambassador to the United States. Talks between Secretary of State Cordell Hull and Nomura intensified in the period from March to December 1941 in efforts to avoid war.[4]

In China Japanese papers and soldiers were belligerent, but what of people like the little Japanese-American boy MBS and Augusta Wagner took in to live with them at this difficult time? Briefly he became part of their household and was treated with affection.

December 1, 1940

Our guest room is now occupied by a visitor who will probably stay for some time. He is ten-year-old John Tachibana, whose mother is an American and whose father is Japanese. His mother came over from Japan for medical treatment here and brought him along because there was no one with whom she could leave him at home. After several months she is still in the hospital, and the American in Peking with whom John has been staying is now leaving the city. Augusta met Mrs. T. in the hospital and has been keeping in touch with her. When she heard John had no place to go, Augusta suggested that he come out here to stay with us until his mother is well again.

John understands English but is rather hesitant about speaking it. He is a completely self-reliant youngster with perfect manners and a sweet smile. I believe that his parents are separated, but his mother has stayed on in Japan because she believed her four children should have a Japanese education and would be happier in their father's country than in her own. She has supported them by teaching and doing all her own housework.

Although the campus is still a haven of peace, there have been alarms. The city gates have been closed since Friday, and although foreigners have been allowed in and out and Chinese women are now allowed to go through, no Chinese men are yet able to go through, so busses are not running and food cannot go through the gates in either direction. The story is that an officer was shot and the culprit has not yet been found. It has been fairly inconvenient for a lot of people who found themselves on the wrong side of the gates from where they wanted to be.

December 8, 1940

I wonder in how many parts of the world there is the same peace and quiet that reigns here at least for this one Sunday afternoon. I've just had a good Chinese luncheon, listening while I ate to the very good radio which has been lent to us by a friend, my rice and marrow sour being eaten to the accompaniment of Carroll Alcott's noon news broadcast. Carroll Alcott is an amazing American who gives a news commentary four times a day from Shanghai. He's informal, breezy, honest, absolutely fearless, says what he thinks is right and doesn't care whose toes he is treading on. At least half a dozen countries must be longing to muzzle him, but he keeps right on wisecracking and telling the truth.

December 17, 1940

We now have three busses a day running to the city gate. (Foreigners are allowed in and out but the drivers of our University busses have not been able to get passes.) There one gets out and walks through the gate, but though technically one is then in the city, one is still five miles from where one wants to be. To go from the northwest city gate to the southeast corner of the city where the shops are one then has the choice of a ricksha (an hour's cold ride) or a tram (a worse crowd than the subway because one is more likely to carry some uninvited guests away in one's clothes) or a city bus (not bad though one may have to wait half an hour on a windy corner before one comes along) or a rickety taxi (which has to be ordered ahead of time and may not turn up after all). Coming home one reverses the process and the comparatively greater ease of making connections with the taxi is counterbalanced by having to carry one's bundles about half a mile through the gate to the place where the bus is allowed to wait for homeward bound passengers. All this makes the trip at least as complicated as the Hudson River Tube, but John and I think we will attempt it today with the goal of Christmas shopping and a visit to his mother who is still in the hospital.

John continues to be a most charming guest. He is making great strides in his English. We have not ventured to suggest that he play with any of the Chinese faculty children, but he plays football with the Sailer boys, takes the dogs walking with Bi, and the servants like him tremendously and are ready to play with him while we are out in the daytime.

December 29, 1940

Christmas Day we began with John's stocking. Then six students came for breakfast of waffles and homemade sausages. When the students had gone, Bi came in and we opened our packages, a ceremony that most years waits until the last guest has gone in the evening but that came early this year for John's sake. When the last piece of ribbon had been picked up off the floor, we dashed over to pay our respects to the President and then back again to set the table for eighteen for dinner. Thanks to Augusta's clever planning we were among the very few Peking households that dined on turkey. The guests were the five Sailers, the Shadicks, Nancy Cochran, Bi, Shirley Duncan, Michael Lindsay, Agnes Chen, Chou Kuo-ping, Frank Fulton, and Langdon Gilkey.[5]

John and I went to town in a car so that he could see his mother. We got home again in time to help Augusta fix the table and move the furniture in preparation for the annual Faculty Open House for students. This year more students than ever were here since only a few had been able to go home. Just over four hundred boys and girls passed through our living room in the course of the evening. If they had been evenly spaced we might have had time for more than a hurried "Merry Christmas! Won't you have a cookie?" but since more than two hundred of them came in the first half hour you can imagine the crush!

Voices of War

The war grew worse in Europe, and Americans in China waited to see what their future might be. Whatever the uncertainties, Yenching began another semester, even as most of the wives and children were evacuated. MBS rejoiced that the gardens were flourishing in the cool spring; lamented the phlegmatic, unassertive middle school girls; and tolerated the unspeculative routine of Mission Meeting.

300

January 5, 1941

Father's letter of December first came yesterday telling of the cable apparently indicating that Mortimer Road[6] had been hit by a bomb. I don't know whether it is a good or a bad thing that one's imagination seems to balk at such news. One's indignation flares up hot and violent, but one just cannot imagine fully what it means either for the present or the future, for the individual families or for the country or for the world, that so many neat and pleasant Mortimer Roads, so many comfortable kitchens and cozy nurseries and satisfying drawing rooms have been turned into heaps of plaster and broken brick.

January 14, 1941

Our small Johnny left us yesterday, and the house seems miserably quiet without his cheerful whistle. His mother was still far from strong, but she was able to leave the hospital and had to get back to her job. They went by train and were able to get only third class accommodations and were not even sure of berths all the way to Fusan, so we shall be anxious to hear that they have arrived in Osaka safely and that Mrs. Tachibana did not collapse along the way. She is a plucky little woman supporting her children by teaching English in a number of different commercial schools. She is the only foreigner in the little suburb where they live and has no one to rely on for much companionship except the children.

But if her other boys are like Johnny, she should be content. There's no doubt that we lost our hearts to him completely, and I wish we could be sure that he is going to have enough to eat during these next months. Everybody who met him here liked him. When one small child can so completely cut across all racial antagonisms, one realizes what fools we are to be led astray by national hatreds.

January 26, 1941

I have been in this week to check up with Cook's about passage home and back this summer because I haven't completely given up my hope of coming home for a flying visit, but when I think about it soberly, I don't see how it is to be managed. If the political situation doesn't clear up, I can't leave here, both because I can't leave my job if things are tense and because I can't leave here if the State Department might refuse to let me come back; and on the other hand, if things do clear up, then we must build a new women's dormitory this summer and I'll have to stay right on the job. The only prospect of my really getting home would seem to be if everything busts up and we all come, and we hardly hope for that!

February 2, 1941

The Sailer family, after debating the pros and cons of evacuation for weeks, finally decided that Louise and the boys should go to Cleveland early this month. Ran got flu during exam time, and Louise got pretty tired doing the last of the packing and was in bed with a sore throat on Monday, but the whole family seemed in pretty good shape when they started off on Wednesday morning. Ran was going to Tientsin with them to put them on the little boat for Dairan.

Imagine our astonishment when the boys turned up on Friday saying that Louise was ill in Tientsin and that they had decided not to go to America after all! Apparently Louise developed real flu on the train and was so utterly wretched with a high fever that it was quite out of the question for her to go on, especially on the little cockleshell in which she would have had to navigate the China Seas in January winds.

Now it is February 6th. Louise and Ran are back. Everyone is delighted to have them settle down to stay, although the few remaining mothers with children who are still in the throes of indecision seem a little upset by this sudden right about face.

Augusta Wagner wrote to Mrs. Speer that the Sailer boys "are thrilled to be back and their Chinese friends equally thrilled to have them. They are having a regular social whirl. The Ts'ai boys telephone to ask them to lunch, the Li boys to dinner. I went over to their house to get out some clothes for them to find half the village there." In the same letter, Augusta asked, "What will the new term bring? Our neighbor moves southward on her aggressive march. Tokyo warns us to stop acting 'arrogantly or the results will be truly dreadful.' Hitler breathes fire and slaughter on Britain and means it and will the United States be in time to help? Meantime we do the day's work."[7]

February 11, 1941

Registration is over and here we are well started on the next lap. All fall we kept saying optimistically, "Well, at least we hope to be able to finish the first semester without interruption." Now that we have accomplished that and have begun the spring semester we have a new goal. "In the spring things will be clearer and we'll know better where we are," has been a maxim for the last three years. It's never true but it always sounds reassuring.

Just now what everyone is really waiting for is to see what happens in the next two or three weeks as the outcome of Admiral Nomura's first negotiations in Washington. Apparently Bishop Reifsnyder doesn't have much faith even in these negotiations, for the latest news is that he is advising all the American Episcopal missionaries to clear out of Japan bag and baggage. The stream of women and children evacuating North China continues to trickle out, but the contagion hasn't yet spread to people with jobs.

It is interesting to see how, little by little, the magnificent courage of the British is arousing an entirely new attitude of wholehearted admiration among the Chinese. The feeling of most of our faculty used to be that of course there were some fine Britishers like the few English men and women on our faculty but that on the whole the British were dyed-in-the-wool imperialists and should be regarded with suspicion. The Opium War and the famous Shanghai park sign, "Chinese and dogs not allowed" were not easily forgotten and forgiven. But all that is changed now.

Bi had a most interesting letter today from London from Bertha Spicer (one of Sir Albert Spicer's large clan) with much to be read between the lines about the necessary readjustments of daily life in London.

February 16, 1941

We are having a new wave of excitement about evacuation. The State Department has reminded us again that women and children are supposed to go, although "highly essential men" may stay. The people at the Embassy here pass the word along but don't do much urging except for people with small children. Mrs. Galt, one of our near neighbors, left yesterday. She and her husband, who are under the American Board, are due to retire a year from this summer, and she has not been very well for the past year, so the Mission has urged her to go, but it seems rather hard, for it means saying good-by to China for good now and being separated from her husband for eighteen months.

The Sailers are still waiting for word from the China Council, but I am afraid that with this latest reminder from Washington, they'll have to go sometime before Easter. Mrs. Frame and Rosamond have passage for next month. It's hardly a pleasure jaunt for the boats have cots in the public rooms and probably have children sleeping in the barber chairs.

It's fun to see how the foreigners who aren't going behave. There are the wistful ones who wish that they had just a little better excuse so that they could leave their jobs and go too. And there are the fire-breathers who think that it is all nonsense and are either very patronizing or very contemptuous toward the poor weaklings who are leaving. And there are the heroes who bravely face any risk in order to be able to stay in their comfortable houses and pursue their comfortable daily routine.

But after all, these are all very small groups, and most people go about their daily business, very sad that so many friends are leaving, realizing that the moment may come when the rest of us will have to follow, but hoping for everyone's sake that sanity will prevail. It is really terrifying to think of what would happen to thousands of people if institutions like the PUMC and Yenching had to close. If salaries and jobs stopped for the members of the staffs, it would mean unemployment not only for them but for thousands more servants and shopkeepers and *k'ungchang* workers. And the closing down of clinics and classrooms would be still another story.

February 23, 1941

This has been another week of saying good-bye and having farewell parties and trying with a little tactful cheer to hearten the husbands who have come back from waving good-bye to their wives and children at Tangku. But I think this is the last batch of evacuees leaving Yenching until April or May when the Sailers must make up their minds whether they are going to go or are to stay.

The papers have news that all the Methodists, including men, are being ordered out of Japan, Chinese-occupied territory, and Korea, although the Methodists here have not yet had any such orders. Evidently something has been brewing in the South Seas, but since the lid hasn't blown off there yet, many people think the tension is relaxing and there isn't going to be a crisis in this part of the world just yet.

Leighton Stuart has been in Shanghai for two weeks and just got back this afternoon. He went and came by air, which is much the most comfortable way of making that trip now, though one cannot always be sure of getting a ticket on any particular day, since the military have first claim on all the seats.

March 11, 1941

Mrs. Frame and Rosamond have been here with us for their last weekend in China. We tried to do everything possible to make it a happy time for them both. We wanted to give Mrs. Frame a chance to see as many of her old friends as possible and to show her how strong an affection and admiration there is for her still in her old haunts, so there was a steady stream of guests at every meal but breakfast and a presentation of a little carved ivory figure from the old timers on the Women's College faculty.

And at the same time there were two other rings to the circus because we wanted to gather in some of the young fry for Rosamond's benefit, and it turned out that Saturday night was the only time that Ruth Woodsmall, Secretary of the World YWCA, who was in Peking on a flying visit, could come out to Yenching. She had many interesting things to say. She was in Chungking a few weeks ago and in Europe a few months ago and confirmed what we knew already that the sort of occupation we have had here for the last three years, even though we are not very fond of it, is not a patch on true occupation, 1940 style in the small countries of the continent.

Yesterday I went in to speak to the senior class at our Presbyterian school and came away as always wondering just what it is that is wrong with girls' middle school education in this country. This is really a good school and getting better all the time under Grace Y's leadership, but the stolid unexpressiveness of the girls' faces is really appalling.

Grace had warned me that this particular class is rather shy and mediocre, but after making all allowances for that and for the fact that they are not used to anyone speaking English except their English teacher, and after acknowledging that there were a few bright alert faces among them, it still seems wrong that any group of eighteen-year-old girls should look so blank. Individually they are bright enough, I am sure, and outside the schoolroom they chatter and play like high school girls anywhere, but there seems to be something absolutely deadening about classroom routine in Chinese middle schools. Whatever it is, it carries over into our college classes. The girls seem to feel that if they betray the slightest gleam of interest, they may be called on, and that is a horror to be avoided at all costs. There are only a few schools in the whole country that don't turn out these mask-like faces, and you can spot a girl from one of them in the first five minutes of any freshman class.

March 16, 1941

An Englishwoman from the Anglican Mission in a little border town in Shansi came to lunch with us today. She has been matron of the mission hospital there for about ten years and was very kind to us when we spent a weekend with her about five years ago. Even then it seemed to me to be as nearly literally God-forsaken as any town on God's earth can be, but from her accounts of what has happened there since the occupation, it must now be ten times more desolate. After long and fruitless negotiations the Mission has had to give up the hospital, turning it over to the new authorities for a nominal but totally inadequate compensation. The hospital will continue to run, but no longer will it serve the poor and the penniless and the undernourished. Our friend has naturally had to leave the hospital compound where she has lived so long, but she is going back after these few days of holiday in Peking to live next to the city chapel, although she will be the only Britisher in the town and although the present restrictions on travel will make it very difficult for her to get out again once she is there. She has red hair and a twinkle in her eye and doesn't seem to think she is doing anything heroic.

Augusta Wagner wrote on the same date to MBS's father about the changes in Peking: "Our American community in Peking and nearby steadily grows

*smaller as more and more women and children leave. At the same time
the influx of Germans is very noticeable. Dr. Stuart told me the other day
that whereas the German Embassy formerly was conducted by four men
it now needs and has thirty. The newspaper is full of their doings, the
hotels and hospices are crowded with them, one encounters them in all
the shops."[8]*

March 23, 1941

Last Sunday we listened to President Roosevelt's speech on the
radio; there was not a word in it which did not sound like the voice
of a country already at war. I do not see how we can help fighting
sooner or later, but it is dreadful to talk as though our only aim was
the annihilation of the German people. Our only Peking English
language newspaper is pro-Axis, and its correspondence columns
are full of letters, usually signed with pseudonyms, from English
and German sympathizers calling each other names. I'm afraid
the British letters seem as arrogant to the Germans as their letters
seem to us; but however nasty and misguided the German letters
sound to us, it's quite clear that they think they are fighting for
their lives.

April 2, 1941

I didn't write on Sunday because it was such a heavenly spring
day with the first white veil of the peach blossoms over all the
gardens that we decided to enjoy the noon sunshine on the back
hillside of the Summer Palace. The front courts of the Palace were
jammed with Japanese soldiers and sightseers, but the north hillside where the blossoms are out we had completely to ourselves.

Thank you so much for all the things you have sent. I don't
know by what magic you managed to persuade the Lakeville post
office to accept the parcel of coffee. No one else here has got any
packages from America for months, and a number of people have
had letters from friends at home saying that packages which they

have tried to send have either been refused by the post office or have been accepted and then returned a few days later. It's silly because the prohibition originated in Chungking, which wanted to restrict its imports to bare necessities. There is no real reason why it should affect us here. Apparently the Lakeville postmaster is the only one with sense enough to discriminate—or perhaps you have instructed him in the geography of China?

We have been hanging on the radio the last few days, trying to understand what is really happening in the Balkans. We were pleased to hear Fred Whyte last Saturday night commenting urbanely and with humor on the Far East and the Axis. There was a radio report a few days ago of the arrest of a number of missionaries in Korea, but we have heard no confirmation or details.

April 9, 1941

The news from the Balkans is not too good. We have just been listening over the radio to a courageous Norwegian in Shanghai speaking on the first anniversary of the German invasion of Norway. He spoke his mind regardless of the many Nazis in Shanghai who might take a pot shot at him from a dark alleyway. We're waiting now with much interest for Matsuoka's return to see whether it will bring fateful developments.[9]

April 27, 1941

The winds have dropped a little the last few days, and the campus has been simply heavenly. In our own garden we have lilac and yellow roses, wistaria and crab apple, as well as two crimson tulips and all the little white blossoms in the strawberry bed. The campus has great masses of color everywhere. Augusta is chairman of the Landscape Committee this year and spends lots of time working on some of the back corners that still need planting and trimming.

It's Monday evening now and I am yawning dreadfully since

we got up at four this morning to hear Churchill's broadcast. It came through clearly. His strong, tired voice, acknowledging that the path is long and stony, sounded very different from Hitler's blustery shouting. He ended with Clough: "For while the tired waves, vainly breaking, Seem here no painful inch to gain...But Westward, look, the land is bright."[10]

May 11, 1941

This year the Chinese calendar predicts a very hot summer, but there has been no faintest sign of it yet. This has been the coolest spring that anyone can ever remember. The garden looks fresh and flourishing without the rank air that it always acquires when the weather gets really hot and the rains begin.

I have been interviewing seniors about their plans for next year and trying to put them in touch with the best opportunities. Ran [Sailer] and I have been spending a good deal of time on a freshman girl who tried to commit suicide in January and is threatening to do it again. We have been having Council meetings with hot discussions of a new and better freshman curriculum, Scholarship Committee meetings with long discussions as to whether so-and-so is really in desperate need or just trying to get a little more pocket money, Deans' Committee meetings to decide on the honors to be announced on Honors Day this week, and the annual crop of class plays and graduation recitals of the music majors. Field Day and Alumni Home-Coming Day and similar pleasant occasions fill in all the chinks.

May 18, 1941

Tomorrow I go down to Paotingfu for three or four days of meetings of the Mission and the Executive Committee. The Mission group has shrunk to only about half its normal size with the evacuation of all but one of the mothers of young children. It is a real question whether some of the younger men who are on furlough this year will want to come back this fall, leaving their families behind indefinitely, so that we have to face the question of whether the work in a small station like Shuntehfu can go on without terrible overstrain and overwork for the few who are left.

I feel ashamed of living in the luxury of this pleasant comfortable house and the even greater luxury of working with people who speak the same intellectual language, more or less. The people who work out in the country and inland towns and villages have to make physical and mental adjustments every minute of the day and night.

We have had pretty good luck lately with the San Francisco broadcast on Sunday evening. Why not try sending us a message sometime. Messages should be personal, clearly written, not more than fifty words and should be sent to The Mailbag Program, General Electric Station KGEI, Treasure Island, San Francisco Bay. Messages should reach them on Thursday to be broadcast on Sunday morning their time. Sorry there is no station that broadcasts messages in the other direction across the Pacific.

MBS explained many years later about the Sunday evening program called Mailbag, a broadcast from the San Francisco station which allowed people in the United States to send messages to China after the mail service was cut down. "On one Sunday the messages would start to addressees beginning at the front of the alphabet; the next week they would begin at the end of the alphabet. By this time we had a fairly good radio, and we would gather around it every Sunday evening, armed with paper and pencil. Reception was far from regular and there would often be large gaps in the program, so if we heard a message addressed to anyone we knew in China, we would write it down and send it on."[11]

In May MBS wrote and sent home her annual "Report to the North China Mission," introducing it by speculating whether such a report should record how her time had been spent, or should be "a statement of the things one has tried to do, thus running the double risk of over-optimism and lack of realism?" Or perhaps, she added, it should sum up the work of the whole Mission of which she was a small part. In any case, she could report (without emphasizing what an extraordinary accomplishment it was in 1941) that "Yenching has happily been able to continue for another year.

"The credit for Yenching's uninterrupted work goes entirely to President Stuart. It is his skill in navigating a dangerous course that has made it possible for the University not only to keep open but to grow in more than numbers. Again and again during the past few years he has said mildly that he hoped at least to finish the semester without interruption, but one semester after another has been safely finished, and the class that is now ready to graduate this June is the class that sat for entrance examinations during the first bewildering gunfire of the summer of 1937. Not a bad achievement for the step-by-step policy!"[12]

June 1, 1941

Mission Meeting at Paotingfu was very successful. It seemed to me that perhaps we spent a little too much time talking about immediate details and not enough trying to take a long look ahead to see if times like these demand some radical change in policy, but probably it is just as well not to spend too much energy trying to foresee what is going to happen. If anything spectacular does happen in the next few months, it will probably take a form that will be highly surprising to everybody. And there is always the danger that planning for emergencies creates emergencies. In one of the missions here in Peking people spent so much time talking about what they would do if they all had to evacuate that they practically hypnotized themselves into going home.

Surprises

Nothing had prepared MBS for the unexpected announcement of another Yenching wedding, an international one. Once more MBS and Augusta Wagner managed the details of ceremony and reception, even as MBS struggled with Chinese families who expected their Yenching-educated daughters to submit totally to their fathers at home and accept arranged marriages.

June 1, 1941

Last evening we had a surprise from which I haven't recovered. One of our younger instructors is Michael Lindsay,[13] son of the Master of Balliol. He is an odd sort of creature, clever, shy, owlish, untidy, friendly, but not really at ease with people. He called up at supper time to make an appointment with Augusta, supposedly to talk about some exam questions.

When he came in, I was standing precariously balanced on a stool on top of a table trying to fix a high electric light wire. I didn't even notice that he wasn't alone until I heard him say to Augusta without any preamble, "Hsiao-li and I have decided to get married." I turned around and saw that he and one of our seniors were standing in the doorway hand in hand. I must have better equilibrium than I ever imagined, for I did not fall off my high perch!

They were both so extraordinarily happy that there wasn't much one could do except to wish them well and be as sympathetic as possible in talking over their plans with them, but just the same one's heart contracts at the thought of all the difficulties that lie ahead. She is an extremely nice girl but knows almost nothing of the world of ideas and music that Michael inhabits, and he knows equally little of her old-fashioned Shansi background. But though they have taken everyone completely by surprise, it is evidently not sudden or hasty on their part, so we're having an announce-

313

ment party for them here Wednesday, and I must write at once to Lil Haass that the YWCA will have to look around for someone else for the job they were counting on Hsiao-li to do after Commencement.

The last two days I have been rushing about trying to find a tactful mediator to help one of our brightest juniors whose parents are determined to marry her off. Her father has plenty of money but his concubine wants it all for her children, so he has arranged what he considers a good marriage for this daughter. She has just finished her pre-medical course here and is ready to take the PUMC exams. The boy her father has picked out is only half way through middle school! For the past two days she has shut herself up in her room in the dormitory refusing to see her father, who stands at the dormitory gate, feeling sure that she will eventually emerge, while the poor matron shuttles back and forth between the two and one of our patient Chinese instructors tries to make the horrid old man see reason.

Another of our students is on the brink of desperation because of the utter stupidity of her parents. Her father is on our faculty, is supposedly Christian, is certainly famous and respected, but I can hardly speak to him politely after hearing the girl's account of the slavish submission he requires of all his family at home. Most of these misguided parents make themselves just as miserable as they make their children, but they seem to be in the clutch of a selfishness that they can't break.

The great excitement of the past week has been Michael Lindsay's wedding. I think I wrote you about the bombshell of his engagement to one of our seniors. The wedding was the day after Commencement. Augusta had to manage all the details of the reception because of course Hsiao-li hadn't the faintest idea how to go about it, and Michael is the typical absent-minded professor. He appeared ready to go away after the wedding in one white shoe and one brown one. Everyone rallied around loyally to help.

I don't know whether we were more taken by surprise by the news from Russia than you were.[14] There had been a few rumors of course, but no one had believed them. We had some students for supper last Sunday night, two seniors, one with his bride, the other with his fiancée, and idly turned on the radio before supper. We could hardly either eat or talk the rest of the evening, but hung around the radio listening to one broadcast or another. Tokyo was even more surprised than anyone else and hasn't yet been able to make up its mind what to do or say next. Although no one attempts prophecy, it begins to look as though the summer might go by without disturbance here, in which case I could have come home after all, except that the boat on which I had passage from here left two weeks late, and the boat on which I had return passage has been taken off entirely!

Lacking passage home, MBS with some her friends, Western and Chinese, vacationed once more in Peitaiho

July 8, 1941, Peitaiho

We have rented a very nice house here for a month. Augusta and Agnes Chen and Chou Kuo-ping, one of our very nice young English teachers, came down a week ago and had all the work of getting the house opened and in order. They brought two servants with them, Pao Ch'ing, who was our boy for so long, and his cousin, Pao Sheng, a nice cheerful youngster. Mary Ferguson and I came down on Friday. Now, after three days of eating and sleeping and alternately sitting in cool breezes and lying in the sun, I feel made over.

The mountains and the sea are what make Peitaiho a nice place, and I never care very much about what people are here as long as there are a few good friends. But this year the place is distinctly less "horde-ish" than usual. The real estate office claims that most of the houses are full, and on the whole rents are fairly high, but of the houses I can see now from the porch nearly half are still shuttered. At church on Sunday the meeting house was only about one third full, and along the roads one hears Swedish and German more than Chinese and English. But the most noticeable thing of all is that there are so few children. The beach that used to be dotted with little white hats bent busily over sand castles now seems bare and deserted.

Prices are double what they were when we were last here five years ago, and the red tape necessary for everything is terrific, but we think constantly of our good fortune in being here in this peace and coolness, looking out at the long jagged line of mountains and the silvery purple sea stretching out beyond Shanhaikuan. People in other occupied areas do not fare so well, nor does everyone in this one.

Augusta Wagner wrote to Mrs. Speer that Peitaiho was different from the old days. "There has never been a car to spoil the peace of our days, but as I write this a truckload of Japanese soldiers has gone roaring by. We have no Japanese neighbors at this end of Peitaiho, but we have Germans and Italians in many houses where we used to have American neighbors.

"I had a nasty experience coming down here a couple of days before Marnie to open up the house. The servants and three Chinese friends were with me. Chinese people are subject to search at any time these days, but we were surprised when one plainclothesman and two soldiers, all Japanese, out of all the crowded railway car descended upon us, demanded our permits and snatched one of the girls' and my handbags. We made no protest, and I held myself in leash while the head man started to terrorize the girls by shouting and yelling at them while they answered his snarling questions with the greatest quietness and poise.

"I saved the day, however, by a God-given flash of insight. When I just was at my wit's end what to do to help them, just as he had ordered one of them to go with him, I quietly said, in a Chinese so fluent that the

girls said they never knew I possessed it, 'I have always heard that the Japanese are the most polite people in the world. I have a Japanese friend who is the most courteous person I know. I know from her that it is true.'

"For a second he stood there abashed and then in a grinning embarrassment said, 'I don't understand.'

"'Yes, you do,' said I. He grinned in sheepish embarrassment, turned his attention to questioning me but stopped terrorizing the girls, and forgot completely his order to the one to go with him. He didn't like the institution with which we are connected and proceeded to tell me what he thought of us. The three of them finally left us without anything untoward happening. All they finally did was to tear in half and take away half of a scrap pad I had in my bag, the pad being made up of old manuscripts of articles from our journals.

"But I started out to tell you of the administrative red tape that makes travel such a joy now. Having fortified ourselves with the necessary photographs, been finger-printed and secured the permit after a couple of trips to town, we had only begun. On the train as we approached Peitaiho, we had to fill in a blank giving age, marital condition, nationality, purpose of visit. When we got to the house, we had to fill in an identical blank. Then we had to take our passports to the police station and pay out $5.00 to them. For that they promise to grant us next week a permit to leave. Without it we cannot buy a railroad ticket. The day of leaving we must again fill out the blank giving age, marital condition, nationality, only this time for the purpose of leaving."[15]

July 19, 1941, Peitaiho

The days here in this peaceful place have gone very fast, and it is hard to realize that our few weeks here are now more than half over. We have been very quiet and lazy. Agnes and Kuo-ping went back last week, and Mary Ferguson followed them a few days later. Bi is here now, and in a few days Ruth Chou (one of the famous Huie family), the owner of this house, will probably come down with her two youngest children.

It has become a tradition to have Friday evening entertainments in the Assembly Hall here, a little more formal than the telling of tall tales in the Assembly Hall at camp but not much more so. I hadn't realized quite how predominantly British this small community is this year until last night when all the performers were British—and a jolly good show they put on. There was nothing in the outward gaiety to show what a strain they cannot help being under.

Everyone has theories about the significance of the Cabinet changes in Japan but really we are all totally in the dark as to what the next move of any nation will be in this part of the world. Missionaries from Manchuria have many interesting and some frightening things to say about all that has happened to them and their work.

July 25, 1941, Peitaiho

In a few days more we shall be packing up to go home. The chief topic of conversation on the beach or wherever two people meet is the train service: which trains failed to run yesterday or the day before and a swapping of rumors as to the possible causes. All through communication between Peking or Tientsin and Japan seems to have been cut off entirely, and the four or five trains a day running up from Peking or down from Mukden have been cut in half. The most plausible explanation is of course the movement of troops up to the Russian border, but no word of that appears in the daily papers. The servants tell us that lots of Japanese have left this area in the last few days. We had been hoping that perhaps our small Johnny would come over to spend part of the summer with us, but I am afraid that is definitely out of the question now.

We have been seeing a number of Irish and Scottish missionaries from Manchuria. They are all very sturdy and fairly philosophical, but life hasn't been much fun for them these past few years. They speak with the greatest calmness and cheerfulness of sons in the Air Force and daughters who are nurses in the casualty wards of the big hospitals and the only serious hardship that they mention is that letters so often take three months to come from England. The British ability to "take it" not only with determination but with humor far surpasses even the Chinese ability to weather storms.

Vacation over, MBS went to work making space for even more students for the coming year. Her personal anxieties were money, with American credit frozen by the Japanese, and mail, cut to shreds by censors.

August 3, 1941

Vacations are very pleasant, but it's always nice to get home again, particularly so in times like these when so many rumors are flying about. Peitaiho is a famous breeding ground for rumors, and there are plenty in Peking just now, but at least here it is a little easier to verify them. We came down on Wednesday, one of the hottest days of the summer. The trip takes twelve hours now instead of eight as when we went up four weeks ago because all the fast trains are being used for military movements to the north. But we felt very lucky to get through without mishap or delay or serious inconvenience because other travelers these days have not been so lucky.

When we got last Sunday's newspaper announcing that America was freezing Japanese credits, we realized that Japan would naturally have to retaliate at once, but we could only wait to see what form the pinpricks would take.

The first blow was to be told at the railroad station on Tuesday that orders had just come that no baggage was to be checked for Americans or Britons. Since we had taken down bedding for ourselves and three guests as well as a lot of books, we had visions of having to abandon a lot of useful possessions which we could not possibly carry by hand on the train, but fortunately a friendly person suggested a way out which I won't elaborate here, and we got our baggage safely. Numbers of people who left Peitaiho the day before were not so lucky for they were allowed to check their baggage there but when they tried to claim it in Peking they were told it was frozen! The Embassy has been protesting about this and a number of similar nuisances and perhaps they will be modified.

I've been busy the last few days with the business of admissions and ordering extra tables and chairs and double-decker beds for the thirty extra girls that we are planning to squeeze into our already bursting dormitories. But while we go ahead with the routine for the beginning of the new term we keep wondering how soon everyday activities will be seriously upset. "They say" that the present supplies of gasoline in Peking are nearly exhausted and that when they are gone there won't be any more. Rickshas and bicycles and legs are still perfectly good means of transportation, but our life will change a good deal if our busses between the campus and the city stop running. Far more important are the diminishing supplies of other oils used in the University power house. If our electricity gives out, we can light our houses with candles, but the laboratories would be completely crippled.

And most urgent of all is the question of money. The general principles for freezing American and British credits were announced over a week ago, but the local authorities haven't yet been able to settle all the details, so we don't know whether the present orders will be modified or tightened. At present Americans with money in the bank may not draw out more than $500 local currency a month. Ordinarily that would be ample for our way of living here, but this particular month it doesn't begin to be enough to cover the extra expenses of vacation, rent for the house at Peitaiho, etc., not to mention the winter supply of coal which usually has to be laid in and paid for at this time.

And if you don't have much money in the bank, how are you going to get any more if gold checks cannot be cashed and if the University funds and the Associated Mission Treasurers' funds are all frozen? So far, the University has a moderate amount of cash on hand, but all its bank deposits are frozen, and though some adjustment may be possible later, none seems to be possible for the moment. Everyone is very cheerful about it and anyone with five dollars offers to share it with his neighbors. So far no one has had to go hungry!

The mails have been more irregular than ever lately. There is a lot of dark talk about additional censorship and unwarranted interference, but it's quite likely that the chief trouble is simply the shortage of ships on the Pacific.

August 17, 1941

This last week brought Mother's letter of July 6, Father's of July 12, and one from Bob written at Crinon on May 19. The censor had a good time with his (or her) scissors on Bob's letter and three of the five pages looked like a very pretty stencil pattern. For the most part the bits cut out did not seem very important, but one whole paragraph of half a page was missing, giving no clue before or after as to what it contained. Father's letter also had a British censor's seal on it, as many American letters do nowadays, but the censor had fortunately not felt obliged to delete any Rockledge news. Mails travel by such curious routes nowadays that I don't know whether it is in Vancouver or Hongkong that they fall into British hands, but so few boats are still on the Pacific run now that we don't mind at all if a British ship has helped the mails along the way.

We have been trying to get our nice faithful young dietitian off for a year's study in America, but the amount of red tape is terrific. Washington set up new and very strict regulations governing the granting of visas to aliens, which went into effect on July 1, but on June 27 the Consulates here had not yet received the details, so when we at last learned that there had to be two guarantors in America and money had to be actually in the bank there, and lengthy biographies had to be sent to Washington, it was very late to get all the machinery started. We feel somewhat disgruntled that our New York Office has not been able to get the permits for Yenching people while the PUMC people were all able to sail on the *Coolidge* this week, but there are dark rumors that the Rockefeller Foundation has special pull in Washington!

With this last letter the Speers filed a bulletin sent on August 25, 1941 to "Relatives, Friends and Supporters of our China Missions and Missionaries" by The Board of Foreign Missions of the Presbyterian Church in the U.S.A. and signed by Lloyd S. Ruland, Secretary for China. This bulletin sums up information gathered by the Board of Foreign Missions from the Department of State and from missionaries in Japan, and it gives details of the travel arrangements of missionaries to and from China—not mentioning Yenching's difficulties getting a visa for its Chinese dietician.

At this time, reported Ruland, "The prevailing opinion in Washington is that there will be no war with Japan...It is felt that Japan, already with her hands full in China and with increasing distress at home, will not attempt anything so foolhardy. Of course, with such a tense situation, there remains the danger of an uncontrolled incident or of a last desperate step taken by a military regime that does not wish to be discredited."

The bulletin confirmed that those who were due to come on furlough or leave had all arrived in the United States "except Miss Margaret B. Speer who had expected to return for the summer but decided not to make the trip" and three others who stayed in China for various reasons.[16]

Frozen Funds, Scissored Mail

At Yenching a new term was beginning, and missionaries in Asia were finding the Mailbag Program on radio sometimes the only means of keeping in touch with people at home.

September 1, 1941

We sat up late last night listening from 11 to 1 to the Mailbag Program. It has become the great Sunday evening pastime of everyone in these parts who has friends and relatives in America. If you have a radio you listen in, and if you don't have a radio you plan to spend Sunday evening with some one who has.

There is always an exciting element of chance, for most of our radios out here are temperamental in one way or another. When we first started listening in the spring, the chances were about fifty-fifty that we wouldn't hear any of the messages clearly, but the station that sends the messages got a new powerful transmitter early in the summer so that we hear pretty well now unless there is a thunderstorm or—what is most maddening—our electric current goes off entirely.

Some of our neighbors have radios that work on University current (a different voltage from city current). In that case the current is not likely to fail accidentally, but it goes off finally and entirely at 11 o'clock. Our radio does not fit the University voltage, so we have installed one wire and one plug of city current, which works pretty well on the whole but is exasperatingly uncertain at times.

Last evening our living room filled up with expectant neighbors—four husbands hoping to hear from their wives and one mother hoping to hear from her children who arrived in San Francisco alone this week—but when we turned on the radio there was only blank darkness and silence. Three of them gave up hope and went home, but the current accommodatingly came on again about five minutes of eleven. The messages are read alphabetically, sometimes from A to Z and sometimes backward. Stanley Wilson, who has had a message from his wife every week all summer, listened patiently last night until the last W at two minutes to one, but didn't get a message after all.

However, it's good fun to listen even if you're not expecting any personal word. Last evening, partly to keep myself awake, I kept a record of the messages and their destinations. In the two hours messages were read for 172 people, most of them for people in China but some for passengers on ships at sea, others for Siam, Burma, Malaya, the Philippines, South Africa, Java, Guam, and New Guinea. Twenty-two of the messages were for people I know and many more were for people who now seem like old friends, although I have never seen them.

Since there is always the chance that the person to whom a message is addressed may not have a radio or that he may not have been listening in, one tries to write down many of the messages to people that one knows and send them on by postcard next day. It is the old rural sport of listening in on the party line on the grand scale.

The check which came from Mother several weeks ago is frozen so solid that there is no prospect of thawing it out at this end. Since there are rumors current, possibly unfounded but still persistent, that it is now considered illegal for us to send US checks through the mail, I am not attempting to send it back but have torn it up. In case you would still like it to go for relief work in this neighborhood, you could send it to Mr. Evans at the New York Office and ask him to transfer it to me through the regular University account.

Certainly there will be plenty of relief work needing to be done in these parts this winter. After many deliberations and searching of conscience, the group of faculty wives who run our *k'ungchangs* have decided to close up all that work. All the American *t'ai-t'ais* who used to help have now gone home, and, although some of the Chinese women like Freddy Li have worked like Trojans, they feel overwhelmed by the complete responsibility for all the designing and selling. The freezing of course has been the final straw. I don't know exactly how many women from the surrounding villages have been employed, but probably somewhere about two hundred, many of the chief supports of their families. Some of course can find other work, but many will be desperate.

The 'K'ungchangs' were workshops where women of the community came to sew. The Yenching faculty wives had made a great improvement over the ordinary embroidery which was for sale to foreigners in Peking. They ordered good linen from Ireland, good thread from France, and helped the women with the arrangement of old traditional designs as well as with new ones. The products were sold usually to tourists who came to Peking and the profits all went into relief work for the community.[17]

Another threatened change in life at Yenching was the cutting off of American magazines and newspapers. With her next letter MBS included a clipping from a Shanghai newspaper dated September 3, reporting that bags of mail with printed matter from the United States had been returned by the Chinese Postal authorities and that hereafter such mail would not be accepted by the Post Office there.

September 14, 1941

The enclosed clipping has filled us all with consternation for we should feel really isolated if all American magazines and newspapers were cut off, but I can't believe that the Chinese Post Office could really take any such action. But mails are certainly far from rapid. The *President Garfield* got into Shanghai two weeks ago but so far there is no sign that she brought any letters for us in Peking.

One can understand some of the delays after talking to Louis Wolferz who got here this week. He came on a Dutch freighter that was scheduled to leave San Francisco on July 8. It was delayed two weeks there before it finally sailed and then set off for Manila as they supposed by the Great Circle route, but after a week they found themselves in Honolulu. A bit later they were able to wave to some tropical isles and at last they came shivering into Brisbane and then north from there to Manila, all the time sailing with a complete blackout at night and with no idea of where they were except so far as the passengers could themselves make a few guesses from the stars.

Our first week of classes are over, and we are managing somehow to get along with our mammoth enrollment, already 340 girls and nearly 800 boys. By the time the last few stragglers on the waiting list have registered we'll probably have a total of 1150.

September 21, 1941

There was a good batch of American letters this week, but still no second-class mail, so that we are almost beginning to believe the rumors that all printed matter from America is to be barred henceforth from this part of the world.

This week has had a number of special occasions. Our neighbor Dr. Galt, who has been one of the pillars of Yenching and its mother institutions for over forty years, celebrated his sixty-ninth birthday on Monday. According to Chinese reckoning this counts as the seventieth birthday and calls for a really grand celebration, so the South Compound had a grand Chinese dinner for him as a surprise. It was here at our house, suitably decorated with a gorgeous golden "long life" character on a red satin background hung over the fireplace. Afterward there was a skit with Augusta and Ran and Harold Shadick showing Dr. Galt's hoped-for retirement in California being constantly interrupted by calls for help from Yenching over the trans-Pacific telephone.

The combination of pleasant fall weather and the shortage of gasoline have made me think longingly of owning a bicycle again, but it is practically impossible to buy a good wheel of my size now so I have borrowed Barbara Hayes's, which she didn't take to Baguio with her. The gasoline shortage has one great advantage in that it has cut down the traffic in trucks and taxis, thus making it quite possible to ride a bicycle to town without endangering one's neck.

A Fortnightly Letter by Nancy Cochran, the Smith College graduate who was teaching English at Yenching, included a description: a "very old bicycle, with an exceedingly high seat upon which [Marnie] tools with dignity about the campus."[18]

October 5, 1941

Lucius Porter got back yesterday after a circuitous journey on a Dutch boat. He left Grace Boynton in Hongkong from which she was planning to fly to Chengtu. He said her passport was exactly like his so that presumably nobody would have stopped her if she had tried to come North, but she was honor bound to the State Department and to Nanking University not to come to Yenching this year though we hope she can surely find a way to get here next summer. She will be happy to have a chance to see Wan-ying, who is in Chungking. We hear rumors that Wan-ying's tuberculosis is active again. I wish there were some way we could get her to a spot where life would be less Spartan and she could have some nourishing food again.

Grace Boynton did not return to the Yenching campus in Peking but made her way to Chengtu in "Free China," where she taught at what became Yenching-in-exile during World War II.

Michael Lindsay describes a meeting of the foreign faculty he says Leighton Stuart asked him to call to see who might want to move Yenching to Chengtu. "However, almost no one was interested. Miss Boring of the Biology Department said that she had made one trip into the countryside in winter and the water in the teapot had been frozen in the morning.

General opinion was that the United States would be able to defeat Japan in a few months and that a short internment was preferable to facing the discomforts of the Chinese countryside in winter."[19]

Later, when the Japanese closed Yenching in Peking, the University re-opened in Chengtu.[20] *But in October 1941, Yenching and Peking continued to hold luncheons, listen to the radio, plan trips to the Western Hills, and wait for mail.*

On Saturday we had our annual luncheon of the Peking Association of University Women. In spite of the long slow trickle of evacuation there were about twenty-five foreign women there and twice that number of Chinese. In the roll call of colleges the first name was the University of Amsterdam, which brought a spontaneous burst of applause when our one Dutch member stood up. (She was in Amsterdam with her children at the time of the invasion but has since managed to get back here to join her husband at the PUMC.) It was painfully ironic that the next name was the University of Berlin, which was greeted politely but with an obvious lack of warmth. We are hoping that the program of the club this winter will include not only our own "cultivation" but at least some small effort to help some of the refugee university women both in Europe and the Orient.

No American letters during the last ten days, but thank you very much for the two pounds of coffee which arrived in their neat and shining blue tins just six weeks after they were mailed in Lakeville in the middle of August.

The radio continues to bring us many good things. The Toscanini NBC Symphony concerts are being broadcast on Sunday afternoons, not directly from America but from Shanghai by some mysterious (to me) recording device that is as clear as if we were sitting in the NBC studio. Last week we heard very clearly the special Presbyterian broadcast from San Francisco, the first of six monthly ones. Several people spoke, bringing news of the Board and "inspiration"—why does that word so often ring a little hollowly?

We have a welcome holiday on Friday and Saturday, the Double Tenth (the tenth day of the tenth month), founding of the Chinese Republic, and still a celebratable occasion. We are hoping to get off for a trip to our favorite temple in the Hills, but there are mountains of work to be cleared off my desk first.

This was the last letter the Speers received from MBS until February 1942 when the following letters reached them, according to penciled notes on the letters: "Rec'd Feb. 11."

Mail had been slow all during 1941, events overtaking transport. MBS was still receiving mail, knowing, however, that it had passed through censors' hands.

October 20, 1941

A nice fat bunch of American mail this week—three letters from Father and two from Mother, the first dated August 28, the last September 14. I am relieved that most of my June and July letters got through even though some of them had spent nearly three months on the way. I don't know whether it is censorship or lack of transport that holds them up so long.

I heard a good tale about censorship this afternoon. A woman whose husband was in the interior wanted very much to go in to join him because he had been ill but she was absolutely refused a travel permit. Finally she prevailed on the authorities but they said that for her safety they would have to provide her with a special escort for the last lap of her journey. When the time came, she was met by a most courteous man who said, "Mrs. Johnson? Ah yes, Mrs. Grace Johnson, you are a very old friend."

"Why," she said, "who are you? I don't think we have ever met."

"Oh, but I know you very well indeed. I'm the censor and I've read dozens of letters from your husband all beginning 'Grace, my dearest angel!'"

Our chief concern at the moment is the new Japanese Cabinet. Everyone asks everyone else whether it will mean a change for the better or the worse, and the most profound reply that our most respected prophet can give is, "Well, it will surely be one or the other." But we have all long ago made up our minds to leave the future in better Hands than ours and as long as there is work to do there is no point in worrying.

In October 1941 Japanese Prime Minister Konoye resigned and General Hideki Tojo, the War Minister, was appointed in his place, signaling a tougher stand toward the United States. Diplomatic settlement with the Americans seemed unlikely, "since the United States neither could nor would understand the reasons why Japan must maintain a strong protective position in China."[21] War seemed likely, but temporary tranquility and good weather tempted MBS and Western friends to go once again to the Western Hills on holiday.

October 20, 1941

We had a perfectly gorgeous weekend a week ago. A national holiday fell on Friday, and the University happily decided that it wouldn't hurt us to take Saturday as a holiday too, so we went off to the Hills on Friday morning and didn't come back until Sunday afternoon. For the first time since 1937 we went to stay at a temple that is farther away than the first ridge of hills around Wo Fo Ssu and the Hunting Park. It is the "Platform of Heaven Temple," a lovely little place where we often stayed in the old days. It is not much more than five miles over the ridge from the motor road and the beaten track, and from its terrace at night you can see twinkling off in another fold of the hills the lights of the little mining town that supplies Peking with its coal and its electric power, but the priest told us we were the first party of guests they had had in four years.

Part of the temple was burnt, nobody quite knows how, in the first months of confusion in 1937, but it is being rebuilt, and the valleys through which we walked could not have been more peaceful. There were eight of us in the party: Harold and Nellie Shadick, Bi, Ran Sailer, Mary Ferguson, Willet Dorland—an odd free-lancing writer who has drifted into Peking—Augusta and I. The weather was more temperamental than usual for a North China October and gave us everything from bright sunshine to drenching showers and a howling gale, but the rain came only when we were safely under a roof and the unusual Scotch mist brought out the tawny russet shades in the hills more than the familiar sunshine.

October 26, 1941

No American letters this week. Probably we must resign ourselves to having not more than one or two American mails a month now. I hope letters are getting to you without too many and too long gaps in between.

I wonder if this will reach you before Thanksgiving. We are planning to celebrate on November 27 though there have been varying reports as to whether the President is proclaiming the 20th or the 27th as the day. Our party here will include the Shadicks; Lucius Porter and Sherm Wilson, both just back from America without their wives; Shirley Duncan; Stuart Mitchell; Dr. Brown, spryer at seventy-three than those of us who are thirty years younger; and Agnes Chen and Chou Kuo-ping. We'd like to have the Fergusons come out, but it may not be possible to get gasoline for a car, and they probably wouldn't care for rickshas in the late November weather.

Pearl Harbor

In the late fall of 1941 doubts about the future of Americans in North China intensified. MBS and Augusta Wagner went into Peking to see American and Chinese friends and came back full of duck and rumors. There was still no mail and not much money, but when she wrote to her family on December 7, MBS was planning Christmas festivities.

November 2, 1941

The dwindling American community in Peking is suddenly going through the throes of another wave of evacuation talk. It may turn out to be nothing but talk because of the extreme difficulty of making connections between here and Manila, which now seems to be the President liners' nearest port of call. Yenching and the Presbyterians are still unaffected and go serenely on, but there has been a little flurry among the handful of foreign nurses still left at the PUMC, and apparently at the American Board quite a number of the men may leave to join their families who went home last winter.

No one can quite see what change there is in the situation to justify any of this, but it seems to have been precipitated by a cable from the American Board office in Boston saying that any of their people who were expecting to go home next summer are free to start at once if they wish since travel may become impossible before June. That can hardly have been news to anyone, but of course as soon as one person decides to leave, two or three more begin to reconsider their plans and soon there is a nice little crop of rumors.

Dr. Stuart feels quite confident that "nothing is going to happen." I don't feel sure that there is any basis for such optimism, but neither do I see what justification there is for all of us to pull up stakes at this juncture. But every fellow must decide for himself, and no one can blame the men who have to consider an indefinite separation from their families.

November 9, 1941

We spent last night in town at the Fergusons' having been invited to dinner last night and to luncheon today by different Chinese friends. We have come back to the quiet of the campus not only stuffed with good Peking Duck but also full of all the latest rumors that circulate about the city. Because we didn't want to wait for the one and only Yenching bus which leaves town rather late on Sundays, and because the municipal bus was packed to the doors with soldiers twenty minutes before it was scheduled to start, we came out by the new bicycle rickshas which have lately flooded Peking. Although they are impossible in the narrow *hutungs* and are somewhat dangerous in crowded traffic, they bowl along very smoothly and quickly on the main roads. Coming along in the warm sunny afternoon light, with the Western Hills blue and purple in the distance, it seemed hard to see much sense in the new epidemic of evacuation fever, and yet in town, where rumors and facts and good and bad prophecies are almost indistinguishable, one finds it fairly easy to imagine what some of the inconveniences of internment would be!

Still no more American mail this week, but since it is now over three weeks since there has been any, we feel sure there must be some soon, for surely there is still enough shipping to get us at least one mail a month. The radio is certainly a miracle, but its ways are sometimes very mysterious and maddening. The Sunday evening group that gathers in our living room to listen to the Mailbag Program was very disconsolate last Sunday, for there were at least three people here who expected messages from their families, but we could only get a few faint inaudible mutterings.

The complexities of the freezing regulations continue to work out in inexplicable or unexpected ways. A couple of months ago the University didn't know whether its next dollar was going to be able to come through or not, but those of us on missionary salaries seemed to have no more to worry about than a little extra delay.

Now the University has at last got a license that seems to take care of its needs very satisfactorily for the present, but we Presbyterians are rather in the soup. First the American currency has to be changed into Shanghai currency at the Stabilization Board rate, which is less than half of the black market rate, and then it has to be changed to Peking currency at an exchange rate which has dropped to only 28 percent of normal, so the long and short of it is that our salaries are now about 40 percent of what they were. We can manage all right for a few months at this rate but not if it keeps up for too long!

December 7, 1941

There is an excellent chance of this letter really reaching you in less than two months, since the *President Harrison* is coming in to Chingwangtao to take off the Marines who are withdrawing from Peking and Tientsin and is also taking a few civilians who think this will be the best chance for some time to come to leave North China. Mary Hutchison, Dr. Stuart's secretary, is the only Yenching person leaving on this ship, but she has generously agreed to take all the letters we can write between now and Tuesday. Goodness knows when there will be any more shipping to take the letters we so trustingly drop into the mailbox. Yesterday at last there was a big fat American mail, greedily welcomed by everyone, even though the latest date on any letter was September 26.

This past week, a week of listening for the latest news of the Washington-Tokyo negotiations, has been a time of endless conversations, some informal, some official, about what the consequences of the apparently imminent break between Japan and America will be for us as an institution and as individuals. Father's good old Swift Diamond motto about preparing for the worst, expecting the best, and taking what comes, is still good advice in its last two thirds, but its first section is somewhat impractical under these circumstances when one's imagination, if given free rein, can envisage so many and such different "worsts."

Some of our friends have what seem to me to be fantastic eleventh hour schemes for avoiding the possibility of internment. The only sure method of doing that that I can see would be to have left Peking a few weeks ago and headed straight for San Francisco. Since we have all preferred to keep on with our normal occupations, we shall just continue to do so unless or until something happens to make it impossible to keep on any longer. Then we shall have to weather the storm as best we can. It renews one's faith in human nature to see how calm and serene everybody is.

Of course absurd rumors fly about. One of our Chinese neighbors came in at breakfast time this morning to say that her cook had heard from the bus driver that all the Americans had been at a meeting at the Embassy yesterday afternoon where they had been told that Roosevelt had given Japan a twenty-four hour ultimatum and that consequently all Americans were packing to leave within a few hours! We were able to reassure her that we had not left the campus yesterday afternoon, and that the only Americans who had braved the discomfort of the crowded Saturday busses were a few people who had gone to a Phi Beta Kappa meeting!

The outcome of this present crisis will no doubt be clear long before you get this letter, but don't worry about us whatever happens. In case we should have to leave the campus but should not be told that we must go anywhere else, we have a standing invitation to go to the Fergusons', and all Dr. Ferguson's resources of experience will be available for us. Actually I think everyone feels that we have lived so long in luxury and security that we now would welcome the thought of sharing some of the discomforts of the rest of the world.

At the same time we go on with all our normal plans for Christmas. Christmas presents will be cut to the minimum, for the freezing regulations and the present exchange rates do not leave anyone with any extra cash beyond ordinary living expenses, but we are expecting to have sixteen here for Christmas dinner and the usual open house for mobs of students in the evening. Plans for pageants and candlelight services and Sunday School parties go on as usual.

Later MBS added the rest of the story of Yenching's fate when the Japanese in a surprise attack bombed Pearl Harbor and the United States entered World War II. "In America people think of December 7th as Pearl Harbor Day since the news of the attack on Honolulu reached most people that Sunday afternoon. In China the attack came in what was early morning of December 8th, so my December 7th letter was the last one before upheavals.

"Dr. Stuart usually knew what was going to happen, but he evidently did not think there would be any new developments that weekend, for he went off to Tientsin on University business. People who knew what was going on in the embassies felt sure something was about to break. All leaves for the Marines and all leaves in the Metropolitan Police Force were canceled for that weekend. On the campus some people had decided that if a break came they could set out for the Hills. Augusta and I decided that as far as we were concerned this would be ridiculous. We didn't believe such an exodus would get people to any place of real safety, but far more important was our sense that our responsibilities lay right at Yenching until something should cut us off entirely.

"After writing my December 7th letter, I had spent the evening with others listening to the Mailbag Program. It was over at about twelve o'clock, and twiddling the radio dials we suddenly found that we were getting a news broadcast from New York. The announcer said that Prince Konoye and Roosevelt had had a conference and that Roosevelt had appealed to the Emperor. This made everyone think that there would surely be a respite for a day or two until the Emperor could send some reply. Little did we know that the Japanese aircraft carriers were already almost at the Philippines and Hawaii.

"We went to bed feeling quite calm. The next morning at breakfast we turned on the usual eight o'clock Shanghai broadcast, and instead of

the announcer's ordinarily cheerful greeting, he said in a solemn voice, 'I have an announcement from the Commandant of the Imperial Japanese Army in Shanghai: "In view of the state of war now existing between Japan and the United States and Great Britain, all American and British citizens are ordered to keep off the streets today." '

"Breakfast forgotten, I telephoned to Dr. Galt to tell him the news and found that he did not know that Leighton Stuart was not on the campus. He said we should have an Administrative Committee meeting at nine o'clock. As I hung up the telephone, Nancy Cochran appeared at the door to ask if she could borrow some bread, since she was one of those who had decided to head for the Hills at the first opportunity. We gave her a loaf, but she never got off and in the general confusion her dog ate it.

"As I reached the Administrative Offices at nine o'clock, the Japanese troops were already coming in the front gate of the University. Announcements were made that all foreign members of the Faculty should meet as soon as possible in the President's house, all Chinese members of the Faculty in another place, and all students in the main Assembly Hall.

"A Japanese major in an elegant grey cloak with his sabre at his side spoke to us through an interpreter and told us not to worry. He had nothing to say about the future but said that we should all immediately go home and write out an inventory of all our possessions and all our money reserves. This posed the first strange question of wartime. Should one continue one's normal habit of telling the truth or was this an occasion when it would be wise not to tell the truth? How could one decide whether, if one listed all one's belongings, the Japanese would then seize them, or if one did not list them and at some future time were to move away, would one be allowed to take anything which had not been listed? It appeared that telling the truth is much simpler and less troublesome than deciding what lies to tell.

"The rest of the day was busy indeed. One felt as though a large heavy stone was lodged in the pit of one's middle. The servants had

337

disappeared and the house was getting cold. One had no idea whether they had gone for good or would be back before long. It turned out that they were ready to come back by evening but all sorts of red tape had to be cut through for all of them to get passes and permits to go and come.

"Of the people who had considered taking to the Hills only two couples actually did so, and they were people who had made serious preparations long before. They were Michael Lindsay and his wife Hsiao-li and a young British physics professor and his wife.[22] Both Michael and Bill Band had been helpful to the guerrillas in previous months, getting them parts for their radios and other supplies that they needed. They knew that they would be immediate objects of Japanese interest and had arranged for a car to be ready to take them on the first lap to the Western Hills whenever war should be declared. They left the East Gate of the campus just as the Japanese soldiers were coming in the West Gate and got over the first range of hills before evening. Michael and Hsiao-li stayed in Yenan for some time, and their first child was born there. The Bands, I believe, went on to Chungking.

"For the next few days one of our problems was the need for interpreters, since we had only one or two Japanese-speaking people on the campus. The chief interpreter for our guards was a Korean, and though at that time most of the Koreans in Peking were ruffians, this particular young man did his best for us.

"Dr. Galt and I spent part of the afternoon persuading the Japanese that the women's dormitories need not be searched that evening. The Japanese evidently had instructions to try to keep the University running but this was something we violently opposed. We were not ready to be another puppet institution in Peking. We asked that students be allowed to go home, but the Japanese said that would be impossible. However, they reluctantly said that any student with a home in Peking might go home for a day or two. What a mistake! The obvious result was that every one of our 1150 students, although many had come from the most distant provinces, all discovered that they had homes in Peking, and on Tuesday morning they began to leave. By noon there was not a student left on the campus.

338

"Tuesday was an unusually mild and sunny day, very different from the usual bitter winds of early December. I had gone on Monday evening to the women's dormitories to say good-bye to the students, assuring them in my optimistic way that this interruption in work couldn't possibly last more than six months. Tuesday morning Augusta and I went down to the gate as the students streamed out of the campus. Some had their bedding piled on bicycles, a few had rickshas, some waited for the public busses, some had got wooden carts, but all went off in remarkably good spirits and all very helpfully doing what they could for one another.

"The next few days were extraordinarily busy. We learned that Dr. Stuart would not be able to return to the campus except for an hour to get some of his belongings. He and Dr. Houghton of the PUMC and Dr. Snapper, the wonderful Jewish doctor from Amsterdam who had recently come to Peking, Mrs. Snapper and Mr. Bowen, the business manager of the PUMC, were all put under house arrest in Peking. The Snappers were released some time later, but the three American men were kept in confinement until the end of the war.[23]

"As time went by we learned that one after another of our leading Chinese professors was arrested by the Japanese. These men had a bad time for the next six months. One of our chief concerns was to help their wives and children.

"It became clear that the Japanese wanted Westerners who lived in different parts of the campus all to congregate together, and the best place for this seemed to be the South Compound. So plans were made in our house for Lucius Porter and Mr. and Mrs. Howard Payne, a British couple who had come from Tientsin to help in our Treasurer's Office, to come to live with us at '57.' Altogether we collected twenty-nine American members of the Faculty in the South Compound plus several Britishers and one German. We were to be a little community, almost a commune, there in our own compound until August 1942."

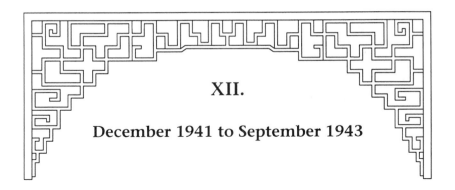

XII.

December 1941 to September 1943

A Thick Curtain

L etters and packages sent by the Speers to China in December 1941
were returned to them marked "Service suspended." Mrs. Speer wrote
to friends, "A thick curtain has dropped."

The Speers did get indirect word that MBS was probably still on the
Yenching campus. A dispatch from the Chinese News Agency Board of
Information of Republic of China in Chungking confirmed that the American and British faculty were confined to the South Compound and added:
"It was understood that some Japanese favor converting Yenching into a
hospital, while others advocate taking over a part of the school and oper-
ating it with a Chinese faculty, but under Japanese supervision. The
latter proposal, however, is handicapped by the fact that some of the
Chinese faculty members have already left the campus and others refuse
to serve the Japanese."[1]

Of course the interned Westerners were aware of the anxiety of their
families. By mid-January there was a rumor that the post office would
accept letters for abroad, and so MBS wrote to her parents—a letter that
reached them a year later, January 16, 1943. Red Cross messages sent
later were similarly delayed, but read chronologically as written tell something of the story of life under the Japanese—carefully phrased for the
eyes of the inevitable censors.

January 15, 1942

The main thing to tell you is that we are all well and happy and extremely comfortable. During the autumn we often joked about internment but never dreamed that our outward conditions would be as comfortable as they have been. The first week was full of excitement, but the officers who took over the University were extremely courteous and everything has been made as easy as possible for us.

The students were all sent home at once. The British and American members of the faculty were told that we should concentrate in one or two places, so all those who lived in scattered parts of the campus moved into the South Compound. Those who lived outside the campus have been allowed to stay in their own houses. Because of the necessity of gathering together and also in order to save money on fuel and household expenses we have all doubled up. There are five of us in our house: Lucius Porter and the Howard Paynes and Augusta and I, and we all enjoy our community living immensely.

Although in times like these no one feels exactly carefree, yet aside from the war we have all the elements of a nearly perfect life—good companions, the beautiful campus, and the first leisure many of us have had for a long time. Since we are in our own homes, we have plenty of books, and most of us are using this opportunity for language study, spending five or six hours a day studying Chinese. We only wish we had news of you and that you could look in to see how well off we are.

There are of course one or two hard things. The lack of letters from home is the worst, but it is something that has to be accepted as inevitable for the present, and we know that God's loving care surrounds you as it does us.

The problem of money is not so immediate as it seemed at first, but it will of course become an acute problem in time unless it is possible for the International Red Cross to arrange some sort of transfer of funds. In the meantime the authorities have allowed the University bank balances to be used to pay our December and January salaries, and we have made an arrangement among ourselves for a joint sharing of all our resources. We are eating simpler food than before but by using the local whole grains and by making the most of the knowledge of the diet experts among us we are getting an extremely wholesome diet. Augusta and the cook manage to make it taste perfectly delicious.

From a purely personal point of view the hardest thing so far has been parting with the dogs. If I had known during the first few days that we were going to be able to stay on in our own house, I doubt whether I would or could have done it, but decisions had to be made in the midst of the first confusion, and it seemed then better to have a quick and peaceful end than to run the risk of having to leave them suddenly without being able to make any provision for them. But I miss them more than I can say.

A trip to the city has now become a great event, but the authorities are quite ready to give the necessary permit to go through the city gate whenever there is any real need such as seeing the dentist. There is lots more to say but perhaps one sheet of paper is enough for this first attempt.

MBS added in her 1982 memoir what she could not safely write in 1942. An immediate, sad decision to put down the dogs was made partly because at a time when people were having trouble getting enough to eat it seemed unwise to feed pets. "So Bi and Harold got some chloroform from the Infirmary and managed the sad job for the Shadicks' dog and ours."[2]

The complimentary description of the Japanese soldiers in her letter did not include some of the details she recalled later. "During the first days there were many astonishments. Every few hours some Japanese soldiers would charge through the front door and walk through the house. Their only explanation was that they were counting the light bulbs. They seemed to do this two or three times a day for a week.

342

"There were times when the Japanese guards seemed rough and uncouth, but there were several pleasant instances. Nancy Cochran's household at that time included a Chinese member of our Faculty, his American wife and their infant son. One morning at breakfast a Japanese soldier arrived at the door and asked if there was a baby in the house. Somewhat hesitantly they said, 'Yes.' Whereupon he opened his jacket and produced a bottle of milk. (The University dairy had been taken over by the Japanese on the very first day, and we had not been able to secure any milk for ourselves. They were astonished and thanked him heartily. He stood looking about the room hesitantly and saw a Victrola in the corner. He asked if they would play some records and if they had Debussy's 'Afternoon of a Faun.' In their confusion they put on the second half of the record. Whereupon he politely said, 'I think that is not the beginning.'

"Another time Augusta and I had received permission from the guard to go to the dentist in Peking, the first time in some weeks that we had been off the campus. Not knowing whether we could get a ricksha or a place on the public bus, we were standing outside the University gate when a Japanese Red Cross truck came down the road and asked if we would like a lift to town, which we gladly accepted.

"There was one exciting morning when I went to the Administration Building with some requests to the Japanese there and saw that the door of our Treasurer's office was open and that Mary Cookingham, our bursar, was being questioned closely by a Japanese officer. Stephen Ts'ai, our controller, was standing in the room and motioned to me to come in.

"The office had a large walk-in safe or strong room whose door was around a corner and could not be seen from the hall or by the Japanese in the room unless he had turned completely around. Stephen motioned me into the safe and said, 'Look, Marnie. These are all things that belong to people on the campus, left here for safekeeping. The Japanese will want to look in here in a short time. See what you can take and take it away and come back as soon as possible.'

"I therefore stuffed the pockets of my Burberry coat with wrist watches

343

and bunches of cash and walked home nonchalantly. It was beginning to snow, and I hoped I would meet no one on the way. Rushing into the house, I emptied my pockets on the bed, told Augusta to put everything in the closet, and sped back to the office for a second load.

"Stephen said,'You'd better not come back again but do what you think should be done with these things.' Later that afternoon poor Stephen was badly beaten by the Japanese because they found a small satchel of ammunition on the top shelf of the safe, something which a previous member of the faculty had used years before for duck hunting.

"As soon as I got home I took the money to Dr. Galt and we decided later that it should be apportioned among the wives of the Chinese faculty who had been imprisoned. The wrist watches and other things were labeled and we were able to get them to their proper owners."[3]

According to Dwight Edwards, when the Japanese took over the Yenching campus, several of the Chinese faculty and staff were arrested and incarcerated. "Seemingly the whole purport of the arrest was to extort from them a confession that Yenching was subsidized by the American government to foster pro-American sentiment and inculcate dangerous democratic ideology, contrary to the 'kingly way' of the Orient." The Chinese faculty were cruelly treated but refused to make the confession demanded by the Japanese.[4]

And for the Westerners to live "a relatively placid and uneventful life in our own houses" was "an unreal life and we felt a useless one." Even with permission from the Japanese authorities getting into Peking was difficult. "Chinese friends from the city and from the village of Haitien were sometimes able to come to see us bringing news of other friends, but as the spring wore on more and more of our Chinese friends began slipping off to Free China."[5] The real cause for concern was still the families of the Chinese faculty who had been arrested. These families were not allowed to leave the city, and Yenching's Chinese friends in trouble were cause for apprehension.

The detained Western faculty studied Chinese, read, discussed theology, played games, and prayed. The sharing of money and food was *not always easy, and health problems increased.*

Communication with the outside world was limited. "We had a radio for the first few months, although much of the news was disheartening—the fall of Hongkong, Japanese naval victories. There were no letters at all from the United States, and there was no point in our writing letters except when now and then there was a rumor that some diplomat had some way in which news could get out.

"We learned in time that we could write to Free China and one of our friends there might be able to send on our letters, or at least the news in them, to America. Naturally such news took months to arrive. At first we were told we could send postcards. But when we had used our tiniest handwriting to squeeze the most news onto a card we were told that no card could have more than twenty-five words. The Red Cross had a system for sending messages that seemed possible but was not very practical. One could send twenty-five words once a month. The messages we concocted were non-committal but reassuring. Some of these got through to their destination in three months, others took more than a year."[6]

Augusta Wagner wrote a tightly packed postal which got through to the Speers eventually. It was, she said, cheaper than letter post and open and easier to censor, but her messages went through untouched. She noted that they were amazingly busy "in spite of the fact that our regular work is no more. Living collectively involves one in much extra consultation, accounting, etc. We are surrounded and uplifted in heart by the kindness of our friends, who are, many, in great sorrow and anxiety over the unknown fate of their loved ones." The Speers would know that the friends were probably the families of the Chinese faculty who had been imprisoned. She reassured Mrs. Speer that the authorities were treating the prisoners with consideration in many respects and concluded "Our chins are up!"[7]

MBS kept a four-lines-a-day diary during 1942 which survived the war stored with other possessions at the Fergusons' house in Peking and later brought to the United States by Mary Ferguson. In minute handwriting she recorded that the Japanese soldiers were at times curt, boorish, and demanding. Later she recalled that "One part of our lives which caused a good deal of discussion and some recrimination was how we responded to our Japanese guards. Any politeness on our part was considered by some of our fellow 'internees' as collaboration. It was a question of how far we should be pragmatic and how far we might attempt Christian friendliness." There were also differences of opinion about money and supplies, aired at a two-hour community meeting "with hot discussion on sharing versus hoarding."[8]

During the winter of 1942 the Westerners were still able to listen to the radio, but telephone service was cut off February 8. MBS spent a good bit of time and energy rushing about getting supplies for the cook, but the Yenching spirit was still unquenched. On February 7 they had a triple birthday party for Bi, Stanley Wilson, head of the Chemistry Department, and Langdon Gilkey, who had come to China from Harvard for a year but was to be there until the end of the war.[9] On February 21 MBS and Augusta Wagner had thirty-nine people for dinner for a "Valley Forge Banquet" with skits and scenes from George Washington's life. Parties and celebrations were a way of preserving equanimity, as they had always been. "Everything that could be done without costing anything helped to punctuate life with something entertaining or amusing."[10]

There were further restrictions in the spring but also hopeful possibilities for their release. In mid-March their radio was confiscated as well as the pass allowing them to go out the East Gate of the campus. But at about the same time there were rumors of possible repatriation. At the end of March MBS sent a letter to Miss Woodsmall, General Secretary of the World YWCA, at the neutral Geneva headquarters, hoping it would get through, since Switzerland was neutral, and could be sent on to the Speers, which it was, although it did not reach Geneva until August 29. When the Speers received their copy was not recorded.

MBS tried again on May 7 because there was a chance of getting a letter to her parents "by various devious channels." At this point she could truthfully reassure her parents that she and other Yenching Westerners were being well treated by the Japanese.

May 7, 1942

I am sitting writing now in my own sunny bedroom looking out into the garden onto flourishing rows of radishes and lettuce and a luxuriant strawberry bed. Who ever dreamed that internment would be like this? There are twenty-five foreigners left here in the South Compound, with another dozen in nearby houses just outside the campus, and although there have been ups and downs and moments of uncertainty, there still seems to be a reasonable expectation that we may be allowed to stay on here.It's an extraordinary life. We have the comforts of our own homes (at least about half of us are in our own homes and the other half have moved in with us); we have servants, the beauty of our gardens and the hills around, a simpler diet than in the past but still more than adequate, and more or less assurance of a monthly dole from the Japanese Embassy through the local American and British Relief Committees for the duration of the war.

MBS described the minor irritations of restrictions, her sorrow for the Chinese faculty, and her frustration at not being able to work. This letter did get through. A postscript to the letter read:"If we do have to leave this house, we have a haven at the Fergusons'."

The diary shows that before MBS wrote this letter, the internees were aware that they might have to move off campus because the Japanese intended to use it for a research institute. Lucius Porter began negotiating for housing in Peking, possibly at a Mission Compound. MBS records that he and others were talking about a future Yenching and whether it should be radically different from the old one.

MBS also went to Peking, by bicycle now, where she was able to see C.W. Luh, one of the imprisoned faculty, at the Mission Hospital, reporting that he was "as emaciated as Gandhi." On June 18 those who remained in prison were released and MBS went to Peking to see them. Lin Chia-t'ung, Dr. S.T. Wang, and Stephen Ts'ai, who looked very white, but all were in good spirits and said their days of imprisonment had been a wonderful experience.[11]

On June 24 MBS reported that Japanese soldiers were moving into the women's dormitories, and it was rumored that all the Women's College buildings were to be used by the Japanese army. In July the Western faculty's move was announced, and there was great confusion. It was unclear what they could pack and take and how the baggage would be moved. Life was no longer comfortable. There were roll calls and rumors, and everyone was tired. Augusta was ill. There were arrests in the village and a stockade erected around the Compound. "All combined to cause general uneasiness."[12]

The Move to Peking

On July 28 MBS and Augusta Wagner made a ten-mile move into the city, "really a new world."[13] The new quarters of the American group from Yenching were in San Kuan Miao, an old temple in the center of the Legation Quarter in Peking, which had been remodeled for American Embassy junior staff. MBS and Augusta were able to bring their furniture from Yenching and once again were reasonably comfortable. MBS finally received a letter her mother had sent in February, a very great treat, and was able to send a reply.

August 6 [1942]

We have certainly been lucky beyond all expectation in general living, and the crowd to live with a fine one too. All the latter part of spring there were rumors of having to move, including a definite order that was rescinded, and finally it came to a head the end of last month, so in we came, with a few staying in houses in the village there. These are old Embassy quarters for attachés and such, old Chinese houses with mostly big rooms, and very run down and patched roofs and installations—the lights constantly out of order. But rainy season will soon be over—it came late after a very hot June. Winter will be awful to heat, but we hope to be out. But even then it will be comfortable enough. No sickness worth mentioning since last Fall.

I may start in Language School in a few days, if not, will study language here. Read and maybe see some sights. Most people [Westerners] in Peking still in their own houses but may be gradually concentrated to free the houses for other uses. Perhaps crowding many in here. We now wear red arm bands but are free to go anywhere in the city.

The Embassy quarters were available because the Embassy staff had been repatriated on the first trip of the "Gripsholm."[14] At first MBS and other Yenching people heard that a second repatriation trip was imminent, but it turned out to be only for the British. Bi and the Paynes left on August 10, leaving MBS with a "gloomy feeling of final separation, of the end of a stage in our lives."[15] Bi carried with him in his pockets letters from those staying behind, and he was able to keep them from the guards. One reached the Speers November 14, 1942.

8 San Kuan Miao
Legation Quarter, Peking
August 9, 1942

I never in my life expected to be living in American Embassy property but here we have been for nearly two weeks, all moved and settled, bag and baggage, furniture, books, and servants. We are not "concentrated" or "evacuated" or even "refugeed," but after a number of false alarms about having to leave our Yenching houses we were suddenly told three weeks ago that we were to be ready to leave within forty-eight hours. You can imagine the bustling and hustling! In the end it was nearly a week before the first households trekked into Peking but in the space of the next five days (one of them pouring torrents of rain all day long) the twenty-six of us who had been living in the South Compound transferred ourselves, our retinues, and our household goods down to the last precious curtain pole and piece of kindling wood into our new quarters.

This property is now officially under the care of the Swiss Representative in charge of British and American interests, but our good Presbyterian Sam Dean is now the actual custodian, and the houses have been put at the disposal of the Americans in the city who have had for numerous reasons to vacate their own houses.

Talk continues of the possibility of another repatriation boat for Americans, but no one knows whether there will really be one or when it will leave or how many it will carry or what route it will take. Some of the wishful thinkers among us spread reports that there will be a boat by Christmas and that the exchange this time will take place by way of Honolulu instead of Mozambique. On the various occasions when we have had to state our wishes about repatriation I have said that I would be glad to go provided there seems nothing for me to do for the University here. At first I thought that there would be jobs I could do but as the months have gone by I have come more and more to the conclusion that I could be far more useful at home than marking time here, and whenever the day comes when reconstruction is possible I could still get back in time. It has become more and more evident that the process of picking up the pieces of the University after this complete "abolishment" is going to take a long time.

Not knowing whether earlier descriptions of the "really happy months in the South Compound" had ever been received, MBS repeated some of what she had written earlier about the comfort, friends, and leisure, discussion groups and "Saturday evening fun," and an "hilarious tennis tournament in which I, about the third worst player in the group, was partnered with Lang Gilkey, erstwhile captain of the Harvard tennis team"; as well as the pain of being "cut off from nearby friends because of arbitrary distinctions of nationality" and from "far away friends by mail-

less oceans and continents." She detested being powerless to help her suffering Chinese friends, and being ignorant of what was happening in Europe. They had managed to meet financial problems and "Augusta, who is a genius in planning food, provided us with much more palatable and varied menus than most of our neighbors," a diet of local grains and very little meat.

Leighton [Stuart] is the only one of our American group whose liberty has been curtailed. During the winter and spring he was allowed occasional visits to the outer world, but it is now several months since we have had any communication with him except by writing. Twelve of our most prominent Chinese faculty members were "detained" on December 8 and held for nearly six months. The experience was a bitter one for their families but most of the men themselves found that confinement did for them what it did for John Bunyan.

To her brother-in-law Bob Barbour in England MBS also wrote a letter, hoping he would be able to send it on to the Speers in America. In this letter she said more about the Chinese students and faculty.

August 8, 1942

Eight months today since we got up from the breakfast table to turn on the radio and heard the first word of a state of war between Japan and the US. Within less than an hour the campus had been occupied and the University as a university was abolished.

The students all left the campus the day after the "Accident," as one of the interpreters happily and unconsciously christened the outbreak of hostilities. Some of the Chinese faculty moved away almost at once; others stayed on in their houses until early April when they were told by our gendarmerie guards that they would have to vacate University property.

*Among other letters Bi carried was one from Nancy Cochran, a member
of the English faculty at the Women's College of Yenching, to her family. She asks them to "let Marnie Speer's family know that she has been
a Rock of Gibraltar to us all."* [16]

*MBS herself described the Peking period of internment as a time when
they were "free to move about the city and to see friends although we felt
we should not be too conspicuous in visiting Chinese friends. We lived
simply but had many guests for meals and for tea, such as the time when
Mary Ferguson brought Père Teilhard de Chardin for a high tea.*[17]

*But there was the summer heat, and Augusta's illness, and "con-
stant changing rumors." In an International Red Cross message to her
family, she wrote a hopeful message they received in April 1943.*

September 10, 1942

Expecting repatriation next boat. Preparations all made to leave
last week but sailing postponed. Hope to be home for Christmas.
Dear love. Happy birthday, Father!

*On October 12, the Speers received a letter from Bi, who had reached
Durban on the way to Australia. He repeated the news of the move from
the South Compound to Peking. He too noted "Needless to say Marnie
all through has been a tower of strength." He was, as he wrote, the only
one who successfully got away. All the British repatriates except Bi were
left in Shanghai, as a result of mismanagement and confusion. "I felt
like a deserter, though the desertion was practically under orders and it
has been heartbreaking being torn away from one's life work and leaving
Yenching where one has had so many very dear friends.*

*"Marnie has been splendid. She is I am sure the mainstay and cen-
ter of the group, so wise, so full of common sense, and very able, so
helpful and patient. Of course she is all that to me and more."*[18]

*For whatever reason, in December Mr. Bevan had not heard from the
Speers and cabled from Melbourne: "DID MY AFRICAN LETTERS AR-
RIVE ARE MARINE AND COLLEAGUES REPATRIATED HEARD NOTH-*

*ING SINCE LEAVING PEKING AUGUST ANXIOUS." The transforma-
tion of MARNIE to MARINE came to the attention of the Office of Censorship, The Cable and Radio Censor, in New York who wrote to the
Speers demanding an explanation and identification and references. One
suspects that even though they too were extremely anxious, the Speers
were amused. They responded the next day explaining and including
impressive references. They had cabled Mr. Bevan that they had received
no reliable information. To the Office of Censorship, they added, "When
Mr. Bevan left Peking in August there was reason to hope that all Americans in North China would soon be repatriated, but this has not taken
place. Evidently no word of this delay has reached Australia." Meanwhile, MBS continued faithfully to send Red Cross messages, rejoicing
when she received the rare communications from home, and always
expressing hope that she would soon be allowed to return to the United
States.*

October 8, 1942

Mother's welcome news of Beryl received last week. Leading
simplified life with belongings all packed ready for repatriation.
Expect surely be home for Golden Wedding.

*At the same time, MBS sent a letter to her family—continuing to try all
channels—to Grace Boynton in Chengtu, who received it November 15
and sent it on. It reached the Speers on January 16, 1943.*

October 11, 1942

Your letter telling of the arrival of the latest granddaughter came
last week and was hailed with joy unbounded not only for its good
news but because after more than ten letterless months the very
sight of your typewriting brought joy to my heart.

For the last seven months I have been sending brief letters at
regular intervals but how many of them reach you or how long
they take I haven't the faintest idea.

Again she repeated the news of the uneventful period in the South Com-
pound and the tumultuous move in the heat of summer and rainy season
to one of the Embassy houses in Peking, "a vast rambling Chinese house,
which for all its diplomatic status was nevertheless dilapidated, leaky,
and really filthy." She told again of being instructed almost immediately
after the move to get ready for repatriation "within a few days" and
then, when possessions had been given away or sold, being told that the
"whole repatriation scheme was indefinitely delayed."

That was six weeks ago and we have lived in a state of suspension ever since, revelling in the beauty of Peking in the autumn sunshine but perpetually wondering when the next orders would come and hearing endless rumors about quotas which might exclude half of us. Mary Ferguson, who is doing a magnificent job as assistant to the Swiss Representative in charge of British and American interests, has a neat little red sign on her desk, "No News Today," and we have learned to treat every tale as a fairy tale until we hear it from her lips. We have been exceedingly thankful that this change of plans came while we were still here and in our own establishments, no matter how bare they may be, instead of being stuck in Shanghai, as happened to many of our British friends who left here in early August expecting to sail from Shanghai at once but who are still there packed like sardines into temporary quarters.

The nice Paynes are among those languishing in Shanghai, and Lucius did not move into town but is living with two others in the village near the campus. Our new housemates are Shirley Duncan and Dorothea Hanwell, two nice girls in their middle twenties.

The Speers received at some point a copy of a letter written by Alice
Boring to her family on November 15, 1942, repeating much of what
MBS had written but with a few additional details of the life of the

Yenching people in Peking: "Here 25 of us who are Americans are grouped into five households: one is a family with two children, one consists of nine bachelors and grass widowers, whose families returned to America a year ago, the other three are single sisters.

"Here we have complete freedom within the city walls. We carry identification cards, but they are seldom asked for—once or twice when I leave a letter or package at the gate where J. Leighton Stuart is confined. As I have not lived in the city since 1926, and was very busy when I did live here, it has been great fun seeing the sights of Peking, and we have done it thoroughly; temples, palaces, museums, ancient sites, parks— there are endless attractions in Peking, and we have had time to burn. The chief difficulty about our situation is that we do not know at what minute we may be told to be ready in two days for evacuation." She had put her name on a list of those who would wait for a later boat, since it was anticipated that there would not be room for all in the first repatriation. According to a letter from Augusta Wagner written about the same time, the Yenching group had heard that Leighton Stuart was not to be allowed to go with repatriates. "He sent out a rather despairing letter which upset Alice (Miss Boring) terribly and she is raising heaven and earth to be allowed to stay."[19]

But Alice Boring was also energetically working on Chinese Amphibia, planning publication. She had given away her books to the YWCA except for biology books, which she gave to a friend who has been lending them. "Perhaps I shall never see many of them again but they will have been useful during this emergency when many students have no books. We are not supposed to see our Chinese friends, but as a matter of fact, we do. They come here frequently, and that makes us very happy. No vicissitudes can break down our Yenching friendships. Freddie [Li] and I see each other once a week, alternating between her coming here and I going to her home for lunch. Stephen [Ts'ai] dropped in yesterday for tea, and I spent one whole morning with William and Rhoda [Hung] at the end of which they insisted on keeping me for lunch. So you see there is some point in being here, and it is better being in the city than it was outside from that point of view."[20]

Although she too stressed the sociability of life in Peking, MBS recorded in her diary in October and November that prices were up, coal and food were problems, and the weather was colder. They heard constant, hopeful (but erroneous) reports of American air attacks on North China, as well as ominous rumors that "concentration camp is imminent."

November 17, 1942

Settling down to hibernate. Still hoping early repatriation. Three letters received: Mother's of June, July, Daisy's May. Busy studying language. Well, hopeful. Love to all.

Two days later MBS received a Red Cross letter from her mother—sent March 30, 1942—and replied "All well and cheerfully adjusting to city life and economical living."

Hopes of early repatriation were fading. The Speers received a letter from The Board of Foreign Missions of the Presbyterian Church in the USA dated December 18, 1942, deeply regretting the long delay and lack of any definite information. "However, we can report from a reliable source that the Department of State is pressing very hard for a completion of the negotiations, and there is some reason to hope that within the next two weeks the official list of those to be repatriated may be released and the 'Gripsholm' start on its voyage." This letter also noted that "Some feel that it is probable Miss Speer is now in Shanghai."

The letter held no hope at all for getting "anything like parcels" to the Yenching faculty in China. "The United States Post Office will receive first-class messages for those officially listed by the Japanese as 'interned,' but our missionaries are not regarded as in that category.

"We are therefore, suggesting that no further attempts be made to communicate with these friends until the list is released. Then, if Miss Speer's name is not included, we shall be glad to assist you in every way possible in trying to reach your daughter by Chinese channels through Yenching people in Chengtu."[21]

In spite of the fading hope of repatriation, MBS celebrated her birthday with her Yenching friends, preached at Union Church, ate a bountiful dinner at the Fergusons' on Thanksgiving, and had tea at the Presbyterian Mission. She continued Chinese lessons. And of course they celebrated Christmas with presents, a service at the British Embassy Chapel, twelve for lunch, "high, high tea in the living room" with carols. "Really a good day."

December 29, 1942

Happy Simple Christmas. Service British Embassy chapel. Friends, carols. Dined off home-raised chickens. Hoping for Easter, Rockledge, preached at Union Church last month. Love.

This bears an American Red Cross Stamp Sep 21, 1943, an earlier stamp, probably from Geneva, 2 Mai 1943, and a note: "Rec'd Lakeville, Oct. 7th, 1943. A comfort to get even tho so old!" Any message was a comfort: the following January reassurance actually reached the Speers in September 1943, before the Christmas message.

January 27, 1943

Regular routine: eating enough; sleeping adequately; studying hard; reading moderately; exercising little; church-going regularly; talking cheerfully; planning optimistically; praying, thinking of you unceasingly. Dearest love.

Attempting to get news through to America was a steady occupation. In February 1943 MBS wrote another letter to Miss Woodsmall at the neutral YWCA Geneva headquarters. Once again, MBS described the move from Yenching to Peking in a caravan of carts. She reiterated reassurances that the little Yenching community was comfortable and well-fed but in constant disarray and anxiety over the news first to get ready to start for home almost instantly, then to delay briefly, and then to find that the delay was indefinite and that there would not be room for all

who wanted to leave. MBS, however, was not one to surrender to sloughs
of despond.

February 5, 1943

In spite of having lived so long on a perch, with one's wings ready for instant flight, we have had a pleasant winter. Books were unpacked; church services have gone on; many of us have worked steadily at language study; there have been chances to see old friends and make new ones; some people have acquired brand new skills; and we have all been thankful to have houses of our own and the comforts which we used to take for granted but which have been taken away from so many inhabitants of the world in the last few years. The chief hindrance to real satisfaction is that one feels so much like a squirrel in a box while all the other creatures of the forest are doing what really matters, but one takes comfort from Milton's sonnet on his blindness and tries to believe that, not being idle, neither are we useless.

In the early spring life for the Americans in Peking was fairly uneventful.
Leighton Stuart was still under house arrest, but MBS and her friends
were free to move about the city, as long as they wore red armbands.
They left gifts and messages for Yenching's president on his doorstep. To
Grace Boynton in Chengtu Alice Boring wrote that she and Leighton
Stuart had become friends with the interpreter of the guards "so letters go
through promptly."[22]

An equal or greater concern was for the families of the "detained"
Chinese faculty, who could not leave Peking. As foreigners, the Ameri-
cans received relief funds, but these were not available for the stranded
faculty families. MBS with Howard Galt and others managed to make
arrangements with well-to-do Chinese families to give the funds they
were unable to send to their children studying in America to the Yenching
administrators in detention, which they in turn distributed to the Yenching
faculty families in need. "All our arrangements were verbal, showing

both our mutual trust and our optimism," remembers MBS. "The accounts for all these transactions were finally typed by me onto pieces of white silk which I sewed into the hem of one of my tweed skirts, knowing that they would be confiscated if found by the Japanese if and when we were to leave China." [23]

Leaving China was a continuing hope, however conflicting the orders and rumors. "We had no idea whether it might be possible for us to be repatriated soon or whether we would be packed off to some sort of internment center. One set of orders from the Japanese said firmly that we were not to take anything with us, we were not to leave anything behind, we were not to sell anything, and we were not to give anything away!" Cherished furniture, silver, linen, porcelain were given away in spite of the conflicting Japanese commands.

Eventually the Japanese determined that the Americans and British in Peking were to be interned. What could they take? The Japanese replied that they could take what was "reasonable." Finally it was agreed that two steamer trunks were reasonable. "We were also told to take our own beds. The Fergusons lent us two sturdy narrow iron beds, and we left our own slightly wider beds with them. We were glad of this when we found ourselves in crowded camp quarters."

The official order for internment was issued in mid-March. Later MBS reflected that "It was hardly surprising that the Japanese decided to intern enemy aliens, particularly Americans. It was partly for their convenience, partly for our safety, and partly a natural reaction to the shameful internment in the USA not only of Japanese citizens but of American citizens of Japanese ancestry."[24]

Weihsien

March 20, 1943

Leaving Twenty-fourth for group life at Weihsien with rest of North China Americans. Expecting entertaining experiences. Renewed admiration Saint Francis. Know you don't worry. Love.

The story of the trek to Weihsien and of MBS's internment there was recorded in her 1982 memoir: "When the day and hour were announced for our departure, we were told that we would have to walk to the station carrying our possessions with us. This being quite impossible, it was finally agreed that a couple of carts could be loaded with the heaviest luggage. We had the feeling that the walk to the station, perhaps three quarters of a mile, was supposed to humiliate us all. The Chinese crowds who lined the streets, however, were friendly and sympathetic and there was no jeering.[25]

"The journey from Peking to Weihsien took twenty-four hours. It is not exactly comfortable to sit upright for twenty-four hours, and before long some of the lighter members of our group climbed up into the luggage racks above our heads where they could stretch out. Fortunately only the thinnest people tried this. I found that I could be comfortable by sitting on a small folding stool about ten inches high. My legs could then stretch out into the aisle, and I would lean my head on whoever was sitting in the seat nearest me.

"The internment center for all the enemy aliens in North China, that is from Tientsin, Peking, and Shantung, was the large former Presbyterian Mission compound at Weihsien. This was an area about the size of a city block. Japanese officers lived in a separate small compound where the missionaries had once lived, among them the family of Henry Luce. In the main compound were a church, a hospital, a boys' school, a girls' school, and a Bible school. The hospital had once been an excellent one, but after the area had been fought over several times it was practically stripped.

"The only entrance to the compound was up a long ramp. As we struggled up this, lugging our belongings, the people who had arrived before us were gathered on the parade ground where they could look down on us and greeted us with mournful shouts of 'You don't know how awful this is.' We determined then and there that when our friends the Shadicks and other British nationals arrived in a few days we would not

greet them so dolefully.

"The first few days were chaos. But it was remarkable how quickly people settled down, ready to accept the inevitable and to be as helpful as possible. When we compared notes later with people who had been interned in Shanghai and elsewhere, we concluded that the Weihsien compound was an infinitely better place than the other internment camps. (The Japanese called all these camps 'Civilian Assembly Centers.') Many of the families in Shanghai were massed together in old warehouses where the only possibility of privacy (visual only) came from hanging sheets between different family groups.

"In Shanghai the Japanese separated the young single men from the older people and from the families with children. At Weihsien we were a totally mixed group: not only English, American, and Dutch, but also people of all ages, missionaries of all persuasions, business people, doctors, nurses, saints, and bounders. There were many children of all ages. Babies presented problems for their parents, but the adolescents presented problems both to themselves and to everyone else.

"The conditions for our life at Weihsien from March to September of 1943 were very different from later conditions for those people who had a much longer time there. Our life was rugged, but for the people who had thirty months there instead of six, it was more than rugged.

"There were 1800 people in the Camp, all from North China, mostly from the cities of Peking, Tientsin, and Tsingtao, but with a few groups from the interior. More than 400 of these were Catholics, some young American priests, groups of Flemish and Dutch friars and nuns, a very cheerful group of American nuns from the Middle West. There were conflicts sometimes between missionaries and business people, and there were many surprises. Some of the missionaries turned out to be poor sports; some of the beachcombers turned out to be useful citizens.

"Our main problems were quarters, food, and cleanliness. It was interesting that the Japanese presented our leaders (chiefly Billy Christian, head of the American Tobacco Company in China) with plans for organization. They said they wished representatives from our group to

deal with them in nine areas: General Affairs, Quarters, Labor, Discipline, Education, Finance, Medicine, Supplies, and Engineering. Mr. Christian said that we would prefer to have committees in each of these areas. 'No,' said the Japanese. 'Only one representative.' However, we did have committees of four people, one each from the Peking, Tientsin, Shantung, and Catholic groups, and the chairman of each group was the only person the Japanese had to know about.

"The single women from Peking were all housed in a three-story building which had been the Science Building for the Boys' School. Our room was quite pleasant with high windows on two sides. There were nine of us in this room, with an inner room housing six more who had to come and go through our room. In our room there were six Yenching people and also Lelia Hinckley of the YWCA; an Englishwoman, Mrs. Jowett, who spent her days gardening; and an extraordinary well-known Peking figure, Magdelene Lloyd Grant—a rather notorious beauty. She had spent the week before leaving for Weihsien drinking, so that she had not paid any attention to her belongings. She brought with her a trunk full of food and only one change of clothing; however, she always looked immaculate and walked around camp with the grace of a panther in slacks that always looked clean and fresh.

"We made our room quite comfortable when we salvaged the crates in which Ruth Stahl and Cookie [Mary Cookingham] had packed their beds. By turning them on end and using some of our curtains, we made a useful 'closet' and also made a corner of the room into what we called the bird bath: a shelf and a washbasin behind a curtain provided some privacy for our ablutions. We felt vastly superior to the women in the room over us where no one would give up an inch of private space for communal use and therefore everyone had to wash in public with her washbasin balanced on her trunk.

"We found a long table in the room and were able to set up two folding chairs which Augusta and I had brought. These were our greatest luxury, since otherwise there was nowhere to sit except our beds. Our room was lit with two 25-watt light bulbs. In the long days of summer *this was adequate. One of the lights was directly over my bed, and I remember reading 'Moby-Dick' under it in the late summer evenings. All lights went off at 10:00. I can imagine that during the two long winters that other people were still at Weihsien the lack of light must have been a great hardship.*

"The question of living quarters was soon settled, but the permanent and most important problem was food. The Japanese provided the raw materials. We did the cooking and serving ourselves. The camp had three mess halls, one each for the Peking, Tientsin, and Shantung groups, with an extra one later established in the hospital for people who were on special diets. Our Peking group consisted of about 400 people in the kitchen that had been used by the Bible School in earlier Mission days. The kitchen equipment consisted of two huge cauldrons which had been used chiefly for rice or soup.

"At first none of us knew how to cook with this equipment or lack of equipment. Pretty soon some volunteer cooks came forward, including one who had been a Navy cook. The food at first was pretty dreadful, but one day one of the Dutch Sisters who was able to speak German told Augusta that her nuns were used to this sort of equipment and would be glad to volunteer. At first the men said women could never manage, but before long we had developed three teams of cooks, each taking a week, the Dutch Sisters managing with Augusta as their representative to deal with the Japanese about food supplies.

"Everyone looked forward to the week that the Dutch Sisters were on duty when the food was far better and more imaginative than the meatless stew which was served for luncheon and supper during the other weeks. The Sisters worked harder than the men cooks and had many ideas to improve our Spartan diet; for example, breakfast had been nothing but cold bread and tea until the Dutch Sisters suggested that if everyone who had an orange from the canteen would save the skin, these could be dried and grated and added to hot 'porridge' (soaked bread) for breakfast every morning.

"Doctors worried that the milkless diet was inadequate for the chil-

dren so we asked everyone who had an egg (either a legitimate egg given to so-called invalids via the hospital or an illegitimate egg secured through our so-called black market) to turn in the shells. Some of the older people had the job of grinding up the shells into fine powder which was doled out to the children on Saturday mornings as a source of calcium.

"Vegetables consisted very largely of potatoes, sometimes potatoes that had been frozen and were almost rotten, and a very few green Chinese vegetables. One, a rather bitter vegetable, looked somewhat like thin asparagus. Augusta and other 'kitchen managers' complained to the Japanese guards about the lack of food. He said he couldn't understand why we were complaining when so much of this vegetable was found in the garbage. Augusta said we simply didn't like this vegetable except in small amounts. 'It is bitter, and its name doesn't make it more attractive.'

'What is its name?' demanded the Japanese.

'Haotzekar,' said Augusta. Literally translated this means 'rats tails.'

'In Japan we call it spring chrysanthemums.'

"We still didn't like it!

"Every five days during the summer the Camp got a small supply of fish sent up from Tsingtao. There was not enough for any one of the kitchens, so we made a deal with the Tientsin kitchen. They took our supply one week and we added theirs to ours the next week. Because the fish had often been on the way in hot weather with little ice, cleaning it was an unsavory job. Stanley Wilson, who had grown up in Maine, was the leader of the fish-cleaning squad, which I gladly joined. The clothes we used for this job were never quite the same again.

"Although we constantly wished for more and better food, we were made aware that we were fed far better than the village people all around the Camp. The only time that any of us were allowed outside the main gate was once a day when men from each of the mess halls took large cases of garbage to dump outside the Compound walls. These were chiefly vegetable peelings, now and then some bones. The men were hardly outside the walls when they were surrounded by villagers wanting to pick

364

over these to us utterly inedible bits of food. We had to be fed by our Japanese guards. The village people did not have to be fed by anyone.

"Cleanliness was not easy to achieve. For our own personal laundry we went to a nearby well for a pail of cold water and then to the camp hot water supply where we would be given two-thirds of a pail of hot water but no more. We supplied our own sheets but when they came back from the Japanese laundry smelling intolerably of fish (I suppose because of the wartime soap) we decided to wash our own. This was quite a feat but we learned to accomplish it with one washbasin and one small washboard. Once one's sheet was washed and hung on the line, one had to watch it until it was dry or it would vanish. 'Scrounging' was a camp habit.

"There was very little time for leisure. One had one's own belongings to keep clean, and everyone in our building had to take a turn at sweeping the stairs and hallways. For each mess hall many workers were needed, not only for cooking and serving but also for stoking the stoves and washing the kitchen cloths, which I did quite often at six in the morning, a nice quiet time in camp.

"A large crew of 'vegetable women' was needed every morning and afternoon. Since we had no refrigeration, vegetables had to be peeled and prepared for each meal. Machines for making noodles were discovered in Camp, and groups of people worked at that now and then.

"A sewing room was set up to mend people's hard-used clothes. The carpenter shop was presided over by Bishop Scott. One member of our Mission turned out to be a champion lock-picker and was often called on by people whose trunks wouldn't open.

"The doctors, of course, were busy. It took time to get the hospital in some sort of shape. A few bedsteads were available but anyone admitted as a patient had to bring his own bedding. I seem to remember one death during the summer. Most of the illnesses, however, were of types of dysentery and were cured by rest and 'hsi fan' (rice gruel).

"Augusta and I each had a brief sojourn in the hospital, and I remember with gratitude how some of the young Yenching men carried me *in a chair the length of the compound from our building to the hospital. Once Augusta broke a couple of ribs working in the kitchen. She said that three doctors held what you might call a mathematical consultation for half an hour deciding how to strap up her ribs using the absolutely minimal amount of precious adhesive tape.*

"The biggest building in the Weihsien Compound was the church, which had constant use, both religious and secular. On weekdays it was used for many of the children's classes. On Sundays there was a succession of services. It was also the scene of many entertainments. I remember particularly a performance of 'Pride and Prejudice' in which Augusta was Mrs. Bennett, and also a marvelous Fourth of July with every part of the camp providing some sort of skit and ending, to the astonishment of the Japanese guards, with a sudden display of the Stars and Stripes and everyone singing 'America the Beautiful.' That was the day that part of the compound wall collapsed in a heavy rain, but no one tried to escape. What would have been the use?"

From Weihsien MBS could write to her family only in twenty-five word monthly International Red Cross messages, and, as before, sending the messages did not carry any assurance that they would be delivered. Messages sent in June and July of 1943 through the Red Cross reached the Speers only in January 1944. It was still possible for the internees to write letters to friends in Free China, which could be forwarded to the United States. In August 1943 MBS's family finally heard from her in a letter sent to Grace Boynton in Chengtu.

[May 1943]

After two months here we have grown fond of our new "assembled" way of life. Spring climate very pleasant. Summer rains and rigors of winter will bring new problems. Share room with Augusta, Cookie [Mary Cookingham], Ruth [Stahl], Martha [Kramer], Shirley [Duncan], Lelia [Hinckley], Mrs. Hardy Jowett, and Magdelene Lloyd Grant. Augusta and Lelia are mainstays in the kitchen. Nellie [Shadick]is queen of the latrine cleaners. I am apprenticed to Stanley [Wilson] as fish cleaner and help with so-called adult education when not cleaning vegetables, floors, or clothes. The first weeks were appalling but the more insurmountable the difficulties, the higher the spirit, and our Peking group has come through with colors flying. The two Alice B's [Alice Boring and Alice Barlow-Brown] have a little room together and are both flourishing, having borne the difficult uprooting as well as anyone. We are all learning new skills, chiefly how to make bricks without straw or how to make a happy community without even a modicum of equipment.

June 24, 1943

Camp conditions slowly improving. Still much to do. Now expert dormitory living, fish-cleaning, quick lunch serving. Thinking of all on summer birthdays, especially Caroline's.

July 23, 1943

New rumor of possible repatriation. If not on first boat surely hope for second. Well. Life busy, strenuous; bearable now, but winter will be difficult.

Toward the end of August repatriation seemed closer. The big question was who would go. From the beginning of their confinement at South Compound after Pearl Harbor, the authorities had asked the Westerners whether they would accept repatriation if and when it might be offered. Some felt then that the war would not last a long time, and they preferred to stay in China. (Some were missionaries from inland China, others had business in China.)

Those who said they would accept were listed in nine categories. The first priority was to be given to people who had been in prison, but in the end Leighton Stuart and the others in Peking were kept under house arrest. Alice Boring did not succeed in staying in China. The American women from Yenching were repatriated with the exception of two who stayed with their husbands. Several British women from Yenching remained in Weihsien, and Nellie Shadick stayed with her husband Harold.[26]

MBS described her trip home many years later: "We heard that the exchange of American and Japanese internees would be made in Goa, the Portuguese enclave in India. Consequently those of us who were going were dubbed Goa-ers and the rest Stay-ers. The Goa-ers naturally gave away all their belongings: beds to the people who had broken camp cots; all books, since no printed matter could be taken; precious wash basins and pots; sheets and blankets.

"We were each allowed to take our two steamer trunks, although there was almost nothing to put in them except ragged clothes. When the trunks were packed, they were collected in the churchyard for inspection by the guards. Several British friends had given me letters to mail when we should reach freedom. I hung around the church yard until I saw that my trunks had been inspected. Then I slipped the letters into the pockets of my Burberry, feeling that they were now safe. However, in Shanghai, our trunks were inspected again, and I just barely had time to extract the letters before the inspectors came and put them back in again after the inspectors turned their backs.

"The journey from Weihsien to Shanghai took 48 hours, a much more uncomfortable trip than our trip from Peking to Weihsien six months before. But we were on our way, and that made all the difference. We were so tired from sitting up that when we changed trains in Nanking— or maybe it was Pukow—some of us just put our steamer rugs on the station floor and lay flat until we heard the 'All Aboard.'

"From Nanking to Shanghai the train seemed to go backward as often as forward. We were told each time that this was because the guerillas had torn up the tracks. Our feelings were mixed about this. We were glad they were successful but hoped they were not going to ruin the railway before we got to Shanghai.

"On the train we found Mary and Dr. Ferguson, who had been confined in the British Embassy grounds in Peking all the time we were in

Weihsien. Mary was distressed in Shanghai when the Japanese guards inspecting our hand luggage tore out the flyleaf of her mother's Bible, the only book she was allowed to take, saying that no handwriting was allowed. We were supposed to be isolated at St. John's University overnight but were cheered in the morning when outside our window two Chinese friends, last seen in Peking, appeared with a carton of ice cream to say good-by.

"Early on a hot morning we were moved down to the Bund. We could see the ship waiting for us, but there was a day-long delay. Some people had saved precious bits of canned food, and when the word went around as we sat on the Bund that no food could be taken onto the ship, everybody opened tins and we all had a picnic.

"Another rumor was that no medicines could be taken. The reason for this we assumed was that the Japanese wanted the medicines themselves to eke out the shortage in Shanghai. Harold Loucks, one of the chief physicians of the PUMC, a wonderful man, intervened in several cases in which people were absolutely dependent on medical supplies.

"The ship that was to take us from Shanghai to Goa was the 'Teia Maru'. It had originally been a French cruise ship. Its sister ship had burned up in the Indian Ocean, we were told to our dismay. The 'Teia Maru' had been used for some time as a Japanese troop ship. Its staterooms were comfortable, but its original accommodations for 400 people had to be increased to take care of about 1500. The quarters for those of us whom the Japanese called 'loose women' were on the forward part of the main deck. Double-decker platforms had been arranged with thin straw mattresses about 18 inches wide for each person. Women were assigned alphabetically, and Augusta and I were delighted to find that we were side by side on the lower layer.

"The 'Teia' voyage took about a month, stopping first at Hong Kong where we took on people who had been in Stanley Prison, among them the famous Emily Hahn,[27] and then on to the Philippines and to Saigon. In the Philippines Barbara Hayes appeared with her two younger children but did not find her husband John with us. He had stayed in Shantung *to care for his elderly parents. When the ship was tied up in the Mekong River, people swarmed over the side selling bananas, which we rushed to buy until the Japanese authorities chased the sellers off. Although we had nothing to read and almost no place to sit down and the food was not very good, the month on the 'Teia' was a time of good spirits. We were on the way at last.*

"At last we reached Goa and were tied up alongside the quay wait-ing for the 'Gripsholm' to arrive. Never was there such a glorious sight as that shining white ship as it came over the horizon. We were at Goa for a week altogether—the first part on the 'Teia', the latter part on the 'Gripsholm', as there were many formalities for the interchange. We were not allowed to leave the 'Teia' until we could go straight aboard the 'Gripsholm', after quarters had been assigned on each ship. I'm afraid that the feelings of the Japanese women going home were very different from ours. On the 'Teia' we women had relatively good quarters while our single men had been given mattresses down in the hold. It appeared that the situation was reversed for the Japanese. The women were given the dark quarters.

"Although we were still confined to the 'Teia' for two days after the 'Gripsholm' came alongside, we leaned over the rail and talked to the 'Gripsholm' sailors. Some of them tossed sandwiches and grapefruit up to us. When some of these fell in the water it seemed like a catastrophe, but the sailors assured us that there were plenty more and we could soon eat our fill. This was indeed true, but it took us days to believe it."

The "Gripsholm"'s first stop was at Port Elizabeth, and there MBS was able to mail a letter home—which reached her family two weeks after she did!

November 2, 1943

The Government has treated us royally on the *Gripsholm*, and I only hope that as a boatload we are worth it. I didn't know any-body could still have such good food in wartime as we have had three times a day. The month on the *Teia Maru* was pretty grim but the pounds lost there and in Camp are being rapidly regained. The parcel sent via Polly Willcox and the Red Cross was delivered almost as I stepped aboard the *Gripsholm*. What angels you were and what a center of envy I was, particularly for the hat to wear on landing in New York!

Later, November 4. We have been ashore for a day (me attired in your brown hat and nice beige dress) and have been showered with such kindness that we were completely overwhelmed. The whole town has opened its doors to us, fed us, practically kidnapped us to stay over night and get a good sleep in a soft bed, and somehow made us feel as if we were real heroes and heroines, which we certainly are not. They are a wonderfully kind, open-hearted people.

MBS later described the six-week trip on the 'Gripsholm' as "a long, unreal period of apparent suspense in space and time and then of gradual adjustment." [28] *She wrote again on shipboard between Port Elizabeth and Rio.*

November 11, 1943

The days are flying by and we are due in Rio on Sunday or Monday, but our first hope of getting home for Thanksgiving is apparently impossible. This ship is still a miracle. Cleanliness and order and good food and freedom to do as one chooses are no longer commonplaces to be taken for granted. They are wonderful, rare things.

We all wonder how we are ever going to adjust to reality after this dream world existence of sunny deck chairs. Everyone tries feverishly to get caught up on all the recent magazines, and there are discussion groups and lectures. Many of us have been kept busy with reports of various kinds for the State Department, but altogether this is hardly a life of action, and everyone is a little worried about how to fit into wartime life and wartime ways. The world behind us seems very far away and the world ahead is curiously unknown.

371

When we get to Rio we will have been on our way just two months and we'll be just as near home as if we were still in Shanghai, but what a difference in feeling! Think of no longer having the gendarmes telling us what we mustn't do!

In Port Elizabeth, MBS recalled later, "We had been looked after by friendly strangers all organized to make us welcome. In Rio we were happy to find an old friend, Gertrude Hodgman, former supervisor of nurses at the PUMC, who invited a large group of us to supper. From Shanghai to Rio we had sailed on sunny seas, but before long the gales and fogs of the Atlantic surrounded us. The 'Gripsholm' docked in Hoboken on December 1st. Arrangements had been made for our families to wait in their own homes or hotels until we could get through Customs and be taken in Red Cross cars to our destinations. Father and Mother had been invited by Mrs. Finley to stay in her apartment on Gramercy Park, and there we had a joyful reunion."

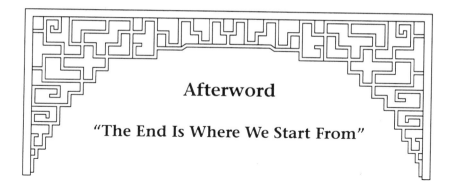

Afterword

"The End Is Where We Start From"

"What we call the beginning is often the end
And to make an end is to make a beginning
The end is where we start from."[1]

T.S. Eliot

November 1943 to August 1945

S tarting anew in America, MBS was mindful of four worlds: her present life, reunited with her parents, free, no longer hungry and in rags; the life of internment where friends were still waiting for repatriation or the end of the war, "doing without privacy, struggling with monotonous and scanty food and an endless struggle against dirt"[2]; Occupied China, "where our Chinese friends and former colleagues are having to make the daily choice between starvation with a clear conscience or compromise in order to get a job that will barely keep the family alive"[3]; and Free China, 2000 miles from Peking, where Yenching and other universities were continuing to educate students who could get there.

Carrying thoughts of China in her heart, MBS picked up the ends of her life to make a new beginning. She had told the Mission Board that she would return to Yenching, after the war, if way opened. Meanwhile she spoke to church and college groups about her experience and considered how she should live now. In June 1944—on D-Day, making it a memorable date—she was approached about a new job, Headmistress of The Shipley School, a preparatory school in Bryn Mawr, across the street from the College.

Shipley was not unfamiliar to her. "The year I was a warden at Bryn Mawr [before going to China] my sister was a senior at Shipley. I was at Rockefeller Hall and she used to come across the street and raid my larder—steal my apples and what not. So I was sort of back and forth at Shipley then. But I didn't know a great deal about it, and actually when I saw the Trustees early in June we were obviously just exploring from either side."[4]

In July she was offered the position and accepted. Her father was not very well, and she felt that her mother "needed her to be not too far away."[5] Her sister was living in England, and her brother Bill was in the Navy. By August 1945, when the Japanese surrendered, MBS was absorbed in her work at Shipley; in the fall of 1945 Augusta Wagner joined her there as associate head after a year in Washington with the State Department. Shipley had always had more than one principal, so the tradition was continued.[6]

While MBS was working with "a school populated by sheltered, eager, restless boarders and daygirls, growing up during a war they knew only remotely,"[7] the women and men of Yenching University had been struggling to continue the life of the University in Free China. Urged by its alumni in Chungking, the wartime capital of Nationalist China, Yenching's Chinese Board of Managers had voted in October 1942 to reopen the University in Free China.[8] The news that the University was to reopen "was transmitted, in devious ways, to the teachers and students in North China so that they would know what to expect, and reception stations were set up with the cooperation of the local alumni along the different routes so that the hardship of those who managed to come across the lines might be reduced to the minimum."[9]

The 2000 mile trek was arduous. "The students did not arrive in Chengtu in marching columns or under flying colors." Traveling two or three together, dirty and hungry, they had to placate Japanese soldiers at the border. Many became ill, and all were poor. A remarkable number were women. "The modern Chinese girl had come a long way indeed from where her grandmothers stood."[10]

Yenching reopened in Chengtu in September 1942. MBS noted that the teaching staff were largely Yenching graduates, including Agnes Chen, "who is taking my place as Dean of the College for Women."[11]

August 1945 to October 1949

After Japan, battered by American atom bombs, surrendered on August 14, 1945, the first impulse of the Yenching community in Chengtu was to return to Peking, but difficulties of transportation and the devastation of war, led the administration to decide to continue in Chengtu for one more semester.[12] Meanwhile, the Yenching faculty and administrators in newly freed Peking immediately made plans to reopen the campus there. On August 27, thirteen days after the end of the war, Stephen Ts'ai, representing Leighton Stuart, officially repossessed the Yenching campus just outside Peking. Stuart had been released by the Japanese on August 17, and he met with the committee of Chinese faculty "who were the last relic of Yenching administrative planning," and asked them to consider themselves "The President's Advisory Committee."[13] The University officially reopened in Peking on October 10, Chinese Independence Day.[14] For one semester there were two Yenching campuses.

MBS's colleague in Yenching's English Department, Harold Shadick, and his wife Nellie were among the Westerners who returned to the Peking campus from Weihsien in the fall of 1945. They found Yenching essentially changed: they had been used to good students, and the post-war students had poor training.[15] There were many strains and tensions.[16] Nellie Shadick sent candid letters to Augusta Wagner about the difficult situation for Westerners in spring 1946. She wrote of her impatience with the students and faculty of the Women's College who were pressuring MBS to return. "I must say I get awfully irritated when I hear people talk about the need for Marnie's presence. I quite agree that she could do things no one else would bring about; but it seems so dreadfully feeble that out of the whole mob of people here no one can do anything properly."[17]

The pressure to return continued. MBS's old friends, Chinese and Western, implored her to help with the rehabilitation of Yenching. "One after another, old members have come back, but thus far we are without you."[18] But by this time MBS was "rooted at Shipley," immersed in her work there and concerned for her aging parents, and she did not return. The Shadicks left Yenching in the summer of 1946 and settled at Cornell where Knight Biggerstaff, the young Harvard-Yenching Fellow who had married MBS's Yenching faculty friend, Camilla Mills, was developing Chinese studies. Bi (L.R.O. Bevan) had planned to come from Australia to visit his American friends, but he was killed in an automobile accident in 1946. "He should have survived and come back to us," lamented Harold Shadick. "He was a very dear friend, and his wit was missed."[19]

Alice Boring, who with Grace Boynton had entertained MBS, Augusta Wagner and two young Chinese faculty at Friday Lunch in pre-war days at Yenching, was more optimistic about revitalizing Yenching. Boring had sailed July 12, 1946 for Yenching. Her letters, printed in the *Bryn Mawr Alumnae Bulletin*, gave MBS a picture of post-war Yenching. The "most beautiful campus in the world" was so no longer. "In the Chinese faculty houses we miss the beautiful carved redwood furniture and the fine porcelain—most of it has had to be sold to buy food. 'Tokyo style' furniture, left by the

Japanese when they hastily departed, is low and small and cheaplooking. In our Biology Department, not a microscope was left." But she knew that her readers in America would be more interested in China's civil war than in the wartorn campus.

"Of course you want to know about the political situation, even if it may all have changed by the time you get this letter," she wrote on November 15, 1946. "It seems to remain critical. Dr. Stuart, whom we still consider our President, on loan for an emergency, has been planning a visit for several weeks, which has had to be postponed each time. Our Chinese faculty are getting to be less and less in sympathy with the Reds. Agnes Chen, Ph.D. in politics from Bryn Mawr, says that there are three groups within the party: (1) the older originals who emphasize agrarian reform, led by Chou En-lai; (2) the Moscow-returned group who are more interested in factory workers and follow Stalin; (3) the Military group, led by Chu Teh, who go right on fighting and trying to claim more territory, regardless of orders from Mao Tse-tung (the head of the whole party), or Chou En-lai, who is making negotiations. As they have been entering new territory lately there has been the same old wholesale slaughter of land-owners and impressing of the poor into service that preceded the present peaceful, well-organized regime at Yenan, so lauded by American journalists. Within the Kuomintang, of course, there is lots of graft, but not so much gestapo business as is generally supposed in America."[20] She has hope for "a fine group of elder statesmen called the Political Sciences Group" but notes that the Youth Party has joined the Kuomintang and the rest the Reds. "Now that the Reds have lost so many cities, we hope that they will consent to take part in a coalition government. Dr. Stuart is still optimistic. On this campus, we go ahead with our work as though no civil war were going on almost at our very gates. The morale here is wonderful....Do you wonder that I am glad to be back?"[21]

Yenching was used to having fighting going on just beyond its

gates. Absorbed in teaching biology, Alice Boring no doubt missed John Leighton Stuart but accepted the changes in the Yenching administration. In June 1946 Stuart had been appointed American Ambassador to China, and an administrative committee with Chancellor Luh as chairman had been established to govern the University. Yenching had by 1948 decided to continue under the imminently approaching Communist regime.[22] The University was named one of the four to continue in the Peking area, and Chancellor Luh and Kit King Lei from the Women's College Faculty were appointed to a Commission on Higher Education.[23]

The Chinese Communist Party, "the Reds" to whom Alice Boring referred, were steadily dislodging Chiang Kai-shek's KMT from Northern China. In September 1948 Boring reported that North China was still a part of the Chinese Republic, but "The Reds come and go in the neighborhood." Trips into the mountains were no longer possible. "Along with teaching Biology, I try to urge social responsibility as a necessary foundation for democracy."[24] In December she wrote that "Despite the continuing Civil War, Yenching keeps hopeful. Nine hundred idealistic students encourage faith and hope. It is on them that the future of China depends."[25]

By 1949 Chiang's government, recognized during World War II by Western powers as the official government of China, had lost what power it may have had. Undermined by personal corruption and conflicts as well as destructive inflation, Chiang and his supporters retreated to Taiwan. On October 1, 1949 Mao Tse-tung officially announced the founding of the People's Republic of China.

Alice Boring had confessed in April 1949, "I am surprised to find myself carried along on the tide, as none of the dire results expected by cautious people like myself have as yet happened. So I am beginning to hope that perhaps a synthesis of ideologies may be accomplished by the Chinese with their gift of reasonableness and practicality."[26] She stayed until the summer of 1950 when she was 67, hale and hearty. "That means I stayed for a year and a half under the Communist regime of the People's Republic of China. It may be hard for you to believe it, but the Chinese were not as badly off as usually depicted! Most of the citizens now have physical advantages never known before: widely distributed education and medical care, better food and housing, better transportation and clean city streets, whereas the lack of freedom of thought and expression does not as yet mean much to them."[27]

Grace Boynton had also returned to Yenching, adjusting to the takeover in 1949 positively but turning bitter when the Korean War stirred anti-American feelings.[28] Others of the Western faculty had left earlier. Lucius and Lillian Porter, whose house MBS and Augusta Wagner had so much enjoyed, waited to see what might be possible, but they left Yenching July 18, 1949. To his class at Beloit he wrote that most of the students and intellectuals of China saw the Communists as liberators from incompetence and corruption, from hunger and fear. The students' "enthusiasm for helping the people is a great good. They want, now, to identify themselves with the people, and get close to them, more than any other student generation I have known in my 41 years in China."[29]

Leighton Stuart, on leave from Yenching to serve as United States Ambassador in Nanking, perforce recognized the Nationalist government, but he was open to discussion with the Communists, arranged by Yenching alumnus Huang Hua, known in his student days as Wang Ju-mei, now a CCP official. Finally, in October 1949, stunned by the realization that there was no hope of understanding between the United States and the CCP, Stuart returned to Washington. In November he was disabled by a stroke.[30]

Western missionary educators were no more welcome in China than the American ambassador. In the spring of 1950 Premier Chou En-lai met with a group of church representatives to announce that as missionaries' passports expired they must leave. In 1951 the Commission on Education was asked to take over the financing of Yenching, and it was amalgamated with National Peking University.[31]

All Americans left by the spring of 1952. Last to leave of the Western faculty were the Lapwoods from London, who stayed until the fall of 1952.[32] By that time the Korean War had brought China and the United States into conflict. Hostility toward foreigners intensified in China, and antipathy to communism grew in the United States in the poisonous McCarthy years. Correspondence with former Yenching faculty friends—MBS thought especially of Agnes Chen, Hsieh Wan-ying, and Freddy Li—was no longer possible.

November 1949 to October 1971

Cut off from her Chinese friends, MBS kept China in her heart and in her Chapel speeches at The Shipley School. One student wrote many years later, "Chapel mornings I used to swear under my breath: 'I wish to hell that I would hear no more of China,'" but Michael Nylan graduated from Shipley and went on to take her doctorate in Chinese Studies and to teach that subject at Bryn Mawr.[33]

Another former student from Shipley wrote to MBS that in retrospect "I had always thought of the China years and the Shipley years as representing two totally unrelated aspects of your life. But in so many ways, the work at Shipley was related to the work at Yenching" for in both MBS had found "friends and colleagues who understood that 'God means all good life to be happy and full of fun' and that as long as there was a job to do that she could accomplish, she was at peace with herself."[34] Her Chinese students were never far from her mind. Retiring after twenty-one years at Shipley, MBS reflected on the contrast between Shipley where "everyone has been so endlessly kind in saying good-bye to me" with "the abrupt good-byes that marked my parting with my Chinese students."[35]

MBS also continued her concern for Chinese students through the Bryn Mawr Chinese Students Scholarship Committee. This group of alumnae had been organized in 1916-1917 to bring Chinese women to study at the College instead of sending financial support to Chinese colleges, "sisters over the sea," as Wellesley called the women at Yenching. The purpose of Bryn Mawr's project "was to deepen the understanding between China and the United States by bringing to this country the type of student who would represent the highest Chinese traditions, and who would in turn interpret to China our Western civilization." It was entirely based on the premise that Western ways were the answer to China's problems. "...with the gradual awakening of China, there is a great and pressing need for women trained in Western methods to direct the reorganization of Schools to meet the demands of the people for education."[36]

Liu Fung-kei, the first Chinese Scholar, had entered Bryn Mawr in MBS's class, graduated in 1922, and returned to open a school of her own in China, keeping in touch with her American friends on the Committee.[37] Almost every year a bright young Chinese woman had come to Bryn Mawr, supported and befriended by the alumnae on the committee. In the Class of 1935 the Chinese Scholar was a petite chemistry major named T'ing Vung-yüin, the only Chinese student on campus. Her aunt was Dr. Vung T'ing, the physician who headed Tientsin's Women's Hospital and who had been at one time a member of the Yenching Women's College administrative committee. It was Dr. T'ing's courageous conviction that "Chinese women are like good steel," that MBS quoted in a March 1939 letter. In June 1939, the last Chinese Scholar from Mainland China for many years, May Chow (Chou Shan-feng) received her A.B. in English.

In 1940 Agnes Chen (Ch'en Fang-chih), a 1935 graduate from Yenching, received her Ph.D. in politics and history at Bryn Mawr. She returned to teach at Yenching and escaped after Pearl Harbor to Free China, where she was the Dean of the Women's College. Agnes Chen "is taking my place," MBS wrote with pride,[38] taking her own place as a member of the Executive Committee of the Chinese Scholarship Committee.

The next thirty years were a time of "dissent at home and deep separation from our friends abroad." Political changes in China made it necessary for the Chinese Scholars to come from Hong Kong, Taiwan, from Chinese families of the embassies and the UN, among them many who had fled Mainland China. The Committee at Bryn Mawr after fifty years changed its purpose: what they now sought was not to westernize the Scholars "but mutually to share interests and experiences, and to help provide them with tools that will assist them in serving their own people and others wherever they may go. Bryn Mawr College believes as we do that its students have much to gain from experiences shared with students of other lands and other cultures."[39] This was MBS writing with Margaret Wood Keith, joint chairs of the committee since 1963, one of the first of twenty yearly reports they wrote.

In these years when the Westerners from Yenching were cut off from China, the older circle realized that they would never return. Alice Boring attended her Fiftieth Reunion at Bryn Mawr in 1954 and was seen as one of the youngest, physically and in spirit, but she died September 18, 1955 in Cambridge, Massachusetts, spending her last days with Yenching friends and memories of the rich years in China.[40] To the full page memorial notice in the *Bryn Mawr Alumnae Bulletin*, Edwin Boring added a few notes, among them that "AMB was a close associate of J. Leighton Stuart, President of Yenching University and later U.S. Ambassador to China. He had great influence on her in molding her enthusiasm for the new China (not then Communistic China) which AMB was sure she was helping to create."[41]

Leighton Stuart himself, whose autobiography, written with help, was published in 1954, died in 1962. Preparing to speak at the services for Stuart, MBS looked over her diary from Yenching years and "was struck once more by the warmth of the friendships that truly illumined our lives, friendships that united people of many nationalities and totally different backgrounds and widely separated in age. One might say that this came from a common Christian purpose, but not all those who lived and worked within the long wall around the Yenching campus were Christians. There was probably no single explanation of the spirit of comradeship and united effort, but Leighton Stuart was at the heart of it."[42]

Grace Boynton lived on in Cambridge until 1970, depositing her journals at Radcliffe's Schlesinger Library and sharing her Yenching memories with Philip West, giving him a "feel" for life at Yenching[43].

October 1971 to May 1993

Even before the end of the Cultural Revolution from 1966 to 1976, when Mao let loose the young Red Guards against the old bureaucracy, scarring the country and the people forever, the People's Republic campaigned successfully to win in October 1971 the UN seat and Security Council vote held by the Nationalists from Taiwan. In November 1971 Huang Hua, Augusta Wagner's former economics student, was named permanent representative to the United Nations. Augusta Wagner remembered him as her former student Wang Ju-mei, and he remembered his teacher with respectful Chinese deference and invited Augusta Wagner and MBS to lunch with him and his wife in New York. They talked about his children—his son was in the Liberation Army and his daughter wanted to be a barefoot doctor—and the fine food in the restaurant. They did not, MBS remembers, say much about the Chinese government.[44]

MBS and Augusta Wagner began to hope they might re-visit China and see old friends, but in 1976 Augusta Wagner died after several years of ill health. "Her greatest disappointment in recent years," MBS wrote to Friends of Augusta Wagner, near and far, "was that doctors and friends discouraged her from asking for a visa to go to Peking. She was always ready to go to far places and to tackle new tasks."[45]

MBS herself returned to Yenching for a two-day visit with a group from Shipley in 1979. She saw her old friends Freddy Li and Hsieh Wan-ying(Bing Xin) and Chinese Scholars May Chow and Agnes Chen. For 36 years, from 1943 until 1979, American and Chinese friends had not been able to keep in touch, as MBS reminded Americans who asked incredulously about her 1979 visit to old friends in Peking. But the ties were strong: "Old friends, last seen when Yenching had to close its door the day after Pearl Harbor, are good friends still. One whose English had grown rusty with disuse wrote me that they were 'jubilating' at the thought of seeing me again. There was no less jubilation on my part." In March 1979 "years of separation were forgotten and we hugged one another."[46]

Word was coming through of the achievement of some of the Chinese women from Yenching. Several had "disappeared" during the Cultural Revolution but now resumed their work. In addition to Bryn Mawr graduates May Chow and Agnes Chen who were at Peking University, MBS's friend Kit King Lei, (Lei Jieqiong), who had taught sociology at Yenching, had become a high government official in Beijing.[47] One of the activist students at Yenching in the 1930s, Kung P'u-sheng (Gong Pusheng) worked for the United Nations and was appointed ambassador to Ireland in 1980.[48] Most widely known was MBS's longtime friend Hsieh Wan-ying, graduate and teacher at Yenching, writing as Bing Xin, still as courageous as when she was an activist student involved with the May Fourth Movement in 1919.[49] They were like good steel, these strong women in China.

New cause for MBS to rejoice came in the fall of 1980 when the Bryn Mawr Chinese Scholarship Committee joyfully welcomed Jie Li from Peking University, first to come to Bryn Mawr from Mainland China since May Chow and Agnes Chen. The threads were powerful: May Chow, who had been professor in the Department of Western Language at Peking University for many years had been interviewing and advising students interested in coming to Bryn Mawr.[50] But for Jie Li and two others who came in the early 1980s the future was uncertain. "The political situation is more open and liberal,"one of them said in 1984, "but we don't know what will happen in the future."[51]

In the early 1980s there was hope. The Cultural Revolution was over, and the repression of the Democracy Wall protests in 1978 was in the past. In 1984 a Beijing chapter of the Yenching Alumni came alive, and in May 1988 the Beijing Yenching alumni began publishing a series of books entitled *The Historical Records of Yenching University,* containing reminiscences, recollections, sketches, biographies by alumni and faculty. The Yenching alumni welcomed Harold Shadick, MBS's colleague and neighbor at Yenching, in 1986 with feasting and fetes in Peking, Tientsin, Shanghai, Canton, and Hong Kong. He had "extended conversation with old and new friends," including many of his former students. "The treasured friendships proved to be intact."[52]

Agnes Chen was one of the friends Harold Shadick saw. She continued to write regularly to MBS. Two years after Tiananmen Square she reflected: "Time flies, as Confucius says, 'like the current of a running stream.' Somehow Yenching days, to you shorter than Shipley and to me only half of that of Peking University, remain something unique in our hearts. Mr. Shadick joyfully agreed when we met in Hongkong several years ago, and I told him all the Yenchians that I have seen said, 'Yenching is the best part of my life,' be they faculty or students, Chinese or Westerners, Kuomintang or Communists."[53]

In 1993 Agnes Chen reported that Kit King Lei, MBS's colleague from Yenching, was chairman of the Yenching Alumni Association in Peking, as well as vice-chairman of the Chinese central government legislature, "All People's Congress, the highest post a non-communist can reach.... Recently the Yenching people talk seriously about establishment of a Yenching Graduate School."[54]

In 1992 Zhang Jiqian, Professor of History at Peking University, came to do research at Yale on the history of Yenching. By good fortune or a special beneficence Caroline Rittenhouse was seated next to her. The workspace at the Day Mission Library at Yale is very limited, encouraging communication between scholars, so MBS was mentioned, her letters and her still vigorous life. "Still alive!" shouted this Chinese woman historian from Peking University with joy and astonishment. MBS is herself like good steel, yes, still alive, a wary China watcher, who said, wisely, alas, as a friend rejoiced at the jubilation of the students in Tiananmen Square and the joyful rise of the Goddess of Democracy and Freedom heralding a new China, "We'll just have to wait and see."

Notes

Introduction

1 See Jane Hunter, *The Gospel of Gentility: American Women Missionaries in Turn-of-the-Century China* (New Haven: Yale University Press, 1984) and Patricia Ruth Hill, *The World Their Household: the American Woman's Foreign Mission Movement and Cultural Transformation, 1870-1920* (Ann Arbor: University of Michigan Press, 1985).

2 Interview with Margaret Bailey Speer, June 7, 1983. Miss Speer, Marnie to family and friends, suggested that she be referred to in text and notes as MBS, her professional signature.

3 Christine Hammer, "Emma Bailey Speer," typescript, Bryn Mawr College Archives, p. 1.

4 MBS interview, September 22, 1982.

5 Hammer, EBS, p. 2.

6 This was the goal of the Student Volunteer Movement.

7 E.D.B.'94 "Collegiana," in *The Lantern*, June 1892, p. 111, Bryn Mawr College Archives.

8 MBS interview, September 28, 1982. For MBS's family life, see "It Was a Nice Family" in *Recollections of Miss Speer*, edited by Trina Vaux (Bryn Mawr, Pa: The Shipley School, 1990), pp. 3-27.

9 MBS interview, September 28, 1982.

10 MBS interview, September 28, 1982.

11 MBS interview, September 22, 1982.

12 "What's Past Is Prologue," Class of 1922 Fiftieth Reunion presentation, Bryn Mawr College Archives.

13 *College News*, April 15, 1919, page 5, Bryn Mawr College Archives.

14 *College News*, January 15, 1920, page 1 , Bryn Mawr College Archives.

15 Quotations on going to China from MBS interview, September 28, 1982.

16 John Leighton Stuart, *Fifty Years in China: The Memoirs of John Leighton Stuart, Missionary and Ambassador* (New York: Random House, 1954), p. 26.

17 MBS recalls Ran Sailer as a "next door neighbor from early childhood until he went off to college, two years before I went to Bryn Mawr. A few years later we found ourselves neighbors again at Yenching, where he taught psychology. At times of student protests Ran was trusted by the students and very sympathetic to their many causes. My admiration for him was great." Conversation with Caroline Rittenhouse, August 18, 1994.

18 "Sisters over the Sea," pamphlet in Yenching folder of President's Office files, Wellesley College Archives.

19 Alice M. Boring to her family, December 15, 1922 and March 4, 1923, Archives of the United Board for Christian Higher Education in Asia, Manuscript Group 11, Special Collections, Yale Divinity School Library. Hereafter UBCHEA.

20 For the history of China, see Jonathan D. Spence, *The Search for Modern China* (New York: W.W. Norton & Co., 1990) and John King Fairbank, *China: A New History* (Cambridge, Mass.: Harvard University Press, 1992), excellent recent single-volume histories of China with bibliographies.

21 John Leighton Stuart to friends, written in Nanking, June 16, 1919, quoted in Philip West, *Yenching University and Sino-Western Relations, 1916-1953* (Cambridge, Massachusetts: Harvard University Press, 1976), p. 54 and note 140. West's study of Yenching examines "the range in attitudes and behavior of individuals" in the institution over more than thirty years.

22 Dwight W. Edwards, *Yenching University* (New York: United Board for Christian Higher Education in Asia, 1959), pp. 91-96.

23 Conversation with MBS, April 4, 1990.

24 Alice M. Boring, "Education versus War in China," *Bryn Mawr Alumnae Bulletin*, June 1925, p. 10.

I. September 1925 to March 1926

1 The Barbours were hosts to the Speer family in 1910 when the first International Missionary Conference was held in Edinburgh. The Speers stayed longer than originally intended because first Marnie, then Pat and Elliott, came down with measles. Later Pat Speer (Constance) married George's younger brother Bob. *Recollections*, pp. 21-22. When MBS arrived in Peking, George Barbour had been professor of geology at Yenching University for several years.

2 Margaret Bailey Speer, "Letters from Yenching"(Haverford, Pa.: privately published, 1982), pp. 2-3. Hereafter MBS 1982.

3 Allan Hunter taught at the Boys' School of the Presbyterian Mission in Peking.

4 Hunter, p. 82.

5 Interview with Harold Shadick: Ithaca, N.Y. July 11, 1987.

6 John K. Fairbank and Edwin O. Reischauer, *China: Tradition & Trans-*

formation (Boston: Houghton Mifflin Co., 1978), pp. 440-441.

7 John Hayes and his wife, Barbara Kelman Hayes, had been appointed to the American Presbyterian Mission in Peking in 1917. He was, MBS believes, the only member of the North China Presbyterian Mission who had been born in China. MBS remembers him as a handsome man who spoke Chinese well.

8 MBS to Bill Speer, November 7, 1925, Margaret Bailey Speer Papers, Special Collections, Bryn Mawr College.

9 MBS 1982, p. 6.

10 T.T. Lew (Liu T'ing-fang) was professor of theology and dean of the School of Religion at Yenching. He was one of the first prominent American-educated Chinese to join the Yenching faculty. He had graduated from Columbia University in 1914, received a B.D. from Yale in 1918 and a Ph.D. from Columbia in 1920 in education and psychology. On Lew, see West, pp. 59-62.

11 Letter to Bill Speer, December 13, 1925, MBS Papers, BMC.

12 Fairbank and Reischauer, pp. 426-427.

13 The Peking Union Medical College was a center for medical education and research supported by the Rockefeller Foundation.

14 Endowment for the Chinese government university in Peking came from the American Boxer Indemnity Fund. Spence, p. 383.

15 West, pp. 92-99.

16 Quoted in West, p. 95.

17 John Stewart Burgess was a Princeton graduate with a Ph.D. in sociology from Columbia. He was a YMCA secretary in Peking, sponsored by the Princeton-Yenching Foundation, and taught sociology at Yenching. Stella Fisher Burgess was the daughter of Henry Day Fisher, a missionary in Japan. West, pp. 32-34.

II. March 1926 to August 1927

1 John Israel, *Student Nationalism in China, 1927-1937* (Stanford: Stanford University Press, 1966) is indispensable for understanding the student movement.

2 John MacMurray was the American Ambassador in Peking. The delegation included Yenching faculty and members of the Presbyterian Mission. For details, see West, p. 94 and note 17, p. 271.

3 Alice Browne Frame was the Dean of the Women's College at Yenching at this time.

4 Spence, pp. 346-348.

5 Henry Killam Murphy was a Yale graduate who designed buildings for the Yale-in-China University at Changsha from 1913 to 1923 before he became Yenching's architect. He was appointed architectural adviser to the Chinese government in 1928 and became the architect for city plan-

ning in Nanking. (Obituary, *The New York Times*, October 14, 1954, p. 29)

6 Born in Hangchow in 1876, child of missionary parents, Stuart was educated in the United States, where he was drawn into the Student Volunteer Movement. He returned to China as a missionary and in 1909 joined the faculty at Union Theological Seminary in Nanking. In 1919 he was persuaded to become Yenching's president. See his autobiography, *Fifty Years in China*, and West, pp. 23-27.

7 Stuart, p. 89.

8 "Leighton Stuart was Yenching," MBS interview September 28, 1982; Yenching's historian, Dwight Edwards, recorded that "Yenching and Leighton Stuart are synonymous terms." Edwards, p. 88.

9 John King Fairbank, *Chinabound: A Fifty-year Memoir* (New York: Harper & Row, 1982), pp. 56-57.

10 MBS interview, September 28, 1982.

11 Natalie S. Low, "The Sisterly Relationship: A Study of What It Means to Adult Women," *The Radcliffe Quarterly*, March, 1990. p. 11.

12 Hunter, p. 70.

13 Interview with Harold Shadick, July 11, 1987, Ithaca, New York.

14 On William Hung (Hung Yeh) see West, pp.74-76, and Susan Chan Egan, *A Latterday Confucian, Reminiscences of William Hung* (1893-1980) (Cambridge: Council on East Asian Studies, Harvard University, 1987).

15 The Boynton diaries are at the Schlesinger Library, Radcliffe College.

16 Stuart, pp. 89-90.

17 Alice Boring to Dear Family, August 29, 1926, Archives of the United Board for Christian Higher Education in Asia, Special Collections, Manuscript Group 11, Yale University Divinity School.

18 Hunter describes turn-of-the-century female missionaries as "staunch cultural chauvinists," p. 148.

19 On the "Nanking Incident" see Edwards, p. 197.

20 Edwards, p. 198.

21 Stuart, April 8, 1927 memo to the foreign members of the faculty concluded with his earnest "hope that Yenching can continue to be a generating center of international goodwill and of reassuring hopefulness during this time of strain and dread." MBS Papers, BMC.

III. September 1927 to May 1929

1 Stuart, p. 68.

2 MBS interview, September 28, 1982.

3 Alice Browne Frame to Emma Bailey Speer, April 11, 1927 in MBS Papers, BMC.

4 "Service of Thanksgiving for the Life of Alice Browne Frame" Yenching University, October 29, 1941, in MBS Papers, BMC.

5 On T. C. Chao, see West, pp. 70-74.

6 On Howard S. Galt, see West, pp. 30-32.

7 The December violence in Canton was part of the effort to eradicate Communists from the Kuomintang in 1927. Israel, p. 15.

8 Israel, pp. 18-21.

9 Edwards, p. 199.

10 Edwards, p. 200.

11 On Lucius Porter, see West, pp. 27-29. Some of Porter's papers are at Beloit College in Wisconsin, including his lecture notes on Chinese philosophy.

12 Interview with MBS November 20, 1991. Biographical information on Stahl can be found in the Archives of the UBCHEA at Yale.

13 On the Boyd gift, see Edwards, p. 121. Mrs. Lee was the Secretary of the Women's Yenching College Committee.

14 MBS 1982, p. 23.

15 MBS 1982, p.26.

16 On Wu Lei-ch'uan see West, pp. 62-66; 130-132.

17 Edwards, p. 309.

18 Edwards, p. 310.

19 MBS 1982, p. 27.

20 Knight Biggerstaff was the first Fellow in China of the Harvard-Yenching Institute for Chinese Studies, which was established in 1928 to help Chinese scholars study their own culture, using Western methods, and to help Americans learn about Chinese culture. Interview with Knight Biggerstaff, July 12, 1987; on the Harvard-Yenching Institute, see Fairbank, *Chinabound*, pp. 96-98.

21 Most of this letter was written December 11.

22 Israel, p. 38.

23 MBS 1982, p. 17. On Bevan, see "In Memory of Mr. L.R.O. Bevan," in the Archives of the UBCHEA at Yale.

24 Edwards, p. 149.

25 Philip West, "Christianity and Nationalism," in *The Missionary Enterprise in China and America* (Harvard, 1974), p. 238.

IV. May 1929 to May 1930

1 Fairbank and Reischauer, p. 446.

2 Returned Students were Chinese who had studied abroad and returned to work in China. Jessie G. Lutz, *China and the Christian Colleges, 1850-1950* (Ithaca: Cornell University Press, 1946), pp. 496-500.

3 Interview with Y.P. and V.K. Nyi Mei, Ithaca NY, July 12, 1987.

4 Interview with Harold Shadick, Ithaca NY, July 11, 1987.

5 Spence, p. 390.

6 John K. Fairbank, *The United States and China*, 4th edition (Cambridge: Harvard University Press, 1983), pp. 322-323.

7 Bettis Alston Garside had been a missionary educator and official of various relief agencies in China, 1922 to 1926.

8 This is one of the "Fortnightly Letters" sent to former members of the Faculty. MBS sent a copy to her mother.

9 MBS 1982, p. 40.

10 Eunice Tietjens, "The Most Sacred Mountain," in *Profiles from China* (Chicago: Ralph Fletcher Seymour, 1917), pp. 39-40.

11 MBS 1982, p. 41.

12 Israel, p. 38

13 On the Japanese in North China, see Lincoln Li, *The Japanese Army in North China, 1937-1941: Problems of Political and Economic Control* (Tokyo: Oxford University Press, 1975) p. 23.

V. September 1931 to June 1933

1 For details and background of the clash between the Chinese and Japanese in Manchuria, see Spence pp. 388-396.

2 Israel, p. 48.

3 Israel, p. 57.

4 This letter was to MBS's brother Bill.

5 See Israel, "The Manchurian Crisis: 1931-1932," pp. 47-87, for a detailed account of student protests at other universities throughout China.

6 For a more detailed report of Wu's negotiations to bring about a compromise between faculty and students, see Edwards, pp. 337-339, and West, pp. 164-165.

7 Stuart, pp. 111-112.

8 Spence, pp. 390-392.

9 Spence, p. 393.

10 Mrs. Speer's copy of this letter exists in the MBS Papers at BMC.

11 MBS 1982, p.57.

12 MBS explained her use of Peiping when she reviewed the typescript : "When Chiang Kai-shek made Nanking his capital, Peiping (Northern Peace) was used in place of Peking (literally Northern Capital)," but she was inconsistent.

13 Spence, p. 394.

14 MBS 1982, pp. 60-61.

15 MBS 1982, p. 63.

16 Spence, pp. 394-395, with a helpful map; Israel describes the disillusionment of the Chinese students produced by the Tangku Truce, pp. 108-109.

17 MBS 1982, p. 65-66.

VI. September 1933 to August 1935

1 MBS 1982, p. 66.

2 MBS 1982, p. 69.

3 MBS 1982, p. 68.

4 Edwards, pp. 125-126; West, pp. 111-113.

5 Cornelia van Asch van Wyck, a Dutch woman who was President of the World YWCA in 1933, came down with paratyphoid in Peking and was hospitalized in the PUMC. MBS visited her there and then took her to Yenching for a long period of convalescence. MBS 1982, p. 68.

6 Maude Royden was an English lay preacher whose secretary MBS had been just after she graduated from Bryn Mawr, when Miss Royden was traveling in the United States. Marion Park was the President of Bryn Mawr College from 1922 to 1942. Dr. Alice Hamilton was a physician specializing in industrial toxicology. Her sister Edith was in Mrs. Speer's class at Bryn Mawr.

7 Pu Yi was chosen in 1908 at the age of three as successor to the throne of the Empress Dowager, whose grand-nephew he was. In 1912 he abdicated, ending the Ch'ing dynasty. After the Japanese set up their puppet government in Manchuria, Pu Yi was enthroned as emperor of the state of Manchukuo.(Spence, p. 802) His story was told in the film "The Last Emperor."

8 Nettie Ssu-tu to the Secretary of the Women's committee, May 9, 1923, Archives UBCHEA.

9 MBS, 1982, p 73.

10 George W. Shepherd, a missionary with the Shaowu Mission of the Congregational Church, was known as an American Chiang Kai-shek trusted. James C. Thomson Jr., *While China Faced West: American Reformers in Nationalist China, 1928-1937* (Cambridge, Mass.: Harvard University Press, 1969), p.76.

11 On Ku Chieh-kang, see West, pp. 157-158.

12 MBS 1982, p. 74.

13 Mrs. John Finley was an important member of the Women's Committee in New York.

14 MBS added when reviewing this paragraph: "Miss Ssu-tu was Chinese by birth, but she had lived abroad so long that she seemed to have lost Chinese ways of thinking and feeling." Nettie Ssu-tu, after resigning from Yenching, returned to Nankai University to teach. Later she became a member of the faculty at St. John's University in Shanghai, and she was Dean of Women there from 1940 to 1947. Edwards, p. 316.

15 MBS 1982, p. 77.

16 Edwards, "Yenching in the Correlated Program," pp. 237-244.

17 Chancellor Wu had resigned in 1933 to teach. At the time this report was written the chancellor was C.W. Luh. Edwards, p. 204.   The Independent Board was a fundamentalist group who caused trouble for

the Presbyterian Board of Foreign Missions and attacked its Secretary, MBS's father, Robert E. Speer. MBS 1982 p.83.

18 MBS 1982, p. 86.

VII. November 1935 to May 1937

1 Israel, "The December Ninth Movement: 1935-1936," pp. 111-156; West, pp. 147-155.

2 For more on student organizations at this time see Jessie G. Lutz, *China and the Christian Colleges* (Ithaca: Cornell University Press, 1971), pp. 337-358.

3 The Hopei-Chahar Political Council controlled these two North China provinces. It was established December 1935 to weaken the influence of the National Chinese government in this area. Lincoln Li, *The Japanese Army in North China, 1937-1941: Problems of Political and Economic Control* (Oxford University Press, 1975), p.4 and note 6, p.15.

4 MBS 1982, p. 94. Wang Ju-mei later took the name Huang Hua. After the CCP takeover in 1949 he negotiated with the remaining foreign ambassadors, including Leighton Stuart. He served on many delegations abroad and was the first representative of the People's Republic of China to the United Nations. See Wolfgang Bartke, *Who's Who in the People's Republic of China* (Munchen: K.G. Saur, 1987), pp. 166-167.

5 Israel, p. 145 and note 106.

6 The Stephen Bakers, friends of MBS's parents, were on a world tour. Student protests and arrests had not yet stemmed the flow of travelers to Peking.

7 H.H. K'ung was the finance minister of the Nationalist government and the husband of Soong Ai-ling, sister of Soong Ch'ing-ling, wife of Sun Yat-sen, and Soong Mei-ling, who married Chiang Kai-shek. In 1937 he became the Chinese chancellor of Yenching. West, p. 133.

8 Hunter, pp. 252-255, records the life of Mrs. Waysung New, based on an interview with her in the United States where she fled in 1949.

9 Mrs. Basil Livingston Learmonth was the wife of the Yenching University physician and herself a medical doctor. Her dispensary provided free medical service in Cheng Fu, a village adjoining the Yenching campus on the east. (Edwards, p. 288)

10 Lucius Porter, "Yenching Celebrates Leighton Stuart's Cycle of Cathay," in Stuart, pp. 94-99, preceded by Stuart's brief description of the event, pp.93-94.

11 September 21, 1936 and continued on October 7, in MBS Papers, BMC.

12 I.A. Richards was in China for the third time from April to December 1936, to involve himself in the teaching of Basic English. On Richards in China, see John Paul Russo, *I.A. Richards: His Life and Work* (Baltimore:

Johns Hopkins University Press, 1989), pp. 417-429.

    13 Spence, pp. 422-424.

    14 MBS was born November 20, 1900.

VIII. June 1937 to August 1938

    1 Spence, pp. 444-445.

    2 Eleanor B. Fabyan, "The Japanese in Peiping," *Bryn Mawr Alumnae Bulletin*, April 1938, pp. 8-9.

    3 Wagner's thesis is still read and used: see Spence, chart, p. 427 and note 19, p. 758.

    4 Stuart to the Board of Trustees, Yenching University, in MBS Papers, BMC.

    5 Cheng To-k'un, Chengtu, April 6, 1938, to Dr. Stuart, in MBS Papers, BMC.

    6 Yu I Li, June 10, 1938, to Dr. Stuart, in MBS Papers, BMC.

    7 MBS uses John or Johnny and sometimes (see November 13, 1938 letter) Jackie. The "J" was what signified.

IX. August 1938 to July 1939

    1 MBS 1982, p. 116-117.

    2 Quoted in MBS 1982, p. 117.

    3 MBS 1982, p. 117.

    4 Stuart, p. 126.

    5 MBS 1982, p. 119.

    6 AW to EBS, November 13, 1938, in MBS Papers, BMC.

    7 Spence, p. 460. For more details of the CCP and KMT military endeavors at this time, see Spence, "Chongquing and Yan'an, 1938-1941," pp. 456-466.

    8 AW, November 13, 1938, MBS Papers, BMC.

    9 Stuart, p. 73.

    10 MBS to Pat and Bob [Barbour] MBS Papers, BMC.

    11 The Kuomintang flag accepted by Sun Yat-sen as the national flag of China in 1928 was red with a white sun on blue in the upper left; in 1938 after the Japanese occupied Peking, a five-barred flag was flown, presumably, MBS suggested, to signify Japan's conquest of the races of China: red for Chinese proper, yellow for Manchuria, blue for Mongolia, white for Tibet, and black for the Muslims of China. The Five-Color Flag, as it was called, had been the flag of the Republic of China from 1912 to 1928. Whitney Smith, *Flags through the Ages and Around the World*(New York: McGraw Hill, 1975) pp. 108-111.

    12 MBS, "Personal Report, 1938-1939," May 1939, p. 3, MBS Papers, BMC.

    13 Edwards, p. 354

X. August 1939 to June 1940

1 Doris Cummings "Fortnightly," November 23, 1939, enclosing the Chiang speech, in the MBS Papers, BMC. It was the custom for each member of the staff at the Women's College to take a turn in writing a fortnightly letter to the Women's College Committee in New York, not an official report but an account of daily life.

2 Augusta Wagner to Florence [Codman], December 7, 1939, in the MBS Papers, BMC.

3 West, p. 175.

4 Stuart, pp. 130-131, in a chapter titled "The Japanese Occupation and an Island of Freedom," pp. 126-136.

5 MBS 1982, p. 158

6 Augusta Wagner to Emma Bailey Speer, July 11, 1940, MBS Papers, BMC.

XI. August 1940 to December 1941

1 Edwards, pp. 357-360.

2 Spence, p. 457.

3 MBS 1982, p. 152.

4 For the intricacies of United States-Japanese relations, see Herbert Feis, *The Road to Pearl Harbor: The Coming of the War Between the United States and Japan* (Princeton: Princeton University Press, 1950).

5 These people were all members of the Yenching faculty. Langdon Gilkey, later a well-known theologian, had come out to China from Harvard in the fall of 1940, planning to stay a year or two. MBS 1982, p. 208.

6 MBS's sister Pat Barbour's house in a suburb of Bristol, England.

7 AW to EBS, February 2, 1941, MBS Papers, BMC.

8 AW to RES, March 16, 1941, MBS Papers, BMC.

9 Yosuke Matsuoka, the Japanese Foreign Minister, had gone to Berlin and Moscow to secure a neutrality pact with Russia. Feis, pp. 180-188.

10 The quotation is from "Say Not the Struggle Nought Availeth" by Arthur Hugh Clough: *The Poems of Arthur Hugh Clough*, edited by F.L. Mulhauser (Oxford: Clarendon Press, 1974), p. 206.

11 MBS 1982, p. 172.

12 Report to the North China Mission, MBS Papers, BMC.

13 Michael Lindsay wrote about his life in China in *The Unknown War: North China 1937-1945* (London: Bergstrom & Boyle Books, Ltd., 1975); the book includes photographs of Lindsay and his bride on their wedding day at Yenching.

14 In June 1941 Germany invaded Russia.

15 Augusta Wagner to Emma Bailey Speer, July 10, 1941, MBS Papers, BMC.

16 Lloyd S. Ruland, "Bulletin No. 21, Confidential," August 25, 1941, Board of Foreign Missions of the Presbyterian Church in the U.S.A., in MBS Papers, BMC.

17 MBS 1982, p. 192.

18 Nancy Cochran, letter to Fortnightly Readers, October 19, 1941 in MBS Papers BMC.

19 Lindsay, *The Unknown War* (unpaged but with chronological sub-heads).

20 Y.P. Mei, "Yenching University in Chengtu," in Edwards, pp. 370-405.

21 Feis, p. 293.

22 Claire and William Band described their escape in *Two Years with the Chinese Communists* (New Haven: Yale University Press, 1948).

23 Leighton Stuart describes his internment in detail in "Incarceration and Release," in *Fifty Years in China*, pp. 137-159.

XII. December 1941 to September 1943

1 C.A. Evans, Acting Executive Secretary to Members and Friends of the Associated [Mission] Boards, dated January 22, 1942, MBS Papers, BMC.

2 MBS 1982, p. 203.

3 MBS 1982, p. 204.

4 Edwards, p. 362.

5 MBS 1982, p. 206.

6 MBS 1982, p. 207.

7 MBS Papers, BMC.

8 MBS 1982, p. 207-208.

9 See Langdon Gilkey, *Shantung Compound* (New York: Harper & Row, 1966).

10 MBS 1982, p. 208.

11 MBS 1982, pp. 209-210; Edwards, pp. 363-364.

12 MBS 1982, p. 211.

13 MBS 1982, p. 211.

14 The *Gripsholm* was the Swedish liner chartered by the U.S. State Department for civilian repatriation. See P. Scott Corbett, *Quiet Passages: The Exchange of Civilians Between the United States and Japan During the Second World War* (Kent, Ohio: The Kent State Press, 1987).

15 MBS 1982, p. 214.

16 A copy of parts of the letter is in the MBS Papers at BMC.

17 MBS 1982, p. 214.

18 MBS Papers, BMC.

19 Augusta Wagner to "Dear Friends of Yenching," September 20, 1942, Archives UBCHEA.

20 Alice Boring to Family, November 15, 1942, copy in MBS Papers BMC.

21 Lloyd S. Ruland to Mrs. Robert E. Speer, December 18, 1942, in MBS Papers BMC.

22 Alice Boring to Grace Boynton, February 28, 1943, Archives UBCHEA.

23 MBS 1982, p. 219. Later these funds were paid in equivalent amounts to the students in America.

24 MBS 1982, p. 220.

25 Langdon Gilkey gives a more dramatic description of the progression to the station, omitting any mention of carts, in *Shantung Compound*, pp. 3-4.

26 Edwards, p. 451.

27 Emily Hahn is an American writer who taught in Shanghai in the late 1930s.

28 MBS, "Back on the *Gripsholm*," *Bryn Mawr Alumnae Bulletin*, March 1944, p. 2.

Afterword

1 T.S. Eliot, "Little Gidding," in "Four Quartets," *Complete Poems and Plays:1909-1950* (New York: Harcourt Brace and World, 1971), p. 145.

2 "Back on the *Gripsholm*," *Bryn Mawr Alumnae Bulletin*, March 1944, p. 1.

3 Ibid., p. 2.

4 MBS in *Recollections*, pp. 114-115.

5 Ibid., p. 113.

6 Ibid., p. 117.

7 "The Class of 1945," in *Recollections*, p. 112.

8 Y.P. Mei, "Yenching University in Chengtu," in Edwards, p. 370.

9 Ibid., p. 373.

10 Ibid., p. 375.

11 "Back on the *Gripsholm*," p. 6.

12 Mei, pp. 398-399.

13 Stuart, pp. 154-155.

14 Edwards, p. 407.

15 Interview with Harold Shadick, July 11, 1987, Ithaca, NY.

16 Edwards, Chapter XLIII, "Rehabilitation," pp. 407-419, describes the dreadful condition of the physical plant after four years of Japanese military occupation, the critical financial situation, the poor food, and political unrest surrounding the campus.

17 Nellie Shadick to Augusta Wagner, March 6, 1946, MBS Papers BMC.

18 Members of the Women's College to MBS, January 18, 1947, MBS Papers, BMC.

19 Interview with Harold Shadick, July 11, 1987, Ithaca, NY.

20 Alice Boring, "Letter from China," November 15, 1946, *Bryn Mawr Alumnae Bulletin*, April 1947, pp. 9-10.

21   Ibid., p. 10.

22   Edwards, p. 425.

23   Ibid., p. 426.

24   Alice Boring, "Class of 1904 45th Reunion Report," 1949, BMC Archives.

25   Alice Boring, letter to Class Editor, 1904 Class Notes, *Bryn Mawr Alumnae Bulletin,* April 1948, p. 19.

26   Alice Boring, April 2, 1949, "Class of 1904 45th Reunion Report, 1949, BMC Archives."

27   Alice Boring, April 1, 1954 to Class of 1904, BMC Archives.

28   West describes Boynton's last years at Yenching, pp. 225-228.

29   Lucius C. Porter to "Sixty-seveners," November 25, 1949, Lucius Porter Papers, Beloit College Archives.

30   On Stuart's last days in China, see Seymour Topping, *Journey Between Two Chinas* (New York: Harper & Row, 1972), pp. 82-90; and Shaw, Yu-ming, *An American Missionary in China: John Leighton Stuart and Chinese-American Relations* (Cambridge, Mass.: Council on East Asian Studies, Harvard University, 1992), pp. 250-274.

31   Edwards, pp. 435-436.

32   Ralph and Nancy Lapwood, *Through the Chinese Revolution* (London: Spalding & Levy, 1954).

33   Michael Nylan, in *Recollections,* p. 83.

34   Frances Dykstra to MBS, January 6, 1983, MBS Papers, BMC.

35   MBS, "Address to the Graduating Class," *Shipley School Letter,* June 1965, p. 6, MBS Papers, BMC.

36   Chinese Scholarship Committee Papers, pencilled date "probably about 1925." BMC Archives.

37   Liu Fung-kei Papers, BMC Archives.

38   MBS, "Back on the *Gripsholm,*" p. 6.

39   "Bryn Mawr Chinese Scholarship Report," 1968-1969, BMC Archives.

40   Grace Boynton to Lucius and Lillian Porter, September 21, 1955, Lucius Porter Papers, Beloit College Archives.

41   Alice Boring alumna biographical file, BMC Archives.

42   Manuscript of talk at Stuart memorial service November 30, 1962, MBS Papers, BMC.

43   West, "Preface," p. vii.

44   Interview with MBS, February 2, 1983.

45   MBS to Friends of Augusta Wagner, February 7, 1976, Wellesley College Archives.

46   MBS, "Another China," *Bryn Mawr Alumnae Bulletin,* Summer 1979, p. 6.

47   Wolfgang Bartke, *Who's Who in the People's Republic of China, 2nd edition* (Munchen: K.G. Saur, 1987), p. 212.

48   Ibid., p. 113.

49 Ibid., pp. 544-545.

50 MBS and Margaret Woods Keith, Chinese Scholarship Committee Report, 1979-1980, BMC Archives.

51 Group interview with MBS and Margaret Woods Keith for the Chinese Scholarship Committee, February 17, 1984, Oral History Collection, BMC Archives

52 Harold Shadick to friends, January 1987, Caroline Rittenhouse personal correspondence.

53 Agnes Chen to MBS April 27, 1991, MBS Papers, BMC.

54 Agnes Chen to MBS, May 4, 1993, MBS Papers, BMC.

Selected Bibliography

Margaret Bailey Speer

Speer, Margaret Bailey, Papers, Special Collections, Bryn Mawr College, Bryn Mawr, Pennsylvania.

Speer, Margaret Bailey "Letters from Yenching," (Haverford, Pennsylvania: Privately published, 1982).

Speer, Margaret Bailey, Interviews with Caroline Rittenhouse, 1982 to 1986, in the Oral History Collection of the Bryn Mawr College Archives.

Recollections of Miss Speer, edited by Trina Vaux (Bryn Mawr, Pennsylvania: The Shipley School, 1990).

Yenching University

Barbour, George B., *In China When...* (Cincinnati, Ohio: University of Cincinnati, 1975).

Biggerstaff, Knight, Interview with Caroline Rittenhouse, Ithaca, New York, July 12, 1987.

Boring, Alice M., "Education Versus War in China," *Bryn Mawr Alumnae Bulletin*, June 1925, pp. 10-12.

Boynton, Grace M., Papers, 1925-1951, The Schlesinger Library, Radcliffe College, Cambridge, Massachusetts.

Dr. Sailer in China [Memorial essays, largely in Chinese] (Beijing, 1985).

Edwards, Dwight W., *Yenching University* (New York: United Board for Christian Higher Education in Asia, 1959).

Egan, Susan Chan, *A Latterday Confucian, Reminiscences of William Hung* (1893-1980) (Cambridge: Council on East Asian Studies, Harvard University, 1987).

Galt, Howard Spilman, "Yenching University: Its Sources and Its

History," manuscript on microfilm, Special Collections, Yale Divinity School Library, New Haven, Connecticut.

Han Suyin, *A Mortal Flower* (New York: G.P. Putnam's Sons, 1965).

The Historical Records of Yenching University, 5 vols. largely in Chinese (Beijing: The Yenching Alumni Association, 1988-1992).

Mei, Y.P. and V.K. Nyi, Interview with Caroline Rittenhouse, July 12, 1987, Ithaca, New York.

Ogilvie, Marilyn B. and Clifford J. Choquette, "Western Biology and Medicine in Modern China: The Career and Legacy of Alice M. Boring" (1883-1955), *Journal of the History of Medicine and Allied Sciences*, vol. 48, no. 2 (April 1993), pp. 198-215.

Porter, Lucius, Papers, Beloit College Archives, Beloit, Wisconsin.

Sailer, Randolph, transcript of excerpts from oral history interview by Midwest China Oral History Project, 1979, Special Collections, Yale University Divinity School Library, New Haven, Connecticut.

Shadick, Harold, Interview with Caroline Rittenhouse, July 11, 1987, Ithaca, New York.

Stuart, John Leighton, *Fifty Years in China: The Memoirs of John Leighton Stuart, Missionary and Ambassador* (New York: Random House, 1954).

West, Philip, *Yenching University and Sino-Western Relations, 1916-1953* (Cambridge: Harvard University Press, 1976).

Yenching University Files in the Archives of the United Board for Christian Higher Education in Asia, Manuscript Group No. 11, Special Collections, Yale University Divinity School Library, New Haven, Connecticut.

Wellesley-Yenching collection and related materials, Wellesley College Archives, Wellesley, Massachusetts.

Missionaries in China

Christianity in China: A Scholars' Guide to Resources in the Libraries and Archives of the United States, Edited by Archie R. Crouch (Armonk, New York and London: M.E. Sharpe, Inc., 1989).

Ferguson, Mary E. *China Medical Board and Peking Union Medical College: a chronicle of fruitful collaboration 1914-1951* (New York: China Medical Board of New York, 1970).

Gregg, Alice H., *China and Educational Autonomy: The Changing Role of the Protestant Educational Missionary in China, 1807-1937* (Syracuse, New York, Syracuse University Press, 1946).

Hersey, John, *The Call* (New York: Alfred A. Knopf, Inc., 1985).

Lutz, Jessie G., *China and the Christian Colleges, 1850-1950* (Ithaca, New York: Cornell University Press, 1971).

The Missionary Enterprise in China and America, edited and with an introduction by John K. Fairbank (Cambridge: Harvard University Press, 1974).

Shaw, Yu-Ming, *An American Missionary in China: John Leighton Stuart and Chinese-American Relations* (Cambridge: Council on East Asian Studies, Harvard University, 1992).

Varg, Paul A. *Missionaries, Chinese, and Diplomats: The American Protestant Missionary Movement in China, 1890-1952* (Princeton: Princeton University Press, 1958).

Missionary Women in China

Beaver, R. Pierce, *American Protestant Women in World Mission* (Grand Rapids, Michigan: Wm. B. Eerdmans Publishing Co., 1968).

Golden Inches: The China Memoir of Grace Service, Edited by John S. Service (Berkeley: University of California Press, 1989).

Harris, Jane "American Missions, Chinese Reality: An Historical Analysis of the Work of American Missionary Women at North China Union College/Yenching Women's College, 1904-1943" (Dissertation in progress, University of North Carolina).

Hill, Patricia Ruth, *The World Their Household: The American Woman's Foreign Mission Movement and Cultural Transformation, 1870-1920* (Ann Arbor: University of Michigan Press, 1985).

Hunter, Jane, *The Gospel of Gentility: American Women Missionaries in Turn-of-the-Century China* (New Haven: Yale University Press, 1984).

Welter, Barbara, "She Hath Done What She Could: Protestant Women's Missionary Careers in Nineteenth-Century America," in *Women in American Religion*, edited by Janet Wilson James (Philadelphia: University of Pennsylvania Press, 1980).

History of China

Bartke, Wolfgang, *Who's Who in the People's Republic of China*, 2nd edition (München: K. G. Saur, 1987).

Boorman, Howard L. and Howard, Richard C., eds. *Biographical Dictionary of Republican China*, 5 vols. (New York: Columbia University Press, 1967).

Borg, Dorothy, *American Policy and the Chinese Revolution, 1925-1928* (New York: American Institute of Pacific Relations, The Macmillan Company, 1947).

Borg, Dorothy, *The United States and the Far Eastern Crisis of 1933-1938:*

From the Manchurian Incident through the Initial Stage of the Undeclared Sino-Japanese War (Cambridge: Harvard University Press, 1964).

Chow, Tse-tsung, *The May Fourth Movement: Intellectual Revolution in Modern China* (Cambridge: Harvard University Press, 1960).

Corbett, P. Scott, *Quiet Passages: The Exchange of Civilians between the United States and Japan during the Second World War* (Kent, Ohio: The Kent State Press, 1987).

Fairbank, John King, *China: A New History* (Cambridge: Harvard University Press, 1992).

——, *Chinabound: A Fifty-Year Memoir* (New York: Harper & Row, 1982).

——, *The United States and China*, Fourth Edition (Cambridge: Harvard University Press, 1983).

—— and Edwin O. Reischauer, *China: Tradition and Transformation* (Boston: Houghton Mifflin Co., 1978).

Feis, Herbert, *The Road to Pearl Harbor: The Coming of the War Between the United States and Japan* (Princeton: Princeton University Press, 1950).

Israel, John, *Student Nationalism in China, 1927-1937* (Stanford: Stanford University Press, 1966).

Li, Lincoln, *The Japanese Army in North China, 1937-1941: Problems of Political and Economic Control* (Tokyo: Oxford University Press, 1975).

Lindsay, Michael, *The Unknown War: North China 1937-1945* (London: Bergstrom & Boyle Books, Ltd., 1975).

Spence, Jonathan, *In Search of Modern China* (New York: W. W. Norton & Co., 1990).

Topping, Seymour, *Journey Between Two Chinas* (New York: Harper & Row, 1972).

Yeh, Wen-hsin, *The Alienated Academy: Culture and Politics in Republican China, 1919-1937* (Cambridge: Council on East Asian Studies, Harvard University, 1990).

Index

A NOTE ABOUT THE EDITOR

Caroline Smith Rittenhouse, College Archivist from 1987 to 1994 at Bryn Mawr College, is a graduate of the College with a Ph.D. in English from Harvard University. She has been an editor of the *Bryn Mawr Alumnae Bulletin* and, as an independent oral historian, has published two life histories: *Four Fifths of A Century*, (1983) and *MacBee Memoirs* (1984). She has been interested in China since 1949 when her father served as guardian for three Chinese children whose family left mainland China when the Communist party came into power.

Book design by Dolores Elise Brien

The lattices of the title page, chapter and page headings were adapted from *Chinese Lattice Designs* by Daniel Sheets Dye (New York: Dover Publications, 1974) an unabridged replication of the second (1949) edition of the work originally published in 1937 by Harvard University Press under the title *A Grammar of Chinese Lattice.* The original and second editions constituted Volumes V and VI of the Harvard-Yenching Institute Monograph Series.